Bearing Arms for His Majesty

BEARING ARMS
FOR HIS MAJESTY

The Free-Colored Militia in Colonial Mexico

Ben Vinson III

STANFORD UNIVERSITY PRESS, CALIFORNIA

Stanford University Press
Stanford, California
© 2001 by the Board of Trustees of the
Leland Stanford Junior University
Printed in the United States of America

Library of Congress Cataloging-in-Publication Data

Vinson, Ben.
    Bearing arms for his majesty : the free-colored militia in Colonial Mexico /
Ben Vinson III.
        p.   cm.
    Includes bibliographical references.
    ISBN 0-8047-4229-4 (alk. paper)   :   ISBN 0-8047-5024-6 (pkb. : alk. paper)
        1. New Spain—Militia—Minorities.   2. Spain—Colonies—America—
Defenses.   3. Blacks—Mexico.   4. Freemen—Mexico.   5. Sociology, Mili-
tary—Mexico.   I. Title.

UA605.M55 V56   2001
355.3'7'0972—dc21   2001020609

Original printing 2001

Last figure below indicates year of this printing:
10   09   08   07   06   05   04   03

Typeset in 10/12 Minion

To My Family

Acknowledgments

"Bearing Arms for His Majesty" began in 1993 as a small summer research project designed to understand the intricacies of race in the 1791 Mexican census. Using a Tinker Foundation grant, I visited the Mexican National Archives for the first time, examining numerous tomes from the Padrones section of the colonial holdings. I had the good fortune that summer of meeting Linda Arnold, who was cataloging the precious repositories of the Ramo Civil. Over coffee and lunch, she provided the crucial first leads to the story that has evolved into "Bearing Arms for His Majesty."

Herbert S. Klein, Deborah Levenson-Estrada, Winston James, Lambros Comitas, and Joan Vincent, were instrumental in commenting upon early versions of this work. Intellectual support at various stages of the project was also received from Daryl Scott, Colin Palmer, Pablo Piccato, Gabriel Haslip-Viera, Leo Spitzer, and Raul Bueno-Chávez. In Mexico, I have benefited from the assistance and insight of faculty at the Instituto Mora and the Universidad Autónoma Metropolitana at Iztapalapa. Particularly, I would like to thank Sonia Perez-Toledo, Norma Angelica Castillo, and Juan Ortiz Escamilla for their cherished insights and friendship. Also, numerous conversations and teas with Clara Garcia Ayluardo at the Librería Ghandi were indispensable in helping me to understand the true meaning of corporate structures in the colonial world.

My understanding of the way Mexicans have come to regard the African presence in their country has been informed by participating in various reunions of Afro-Mexicanists. In Xalapa, I extend warm gratitude to Adriana Naveda Chávez, for her time and friendship. Likewise, Genny Negroe Sierra, Jorge Victoria Ojeda, Maria Guadalupe Chávez Carbajal, Luz Maria Montiel, Padre Glen Jemmot, and Maria Elisa Velázquez have all pointed me in valuable directions. I thank them as well for helping me to maneuver in cities and archives that were previously unknown to me.

Apart from the Tinker grant, funding for this research has been provided by the Fulbright-Hays Commission, the Ford Foundation, the SSRC/Mellon Minority Fellowship Program, the Gilder Foundation, Barnard College, and Columbia University. In terms of managing the mechanics of the research, I extend special thanks to Juan Galván of the AGN, and Patricia Barriaga, my research assistant in Mexico City. For the countless other aspects of this project, I thank Jaime E. Rodriguez, Rhonda Vonshay Sharpe, my friends from the "Casa de Victor" in Coyoacán, John Dwyer, Paul Eiss, Antonio Rena, Omar Farouk-Roque, Claudia Lomeli, Mrs. Merlin, Ilona Katzew, Milady Merette-Polanco, and the memory of Elizabeth Paliza. The support of my colleagues in the History Department at Barnard College and my friends in the graduate program at Columbia University have been inspirational as well.

Very special regard is given to Herbert S. Klein, whose oversight was crucial to the success of the manuscript in all of its stages. His mentorship is deeply cherished. Finally, I would like to thank my loving parents, Ben Vinson Jr. and Lillie M. Hill Vinson. Their lifelong support and nurturing are the real reasons why this research has been possible. My mother's unyielding commitment to elementary education and her early attempts to expose me to "History" have instilled in me a passionate love of knowledge. My father's outstanding military career, selfless physical sacrifice, and life experiences reveal that in writing this book, I am in many ways, writing about my family as well.

New York City, 2001

Contents

Tables

Text Tables

Appendix Tables

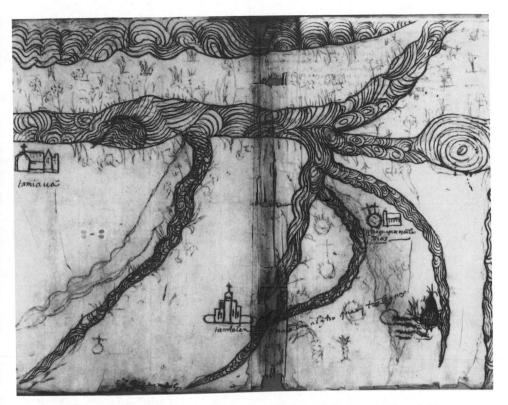

The region of Tamiagua, late sixteenth century, 1583. (Mapa Tamiagua y Tamtolon, signadario Cristobal . . . de Arellano, alcalde mayor, 1583. Archivo General de la Nación, Tierras, vol. 2777, exp. 13, fol. 8. Original dimensions 32x41 cm.)

Overleaf: The Cabecera of Acayucan and its environs, 1781. (Mapa provincial de Acayucan, Veracruz, 1781. Archivo General de la Nación, Tierras, vol. 3601, exp. 7, fol. 5. Original dimensions 31 x 43 cm.)

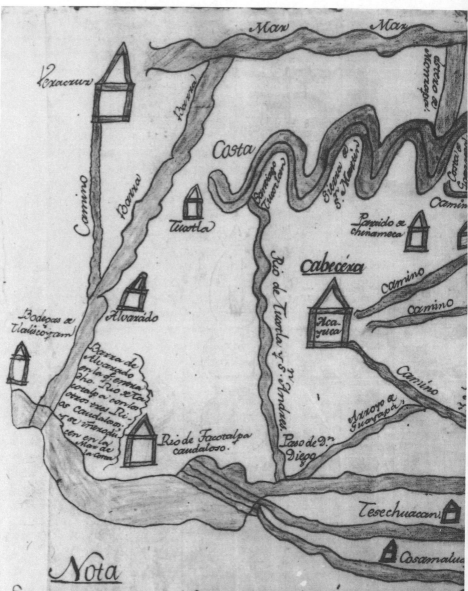

Nota

Se previene que desde la Barra de Goazacalcos y su Rio caudaloso, viniendo desde la Provincia? hasta los Mijes de la Serrania de Villalva, y de otro pasan por tierra todo el Obispado de Oaxaca
de la Provincia de Agayucan con el nombre de S.n Juan Michapan, y otros dos Rios caudalosos y n-
entran con el de S.n Juan Michapan en el Rio grande de Tacotalpan = De este se sigue navegando
Mar de la Costa: Si se quiere desde Tabasco, sin fondear, en el Rio de Goazacalcos, y Paso de A-
lopero nombrado de Monzapa, o Caño de agua que sale del Mar, y desembocan quanto se quiere
hasta? del las Pozas, y embarca? todo en el Rio de S.n Juan Michapan rio arriba hasta los Mijes, Villalva,
pero a que estos contemplo no son practica, y si los que llevo expuestos, los quales merecen mucha a-
tcos, es de los mas considerables que hay en el Reyno; pues solo la Provincia tiene de latitud 80.

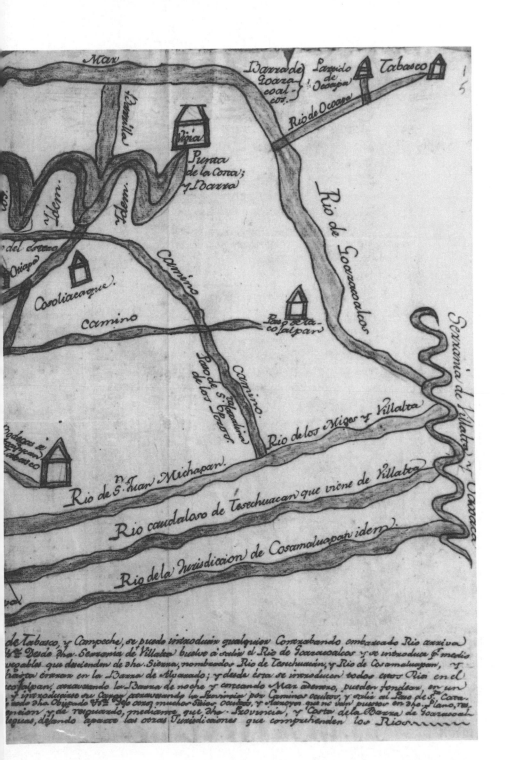

Mar

Barra de Goazacoalcos.

Lamido de Ocoapa.

Tabasco

Rio de Ocoapa

Rio de Goazacoalcos

Ranilla

Vijia

Punta de la Cora; y su Barra

Idem.

Idem.

del eoten

Oxiapa

Cosoliacaque.

Camino

Camino

Camino

Paso de la cosalpan

Serrania de Villalta, y Oaxaca.

Camino

Paso de Sn Pedro Agualtines de los Sres.

Rodigos de Tabasco

Rio de los Migos y Villalta

Rio de S. Iuan Michapan.

Rio caudaloso de Tesechuacan que viene de Villalta

Rio de la Iurisdiccion de Cosamaluapan idem.

de Tabasco, y Campeche, se puede introducir qualquier Contrabando embarcado Rio arriva
y Desde dha. Serrania de Villalta buelve à salir el Rio de Goazacoalcos y se introduce en medio
navegables que decienden de dha. Sierra, nombrados Rio de Tesechuacan, y Rio de Cosamaluapan, y
haren eraren en la Barra de Alvarado; y desde ella se introducen todos eros Rio en el
cosalpan; atravesando la Barra de noche y costeando Mar adentro, pueden fondear, en un
y introducirse su Carga, atravesando la Provincia por Caminos ocultos, y salir al Paso de Sn Cata-
siendo dho. Obispado VE por esto cora muchos Sitios ocultos, y Navegen que no van puestos en dho. Plano, ta-
tencion, y de resguardo, mediante, que dha. Provincia, y Costa de la Barra de Goazacoal-
leguas, dejando aparte las otras Iurisdiciones que comprehenden los Rios

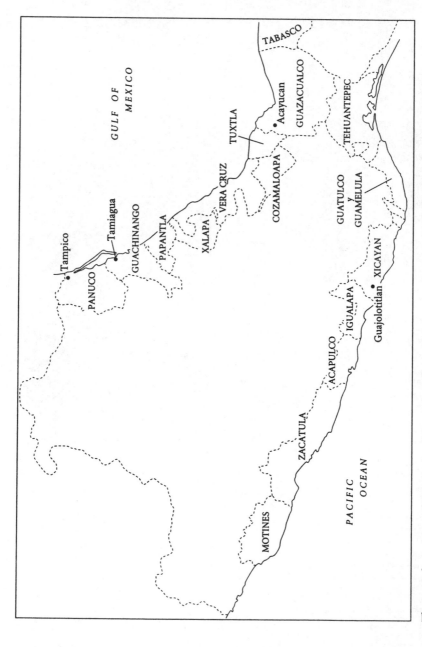

The coastal provinces of New Spain, eighteenth century. (Information from Peter Gerhard, *Geografía Histórica de la Nueva España, 1519–1821* [Mexico City: Universidad Autónoma de México, 1986.)

Introduction

COLONIAL MEXICO represents an important case study for deepening our understanding of black peoples and cultures in the New World. Although slave imports never reached the levels of the United States, Jamaica, Brazil, or Cuba, sufficient numbers of Africans arrived in the colony to make indelible contributions. Indeed, during the peak years of Mexican slavery, from 1521 to 1639, the colony ranked high among the leading New World importers, receiving roughly half of all slaves entering the Indies. Total slave imports for the period amounted to over 110,525 persons.[1] Of course the demographic impact was far more profound than the numbers suggest. Miscegenation gave rise to an array of Afro-mestizos, of whom the most common categories were the *pardos* and *mulatos*, but which also included *morenos* and *moriscos*.[2] By 1742, census records reveal their numbers to have been over 280,000. By 1793, their numerical presence had increased to over 370,000, representing just under 10 percent of the colony's population.[3] Since most Afro-Mexicans by this time were freedmen, Mexico's eighteenth-century free-colored population was among the largest in the Americas.[4]

With such a strong physical presence, especially in coastal regions that were sparsely populated by whites, scores of free-coloreds were called upon by the government to serve in the military. Some were cooks, others were messengers, many were armed soldiers. A few served in the regular army. More served in militia and reserve units.

This book is about the free-colored militia in colonial Mexico. It explores aspects of the lives of the tens of thousands of part-time *pardo*, *moreno*, and mulatto soldiers who served in the colony as volunteers and drafted conscripts. Using a multiregional approach, this study uncovers historical trends and discontinuities in New Spain's major cities and rural coastal areas, such as the environs of Tamiagua, Puebla, Igualapa, Veracruz, and Mexico City. This is primarily an institutional history, but one that marks a departure from many recent works on the colonial military by investigating patterns of militia development that occurred both prior to the Bourbon reform era of the 1760s, as well as events that took place during and after that period. The eighteenth century, particularly the years following 1762, has been traditionally interpreted as a watershed in military affairs. It has been claimed that the policies and innovations introduced under King Charles III in response to losses incurred during the Seven Year's War brought not only substantial increases in overall troop deployment but also in fact formally served to create a stable militia corps in the New World. But in isolating Mexico's free-colored militia as a research focal point, and by extending the time frame of historical inquiry, a different understanding is reached. The late colonial period, rather than being a time of important military genesis, emerges as a period of crisis and decay for the free-colored militia. Since the 1550s, free-colored forces had figured prominently in the colony's military defense scheme, being posted in key strategic locations. Moreover, these units had been evolving on increasingly autonomous grounds throughout the seventeenth and eighteenth centuries. While the Bourbon reforms clearly expanded the military establishment, and specifically the participation of American-born colonists in protecting the kingdom, this growth came at the price of the free-colored companies, both in terms of their numbers and corporate privileges. This study provides a broad historical context for understanding these changes, while documenting some of the particular effects of the reforms.

The decision to concentrate on the free-colored militia as a topic of study centers on several issues. Free-coloreds participated formally and informally in a range of institutions in the colonial world. Confraternities and cabildos have been pinpointed for preserving and developing facets of African-based culture, while providing material assistance to free-coloreds in times of need. These same organizations offered important spiritual stewardship, public visibility during feast days, and opened avenues for developing alliances with church officials who functioned as overseers.[5] Likewise, guild membership offered opportunities for concrete economic gain through acquiring trade skills and cultivating relationships with powerful magnates. Although prohibited by law, a number of blacks entered these organizations and benefited accordingly.[6] However, in a society heavily permeated by corporate networks, few institutions offered the same amount of legal and political strength as did the militia. As an armed, crown-sanctioned entity, militiamen had access to a host of government officials, and could press their demands with force when necessary. Furthermore, in occupying important strategic roles, militiamen possessed bargaining leverage. By threatening to withhold their services, they commanded the attention of provincial and viceregal officials, who feared exposing the colony to the pressures of foreign incursions, Indian revolts, and pirate raids.

While the existence of these militia units has been documented throughout the Americas, very little is known about them, their internal functioning, or their role in colonial society. A broad-scale, colonywide survey answers questions not only about their composition and military value but also their role in preserving internal order within provincial and urban settlements. Even their political involvement can be assessed, as soldiers positioned themselves to acquire privileges from colonial authorities. Political maneuverings to secure tribute relief, courtroom immunities, fishing rights, trading benefits, and access to select agricultural properties took place at both the local and regional levels. The impact of these struggles touched not only the free-colored soldiers themselves but also their families, neighbors, and other segments of the colony's black population. This book examines some of the militiamen's participation in nonmilitary affairs, while assessing the effects of their involvement.

Indeed, in social terms, the underlying importance of the free-colored militia may have rested outside of its specific military duties. A focused study of the corps in all of its capacities has much to offer our understanding of the colony's social profile. Did the militia serve as a significant source of social mobility for its members? In fact, how was social mobility defined for Mexico's free-coloreds? Since the individuals composing the free-colored forces were considered among the lowest members of the colonial racial matrix, mobility to some extent entailed overcoming some of the caste burdens imposed upon them by colonial law. Colonial Spanish American society was stratified along color lines, creating the complex *sociedad de castas*, or society of castes, which situated white Spaniards at the top of the social ladder. Instituted as a social control mechanism, the society of castes assigned numerous labels to the various shades of mixed-bloods and tried to restrict their activities. Under the system, free-coloreds came to assume a discernible legislative status. For instance, all free-blacks were subjected to tribute. They were required to hire themselves out to Spaniards in order to provide a readily available pool of hacienda and domestic labor. To reduce vagrancy, freedmen were then required to live with their employers. They also had to abide by curfew laws and sumptuary legislation. Women were prohibited from wearing gold, silks, and pearls; all free-coloreds were prohibited from walking the streets after certain hours of the night. Additionally, freedmen were barred from the university and had strict educational limitations. Blacks could not hold public office, nor possess access to Indian tribute labor. They were sometimes denied burials in important cathedrals, or ordered to bury their dead coffinless. When attending funerals, they were limited to congregating in groups of eight or less. Even marriage choices were not left untouched, as black and free-colored exogamy was sternly discouraged, both socially and legislatively. These were just some of the general laws passed to inhibit black behavior. Atop these were specific, customized decrees that were applied in particular colonies and regions. The net effect of the corpus of laws was to send a clear message: free-coloreds were not full citizens in colonial society, certainly not in the same light as white creoles, nor even the racially mixed mestizos. The dark shadow of slave status still followed them, although some free-colored families were several generations removed from slavery's chains.[7]

This study offers some insight into the functioning of the caste system by examining how a corporate institution and its privileges offered possibilities for rearranging the social and legal restraints of race. It is true that one can argue about how effective caste restrictions were in actually controlling behavior. In practice, many prohibitive laws were implemented half-heartedly, if at all. Some proved too difficult to enforce consistently, and were applied unevenly throughout the colonies. Economic necessity often directed mixed-bloods, blacks, and Indians into a wide variety of unsanctioned occupations, including several highly skilled positions that were supposedly reserved exclusively for whites. Under these conditions, some have claimed that blacks actually occupied a much vaguer legal status than the law implied.[8] Indeed, generations of scholars have taken on the task of exploring the strength of caste boundaries, producing the caste vs. class debate. In brief, the debate has examined whether, over the course of the colonial period, class structuring outperformed caste as the primary force for shaping social relations. Scholarly inquiry has produced tremendous local insights. We now understand that urban centers tended to have a stronger class-based orientation than rural areas, partly because greater occupational diversity offered better opportunities for deconstructing the confines of caste. We understand that there may have been a fusion of caste and class status in defining one's social station, creating what has been described in the literature as "*calidad*," a direct reference to the combined biological, reputational, and occupational classification of a person. The debate has caused a greater appreciation for "racial drift" and "racial mobility," references to the fluidity with which individuals were able to alter their racial status according to changes in lifestyle, cultural practices, and income.[9]

Few works, however, have directly addressed what race might have meant through the lens of a corporate institution. Given that colonial Mexico was a society where "racial drift" and even "passing" were possible, did the mulatto or *pardo* ever feel a racial identity as such? Did free-coloreds bond or feel a race-based affinity, especially considering that racial discourse during the colonial period was largely defined by and worked for the benefit of others? While the militia opens only one window into the world of Mexico's free-colored population, it is a provocative view. By enrolling in the free-colored corps, soldiers participated in an institution that was often segregated and defined by race. As a result, upon joining, race assumed added meaning in their lives, perhaps more so than for the average Mexican colonist. New networks were established with peers of color. Contacts with civilians were shaped by race, since the militiamen's jurisdictional powers were frequently challenged on the grounds of color. In this sense, specific military duties became understood in racial terms. The corporate entity became the modality through which a racial identity was preserved and expressed.

Any analysis of a corporate institution is likely to uncover corporate identity. However, it is important to stress that the point being developed here is that a militia corporate identity served as a superstructure for racial identity. Many free-colored militiamen in colonial Mexico became vocally attached to describing themselves as *pardo, moreno,* and mulatto because their participation in the military establishment offered them opportunities to reinterpret that condition. Corporate privileges eradicated many of the legal limitations imposed upon the free-colored population. While it may be true that by virtue of custom and practice many blacks were excluded from several of these burdens anyway, the militia formalized the process. The militia also offered an arena in which the soldiers could contest and secure added privileges and status. By erasing many of the legal consequences of color, it became easier to claim that racial status. Rather than racial whitening, I argue that the corporate military identity and privileges fostered a *pardo* and *moreno* racial identity, almost by default. But it was the soldiers themselves who worked out the mechanics and meaning of their experience.

Of course there were limitations to the type of racial identity that was nurtured under the militia. The life and trajectory of the militia as an institution, its corporate structure and privileges, greatly affected identity design. In the early colonial period, especially during the sixteenth and early seventeenth centuries, weaker privilege structures generated a lower degree of corporate-based racial identity than in later periods, when the stakes of privilege were higher. In the eighteenth century, the extent to which certain militia privileges, such as tribute relief, became transferable to the civilian population improved the chances of creating a more enduring identity that could survive the institution's lifespan. A wholesale assault on free-colored militia duty in the late eighteenth century, coupled with increased concern over bringing free-coloreds under taxation, provided key tests for determining the resiliency of the militia-bound, free-colored identity. Numerous legal confrontations took place between the soldiers, free-colored civilians, and the colonial government. But by the 1790s, it was clear that the government challenge had ultimately proved too great. As militia units were being disbanded throughout the colony, the corporate-based racial identity began to fragment, since the privilege structure that sustained it was being eliminated.

Although this book briefly examines some episodes of the early nineteenth century militia in the Yucatán, the study effectively concludes in the 1790s, when the policies of Viceroy Revillagigedo brought about the formal demise of most of the colony's free-colored forces in New Spain's interior. This is a natural closing point for the types of units described in this study. By and large, these forces were noncombatants in the traditional sense. When mobilized, they were involved in limited frontier operations, antipirate activities, ambushes against runaway slaves, strikes against hostile Indians, and internal peacekeeping operations. They were categorically different from the soldiers who fought in the War of Independence, who were inspired by the ideology of revolution and social transformation, who were exposed to concrete plans for secession, and who fought in arduous, sustained campaigns. The latter were mobilized under much different circumstances, had different responsibilities, and ultimately, different agendas.[10] Nevertheless, this book does offer important background information toward understanding the free-colored soldiers of the independence era, both royalists and insurgents, by tracing the tradition of duty and underscoring what military service meant to previous generations of blacks.

The book is divided into two sections. The opening three chapters examine New Spain's free-colored militia in institutional terms. The second half of the book explores the relationship between militia corporate privilege and racial identity. Hence, the overall objective is for the racial analysis to emerge from the institutional analysis. Chapter 1 offers an overview of the free-colored militia from its earliest development through the eighteenth century. In an attempt to be comprehensive both in chronological and geographical scope, the chapter's primary emphasis is on building unit typologies, while generalizing about different theaters of service and the conditions of duty at certain historical junctures. Chapter 2 assesses the internal dynamics and functioning of the various militia types. The operating command structures are highlighted in considerable detail, along with an examination of the officer corps. In Chapter 3, the soldiers are compared to their civilian counterparts. After conducting a study of recruitment procedures, the occupational and marriage patterns are analyzed for select locations. All of the material presented in the chapter attempts to answer this question: Did the militia favorably distinguish its soldiers from civilians, offering avenues for free-colored social mobility? The fourth chapter is the first that isolates discussion on militia-based privileges. Through a wholesale review of the tribute establishment and how the militiamen garnered tribute relief, commentary is presented not just on the impact of the militia for the soldiers but also for free-colored civilians as well. Chapter 5 explores the dimensions of the free-colored military legal exemption known as the *fuero militar*. Again, after delving into the mechanics of the privilege, there is an assessment of the *fuero*'s importance in terms of delivering a greater racial meaning to service. The last chapter considers the meaning of race for the militiamen through a sample of racial referencing, internal relations, and external challenges to their institution.

On a final note, this book uses the words "free-colored" and "black" interchangeably. These refer to the same racial groups, namely the *pardos*, *morenos*, and *mulatos*. While many scholars have utilized various forms of nomenclature to refer to these groups in the past, free-colored is the preferred terminology here, and is the most used. It more faithfully captures the spirit of colonial referencing—*pardos libres*, *morenos libres*, and *mulatos libres*—where "*libre*" stands for freedman's status, instead of free from tax obligations, as some have assumed. I have also chosen to preserve the spelling of Spanish names as they appear in the colonial documents. Consequently, names like José will oftentimes appear as Joseph in the text, as was frequently common in the seventeenth and eighteenth centuries.

CHAPTER ONE

Militia Awakenings

O N N O V E M B E R 3 , 1 7 7 7 , Benito Péres de Santiago, a free-colored officer in Veracruz's all-black provincial company of *morenos*, returned home to his native Cuba after eighteen years of service in Mexico.[1] He had acquired many accolades while in New Spain, among which was the captaincy of his unit. Atop that, he was bestowed with the illustrious grade of *comandante*, a supervisory position that offered charge over all of Veracruz's free-colored forces. Having initially arrived in Mexico as a mere lieutenant, Benito was part of a contingent of black military officers who circulated throughout the Americas as part of the Spanish crown's plan to improve the defenses of its important strategic centers. After his period of solid tenure in Mexico, the royal government accepted Captain Benito's petition to return home and promptly granted him equivalent rank and grade in the Cuban free-colored militia.

In 1807, a Cuban-born, free-colored militiaman died in Mexico. At the time of death, Captain Juan Pastor was stationed in Mexico City, where he had served from at least the 1770s. Unlike Benito, Juan had decided to carve a new life for himself permanently in his transplanted home. He took a wife, Doña Maria Negra, and had five children. Born to a relatively wealthy family in Cuba, Juan succeeded in replicating some of his family's financial success in New Spain, establishing a respectable carpenter's practice in Mexico City. The income allowed him to purchase a home near the "Salto del Agua" quarter, while running a workshop on the street named after Don Juan Manuel. Although Juan owed some money at the time of his death, his home and property were free of mortgage payments and firmly in the hands of his heirs. But by matter of circumstance, Juan was survived only by his wife and son, Ignacio Pastor. Seeking better fortunes elsewhere, Ignacio had already returned to Havana. Given that Juan had named his son as his universal heir, the future of the Pastor estate in Mexico was unclear by the beginning of 1808.[2]

Both of the above examples illustrate that free-colored military service did not exist in a vacuum. Free-colored militiamen did not serve in units that were isolated entities; rather, their companies were integrally linked to the processes and currents of military policy formed at the highest rungs of the colonial administration. Having Cuban militiamen serve on Mexican soil resulted as much from crown directives as from individual volunteerism. Although individuals could take rather independent courses, as with the divergent cases of Juan Pastor and Benito Pérez de Santiago, the fact remained that the lives of the soldiers were conditioned by overarching policies at some basic level. Therefore, any examination of the free-colored corps and its social impact must begin with a fundamental understanding of the changes, direction, and shape that the military institution took during colonial times.

The aim of this chapter is to provide a brief overview of the essential features of Spain's military establishment in the Americas, while situating the specifics of the Mexican case within that material. Surfacing from this backdrop will be the experience of the free-colored militia. The characteristics of the institution as it developed in Mexico will be described in detail, offering a look at the types of units that evolved, their history, and their distribution.

Historiography has traditionally divided the state of colonial military affairs into two major periods based upon the varying degrees of intensity with which reforms to the military establishment were carried out. The first preceded the Bourbon reforms of Charles III, while the other took place during that era. Spain's participation in the Seven Years' War marked the dividing line. In 1762, British expeditionary forces successfully launched sieges against Havana and Manila. Both strikes were cause for serious alarm. Hitherto, each port had been considered impregnable, especially Havana, which was rumored to be the strongest fortified Spanish site in the Americas. Its easy fall exposed the full weaknesses of the existing Spanish defense plan in the colonies, causing wholesale review and overhaul.[3]

Until that point, colonial defenses had relied heavily upon a few fortified sites placed in strategic locations, manned largely by regular army troops from Spain. In the seventeenth century, these units were called *compañías de presidio*, given that their duties were quite specific and limited to the defense of the forts where they operated. In the early eighteenth century, announced by a series of *reglamentos* (military ordinances), the forces were remolded into what became known as the Army of the Americas.[4] Never exceeding fourteen thousand men for the entire New World prior to 1750, this army's core was drawn from peninsular recruits. It was divided into two forces. The bulk received the title of *Ejército de Dotación* and was stationed permanently in the Indies. A smaller "Reinforcement Army" remained on call in Spain to be deployed during emergencies. Their number was maintained at twenty-five hundred for the first half of the eighteenth century.[5]

The military scheme's primary objective was to provide adequate coastal defense while ensuring that all major entry points into the imperial holdings were well guarded. The focus was placed clearly on diverting external threats posed by foreign invaders, especially with respect to the crown's vital commercial interests, which were needed to underwrite Spain's absorbing expenses in Europe. Consequently, places like Cartagena, Veracruz, and Havana emerged as natural focal points for defense. The crown was also interested in controlling important sea lanes, thereby facilitating the movement of the treasure fleets while reducing contraband trade. Maritime deployment was concentrated most heavily in the Caribbean and the Atlantic Triangle, an area encompassing the Azores, the Canary Islands, and the Straits of Gibraltar. There was a smaller presence in the Pacific, consisting of the treasure fleet's convoy and three to four warships permanently stationed in Callao.[6]

Perhaps the defining aspect of the defense system prior to the Bourbon reforms was its gradual evolution, peppered with numerous starts and reverses.[7] A pattern emerged whereby the crown took great interest in providing defense during periods in which it was at war, particularly in conflicts with New World implications. In the intervening times, America's defenses became almost an afterthought, although serious pirate depredations could motivate spending. For example, around the mid-sixteenth century, substantial increases in pirate attacks precipitated greater crown investment in forces and materiel. The same occurred in the wake of the raids of Sir Francis Drake in 1578–79 and 1585–86, as well as after numerous Dutch corsair incursions during the seventeenth century. But no matter what the level of the crown's commitment toward building the military establishment, royal administrators always remained parsimonious in their approach, wedded more to the principles of extracting wealth from their colonies than to pumping precious resources back into the Americas. Moreover, commitments in Europe were always pressing, as new wars brewed right until the end of the colonial period.[8] In lieu of sending masses of revenues abroad, the royal government searched for ways in which the colonies could bear the fiscal burden of defense. Beginning with the reign of Philip II, a great deal of New World military spending came from *situados*, or royal subsidies. Under this procedure, the larger New World treasuries underwrote the defense expenditures of the less vigorous ones.[9]

Most accounts agree that prior to the eighteenth century, protecting the Americas was cheap when compared with other areas where the crown allocated its resources. This was truest during the early years. For instance, during the period between 1535 and 1585, Spain spent just 5 million ducats for its New World defenses. By comparison, the royal government annually spent an average of 2.5 million ducats for its wars against the Dutch during those years. In other words, fifty years of protecting the Americas amounted to just two years of war against the Dutch in the sixteenth century.[10] Spending did increase in the seventeenth century, as did the burden assigned to the colonies.[11] The strain on some colonial treasuries was immense. When the *situado* system failed to provide the needed funds, money was collected from private citizens, usually important local merchants. However, recourse to private loans was more typically a feature of the eighteenth century, when military investment skyrocketed, causing problems in places like Havana, Santo Domingo, Panama, Chile, and Cartagena.[12] In the seventeenth century, although important increases in military spending were registered, total expenditures reached a maximum of only 3 million pesos per year by 1690, as opposed to over 20 million pesos per year a century later.[13]

Thanks to the seventeenth-century defense initiatives, the number of regular army forces posted in the Americas rose to six thousand men by the beginning of the eighteenth century.[14] Yet defenses remained far from adequate. Even the famed Armada de Barlovento, the costly fleet built to protect the Caribbean in the 1640s, did not live up to expectations as a naval deterrent, and it was scrapped in 1748.[15] In the face of the military's obvious shortcomings, the principal source of solace was that Spain's European enemies did not yet have the means to field forces strong enough to subdue the most prized colonial holdings, namely, the viceroyalties of New Spain and Peru. So with minimal forces Spain could still successfully thwart attempts at its key possessions. But numerous territorial losses in the Lesser Antilles to British, Dutch, and French forces revealed other debilities. The fall of Jamaica in 1655 was particularly illustrative of the spotty nature of the Spanish scheme: overcommitment in some areas, leaving others bare. The overextended empire was beginning to pay the price in land. Weaknesses resonated in military technology and organizational structure. In the late seventeenth century Spanish forces were still using matchlock muskets, hackbuts, and pikes, instead of the bayonets and flintlocks that had become standard issue in French armies. The innovative Spanish military formation known as the *tercio*, which had been the terror of Europe in the sixteenth century, was not keeping pace with changes in military strategy, organization, and tactics. Command staff structure was deemed less efficient and modern than those of the emerging European superpowers. Atop these troubles were problems with recruitment. No longer were young Spaniards as willing to serve in the seventeenth century army as they had done previously, causing greater reliance on unpredictable mercenaries.[16] Recruitment pinches at home meant that fewer troops would be available for stationing in the Americas.

Despite being faced with increasing manpower shortages, the seventeenth century crown was hesitant about employing colonists in the New World's regular armies. In truth, the royal government had always been reluctant in soliciting the colonists' military services, fearing that these men might use their weapons to topple the regime. Moreover, prejudices in court circles stereotyped its American subjects as lazy, untamed, and ill fit for martial careers. Consequently, until the Bourbon military reforms of the 1760s forced military planners to re-evaluate their position, the regular army in the Americas was always principally Spanish in composition. Even as late as 1740–60, the proportion of Spaniards never dropped below 62 percent. In some areas, such as Cuba, eighteenth-century laws expressly prohibited the number of American-born soldiers from exceeding 20 percent.[17] Of those colonials who did manage to participate in the army, the crown strongly emphasized that the preferred type of soldier was the white creole. Legislation originating from the seventeenth century banned mestizos, Indians, *mulatos*, and *negros* from enlisting as regulars.[18]

Unsurprisingly, the military could not be so discriminating in practice. Maintaining high numbers of peninsular troops abroad was difficult. Many despised the prospect of serving in the Indies as a dead end for their military careers; to improve their chances for advancement, many requested transfers after having barely touched New World soil. On the other hand, available white creoles were almost as few in number as peninsular recruits, especially in coastal areas that were always in urgent need of capable forces. Nor were white colonists particularly keen on the low pay and hostile living conditions that many New World soldiers faced. Additionally, lessons learned from experience prodded some military officers to question the premise of maintaining standards of white purity in the ranks. Even the revered peninsular soldiers, after years of service in the colonies, could become as licentious and irresponsible as ordinary colonists were reputed to be.[19] By default, in the constant search for bodies, recruitment levies were performed directly in colonial jails; homeless men were unabashedly drawn off city streets and dressed in uniform; taverns were swept after midnight for drunkards who might be enticed to join. The regular army corps became increasingly staffed with a lot that veered far from the ideal social and racial profiles held dear by crown administrators.[20]

Notwithstanding the eager grabs made at New World residents, most colonists participating in the military establishment did not do so in the regular army but in the citizen militias. With all their inherent limitations, these forces became the backbone of coastal defense schemes, providing the manpower base that would meet most local emergencies. The militia's structure and evolution was loose and gradual in the period prior to the 1760s. After the initial work of the conquest, the *conquistadores* retained their private armies under an arrangement known as the *hueste*. Officially, this was a crown endorsement that allowed the *conquistadores'* partisan forces to continue their military services under the name of the king. The appearance of the *hueste* marked the debut of a New World defense force manned primarily by colonials. Eventually, these same *conquistadores* acquired land grants and titles, thereby making the transition to a more sedentary life. As such, they became *encomenderos*—essentially, landed "benefactors" in possession of an allotted amount of Indian tribute and labor. Part of the *encomenderos'* royal responsibilities included fielding troops and bearing arms during emergencies. Until 1582, they were also commissioned to provide manpower for selected forts and garrisons.

Hence, a second type of citizen-based military force came into being. Proto-typical forms of militias, the *hueste* and the *encomendero* armies persisted for only a limited time. The *hueste* functioned from 1493 to 1573, which marked the official duration of the conquest period in Latin America. The *en-comendero* armies endured until the demise of *encomienda* system in the early eighteenth century.[21]

On October 7, 1540, the crown issued a *cédula* (decree) in the Americas that called for colonists to establish the militia as a formal institution. Its creation did not mark a radical departure from either of the two previous citizen-based military structures. But among the most notable changes introduced was a re-duction in the highly personalistic leadership style of the militia's predeces-sors. This is to say that the *hueste* and *encomendero* armies had been financed and furnished by private individuals who proceeded to monopolize com-mand. By contrast, in the new militias all participating colonists provided their own weapons. Command, while still falling upon a core group, tended to circulate more widely among high-ranking colonial officials who resided in the towns of militia operations. If such officials were unavailable, then town councils hand-picked the militia's leaders, occasionally after receiving prior approval from the soldiers themselves.[22] These early militias became known throughout the Americas as "urban" militia companies. This did not mean that the units were necessarily founded in cities.[23] In fact, the majority existed in rural towns. Rather, urban status was simply a means of defining their theater of operations. These units were strictly tied to their localities. When crises arose, militiamen in urban companies were under no direct obligation to participate in campaigns that extended beyond their homes. Consequently, urban units were defensive in the narrowest sense and could not be relied upon for coordination in broader military expeditions.[24]

What we have seen up until this point is the general state of the military in the Spanish Americas prior to the Bourbon reforms: a small group of regular army veterans were stationed heavily at key points, while a larger, loosely regulated militia served as human filler for the remaining areas. New Spain roughly adhered to this pattern. However, the total concentration of soldiers was less than in places such as Cuba or Santo Domingo. As one of the crown's most precious holdings in terms of overall economic value, defending New Spain was certainly of paramount importance. But the colony's special geog-raphy and location dictated that military defenses could be applied unevenly with relatively good results.

Whether consciously or unconsciously, military deployment assumed a re-gional character in New Spain. As was the case with the rest of the crown's pos-sessions, defending the coasts and frontiers was the foremost concern. In Mexico, these heavily underpopulated and exposed areas offered potentially easy access into the interior. To make amends for scattered development, the northern, semiconquered frontier witnessed the implementation of a constantly shifting presidial line: essentially, a loose conglomerate of medieval-style defensive forts that held anywhere between six and a hundred men.[25] Regular army troops and militia reinforcements sent from other areas of the colony played minimal roles in presidial defense, partly because of the harsh conditions of life in these northern outposts. Hardened, home-grown troops, recruited from the local populace became the featured soldiers. Being neither true militiamen nor regulars,[26] the main challenge they faced came from confrontational Indian groups, notably the Apaches and Comanches, but also the Yaquis, Mayos, Papagos, Comanches, Tarahumares, Pimas, Seris, and Sobaipuris.[27] However, as French aggression became more pronounced in the late seventeenth century, there was greater recruitment effort placed in raising militia forces to supplement the defenses of the presidial line. Also introduced were a string of "flying companies" (*volantes*), installed for the fixed protection of select frontier towns.

Even more than the northern frontier, Mexico's Gulf and Pacific coasts were seen as especially problematic defensive zones. At least in the north there was a huge land barrier, the Provincias Internas, which prevented deeper inroads from being made into the important political and commercial centers lying southward. But the coasts provided better opportunities for attack, at least in theory. A surgical strike at Veracruz was deemed most serious, since the best roads inland extended from that port. Indeed, apart from New Orleans, there was reputedly no better means of access to the continent.[28] Additionally, coastal cities were key nuclei for overseas communication.[29] Loss of these sites jeopardized the colony's flow of goods and information. Defense fears were borne out by the reality of countless pirate incursions.[30] However, the dreaded threat of massive foreign invasion never materialized. Any foreign power drafting plans of attack on the viceroyalty quickly came to realize that the odds were against them, no matter what the level of defensive deployment. New Spain's allies, which were its proliferation of climate and disease, threatened to consume any force landing on the coasts. In fact, Spain's own defensive armies convalesced in shore port hospitals while awaiting potential enemies.[31] And if those problems were not enough, then the logistics of supplying and communicating with an invading army bewildered possible foes. Although Mexico was indeed a great prize, Spain's colonial military planners completely understood that with a few forts—namely, Acapulco, Veracruz, and Campeche—the colony could thwart potential, large-scale invasions. Meanwhile, defenses elsewhere could be slackened.[32]

With this geo-strategic framework in mind, as in other settings throughout the New World, core groups of regular army soldiers were stationed in New Spain at the most essential defense centers. Mexico City, Veracruz, Campeche, Mérida, San Blas, Acapulco, Perote, Sisal, as well as selected points along the northern presidial lines all received veteran troops. The number of regulars and their geographical distribution increased after 1739.[33] Militias played the supporting role. Accurate estimates for the total number of men composing New Spain's defenses prior to the 1760s are hard to obtain. But according to Francisco de Seijas y Lobera, who wrote a general treatise on the crown's government in the Indies during the first decade of the eighteenth century, if planned right, Spain could rely comfortably upon nearly 200,000 men to post defense at any frontier or coastal location in times of emergency. At least an eighth of those would be whites.[34]

Although Seijas's projections seem like wild distortions of Mexico's available human resources at the time, what he essentially tried to signal in his proposals was that with a creative yet firm use of colonials as soldiers, the crown could field a formidable army. Seijas himself fully realized that his numbers were exaggerated versions of the actual number of militiamen and regulars found on post. Yet he hoped that by magnifying the dimensions of the colonial military he could prod the crown to tap deeper into the colony's manpower reserves, specifically through incorporating more mestizos, *negros*, Indians, and *mulatos* into the militia. His written ideas about racial inclusion initially appear progressive, but they had their limitations. While Seijas esteemed the mestizo soldier as the military equivalent of the best European white, his perception of the free-colored soldier was far more calculated. Undoubtedly possessing traits of martial valor, blacks and *mulatos* were still to be denied access to firearms, swords, and daggers. In his military design, the free-colored soldier's role figured mainly in the capacity of mounted lancers, armed only with light spears and machetes. Menacing to an enemy, these same instruments were less threatening than guns if aimed at the colony, always a possibility in his mind when blacks wielded weapons. Hence Seijas allowed blacks to be implemented into the military scheme, but in severely controlled fashion. His opinions were reflected in his projected troop proposals. For example, along the Gulf coast stretch known as the Seno Mexicano, free-coloreds were to compose a healthy militia contingent of forty thousand men. Nevertheless, whites and mestizos were to predominate in defending the region, totaling sixty thousand troops.[35]

It is debatable if Seijas's fourteen tomes of counsel were heeded at the time of their publication, much less read by busy crown administrators. Regardless, for our purposes his observations serve to illustrate the types of debates that preoccupied administrators for most of the colonial period regarding the state of the Mexican military. How were the military and militia designs to be improved, if at all? Precisely to what extent were colonists to be brought in for their own defense? What was the potential value of soldiers of different races, and could they be used effectively? It is in this context that free-colored service emerged in the colony.

Free-colored militiamen first appeared in Mexico shortly after the 1540 decree, and were a result of military necessity. In areas where whites were few, or where strategic circumstances demanded a large number of defenders, blacks were called to duty. The summons was made reluctantly. A score of legislative measures were written, beginning in 1537, prohibiting blacks from even carrying arms.[36] If free-coloreds wished to own a dagger or sword, they had to make formal appeal to crown officials, who examined each situation to assess if the weapons were truly needed.[37] As echoed in the writings of Seijas, fears over arming blacks stemmed from the potential threat of rebellion. Especially in the sixteenth and early seventeenth centuries, these were serious concerns in Mexico. Royal administrators wrote numerous letters to the king during this period, expressing how the influx of blacks had reached unmanageable levels. Combined with mestizos, they were said to outnumber whites.[38] Although the scope of the actual threat may have been magnified by nervous crown officials, there is evidence that blacks began slipping from control as early as 1523, when reports detailed how runaway slaves sought refuge in Zapotec communities. In 1537 the first known slave rebellion in the colony was planned just outside of Mexico City. In New Galicia, from 1549 through the 1570s, free-*mulatos*, vagabonds, and mestizos joined forces with runaway slaves and hostile Chichimec Indians to launch a series of menacing highway raids. The same took place in Guanajuato, Penjamo, and San Miguel, during the 1560s. Throughout the sixteenth century, numerous runaway slave communities, or *palenques*, were established in Mexico, such as Canada de los Negros (1576) near León, and lesser-known settlements outside of Antequera, Guatulco, Veracruz, and Orizaba. Perhaps the most belligerent of these settlements were those in the outlying areas between Orizaba and Veracruz. Of special repute was the *palenque* founded by the runaway Yanga. His community harassed the Veracruz area for more than thirty years. Finally, in 1609, the settlement was subdued through a massive, coordinated effort involving soldiers from Puebla.[39] Although collective resistance from runaways and slaves had subsided for much of Mexico after 1618, problems persisted in Veracruz into the eighteenth century, with large-scale rebellions taking place in 1735. Troublesome *palenques* founded during these uprisings continued to plague colonial forces and estate owners for years.

With so much disquieting slave behavior, arming free-blacks was considered dangerous because one could never be sure of their loyalties. The crown tried ardently to persuade free-coloreds to behave as responsible vassals by acting against maroons. Handsome rewards were offered to freedmen who assisted in capturing runaways. Some were given bounties of fifty pesos each, while others were granted the rights over apprehended slaves.[40] These incentives worked to some extent. In the campaign against Yanga, such attractions enticed a large number of *mulatos* to staff a racially mixed military unit of two hundred volunteers.[41]

But on the other hand, there is also evidence that free-coloreds were conspirators in rebellious events, sometimes helping slaves to escape their masters. Rare details on an unsuccessful rebellion planned in Mexico City in 1608 demonstrate that slaves and free-coloreds even collaborated occasionally to plot the coronation of their own king and queen.[42] Free-blacks continued to play prominent roles in civil unrest in Mexico City, notably during 1611, 1612, 1624, and 1665. The 1611 affair involved a riotous protest of some fifteen hundred black confraternity members who bemoaned the death of a female slave who was brutally beaten by her owner. This led to another furtive coronation attempt that was quickly foiled, with the participants hanged and their heads thrust on pikes for all to see. In 1624, blacks joined the widespread urban protests against Viceroy Gelves and contributed to his overthrow. In 1665, there was yet another *mulato* conspiracy to elect leaders from among their ranks to run the colony.[43]

Free-colored violence and unruly behavior in Mexico City impacted policy toward blacks in other areas of New Spain, since legislators residing in the capital witnessed firsthand the bellicose behavior. Countermoves designed to reduce black liberties were particularly prominent under the administration of Viceroy Gelves, who issued a set of austere ordinances from 1622 to 1623. Under them, blacks were not allowed to leave their homes after 10:00 P.M. Unless they were members of one of only a few guilds that officially accepted blacks, they were forbidden from living together with other free-coloreds and discouraged from residing alone. Additional occupational restrictions were imposed atop existing ones, in attempt to maneuver blacks into finding gainful employment under the watchful eye of white Spaniards.[44]

Given this context, the racial climate in which free-colored militia service first developed in Mexico was a hostile one.[45] This influenced the nature in which free-colored units evolved. Since only limited documentary evidence exists on the earliest history of the free-colored militia, a detailed assessment of their beginnings is not possible. However, what is clear is that in the initial phases, the crown exercised caution in utilizing blacks, testing the strength of their allegiances. At the outset, free-coloreds were either employed as auxiliary troops or were incorporated into racially integrated units. They were not allowed to possess autonomous militia companies of their own. In Mexico City, free-colored militiamen served as auxiliaries as early as 1562, just six years after blacks were integrated into the regular army forces of Veracruz.[46] In militia units formed in towns along the Gulf coast, blacks served with whites in racially mixed companies.[47] The cautious approach toward employing blacks as soldiers was not unique to Mexico. In Havana (1555), Puerto Rico (1557), Cartagena (1560, 1572), and Santo Domingo (1583), free-colored militiamen started out in the capacity of auxiliaries.[48]

As the initial fears about black soldiers subsided and the militiamen began to prove their worth, the free-colored militia institution assumed a more definite form. Three basic types of companies evolved: independent free-colored units, companies of racially integrated service, and militias in former maroon communities.

Free-coloreds who had started out serving in auxiliary units eventually had their companies upgraded to nonreserve status, thereby becoming militias of the independent type. The upgrade was facilitated by increased crown support for the free-colored militia's formal existence. For instance, when the process occurred in Mexico City in 1612, the militiamen's rights were protected by a number of *reales cédulas* that worked to legally sustain their use of arms and to shield them from abuses of corporal punishment. The first of these measures took effect in 1608.[49] Generally, the colony's larger cities were sites where independent free-colored companies came into being. Independent simply meant that the units were no longer fully subordinate to other forms of regular army and militia companies. Furthermore, the units were labeled as *compañías de pardos y morenos libres*, and color became one of the main criteria for matriculation. The companies quickly became recognizable as distinct free-colored entities, especially in the eyes of outsiders. Consequently, race became an important aspect of the militiamen's transactions and affairs.

Indeed, these units' importance within the larger framework of free-colored military service rested on their relatively high degree of internal autonomy, as well as the extent to which race served as a signifier of service. The officer corps, even at the highest levels, was drawn almost exclusively from the free-colored castes. By and large, the soldiers raised money for themselves and distributed it as they saw fit. Apart from joint training sessions with white units and occasional campaigns, other functions were seldom shared. When legal problems arose, the militiamen, through their officers, dealt directly with crown and military legal officials without stipulated recourse to intermediaries.

While seemingly intuitive in a caste-regulated society, the rise of companies reserved wholly for free-coloreds needs some explanation, given that not all Afro-Mexicans served in those units. Obviously, the crown's interest in maintaining racial boundaries must have encouraged a policy to create racially segregated forces. But the opinions and prejudices of the colony's white elite may have played a shaping influence as well. Whenever possible, elites sought to preserve social distance from the rabble, especially of darker hue. Many prosperous whites held militia titles themselves, and the mere idea of serving in units alongside blacks threatened to debase the prestige of their commissions. In the eighteenth century, elite concerns over protecting the status of their militia rank often prompted the creation of racially segregated units.[50] Although few documents speak directly to the issue, it is not wholly inconceivable that elites also made similar appeals for the racial purity of militias during the sixteenth and seventeenth centuries, incited by the same status-driven motivations.

Another, less-discussed possibility for the origins of segregated militias deals with certain structural factors of military organization. It is somewhat peculiar that companies of the independent type were primarily characteristic of New Spain's cities. Two factors account for the situation. First, because of their large and diverse populations, the colony's major urban centers were among the best possible locations to bear companies segregated by race. In lesser towns in the rural countryside, smaller populations made it more difficult to raise and sustain companies delineated by caste. Secondly, most militia units founded in cities prior to the 1760s were created and supported by guilds. Because blacks were legally excluded from the majority of these trade associations, there was no possibility for them to be formally included into guild-based militia units. Consequently, military planners probably reasoned that if free-coloreds were to be utilized as soldiers, the best course was to create special companies for them that were categorized by race. In other words, during the seventeenth century, guild exclusivity functioned as a sieve, working to establish separate companies in the cities. Whites served in the companies of tanners, silversmiths, tailors, merchants, and so forth. Free-coloreds, and even mestizos, served in companies reserved for their respective castes.

Eventually, blacks found entry into even the most elite trade associations, becoming master painters and goldsmiths. However, that did not change the disposition of early military planners toward allowing free-coloreds into the restricted, guild-based militia companies. If anything, there was likely more resolve placed on keeping the militias racially distinct. Colonial bureaucrats exerted great effort in trying to regulate society in ways that ensured that the privileges of whites were not lessened by the ambitions of the lower castes.[51] The significant increase in black guild participation, largely illegal, was one such threat that jeopardized the boundaries of caste privilege. Military planners sought to prevent further breeches of free-colored status by prohibiting guild affiliations from providing access into the racially exclusive, guild militia units. Consequently, despite considerations of wealth and artisan standing, all free-coloreds were subject to serving in the *compañías de pardos, morenos,* and *mulatos* as a means of containing their social position.

In time, it proved impossible to preserve complete racial segregation in the guild militias. The frequent employment of *alquilones* (hired replacements) and the gradual acceptance of mestizos darkened the complexion of these units.[52] On the other side of matters, even the *compañías de pardos* came to have a small sprinkling of mestizos and whites. For places like Puebla, Mexico City, Veracruz, Mérida, and Campeche, racially separate militias ultimately developed into approximations of their designated racial status. This is to say that the companies of free-coloreds were mainly *pardo, mulato,* and *moreno* in composition; the companies of whites were mainly white, those of mestizos were mainly mestizo, and so forth. The degree of racial purity at any given moment depended upon recruitment procedures, the timing of militia mobilizations, and occasional crackdowns by crown officials. Haphazard recruitment often resulted in greater racial diversity. Militia mobilizations tended to diminish the presence of duty-shy whites. Realizing the situation, royal administrators called for stricter adherence to racial divisions in cities when, in the 1740s and 1750s, they recognized an increased amount of racial intermingling in supposedly white and free-colored units.[53] Regardless of the racial oscillation that took place, free-colored militia companies of the independent type tended to be more racially homogenous than not.

Companies of racially integrated service, the second major type of company under which free-coloreds served, differed from the independent free-colored companies in that their structure was not based on race. Since these forces were initially raised to include mestizos, blacks, and whites, there were few concerns over preserving rigid racial quotas. Depending upon their location, however, integrated units could become thoroughly staffed by free-coloreds. In such situations, over time, high levels of free-colored participation proved transformative to the militia forces where they served. The case of Papantla is illustrative.[54] Located north of Veracruz along the Gulf coast, racially mixed units were first founded here in the context of a pirate raid in 1649. As white confidence grew, blacks began to assume positions of command while still serving in the town's integrated forces, rather than in free-colored companies of their own. By 1684, all of Papantla's militia officers were *pardos*, except for the ranking senior officer, who was the *alcalde mayor* (district governor) himself, acting as *capitan aguerra* (war captain). Into the early eighteenth century, the number of whites decreased among the Papantla militia's rank and file, making the units more *pardo* and mestizo in composition. Blacks continued serving as militia commanders. In effect, unlike Mexico City, these companies had become free-colored by accretion rather than by direct policy. In name the units were referred to either in racially neutral terms, simply as "militia companies," or occasionally as units of *pardos*, *mulatos*, and *morenos*, despite the fact that other races served in them as well. The choice of nomenclature depended upon changes in local custom and fluctuations over the extent to which free-coloreds had actually come to dominate the militia's ranks. Papantla's situation was not specific to the town but was encountered in numerous rural villages along New Spain's Gulf and Pacific coasts.

There were definitely limits to the means by which free-coloreds could racially transform the integrated militias. Because these companies were initially created without racial guidelines, there were no controls in place to ensure that officers had to be drawn from the free-colored castes. Any evolution along these lines developed purely by custom. Also, the guiding presence of the *capitan aguerra* meant that the voice of free-colored officers, indeed, any officer for that matter, would be muted under the larger concerns of the *alcalde mayor* and his subordinates. As a result, integrated units were left widely exposed to changes in government policy, political influences, and even shifting demographics, as greater doses of whites and mestizos in a region could jeopardize the chances free-coloreds had for exerting effective control.

When a variety of these factors collided, sometimes the solution was to racially segregate a town's "integrated" militias. This appears to have been done in seventeenth-century Tamiagua, where existing rifts between whites, Indians, and free-coloreds were exacerbated by struggles over fishing rights.[55] Between the mid-seventeenth century and the early 1700s, an influx of new white arrivals to the Gulf coast town caused added friction. Wholly polarized, Tamiagua solidified its internal differences through creating separate militia companies from earlier integrated ones; *españoles* served alone, as did free-coloreds. But the structure was never formalized by viceregal approval. Consequently, while the new units were functionally segregated, they were still integrated in legal terms. Obviously, room was open for new problems. In the early 1700s, after the death of the *pardo* captain Nicolas Alexandre, the 750 men who composed the free-colored militia were placed unwillingly under the jurisdiction of a white captain. The *alcalde mayor* himself had ordered the move, so as to quell what he perceived to be increasingly unruly behavior among the free-colored corps. The forces had led a rebellion in 1710 and had engaged in additional tumultuous activities in 1725–26. Moreover, they had proven unreliable in several emergencies. The *alcalde mayor* could justify his actions by relating that there were no legal restrictions forcing him to appoint a free-colored commander.

Several frustrated *pardo* officers sought reprisal by overstepping the local government's jurisdiction. When another opportunity opened in the captains' ranks in 1733, these men eagerly sought the post by applying directly to the viceroy, instead of by first acquiring the necessary recommendation of the *alcalde mayor*. The tactic was an unveiled attempt to subvert the *alcalde mayor*'s efforts at naming yet another white appointee. The free-colored officers supported their actions with evidence. According to their arguments, the militia had fallen into a ruinous state while under white supervision. From time immemorial, free-coloreds had always commanded themselves. It was a preordained rule of nature that like peoples should govern like. Anything else would be illicit by crown law. Therefore, the militiamen demanded that the *alcalde mayor* be pressured into drawing up a slate of three free-colored candidates to assume leadership of the companies. They refused to let the *alcalde mayor* further inhibit the command authority of the town's *pardos* and *morenos*. Unfortunately, the immediate outcome of the matter was not preserved in the case testimony. But other documents reveal that by the middle of the eighteenth century, the companies had again become fully segregated, implying that eventually, persistent free-colored appeals met with success.[56]

Tamiagua's crisis stemmed partly from the fact that integrated militias were not ideal types of units for containing problems in locations where free-coloreds, whites, and mestizos competed aggressively for community resources and military command. Even when the choice was made to adopt a segregated, or "independent," militia framework, further problems could arise when the transition to the new militia order was not clearly defined in legal terms. Tamiagua was not an isolated example. Similar problems occurred in Papantla's integrated companies. The situation came to a head between 1762 and 1764, within the context of Bourbon military reforms. After the outbreak of hostilities with Britain, Viceroy Cruillas commissioned the *alcalde mayor* of neighboring Zacatlán, an experienced military officer, to reform Papantla's militias. After congregating the men into a company of 300, he proceeded to siphon off the pre-existing free-colored officer corps, replacing it with whites. The company was reformed again in 1764, this time under the direction of Don Palacio Pérez, an official member of the Bourbon military reform staff. The newly streamlined company stood at 280 men. Once more, free-coloreds were withheld a place in the upper ranks. Like Tamiagua, the free-coloreds serving in Papantla's integrated militias were extremely vulnerable to policy changes, largely because of the informal role that race played in patterning their units' structure. The Bourbon policy initiatives in Papantla left its company racially lopsided in 1764. Almost all of the ordinary soldiers were free-colored, while the handful of officers were white and mestizo. Arguably, if the same unit had been of the independent type, the Bourbon reform efforts would not have been as successful in eliminating the free-colored officer corps. In light of the changes to their company, Papantla's rank and file responded with an angry letter to their *alcalde mayor:*

Since the beginning, when this company was founded, *pardos* themselves have always been its officers, and these officers have treated us as we deserve; and Your Majesty orders it that way. However, we have experienced a change. Others who are not from our [racial] sphere have only aspired to extol themselves with the grace of the sovereign, and to have us as additional slaves in their businesses.[57]

The *alcalde mayor* read and ignored the plea. Instead, he proceeded to round up and incarcerate its authors. By his actions he demonstrated his full support for the new military program and its light-skinned officers. The event ignited a three-year feud between the free-colored soldiers and the provincial authorities that finally culminated in 1767, when the militiamen proceeded to nominate one of their own for a vacancy in the captain's post. Having learned their lesson, this time they sent all correspondence directly to the viceroy. Unfortunately for them, the tactic produced few concrete results. In fact, the officer corps was left abandoned, with no new officer candidates being accepted for appointment. Even as late as the reforms of 1779, no militiaman in Papantla could be found holding a commissioned grade. Surprisingly, the situation endured despite the fact that additional military reforms had been conducted in 1774, an opportune time to have replenished the officer ranks. With hindsight, one can consider the outcome a modest victory for the free-colored soldiers. Once the originally appointed white and mestizo officers had died, retired, or relocated themselves, they were not replaced with others of their kind. Consequently, aside from the *capitan aguerra* himself, free-colored sergeants and corporals became recognized as the de facto heads of Papantla's integrated militia, although their rank was not of sufficient luster to prove it.[58]

A third and less common type of free-colored militia order was encountered in former maroon communities. In 1607, the *palenque* headed by Álvaro de Baena, on the outskirts of Veracruz, was legitimated in return for the settlement's role in providing coastal defense and protecting against future slave uprisings.[59] Álvaro himself was issued the coveted title of military captain. In 1609, shortly after the heat of battle, Yanga's community was upgraded to town status, becoming the settlement of San Lorenzo de los Negros. As part of the deal, Yanga's forces were required to rechannel their efforts into capturing runaway slaves and defending the zone from hostilities. This meant conferring full militia responsibilities on the community.[60] The trend continued into the eighteenth century. For example, runaways in the town of Amapa were commissioned to serve as lancers for the area of Veracruz in 1769.[61]

Military commissions granted to former slaves and runaways represented an apparent aberration from the cautions exhibited by sixteenth-century policy makers toward utilizing free-colored soldiers. But their actions had a rationale. On the one hand, royal administrators realized the scope of existing manpower shortages in the colony. Areas where runaway slaves had chosen to establish communities were particularly isolated and exposed to encroachment. Administrators felt compelled to rely on black expertise in combating the pressing problems of rural banditry, pirate raids, Indian disturbances, and slave rebellions. On the other hand, the suddenness with which the crown bestowed militia responsibilities on former *palenques* also suggests an attempt at co-opting these former runaways into becoming obliging citizens in colonial society. In this light, the militia must be viewed as an instrument of social engineering, a means of mainstreaming those who had once occupied the fringes of society. Immediately after a *palenque* had been elevated to a township, the colonial government's institutional presence in the settlement was weak. The number of white officials assigned to these towns was low and their influence marginal at best. Issuing high military titles to the prominent leaders of former maroon communities served to tie their fortunes to the crown, obligating them to serve as legates. Having their primacy legitimated through royal channels facilitated the means by which they could substitute for the absence of provincial representatives. Of course, it is debatable to what extent these former slaves actually engaged in carrying forth crown objectives: capturing other runaway slaves and risking their lives at the king's expense. But such observations miss the larger point. What is important is that until increases in mestizo and white immigration to these communities altered the complexion of their racial mix, and worked to assimilate them into the predominant form of rural social order, the militia structure served as a key component in helping reorient these settlements into the pattern of village organization that had been ordained by the colonial government.

As can be inferred from the above typology, free-colored militia service encompassed a wide geographic region in New Spain and incorporated an in-

New Spain and the Diocese of Puebla, Seventeenth and Early Eighteenth Centuries.
(Source: Mapoteca Orozco y Berra, Colleción Orozco y Berra, 1152, varilla 2, Tela
calca manuscrito. Mapa del obispado de la ciudad de la Puebla de los Angeles, gober-
nado por el ilustrísimo señor, Juan Lardizaval y Elorza, 2 ejemplares, autor descono-
cido, sin folio. The map is not drawn to scale.)

determinate number of individuals at any given moment. Commonly speaking, wherever free-coloreds lived there was a strong chance that they participated in the local militia.[62] This was especially true when it is considered that
whites expressed displeasure for military duty, leaving voids in the ranks.[63] Regardless of their individual opinions and prejudices, administrators generally
agreed that blacks demonstrated a greater willingness to take up arms than the
colony's other residents.[64] By the middle of the seventeenth century, the principal regions of free-colored duty began to take shape. The areas possessing
companies of the independent type included Puebla, Mexico City, Campeche,
Mérida, and Veracruz. At a later date, Guadalajara, Valladolid, Acapulco, Orizaba, Cordoba, and Jalapa, among others, possessed these units as well (see
map above). In other words, free-colored service in independent units was
common in the colony's principal administrative and commercial centers.

Significant free-colored participation in companies of the integrated type
was found in the lesser rural towns along the Gulf and Pacific coasts. The same
held true for companies raised in communities of former maroons. A lack of
whites placed the burden of military duty heavily on free-colored shoulders in
those areas, especially since Indians were restricted from militia responsibilities.[65] An impression of the racial imbalance in these coastal locations can be
gleaned through census materials.[66] In the diocese of Puebla, which encompassed a vast region of over 96,000 square kilometers, information from a 1681
census reveals that members of the castes outnumbered whites by a ratio of

TABLE 1
Population of the Central Coasts in the Eighteenth Century

Years	Indians	Whites	Mestizos	*Pardos*	Total
1742–46[a]	26,717	271	54	1,785	28,827
1777[b]	44,917	1,491	1,243	14,362	62,013
1789–93[b]	40,007	5,943	1,240	19,193	66,383

Source: Cook and Borah, *Essays in Population History*, 2: 201–18.
[a]The figures represent the number of families only.
[b]The figures represent the number of persons.

TABLE 2
Militia Units along the Gulf Coast prior to the Bourbon Military Reforms, 1763–66

Location	Number of Companies[a]	Number of Militiamen	Location	Number of Companies[a]	Number of Militiamen
Papantla	1	285	Guejutla	1	147
Tuxpan	1	114	(Huexutla)		
Tihuatlan	1	43	Tempoal	1	94
Tamiagua	3	461	Tampico[b]	2	182
Tamapachi	1	253	Pánuco[b]	2	167
Ozuluama	1	185	Guachinango[c]	2	200
Tantoyuca	2	326	TOTAL	18	2,457

Source: AGN, I.G., vol. 231-B, Luis Bermudo Sorrano, 1763.
[a]All in Racially Mixed Units.
[b]Tampico and Pánuco each had one company reformed by Colonel Escandon.
[c]The Guachinango figure is an estimate based on the observations of Bermudo Sorrano.

TABLE 3
Militia Units in the Jurisdiction of Veracruz prior to the Bourbon Military Reforms, 1758

Location and Unit Type	*Españoles* Companies	Men	*Negros /Pardos* Companies	Men	Racially Mixed Units Companies	Men	Total Soldiers Companies	Men
Veracruz Infantry	4	191	4	268	0	0	8	459
Alvarado Infantry	1	122	0	0	0	0	1	122
Tlacotalpan Infantry	1	182	0	0	0	0	1	182
Veracruz Lancers	0	0	0	0	1	637	1	637
Alvarado Lancers	0	0	0	0	1	65	1	65
Tlacotalpan Lancers	0	0	0	0	1	187	1	187
TOTAL	6	495	4	268	3	889	13	1,652

Source: AGN, I.G., vol. 213-A, Francisco Crespo Ortiz, October 10, 1758, Veracruz.

TABLE 4

Militia Units of New Galicia prior to the Bourbon Military Reforms, 1753–72

Location	Españoles		Pardos, Mulatos, Negros, and Coyotes		Racially Mixed, Indio, or Mestizo Units		Total Soldiers	
	Companies	Men	Companies	Men	Companies	Men	Companies	Men
Guadalajara	4	195	4	309	0	0	8	504
Charcas	7	385	6	330	0	0	13	715
Sierra de Pino	2	100	2	100	0	0	4	200
Tepic	1	50	1	60	1	50	3	160
Xerez, Tresmillo, Taltenango	2	50	0	0	0	0	2	50
Sn. Sebastian, Hostotipac	1	50	1	50	0	0	2	100
Purificación, Tomatlán	2	181	2	102	0	0	4	283
Tequila, Atemanica	2	128	2	90	3[a]	100	7	318
Guastla, Amatitlan	1	50	1	50	1[a]	112	3	212
Nayarit	0	0	0	0	1[a]	69	1	69
Compostela	3	107	1	143	1	56	5	306
Sta. Maria Tequepespam	4	144	1	40	2[a]	65	7	249
Juscauesco	0	0	0	0	4	94	4	94
Zapotlan el Grande	4	240	0	0	0	0	4	240
Tamazula	2	100	1	71	0	0	3	171
Mazamita	0	0	0	0	3	173	3	173
Cuaititlan	2	55	1	49	0	0	3	104
TOTAL	37	1,835	23	1,394	16	719	76	3,948

Source: AGN, I.G., vol. 252-B, Don Nicolas Lopez Padilla, October 13, 1772, Guadalajara.
[a]Denotes Indian companies only.

roughly 2:1 (see map).[67] Upon isolating the rural coastal parishes of Guachinango, Igualapa, Papantla, and Cozamaloapa, covering 14,570 square kilometers, the ratio climbed to 5:1.[68] These were sites that became renowned for free-colored militia duty. After adding the parishes of Acapulco, Nueva Veracruz, and Vieja Veracruz, which encompassed important urban coastal centers of free-colored service, the ratio of castes to whites slipped, but still remained high at 2.3:1.[69]

The free-colored population in New Spain's central coast areas continued to exceed that of whites into the eighteenth century (see Table 1). Loosely defined, the colony's central coasts included the jurisdictions of Tamiagua, Acapulco, Igualapa, Huamelula, Xicayán, and Tehuantepec.[70] The population gap between the races was widest toward the beginning and middle of the century. Between 1742 and 1746, the ratio of *pardo* to white families exceeded 6:1. In terms of individual persons, free-coloreds came to outnumber whites by nearly 10:1 in 1777. During the brief stretch from 1777 to 1793, the white population grew, narrowing the gap to just over 3:1 by the end of the century. But even with white increases, free-coloreds remained firmly in place as the second major population group in the region, and the primary population base for militia duty.[71] Many of these individuals found entry into companies of the integrated type.

TABLE 5

Militia Units in the Archdiocese of Puebla prior to the Bourbon Military Reforms, 1758

Location and Unit Type	Españoles Companies	Españoles Men	Pardos Companies	Pardos Men	Racially Mixed Units Companies	Racially Mixed Units Men	Total Soldiers Companies	Total Soldiers Men
Puebla Infantry	6	995	5	563	0	0	11	1558
Puebla Cavalry	1	164	0	0	0	0	1	164
Cholula Infantry	1	164	1	59	0	0	2	223
Cholula Cavalry	1	114	0	0	0	0	1	114
Atrisco Infantry	1	76	1	60	0	0	2	136
Atrisco Cavalry	1	110	0	0	0	0	1	110
Izucar Infantry	1	164	0	0	0	0	1	164
Chula Infantry	1	111	0	0	0	0	1	111
Tlaxcala Infantry	1	111	0	0	0	0	1	111
Tlaxcala Cavalry	1	74	0	0	0	0	1	74
Guamantla Infantry	1	111	0	0	0	0	1	111
Guamantla Cavalry	1	74	0	0	0	0	1	74
San Phelipe Infantry	1	74	0	0	0	0	1	74
Goaxosingo Infantry	1	128	0	0	unknown	unknown	unknown	unknown
Goaxosingo Cavalry	1	111	0	0	unknown	unknown	unknown	unknown
Tepeaca Infantry	1	128	0	0	unknown	unknown	unknown	unknown
Acacingo Infantry	1	128	0	0	unknown	unknown	unknown	unknown
Quichula Infantry	1	161	0	0	unknown	unknown	unknown	unknown
Tecamachalco Infantry	1	111	0	0	unknown	unknown	unknown	unknown
Chalchicomula Infantry	1	116	0	0	unknown	unknown	unknown	unknown
Chalchicomula Cavalry	1	73	0	0	unknown	unknown	unknown	unknown
Tepexi de la Seda Infantry	1	84	0	0	0	0	1	84
Tehuacan Cavalry	1	164	0	0	unknown	unknown	unknown	unknown
Jalapa Infantry	1	110	0	0	unknown	unknown	unknown	unknown
Jalapa Cavalry	1	74	0	0	unknown	unknown	unknown	unknown
Maulingo Infantry	1	64	0	0	unknown	unknown	unknown	unknown
Maulingo Cavalry	1	64	0	0	unknown	unknown	unknown	unknown
Altotonga Infantry	1	103	0	0	0	0	1	103
Perote Infantry	1	76	0	0	unknown	unknown	unknown	unknown
Azala Infantry	1	83	0	0	0	0	1	83
Xalacingo Infantry	1	153	0	0	unknown	unknown	unknown	unknown
Tecuitlan Infantry	1	255	0	0	0	0	1	255
Atempa Infantry	1	56	0	0	0	0	1	56
Los Llanos Infantry	1	129	0	0	unknown	unknown	unknown	unknown
Los Llanos Cavalry	1	129	0	0	unknown	unknown	unknown	unknown
Zacapoaztla Infantry	1	156	0	0	unknown	unknown	unknown	unknown
Teles Infantry	1	59	0	0	0	0	1	59
Tlaustepec Infantry	1	59	0	0	0	0	1	59
Orizaba Infantry	2	306	1	50	0	0	3	356
Orizaba Cavalry	1	106	0	0	0	0	1	106
Cordoba Infantry	1	106	0	0	0	0	1	106
Cordoba Cavalry	1	106	1	210	0	0	2	316
Coscomotepec Infantry	1	106	0	0	0	0	1	106
Veracruz Lancers	0	0	2	110	unknown	unknown	unknown	unknown
Papantla Infantry	0	0	1	151	unknown	unknown	unknown	unknown
TOTAL	49	5,798	12	1,203	unknown	unknown	unknown	unknown

Source: AGN, I.G., vol. 46-A, Pedro Montesimos de Lara, October 14, 1758, Puebla. Additional companies in which pardos were mixed with whites but the strength was not known included Zacatlan, Galacingo, Piastla, Acatlan, San Agustin Tlaxco, Tulancingo, Amozoque, Tustepeque, Guatepeque, San Andres Guatusco, Tlapa, Coscatlan, Santa Maria Tlapacoya, Olinala, Songolica, Jaliscoyan, San Andres Asala, Tamiagua, San Andres, Tuxtla, Chetla, San Luis de la Costa, San Angel del Palmar, Allustla, Chilapa, Copalillo, and Temalaque.

Tables 2 and 3 provide a detailed look at the strength of the integrated companies along the Gulf coast and in the jurisdiction of Veracruz prior to the Bourbon military reforms of the 1760s and 1770s. To obtain a full sense of how thoroughly free-colored some of these units were, if the military census of 1766 remained a faithful indicator of the troop base that was used to man the companies of Ozuluama, Tantoyuca, Tempoal, Tampico, and Pánuco, then up to 95 percent of their 954 militiamen were free-coloreds near mid-century (see Appendix Table A.1).[72]

Rural New Galicia represents an anomaly in the general dichotomy I have been establishing between urban and rural units (see Table 4). Here, the evidence shows that not all free-colored companies of the independent type were clustered in the province's major cities. Indeed, militia rosters reveal that there were more free-coloreds registered in rural New Galicia's independent companies than in integrated ones. Similarly, there were a score of units reserved only for whites in the countryside. Even in the archdiocese of Puebla in 1758, there were several towns where a significant number of all-white companies operated (see Table 5).

The information apparently indicates that whenever there was a sufficient number of whites in a rural location, strides were taken to separate them into their own militias. This was particularly true if the whites were fairly prominent in their communities and were overtly conscious of their social position in relation to their *pardo* and *moreno* neighbors. However, for the delineation to be made successfully, there also had to be a fairly bountiful free-colored population in residence. This opened the possibility for free-coloreds to either be separated into their own units, as was largely the case in New Galicia, or to be incorporated into integrated companies that held lower-status whites and mestizos. The latter circumstance was found commonly in Puebla, notably in towns located toward the center of the diocese, on the plateau. In these areas there were considerably fewer *pardo* and *moreno* inhabitants than along the coasts.[73] Therefore, it made more sense to include them in integrated companies rather than to isolate them into units that were too small to be of functional value. In brief, what we can surmise is that demographics played a strong role in determining whether integrated or independent forms of militias were to operate in certain regions of the colony.[74]

Free-colored militia service experienced four major periods of development. The early years after 1540, as has been discussed, were the formative years. This sixteenth-century trial period saw extremely limited responsibilities, with free-coloreds mainly manning garrisons and being attached as auxiliaries to other units. With the evolution of the three major types of companies in the seventeenth century, more responsibilities ensued, marking a second period that can be described as one of slow institutional maturity. Yet the duties performed by free-colored militiamen were sporadic and their military privileges were few for most of the seventeenth century. Training sessions united soldiers only once every four months.[75] Militiamen marched together during important religious festivals, but again, these were infrequent. For instance, in small towns along the Gulf coast, such as San Andrés Tuxtla and Acayucan, Holy Week was one of the lone times of the year when all soldiers congregated. Militia inspections were carried out, and the soldiers provided a security force to counter the increased number of fights that took place because of heavy drinking during the holidays. Normally, however, full militia musters in rural areas were inhibited by the great distances that often separated soldiers from their towns of service. In Tuxtla and Acayucan, militiamen and their families resided as far as eighteen leagues from their *cabeceras* (head towns), while in Tehuantepec, some soldiers lived at thirty-four leagues' distance. Furthermore, agricultural responsibilities kept soldiers wedded to their personal *milpas* and *rancherias*. There were five maize harvests in Tuxtla, and cotton was customarily sown from October through December. The constant need to care for crops militated against performing militia service, except in critical emergency situations.[76]

In terms of privileges, tribute relief, an exemption that has been commonly associated with free-colored militia duty, was not in effect for most of the seventeenth century. Moreover, *fueros*, or legal immunities, came about only in the late seventeenth and early eighteenth centuries and were not granted to every location.[77] Even when bestowed, just a handful of soldiers enjoyed *fuero* rights prior to the 1760s—namely, officers and NCOs above the rank of corporal. Unfortunately, not all areas allowed free-coloreds to acquire the commissions of high rank that would allow them to benefit from the *fuero*. The local elite in Campeche jealously guarded against access to officer posts, withholding those ranks from blacks until the late 1600s.[78] For those few individuals who did manage to enjoy the *fuero*, the benefits were applicable exclusively when on campaign, or when the soldiers were fulfilling specific military obligations. *Fueros* could be active (*activo*) or passive (*pasivo*). Under the passive *fuero*, militiamen were immune from prosecution in regular trials. This was the most common type of *fuero*. Under the active *fuero*, militiamen were able to raise cases as plaintiffs, pleading their cause before a special military tribunal, rather than through the ordinary courts. *Fuero* rights were further distinguishable as being applicable either in civil or criminal cases. Militiamen of the highest rank possessed the most complete *fueros*, extending to both civil and criminal proceedings and being both active and passive in nature.[79]

Abridged *fuero* rights and the absence of tribute exemption meant that the seventeenth-century free-colored militia had little social impact in terms of its privileges. Similarly, the infrequency of mobilizations diminished the strength of corporate bonds. Of course, there were exceptions to the rule. Coastal towns that were susceptible to pirate raids posted a twenty-four-hour militia lookout, known as the *vigía*, to alert nearby populations of possible incursions. Free-coloreds were the principal bearers of this responsibility, especially those living closest to strategically situated towns with militia head-quarters. Likewise, in major ports such as Veracruz and Campeche, blacks played regular roles in sentinel and garrison duties, more so than elsewhere in the colony. These tasks increased the soldiers' institutional affiliations. In the 1650s, Veracruz's free-colored militiamen even reinforced their militia ties by founding a confraternity for themselves known as Nuestra Señora de la Purís-sima y Limpia Concepción. Eventually they opened the organization to civil-ian free-coloreds and members of the urban poor. In this way they extended their militia networks beyond the confines of the companies. Yet the soldiers placed provisions in the confraternity's constitution that allowed them to re-tain a measure of control over the brotherhood's top administrative positions. As late as the 1790s, free-colored militia officers were still found responsible for the welfare of the organization.[80] Given the important social role that con-fraternities played in the urban community, the Veracruz militiamen, espe-cially those who ran the brotherhood, came to be seen as important material and spiritual patrons for the lower ranks of urban society. The confraternity provided sick members with care and organized religious ministry and cele-brations. When members died, the confraternity provided limited funeral rites, masses, and assistance with burials. As always, emotional support was given to families during times of crisis. Even small loans were made available to needy members. As the organization's membership expanded, so did its so-cial reach, thereby expanding the influence of Veracruz's free-colored militia-men.

Nevertheless, it should be kept in mind that the effort put forth by Vera-cruz's militia in raising the confraternity was an exception for the period. For the majority of free-colored militiamen during the sixteenth and seventeenth centuries, duty meant little more than a series of occasional gatherings to counter pirate raids, defend ports, capture slaves, or quell Indian uprisings. After those brief duties had concluded, there was little else to sustain the mili-tia or transfer its influence into the wider space of civilian society.

A series of circumstances brought dramatic change to the nature of duty toward the end of the seventeenth century, signaling a third distinguishable period of militia service that stretched until the 1760s. From the 1670s until the early eighteenth century, free-colored militiamen began petitioning the crown for tribute exemption, thereby engaging the soldiers in legal debates that tran-scended their purely military activities. The terms of the agreements that were reached held enormous potential for altering civil-military relations, particu-larly along the coasts. The year 1683 was also one of tremendous consequence. A bold raid made by privateer extraordinaire Lorenzo de Graff, known in New Spain as "Lorencillo," resulted in one of the most punishing events yet experi-enced by the viceroyalty. Landing in Veracruz with a force of nine hundred men, he herded over six thousand of the city's prominent individuals into churches, where his troops held them under a watchful eye. Then his men sacked, raped, and pillaged, killing three hundred citizens in the process and securing over seven million pesos in booty.[81] Although the attack was over within a week and was just one of many pirate expeditions to strike New Spain, its implications were wider. The raiders had made light work of the defenses of the most strategic point in the kingdom, completely exposing the colony's state of military weakness. Alarmingly, the road to Mexico City from Veracruz was an easy one. Travelers moving quickly during the late seventeenth century could cover the distance in three to four days. A heavily packed army might reach the capital in just over three weeks.[82] As soon as the viceroy heard the news, he realized that a siege of the capital could be imminent.

A hasty muster was made to send reinforcements to Veracruz, resulting in streams of troops pouring out from the capital. Summonses were also sent to Puebla, Orizaba, Jalapa, Oaxaca, Atrisco, Cholula, and Querétaro, among other locations.[83] Fortunately for colonial administrators, Lorencillo and his associates were uninterested in the protracted and arduous effort needed to make a deep run into the interior. Easy coastal plunder was more attractive than capturing an entire colony that his small force could never hope to maintain. His raiders quickly moved on, harassing other ports in the viceroyalty. However, the strike reshaped the profile of free-colored militia service. As would be proven on numerous future occasions, nothing was more effective for inspiring the creation of new militia units than a military emergency. To protect against similar raids, and to increase the strength of the inland buffer, new *pardo* and integrated companies sprang up throughout the diocese of Puebla. Additionally, pre-existing free-colored units were reformed in order to improve their fighting capacity.[84] In Puebla and Mexico City the overhaul marked such a departure from the old order that the founding date of the companies in both cities was often erroneously cited as being this date.[85] Also at this time, criminal and civil *fueros* were introduced for officers in Mexico City, with the most comprehensive set of privileges being conferred on the newly elected captain *comandante* (commanding captain). His company was the first one that had been reformed in the city after Lorencillo's attack, and was officially designated as the oldest free-colored unit. *Comandante* rank provided its owner with broad supervisory powers over the other captains and allowed his company to step first in marching order, thereby exhibiting itself as the most celebrated unit during military functions and parades. But for the *comandante* to retain his primacy it was important that 1683 be understood as the militia founding date. All *comandante* privileges hinged on his ability to establish his unit's antiquity in the context of the late seventeenth century's military reforms. This partly explains the commitment, at least by some officers in Mexico City, in portraying the Lorencillo event as the seminal moment of free-colored militia history.[86]

Lorencillo's raid on Veracruz was followed fairly quickly by other major events. These served to solidify free-colored service into important defensive roles in ways that had not been seen previously, especially in Mexico City and neighboring Puebla. Lorencillo struck again in 1685, plundering the port of Campeche. Puebla's free-colored troops were rushed to the scene. In 1692, grain riots in Mexico City caused serious internal chaos that brought important mobilizations of the free-colored and merchant militias, including a *pardo* detachment from Puebla.[87] In terms of the severity of domestic unrest, the 1692 uprisings were matched in scale only by the politically inspired protests against Viceroy Gelves in 1624.[88] Free-colored troops remained stationed at various centers throughout the capital for several months. A few years later, the War of the Spanish Succession introduced more potential foreign threats to the viceroyalty, necessitating additional garrisoning of Veracruz. Free-colored troops from Puebla marched to the port with a force of 106 men in 1701. Preparations for another march were made in 1710. Even in Oaxaca, free-colored units were poised at the ready.

Large-scale mobilizations designed to meet internal and external threats were accompanied by an increased regularization of daily militia responsibilities, thereby transforming the institution from being one of casual participation into being one of routine duty. In the countryside, the shortage of bailiffs and constables, as well as the poor condition of jails, produced a situation whereby local and regional officials—namely district governors (*alcaldes mayores, corregidores, gobernadores*) and their subordinates (*tenientes de justicia*)—relied increasingly upon militiamen as deputies who enforced the law.[89] Moreover, since they were in office for only short terms, *alcaldes mayores* were often unfamiliar with the nuances of their regions, particularly at the outset of their administrations. Dependence on local expertise, especially free-colored militiamen, was considered crucial for achieving effective government in areas where blacks were a significant presence. Additionally, local administrators fell victim to holding a very narrow view of the free-colored population, being quick to believe that they constituted a homogenous group with implicit cohesion. In colonial documents, one constantly encounters administrators' references to free-coloreds as *esa gente, nación, clase,* and *aquella gente.*[90] As a result of this mindset, colonial authorities in rural areas perceived the role of the free-colored militia, particularly the officer corps, in much the same light as the caciques of the Indian pueblos.[91] Both were deemed natural leaders of their respective "communities." They were called upon to serve as interlocutors for the government by shaping opinions, extracting taxes, harnessing labor, imposing the law, and influencing their racial peers through a variety of informal means. These militia functions assumed greater prominence in the eighteenth century. An excellent sense of the role assigned to free-colored troops can be obtained from the words of military commander Don Joseph Fluri, writing about the province of Xicayan in the 1790s: "With the subjection of some of them [free-colored militia officers], they can govern and place the black and mulatto inhabitants under subordination, since only these [officers] can achieve this. Only they can get delinquents into jail and accomplish whatever else that they want to do."[92] Fluri went on to recommend a list of pliant and obedient officers, respected by their community, who he believed were perfect candidates to serve as legates in the government's effort to enhance its control.

Depending upon location, the array of new responsibilities that appeared toward the end of the seventeenth century exceeded the militiamen's normal military duties. Even in racially integrated companies, it always seemed that free-coloreds bore the brunt of the work burden. Soldiers might be called upon for anything. In Jalapa, they regularly escorted the royal silver train that arrived from Mexico City en route to Veracruz.[93] In Xicayan free-colored militiamen doubled as mail carriers, circulating royal decrees throughout the province, especially across the difficult terrain of the cordillera.[94] Soldiers were often required to apprehend criminals and post guard at public buildings. On occasion, certain *alcaldes mayores* required the men to keep watch at their homes, more as a status symbol than to serve any defensive purpose. Similarly, when important outsiders visited the provincial head towns, local officials might call out the militia to perform maneuvers to impress the guests. More often than not, the multiple responsibilities of militiamen in rural towns fell upon the shoulders of those living closest to the sites of duty, which were normally the *cabeceras*. It was not unheard of, however, for men to be summoned who lived at great distance.

Alcaldes mayores and local justices possessed notorious reputations for abusing the privileges of their offices.[95] They manipulated taxes and fees. They charged the populace dearly for performing the most basic public functions, such as measuring land, certifying wills, and taking inventories.[96] In an increasing capacity over the seventeenth and eighteenth centuries, local justices attempted to use militiamen as tools in their exploitative efforts. For example, soldiers who worked as constables were encouraged to be overly zealous in apprehending citizens, so as to collect extra bail money or bribes from those trying to avoid incarceration. District governors and *tenientes* were not always fully successful in recruiting militiamen for their projects. Much like the *caciques*, when free-colored militiamen were asked to engage in these activities, they found themselves deliberating their position as intermediaries. Depending upon the strength of their allegiances to the provincial authorities, the soldiers might aggressively do the government's bidding, sometimes reaping financial gain in the process. Or the militiamen could tailor the demands placed upon them in order to better serve their fellow townspeople. It appears that militiamen frequently balanced both roles. When they opposed government officials, messy disputes ensued.

In Papantla during the 1770s and 1780s, free-colored militiamen protested that the abuses enacted by the *alcalde mayor* were becoming unbearable. Citizens were being charged an average of three to four pesos per legal encounter, a hefty price that amounted to several times the daily wage. The militiamen no longer wanted to play a part in the scheme.[97] But legislation was passed in 1781 that demanded that soldiers remain subordinate to their *alcaldes mayores* in all civil and criminal affairs, dutifully assisting these provincial governors upon request. Using the 1781 codes as supporting evidence, Papantla's *alcalde mayor* reiterated the soldiers' legal obligation to duty and warned of sharp reprisals for those who failed to comply with his wishes. Regardless, the militiamen remained adamant in the face of his flagrant abuses. Rebuffed, the *alcalde mayor* resorted to other forms of coercion. To prod the unwilling men into duty, he began meting out unduly harsh punishments and fines onto the soldiers themselves.

Papantla's situation was far from unique. The late seventeenth and eighteenth centuries witnessed frequent jousting between militiamen and rural authorities as each tried to establish the limits of the soldiers' increasing responsibilities. Especially after the 1760s, when *fuero* privileges increased for the provincial militia's rank and file, thereby granting them a measure of legal immunity from the *alcaldes mayores*, it became more difficult for local officials to gather men for tasks. Under the traditional method of summons, a team of drummers proceeded to a town's plaza and began playing loudly. Upon hearing the battery, soldiers would hastily congregate to see what was needed. However, with the advent of comprehensive *fuero* rights, fewer men appeared. Typically, those heeding the call were either too old for duty or enjoyed other forms of service exemptions. The majority of the militiamen simply remained in their homes. Using the *fuero* as an excuse, they claimed that the only authority they were now required to recognize was that of their company captain. Tensions mounted in these situations as angry rural officials sought other ways to press the soldiers into service.[98]

While in the countryside a score of small and sometimes illegal duties were heaped upon the militia in the seventeenth and eighteenth centuries, in places such as Mexico City, Antequera, Puebla, and Jalapa the expansion of daily militia responsibilities was achieved through the implementation of night patrols. After 1683, free-colored militiamen in all four cities were specified to form small squadrons that would walk the streets from dusk till dawn.[99] They were authorized to carry weapons on their rounds and were required to bear a special insignia to announce their authority. Soldiers alternated patrol duties so that the burden of responsibility would eventually rotate among every man in the companies. Out of fear of losing precious sleep that could jeopardize their day jobs, some militiamen paid their friends to substitute for them. As with most militia labors, night patrols were an unpaid obligation. The militiamen's beats were independent of those of the municipal constables, or *alguaciles*. Yet, like those law-enforcement officers, the soldiers' rounds fell under the jurisdiction of the Real Sala de Crimen, which was the colony's highest criminal court of appeals.[100]

Our understanding of the mechanics of these patrols is best for Mexico

City. The viceroy was initially responsible for first creating the patrols in the capital; through a special commission, he broadly outlined the militiamen's responsibilities. Hence, while soldiers' activities were subject to daily supervision by the Real Sala, the ultimate authority on all matters pertaining to the rounds was the viceroy himself. Indeed, he periodically reviewed the terms of the militiamen's contract and assessed their duties, as in 1701 and 1716, when the free-colored militia's patrolling commission was renewed.

The militiamen registered with the Real Sala before conducting rounds each night, thereby providing city officials with a written record of the soldiers who were scheduled for duty. Generally, the militiamen were responsible for apprehending criminals and maintaining watch only at the outskirts of the city. Limiting their jurisdiction to the outer barrios conformed with contemporary theories of urban planning. The downtown center area, or *traza*, was delineated as a space of principally Spanish domain. Perimeter areas were left to be inhabited by Indians, blacks, and mixed castes.[101] These were artisan neighborhoods and working-class sections of the city. In other words, in its original conception, the free-colored militia patrols were established in such a way that the soldiers would primarily be charged with having custody over others who, socially and racially, resembled themselves.

During rounds, any individuals found loitering were to have their names placed in a logbook. This was to be handed over to representatives of the Real Sala the following morning. No one was to be excluded from entry in the register, regardless of age, race, class, or gender. Sometimes the soldiers captured criminals. These were to be promptly turned over to municipal authorities. Militiamen were prevented from pressing charges against lawbreakers, emphasizing that they were simply the instruments of crime prevention rather than implementers of legal justice.

A revealing situation developed in the early 1720s when the *auditor de guerra*, being the senior military legal officer, simultaneously held an appointment as *alcalde de corte*, which gave him municipal responsibilities over a portion of Mexico City. At the time, the city was divided into six *cuarteles*, or wards. Three of these came under the direct care of the Real Sala, while the others fell under the stewardship of the *alcaldes ordinarios*, the *alcaldes de corte*, and the *corregidor*. The *auditor de guerra*, overburdened with work from both his municipal and military posts, privately contracted the free-colored militia to police his *cuartel*. The relationship proved to be a harmonious one, with the soldiers bringing apprehended criminals directly to the *auditor*. Once the *auditor*'s term as *alcalde de corte* had ended, the soldiers' patrols came once again under the exclusive watch of the Real Sala. The lesson learned was that on occasion, free-colored militiamen might be called upon to perform special duties that were not directly sanctioned by the viceroy or the Real Sala.[102] As a result, soldiers began patrolling areas of the city that were not specified under their original commission, producing a potential source of conflict with municipal authorities. In fact, the militiamen's area of operations had been expanding incrementally ever since 1683. The 1692 grain riots placed the soldiers into the fray along the Calle Real, at the Royal Palace, near the church of San Dimas, and at the Hospital of the Pura and Limpia Concepción. Many of these locations were in the heart of the *traza*. The soldiers' heroic accomplishments in recovering stolen goods and protecting the palace served as a precedent for placing them in other guard positions around the city. Sometimes the soldiers of the *comandante*'s units were even requested to perform military exercises directly inside the viceregal court. In Puebla, similar strides were being made as militiamen were asked to protect the cathedral, jails, hospitals, and administrative structures, particularly after the urban riots of 1729.[103] In short, through their expanding sentry duties, free-colored militiamen were becoming coterminous with the physical symbols of colonial authority. The fact was not lost upon the most ambitious of their number, who used their guard and patrol duties as leverage to support the militiamen's arguments in legal petitions. From a tenuous start at the beginning of the eighteenth century, by the 1760s free-coloreds were found patrolling, guarding, and maintaining bivouacs throughout Puebla and Mexico City.[104]

Unsurprisingly, night patrols evolved into contentious events. Disputes occurred with municipal authorities over matters of proper jurisdiction, especially as the militiamen's arena of operations expanded. Conflicts with ordinary citizens were also common. In 1729, Mexico City's militiamen related that while they had apprehended countless criminals during their tenure and had worked to bring peace to the municipality, in return, they had been treated by the public with cruelty and slandered "with words so indecent that we cannot repeat here."[105] Serious confrontations arose when soldiers attempted to register individuals into the logbooks. Some claimed their *fuero* immunity and physically resisted entry. Others fell back upon their social position, claiming to be above reproach. In one brutal incident, taking place on February 1, 1724, a party of militiamen approached a man walking near the *calzada* de Belén around 8:30 P.M. He resisted interrogation, killing a soldier in the process. Unfortunately, the delinquent escaped and was never brought to justice; however, the free-colored colonel pointed to the incident as symptomatic of the militiamen's woes. In the wake of the murder, he appealed to the viceroy, requesting that a *bando* be published for all to see, detailing the exact jurisdiction of the militiamen and highlighting their right to detain citizens. He urged that circulating the *bando* throughout Mexico City would help deter future calamities against the militiamen. It was not the first time he had made the request, and it would not be the last. From 1725 to 1729, he continually pressed his concerns, only to have his petitions partially heard.

The viceroy passed the appeal on to the *auditor de guerra*, who in turn sent it to the Real Sala. No one wanted to deal directly with the issue. The attorneys of the Real Sala finally determined that it would be unwise to publish a *bando* of militia duties since it might cause unspecified "novelties" in the rounds that would result in more problems. What they really meant was that scandalous situations might result for certain people if they were pressured by viceregal decree into registering in the logbooks. The attorneys sought to protect the city's elite from any potential embarrassment that might occur after an illicit late-night rendezvous.[106] The colonel continued lobbying his case and obtained a clearer decision on matters in 1729. Ultimately, it was resolved that the militiamen were to continue registering individuals into the logbooks. But in instances in which the people detained were publicly recognized secular authorities, the soldiers were to refrain from entering their names. In circumstances in which lesser-known citizens resisted log entry on account of their *fueros* or immunities, they were to be placed on a separate list that was to be handed over to their prelates and superiors. Those authorities in turn would determine the course of action that needed to be taken against their subordinates.[107]

The protracted ordeal demonstrated that the crown's respect for the urban elite prevented it from taking a strong initial stand in favor of the militiamen's patrol duties, even though those militia responsibilities had been originally drafted by royal officials in the first place. Hesitations over clarifying militia policy kept the night rounds in a state of controversy. The 1729 ruling did much to resolve unsettled issues, but the rights granted to the urban elite concerning logbook entry eventually sustained problems on the patrols, as certain strata of society continued to denigrate and question the authority of the free-colored militia.

From the late seventeenth century onward, increased militia obligations in the form of night patrols, sentry duties, and mobilizations inevitably led to a growing militia involvement in local political affairs. Being a member of a certain company could tie one's fortunes to specific factions embroiled in struggles for power and privilege. The case of the town of Acayucan in the 1750s is revealing. Two companies of *pardos* operated there. One was under the command of Capt. Antonio Telles, a favorite of the *alcalde mayor*. The other was led by Lt. Juan Domingo Ramos, a friend of the town's priest, Dn. Buenaventura Urbina. For years, the priest and *alcalde mayor* had clashed over personal matters, jurisdictional authority, and town management. When Domingo Ramos suddenly appeared in Acayucan in the early 1740s, having fled the city of Nueva Veracruz after committing murder, he received nurturing protection from the town's priest. Amid much scandal, the clergyman personally ensured that Domingo Ramos rose quickly through the ranks, providing the financial backing to make him a lieutenant shortly after his arrival. By helping to position Domingo Ramos, he had created the perfect ally in his feud against the *alcalde mayor*. Although a wanted fugitive, Domingo Ramos possessed prior military experience in Veracruz's Dragoon Regiment and could prove useful in Urbina's schemes. It was not long after receiving his officer's commission that Domingo Ramos went about customizing his militia company into a personal army.

He entwined his soldiers through gossip, plots, and jealousy, ensuring that a cadre always remained loyal to him. It soon became clear that anyone affiliated with his unit was politically aligned with the priest, while others were sided with the *alcalde mayor*. Pressure came to a head when the *alcalde mayor* formally denounced both Domingo Ramos and the priest to the viceregal authorities. Domingo Ramos immediately traveled to Mexico City to clear the charges. But the matter did not end there. The Real Audiencia ordered investigations into the *alcalde mayor*'s allegations, and into the nature of several suspicious transactions. Teams of commissioners were dispatched to Acayucan. Tensions flared during one of the visits, leading the *alcalde mayor* to arrest Dn. Cristobal Buitrago, a good friend of the priest. Domingo Ramos retaliated. With the priest's blessing, he turned his house into an armed barracks, hoisted his company's flag, and marched a detachment of *pardo* troops to the jailhouse. There he was received by the *alcalde mayor* and another host of armed *pardo* troops under the command of Capt. Telles. The initial event resulted in a stalemate, but the next day, renewed efforts eventually freed the prisoner.[108] Although merely a single example, the ordeal underscores how the soldiers' allegiances often possessed political implications in their towns. Both Acayucan's *alcalde mayor* and priest used the free-colored militia as pawns in their moves for municipal control. In the process, individual militiamen's careers benefited and flourished, even changing the life fortunes of a wanted criminal.

The 1760s brought a rude change to the modus operandi of New Spain's military affairs, marking the fourth and final period of free-colored militia duty. The crown's laissez-faire approach toward handling the free-colored companies during the seventeenth and early eighteenth centuries meant that these units, especially those of the independent type, conducted much of their business with minimal outside supervision. Therefore, the growing responsibilities and politicization of the companies occurred within a context of relative internal militia autonomy. As if in a feedback loop, the maturing of the militia into an institution with increased privileges, visibility, and social impact worked to further increase its overall autonomy and strength. By the 1740s and 1750s, militiamen in places such as Mexico City and Puebla were quick to challenge the government on issues of rights and procedure that would have been unimaginable at the outset of the century. Some free-colored commanders were in the rare position of requesting the viceregal government to grant them supervisory rights over all the colony's black militia forces.

But after the shock of losing Havana, and with the arrival of the first Bourbon military reformers to New Spain in 1764, the emphasis on improving military quality necessarily involved tightening free-colored militia regulations, autonomy, and structure. Another consequence involved whitening their units. The first steps in these directions consisted of establishing what was known as the "provincial" militia system, installed to replace the older, urban militia forces. Initially introduced in Spain itself in 1734, the provincial militia plan showcased "disciplined" companies that received regular professional training and were regulated according to stringent crown specifications. The details of the new militia order began to take a clear and standardized shape throughout the Indies after the publication of the Cuban *reglamento* in 1769. Essentially, the defining feature of the provincial plan was the stationing of a veteran army cadre in each regiment. These regulars would supervise the militiamen's training, activities, and internal affairs.[109] It was hoped that their guiding influence would take a concentric hold on the general population, as the cadre's ability to control military actions and maneuvers radiated outward through the militia.

The effect of adopting the provincial design meant that free-colored companies of the independent type had to cope with the presence of unwanted white regulars who scrutinized their actions and often brought haughty and prejudicial attitudes to their work. Companies of the integrated type had to put up not only with the veteran cadre but also with a serious increase in the number of white officers placed in the upper ranks, as militia reformers discouraged the presence of free-coloreds in these positions. In the Gulf coast provinces of Tampico, Pánuco, and in the jurisdiction of Huexutla, the 1766 switch to the provincial system saw almost the entire white, adult male population garner the posts of captain, lieutenant, or second lieutenant. A census taken prior to the reforms identified just thirty-two whites eligible for militia duty in those locations. A full twenty-one of their number became officers after the reforms. Of the more than eight hundred eligible male *pardos*, just six were installed as officers, half at the low rank of second lieutenant (see Appendix Tables A.1 and A.2).[110]

The implementation of the provincial system took place in stages in New Spain, thereby affecting the extent and geographical coverage of the military reforms. Lieutenant General Juan de Villalba y Angulo, the captain general of Andalusia, was the first to be commissioned with the task, serving as inspector general to New Spain between 1764 and 1766. Although he managed to raise six provincial infantry regiments, three battalions, and two cavalry regiments during his tenure, his program was doomed to an uncertain future from its inception. There were few guidelines in place regarding the nature of Villalba's authority in the colony, inspiring him to act arbitrarily. Shortly after his arrival he began authoring his own military policy, without consulting Viceroy Cruillas. Needless to say, his independent actions insulted the viceroy, who tenaciously challenged Villalba's reform efforts, thereby complicating the reform process.

When the charge of reform was finally passed to Viceroy Carlos Francisco de Croix in 1767, many of the jurisdictional problems witnessed during the previous two years were resolved. Under Croix's administration, the policy directives of the viceroy were firmly established as superior to those of the two inspector generals, the Marqués de Torre and Francisco Douché. The provincial militia companies of Valladolid, Guadalajara, Pátzcuaro, Oaxaca, Tampico, and Pánuco were created under Croix's oversight. The urban free-colored companies of Mexico City, Veracruz, and Puebla, already changed by Villalba, were placed on a more solid provincial footing. Additionally, mixed legions of cavalry and infantry were formed in Guanajuato and San Luis Potosí shortly after uprisings rocked both cities in 1767. However, as Croix went about establishing new units, he also condensed the troop rosters of the companies founded by his predecessor. In Croix's estimation, Villalba's proposed numbers for militia strength were simply out of touch with the manpower realities of New Spain. Moreover, in light of the 1767 riots, too heavy a reliance upon Mexican-born militiamen could present a new set of problems, as loyalties among the colonists had proven to be divided.

The Bourbon military reforms entered a definable third stage during the administrations of Viceroy Bucareli (1771–79) and Martín Mayorga (1779–83). The period was marked by protracted debate over the extent to which Mexicans would be relied upon for their own defense. Planners were quickly coming to realize that the first decade of reforms had produced a less than satisfactory outcome. Veteran army cadres stationed in provincial regiments had become models of laziness rather than the inspirational backbone of the corps. Within a few years, many of these officers fell victim to their own obscurity. Stationed in remote towns distant from their homeland, they degenerated into petty thieves, drunkards, and public nuisances. Seeing this situation, a number of vocal proponents favored reverting to the older, urban militia forces for defense. These would be recast under the label *sueltas*, or reserve militia units. Aside from the usual differences that existed between the urban and provincial forces, the *sueltas* would be even more casually called upon for duty, serving only as reinforcements to regular battalions in emergency situations. There would be no formal attempt to train these men. Instead, the *sueltas* would be subjected to an annual review by a military inspector, the purpose of which was merely to ensure that a sufficient number of warm bodies continued to fill the militia posts.

The problem with relying too heavily upon the *sueltas* was that it placed too much of the defense burden on veteran forces, particularly those transferred from Spain. Lean royal finances could not foot the bill. As a result, despite the years of strident debate, viceroys Bucareli and Mayorga eventually pursued a moderate course in implementing a military plan. Their proposals were heavily influenced by Inspector Pascual de Cisneros, who was one of the few peninsular-born administrators who placed great faith in the fighting capacity of creoles. Cisneros's tenure as inspector general lasted for the full duration of the thirteen-year period, providing some much-needed stability to military affairs. The reforms he supervised were substantial. Apart from expanding the geographic reach of the provincial program, raw numbers increased significantly, jumping from a strength of 9,244 soldiers to 16,755 (see Appendix Tables A.3 and A.4).[111] Cisneros also improved training procedures and internal militia relations. He required all militia captains to attend weekly training classes. For soldiers, Sundays were to be reserved for assemblies and arms instruction. Abusive punishments inflicted upon the militiamen by their superiors were to be curtailed, and regular reviews of training cadres were to take place. He and his staff were to carry out frequent inspections personally.[112]

Spain's war against Britain (1779–83) during the American Revolution proved once again the limitations of New Spain's army. Fortunately the colony escaped danger. But if an attack had been made, few would have been prepared to provide resistance. In 1783–84, military planner Col. Francisco Crespo designed a scheme to deal with the colony's perceived military shortcomings. However, a series of administrative crises, including the quick deaths of two viceroys, postponed the adoption of his suggestions until 1787, when Viceroy Manuel Antonio Flórez proceeded fully with the Crespo plan. Crespo's sober recommendations represented a compromise of all previous military proposals. The defense of the colony would rely unquestionably upon creoles, interspersed with a respectable regular army force. Provisions for urban, *suelta*, and provincial militias were all included. This meant that there would not be a commitment to abolish the provincial militia order in favor of undisciplined units. During wartime, the combined strength of the veteran and militia forces would amount to a maximum of forty thousand men. Most important, the costs for realizing the scheme were reasonable. The plan received relatively quick approval from Spain. By May of 1787, initial moves were being made to carry out the defense modifications called for by Crespo (see Appendix Table A.5).

But the push for military reform came to a halt under the subsequent viceregal administration of Revillagigedo. Called to take over the colony in 1789, Revillagigedo proceeded to single-handedly dismantle most of the work done by his predecessors. He deeply feared that by arming creoles, the crown was writing its own death sentence for the New World empire. These suspicions were matched only by his contempt for blacks, free-coloreds, and Indians. Acting on his impulses, he seriously downsized the provincial militia system in his plan of 1790 and provided the fatal blows to free-colored forces shortly thereafter. After 1793, free-coloreds served in independent companies mainly in the port of Veracruz, and in severely reduced numbers in a small selection of racially integrated units throughout the colony. While the succeeding reforms of Viceroy Branciforte increased the number of provincial units, for all intents and purposes, the era of widespread free-colored service had ended by the mid-1790s (see Appendix Tables A.6–A.9).[113]

The numerous starts and reversals of the Bourbon military reforms, which can be traced in this policy overview, meant that the organization of New Spain's militia companies after 1764 was almost always in a constant state of flux. However, even the neatly distinguishable policy stages outlined above were played out in a much more scattered fashion at the provincial level. It took time to arrange and send out teams of inspectors that could reorganize existing militia forces and raise new ones. As a consequence, reforms were felt unevenly throughout the colony, both in geographical terms and regarding when specific changes were implemented. In broad view, the reform period from 1764 to 1793 brought about an overall *reduction* in the number of active free-colored militiamen in New Spain, quite the opposite of the much-touted military expansion that was said to have occurred among colonial whites.[114] The declines were felt hardest along the coasts. We have already seen how the transition to the provincial order increased the number of white officers found in Tampico, Pánuco, and Huexutla, to the detriment of free-colored officer access. The changes to the rank and file were apparently more profound.

Lacking complete data for New Spain's free-colored rosters, a few key cases will serve to illustrate the point. In the province of Tuxtla, reforms conducted in 1775 witnessed a substantial decrease in the overall number of active militiamen, more than a 50 percent decline (see Tables 6 and 7). While all racial groups experienced drops, none were as hard hit as Indian and free-colored militiamen. Indians were completely stricken from duty, while the number of *mulatos* and *pardos* dropped to less than half. Even though the end result of the reforms was the creation of highly standardized and uniform units in the region, military participation was now out of balance with the province's demographic racial distribution. Whites and mestizos disproportionately bore the brunt of militia service. The creation of provincial companies in Guachinango had the same effect. Military reforms took hold in 1781, replacing the previously existing squadrons with regiment-styled, racially integrated companies (see Tables 8 and 9). As in Tuxtla, the shift to the provincial order brought about a more than 50 percent decline in the total number of militiamen. Racially speaking, whites experienced the smallest numerical loss, while *pardos* registered at least a fourfold drop. Farther south, in the province of Tabasco, estimates reveal that the militia reforms of 1766–68 brought about a drop to less than half in free-colored participation. The number of free-coloreds incorporated into the region's militias prior to the Bourbon reforms stood at more than thirteen hundred men. After the reforms, the number was curtailed to just five hundred soldiers.

Information from several locations has been grouped together to provide a look at the provincial militias in the Gulf coast region running north from Papantla to Tampico (see Table 10). In these areas, free-coloreds consistently composed three-fourths of the troop base used to form the region's racially integrated companies.[115] The table reflects a 35 percent overall decline in troop

TABLE 6

Militia Units in Tuxtla prior to the Bourbon Military Reforms, 1775

Location and Unit Type	Españoles		Mestizos		Mulatos /Pardos		Indios Caciques		Total Soldiers	
	Compa- nies	Men	Compa- nies	Men	Compa- nies	Men	Compa- nies	Men	Compa- nies	Men
San Andres Tuxtla Infantry	1	83	1	93	1	156	1	77	4	409
Santiago Tuxtla In- fantry	1	73	1	78	1	141	0	0	3	292
TOTAL[a]	2	156	2	171	2	297	1	77	7	701

Source: AGN, I.G., vol. 33-B, Antonio de Saavedra to Dn. Juan Fernando de Palacio, November 12, 1775, Tuxtla.

[a]In addition to the company of *indios caciques*, there were actually seventy-five *indios* serving in the various types of racially segregated units of both towns: six in white companies, thirteen in mestizo units, and fifty-six in the *mulato/pardo* companies.

TABLE 7

Provincial Militiamen in Tuxtla after the Bourbon Military Reforms of 1775

Location and Unit Type	Españoles		Mestizos		Mulatos/Pardos		Total Soldiers	
	Companies	Men	Companies	Men	Companies	Men	Companies	Men
San Andres Tuxtla Infantry	1	53	0	0	0	0	1	53
San Andres Tuxtla Lancers	0	0	1	50	1	50	2	100
Santiago Tuxtla Infantry	1	53	0	0	0	0	1	53
Santiago Tuxtla Lancers	0	0	1	50	1	50	2	100
TOTAL	2	100	2	100	2	100	6	306

Source: AGN, I.G., vol. 33-B, Antonio de Saavedra to Dn. Juan Fernando de Palacio, November 12, 1775, Tuxtla.

TABLE 8

Provincial Militiamen in Guachinango after the Bourbon Military Reforms of 1781

Location and Unit Type	Number of *Españoles*	Number of *Pardos*	Total Soldiers
Tuxpan Infantry	23	73	96
Temapache Infantry	Not Given	Not Given	114
Temapache Cavalry	Not Given	Not Given	63
Tihuatlan Cavalry	24	47	71
TOTAL SOLDIERS	47	120	344

Source: AGN, I.G., vol. 484-A, Tomas Gil de Onzue to Martin Mayorga, June 18, 1781. The 344 men in the table were distributed into four racially integrated companies. Their muster does not reflect the eventual full strength of the Guachinango reformed units, which was slated to reach 663 men.

TABLE 9

Militia Units in Guachinango prior to the Bourbon Military Reforms, 1781

Location and Unit Type	Españoles		Pardos		Total Soldiers in Unreformed Units	
	Squadrons	Men	Squadrons	Men	Squadrons	Men
Tamiagua Infantry	0	0	8	391	8	391
Tuxpan Infantry	1	25	2	73	3	98
Tihuatlan Infantry	1	26	1	48	2	74
Temapache Infantry	Not Given	Not Given	Not Given	Not Given	6	209
TOTAL SOLDIERS	2	51	11	512	19	772

Source: AGN, I.G., vol. 484-A, Tomas Gil de Onzue to Martin Mayorga, June 18, 1781.

TABLE 10

Militia Strength of Selected Gulf Coast Sites before and after the Bourbon Military Reforms

Location	Number of Militiamen prior to Reforms, 1763–66		Number of Militiamen after Reforms, 1766–80	
	Companies	Men	Companies	Men
Papantla	1	285	2	150
Tuxpan	1	114	1	96
Tihuatlan	1	43	1	71
Tamapachi	1	253	2	177
Ozuluama	1	185	2	159
Tantoyuca	2	326	2	156
Guejutla (Huexutla)	1	147	2	140
Tempoal	1	94	1	78
Tampico[a]	2	182	1	77
Pánuco[a]	2	167	1	77
TOTAL	13	1,796	15	1,181

Source: AGN, I.G. 231-B, Luis Bermudo Sorrano, 1763; AGN, I.G., vol. 490-A, August 9, 1766, Gorostiza to Villaba; AGN, I.G., vol. 490-A, Gorostiza to Marques de Croix, October 17, 1766; AGN, I.G., vol. 490-A, Gorostiza to Villaba, October 1766; and AGN, I.G., vol. 484-A, Tomas Gil de Onzue to Martin Mayorga, June 18, 1781.

[a]After additional military reforms conducted in 1780, the Tampico and Pánuco troop levels reached 160 men per town.

strength during the military reform period from 1766 to 1780. Although increases to troop numbers in Tampico and Pánuco were made in 1780, the total number of militiamen remained a fourth less than before the reforms. Given that so many of the troops were free-coloreds, they were the hardest hit by the downsizing.[116]

Closing the doors of participation in the provincial militia had its consequences. Many former free-colored soldiers who had enjoyed militia privileges in the past were left exposed to tribute collection and lost their legal immunities. The situation was piqued in that military planners proceeded to endow the provincial forces with levels of benefits that had never been seen before in the pre-existing urban companies. The centerpiece of the privilege upgrades dealt with the *fuero militar*, being extended to enlisted men for the first time on a widespread basis. At the same time that the crown was expanding the privileges of the provincial militia, it stripped the benefits of unreformed urban militia units. As a result, until reforms had actually reached certain locations, all of their companies were left without their traditional rights. On this score, the period after 1764 was fraught with tensions as free-colored militiamen were faced with some hard choices. Those in unreformed companies could either patiently wait until reformers reached their towns and cities. At that point they would find out if they had made the cut into the highly tailored, provincial militia units. A second option was to abandon service altogether and accept a wholly civilian life. The third option was to raise a legal fuss, fighting to retain their privileges, whether their companies were reformed or not. Given that much of this discussion leads us into other topics of interest, an analysis of these issues, as well as a detailed examination of the *fuero*, will be taken up in later chapters. Suffice it to say here that after nearly eighty years of relative autonomy in their institution's development, the fourth and final period of free-colored militia duty was one of constant external challenges to the terms of service.

The portrait of the free-colored militia seen in this chapter reveals an institution that increasingly acquired its shape, responsibilities, and meaning over the course of the seventeenth and eighteenth centuries. The overview of militia typologies and the periodization of events further reveal that there was considerable diversity in free-colored militia experiences. For example, the experiences of urban-based militiamen were different from those in the countryside. Similarly, militiamen operating in the latter portion of the seventeenth century were involved in significantly different activities than those in the late sixteenth century. In essence, the experimental first century of duty laid the initial groundwork for free-colored militia diversity by setting into motion the individual trajectories that cities, regions, and towns would take. Fairly early on, it became generally clear where units of the independent type, as opposed to those of the integrated type, would operate.

The critical stage for militia growth came during the years 1670–1762. Here, an increase in militia responsibilities arose within a unique framework whereby free-coloreds exercised a strong measure of autonomy over their militia affairs. The state's concerns over defense, and its gradual acceptance of free-colored soldiers as important to the colony's strategic planning, provided the militiamen with important political capital that could eventually be used to garner added privileges and benefits. The story of the 1670s through the 1750s was one of continual institutional redefinition, as blacks worked ceaselessly to determine the exact social impact that the militia would have upon their lives.

With the advent of the Bourbon military reforms, New Spain's geo-strategic plan shifted in new directions. As mentioned above, in this fourth and final stage of the free-colored militia's story, previous social gains made under the militia framework, as well as the future course of the institution, were questioned in light of the new military program.

The periodization of events presented here serves as the undercurrent to all of the discussions found in the subsequent chapters. Next, in continuing the examination of the militia's primary institutional features, Chapter 2 will explore some of the mechanics of internal militia design, both in theory and practice. This will illuminate the description of the unit typologies presented in Chapter 1. Finally, the chain of command will be discussed, leading to a close assessment of the development of the officer corps.

The Contours of Duty: Internal Militia Structure, Finances, and the Officer Corps

T HE RAGTAG GROUP of militiamen who were rushed off from Mexico City to confront Lorencillo in 1683 resembled nothing like the tightly knit, proud, professional Spanish armies that had terrorized Europe in the sixteenth century. The companies had been hastily mustered. As the more than two thousand men marched forth from the city on a hot May afternoon, the only real organizational dynamic among them was that they were segregated by race. At least whites and mestizos either marched or rode mounts as they passed the viceregal palace for inspection on their way out of the city. The free-colored units were the last to leave. As if to accentuate the low position they enjoyed, as well as their lack of firm military structure, Mexico City's *negro* and *mulato* companies rattled past the viceroy drawn by the four wagons used to carry the city's trash.[1]

Matters were not supposed to be that way. In theory, the military arrangement of New Spain's free-colored companies was slated to follow the *tercio* and regiment organizational models, which were the principal military designs used by Spain's Hapsburg and Bourbon monarchs. The *tercio* was the featured military order of the Spanish army during the sixteenth, seventeenth, and early eighteenth centuries. Ideally, a *tercio* comprised twenty-five hundred men distributed into ten companies, each under the stewardship of a captain and unified under the superior guidance of a *maestre de campo*.[2] With the ascension of the Bourbon dynasty to the Spanish throne during the War of the Spanish Succession, the regiment system began to take root on the Iberian peninsula, passing to the New World in the early 1700s. Under the new order, a regiment comprised sixteen companies divided into two separate battalions. The colonel replaced the *maestre de campo* in the senior officer posts. Above him stood a staff of generals ranging from brigadier to captain general.[3]

As seen in the context of the Lorencillo expedition, it is debatable how well any of these structures worked in Mexico. Especially in New Spain's rural areas, a lack of available troops dictated that the isolated company would serve as the principal organizational unit in the countryside, rather than a complete regiment or *tercio*. Individual companies could be found uniting men from several towns, and the total number of troops assigned to each unit was rarely fixed prior to the first half of the eighteenth century. In other rural locations, squadrons were preferred in place of companies. These tended to be smaller in size, although there were no specific rules observed to that effect. The principal difference between companies and squadrons was their command structure. Squadrons were significantly streamlined, not possessing any officers above the sergeant level.[4] As a result, the military influence of the *alcalde mayor* was augmented. Acting as a squadron's *capitan aguerra*, the *alcalde mayor* did not have to deal with the intervening authority of junior officers. But regardless of who was at the helm of the rural militias, the point is that in the countryside, companies and squadrons demonstrated tremendous structural flexibility, allowing them to accommodate the shifting demographic realities of their provinces. Therefore, any efforts to fully incorporate the *tercio* and regiment models did not have to be eagerly pursued.

Prior to the Bourbon military reforms, the closest approximations of the *tercio* and regiment arrangements were found in the major cities of free-colored service, where there were larger population bases to draw upon.[5] In the late seventeenth century, two free-colored companies operated out of Mexico City, one of which reached a strength of 250 men in 1711. By the 1720s, the city's free-colored units had increased in number, totaling up to four companies. Combined, these units were commonly referred to as the *tercio* of *pardos* and *morenos libres*. It is unlikely, however, that more than one company maintained the requisite *tercio* strength of 250 men. Certainly, the complete troop muster was significantly lower than the standard *tercio* of 2,500 soldiers.[6] Structurally speaking, improvements to the militia order occurred when the shift to the regimental footing was made, just prior to the 1740s. From that decade into the 1760s, the units' combined strength consisted of eight companies, totaling roughly 400 men, thereby forming a complete and proper battalion.[7]

The strides made toward implementing the regiment system were clear in Mexico City, but in other urban areas the transition was less evident. Take Puebla, for instance, where neither the regiment system nor the *tercio* arrangement took firm hold. By 1710, Puebla possessed five free-colored companies, totaling 593 men.[8] As in Veracruz, Puebla's free-colored companies were further separated by phenotype, with specific companies existing for *pardos* and *morenos*. Although the companies' racial distinctions were eliminated after the 1720s, the basic structure of five companies persisted until mid-century.[9] In official papers there was confusion on exactly how to refer to Puebla's free-colored militia. Throughout the first half of the century the forces were alternately described as either a battalion or *tercio*.

Obviously, part of the problem accounting for the irregularity in description came from the fact that the structural guidelines for regiments and *tercios* were not fully heeded. Equally as influential was a growing preoccupation among members of the local elite, as well as some colonial administrators, to find ways to accentuate status differences between the free-colored militiamen and their white counterparts. This translated into a policy, quite evident in Puebla, and even in Guadalajara, in which *pardo* and *moreno* militia forces were continually referred to as *tercios* well into the 1760s, regardless of the state of their structural organization. The phraseology served to delineate free-colored militia service as secondary to that rendered by members of the more socially prestigious merchant companies.[10] However, when whites were referred to as serving in battalions and regiments, oftentimes their units' structure did not meet the required criteria, nor was their makeup significantly different from that of the free-colored militias, which were still being labeled as *tercios*. In Puebla, while the battalion of whites consisted of the proper eight companies in 1710, their number fell to only six by the 1740s. In both periods, white companies included a mounted unit, which was not an accepted addition to the regimental infantry arrangement.[11] Yet the forces received the designation of battalion, nevertheless.

With respect to command staffs, free-colored militia units under the *tercio* arrangement were entitled to a *sargento mayor* (major), which became the senior operating officer in militia companies of the independent type until the 1720s. Evidence suggests that the position was not conferred on free-coloreds until late in the seventeenth century. In Mexico City, a free-colored *sargento mayor* was active as early as 1683. In Puebla, the post evolved more gradually, coming into being sometime after 1710. Within the *tercio* arrangement, the *sargento mayor*'s command was second only to that of the *maestre de campo*. Essentially, the *sargento mayor* was responsible for coordinating affairs between various companies in a city, and catered to every aspect of his soldiers' material needs. It was he who made combat preparations and conveyed all superior orders to the *tercio*'s junior officers. He handled militia balance sheets, and even served in the capacity of judge in internal legal matters pertaining to the militia. His was the most visible militia post, and free-colored units possessing a *sargento mayor* enjoyed the greatest degree of autonomy in handling their daily affairs. But when under campaign, or in the midst of crisis, he was subjected to the direction of white superiors. In the 1683 expedition to Veracruz, for example, *Sargento Mayor* Joseph Escobar took orders from the Conde de Santiago, who served as the field army's *maestre de campo*.

Directly under the rank of *sargento mayor* came the junior officers. These included one captain and *alférez* (lieutenant) per company. This was the standard militia arrangement for most of the first half of the eighteenth century; however, the implementation of the regiment system allowed for the additional posts of *ayudante* (adjutant) and *subteniente* (second lieutenant), which were incorporated after 1767. Of the junior officers, the captain steered each company and was its supreme authority in all internal matters. If problems could not be handled by the captain, they were forwarded to the *sargento mayor*. There were gradations in the importance of the captains. Those who had held officerships for the longest time were placed in command of the lower numbered companies. That is to say, the captain of the second company possessed more clout than the commander of the eighth company. Meanwhile, the captain of *granaderos* (grenadiers) was the most illustrious of the group, often doubling as captain *comandante* (commanding captain). Traditionally, the militia company staffed by the *granaderos* was assigned the number of "first" militia company, whereas all other numbered units were simply companies of fusiliers. The captain *comandante* served as the right-hand man of the *sargento mayor*. In areas lacking a *sargento mayor*, the *comandante* stood in his place.

Ordinary captains kept records on their soldiers, noting when they were sick or had deserted. Likewise, during days of inspection and training, captains kept count of the men present and absent in their unit. The paperwork was then submitted to the *sargento mayor*. Captains also signed each soldier's *filiación* papers, which was proof of their militia enrollment, documenting their race, date of matriculation, company number, and distinguishing physical features. When men from their companies became embroiled in legal troubles, captains went to their aid, provided that the soldiers possessed *fuero* privileges.

The *alférez* coordinated affairs with his captain and substituted for him in his absence. He commanded his company's musicians, whose signals instructed the militiamen on how to proceed with military maneuvers. In some cases, the *alférez* soothed differences between soldiers and officers when internal conflicts arose. In all matters, he was deferent to the captain. In the 1750s, the post began to be widely duplicated, as both an *alférez* and *teniente* (lieutenant) could be found serving in companies throughout the colony. This gradually led to the creation of the positions of first and second lieutenant. As free-colored units slowly adopted the regiment order, the positions of *ayudante* and *subteniente* were incorporated into their companies for additional command support. The *ayudante* served as the direct assistant of the *sargento mayor* but still remained under the jurisdiction of a captain. Meanwhile, *subtenientes* served as the aides of a company's *alférez*.

Below the corps of junior officers were the ranking NCOs. Up to four sergeants served per company. A *cabo* (corporal) was assigned to each squad of twenty-five men. The duties of these NCOs placed them in close proximity with the rank and file. Sergeants instilled discipline and maintained limited records on individual troops. They were required to know the military codes from memory. Corporals attended to weapons, making sure that they were fit for use. At least in the regular army, they performed the supplemental duties of visiting sick soldiers, supervising baggage management on campaigns, and inspecting military lodgings.[12]

The year 1719 marked a major turning point in the arrangement and autonomy of the colony's free-colored militia forces. It was during that time when Sebastian Almaraz, a career free-colored militiaman in Mexico City, was bestowed the rank of colonel over New Spain's *pardo* and *moreno* units. For years he had tenaciously petitioned the king for the post, using subtle and coherent arguments. His pleas might have failed had not a precedent already been established for granting the colonelcy to people of color. A number of years earlier, a detachment of black soldiers from "Guinea," stationed in Cadiz, had successfully incorporated the post into their ranks with excellent results.[13] Their experience provided Almaraz with some negotiating room for having the free-colored colonelcy brought to Mexico. Nevertheless, the implications of having the rank adopted in New Spain were much wider than on the Iberian peninsula. Being equivalent in grade to the *maestre de campo*, the colonel would become the virtual centerpiece of the vast network of free-colored militia forces throughout the colony. Also, the city where the colonel operated was to become perceived as the focal seat of free-colored militia authority. When Almaraz was finally granted the colonelcy in 1719, this was the status he brought to Mexico City's free-colored companies. In future campaigns, it would be Almaraz, rather than white superiors, to whom the colony's *pardo* soldiers would defer. Although he would still have to coordinate his activities with white military commanders, his appointment immediately meant increased independence for free-colored militiamen in large-scale missions.

Viceroy Casafuerte proceeded to expand Almaraz's role in 1726, by commissioning him to serve as the military inspector for all of the free-colored companies in the kingdom. Along with a small party of subordinates, Almaraz was held responsible for examining the units' internal structure and ensuring that their officer corps met crown standards. Any officers found lacking the signed, viceregal documents needed to authorize their posts were to be stricken from duty. The same applied to those who had not paid the obligatory *media annata* for assuming their positions. Anyone hoping to retain his rank would have to comply completely with proper military protocol. Over the years it had become customary for *alcaldes mayores* in rural areas to confer officerships by word of mouth, without procuring proper confirmation from the viceroy.[14] This created opportunities for corruption, as fees paid for commissioned posts went straight into the pockets of the *alcalde mayor* instead of to the royal treasury. Likewise, given that many officers owed their rank solely to the spoken grace of the *alcalde*, these provincial governors wielded much more influence over the militia than they should ordinarily have possessed. Sometimes the militia forces became nothing more than the *alcalde*'s private army. Almaraz's commission was targeted at remedying that situation. On his itinerary were the towns of Orizaba, Puebla, Veracruz, Jalapa, "and all other areas of the kingdom where companies of *pardos* and *morenos libres* have been formed."[15] In addition to overseeing the state of the officer corps, he supervised the soldiers' training regimen and assessed their readiness to meet emergencies. Upon departure, he was to leave the militiamen in each town capable of handling weapons and seasoned in the fundamental basics of tactical maneuvers. Naturally, Casafuerte expected Almaraz to encounter stiff resistance to his commission by jealous white elites. After all, Almaraz was not even of racially mixed heritage, but described as a *negro*. Sensing potential trouble, the viceroy included specific instructions for the *alcaldes mayores* in each region to provide the colonel with "all the assistance, favor and support that he will need [for the task]."[16]

The colonelcy remained part of the free-colored militia's organizational structure until the battalion of Mexico City was abolished in the 1790s. Only four men held the title during the entire colonial period. Over time, the influence of the position waned. When Almaraz vacated the post due to a fatal illness in the 1740s, crown officials were quick to point out to aspiring successors that the benefits of office accorded to him were based solely upon the special circumstances of his case. Almaraz had independently petitioned the crown to install the post. Consequently, when the king consented the colonelcy, royal administrators claimed to have understood the rank as a personal contract drawn between Almaraz and the crown. Royal officials apparently believed that the situation differed from the privileges and authority offered to the lower militia grades, such as that of captain and *alférez*. Those positions were well-established and regulated parts of the free-colored militia's design from the previous century. The bulk of their privileges came into being not through individual contracts and unilateral appeals but by official ordinances first conceived of by the crown itself.

Some of the nuances of the crown's position were debatable. When the king granted Almaraz's post, he did not create the free-colored colonelcy from scratch but based it upon the pre-existing model in Cadiz. In fact, Almaraz's responsibilities and *preeminencias* (privileges) were initially identical to those of his Iberian counterpart. But the point that royal administrators emphasized was that through additional appeals, Almaraz had tailored the office to his own specificity. Also, the arguments he used to shape the office had a distinct personal touch. Having logged more than forty years of service by the early 1720s, he had risen successively through the ranks, starting as a foot soldier. His vast experience in every aspect of free-colored militia duty was supplemented by his record as a premier law enforcer, being personally responsible for apprehending a score of criminals in Mexico City, as well as performing dutifully during the grain riots of 1692. On these highly personal grounds, Almaraz pleaded for increased salary and the right to wear a special medal to symbolize his rank. He even requested unrestricted arms use for himself and his soldiers. Given excellent recommendations from members of the viceregal court, the king granted a raise in salary, amounting to sixty ducats per month, equal to that of a captain in the regular army.[17] In terms of Almaraz's other entreaties, the crown exercised caution, not wanting to authorize too much additional jurisdiction and authority to the colonel. On that score, Almaraz's plea for unfettered weapons use was denied. For any future appeals that the colonel might make, the high crown authorities left those decisions open to the viceroy's discretion, always under the rule that restraint was to be observed in increasing Almaraz's status.[18] The crown also made it clear that any benefits negotiated were solely rewards for the person filling the office, rather than a standard aspect of the office itself.

Future aspirants to the colonelcy were hindered by the air of caution surrounding Almaraz's numerous demands, and the perceived uniqueness of his appointment. Nicolas Bertel, Puebla's *sargento mayor*, became Almaraz's successor between 1741 and 1742. Frequent contact between Mexico City and Puebla kept militiamen in both cities abreast of each other's affairs, spurring Bertel to seek the post shortly after its vacancy. His credentials certainly were equally as illustrious as his predecessor's, if not more so. A twenty-one-year career had taken him to the leading post in his city. Unlike Almaraz, he had entered the militia as a captain and had directed all of his male children into the ranks as well. Each son served as an officer, either in the position of captain or *alférez*. In 1739, Bertel successfully petitioned the crown to augment the authority of the *sargento mayor*'s post. Ever after, he had exercised his commission with sagacity and flair, inspiring countless civilian free-coloreds to join the corps by means of his august personal example. According to his own accounts, municipal officials often remarked on the elegant performances exhibited by his soldiers on public holidays. To Bertel's credit, the style in which he executed leadership was complemented by the defenses he provided during critical moments in Puebla's history, especially during the riots of 1729. Although some men under his command were killed in the crossfire, his efforts prevented aggression from spreading widely throughout the city. During his tenure, he had also organized numerous punitive raids to uproot illegal businesses. Additionally, he protected the main plaza from criminals who delighted in robbing helpless women after Mass. On occasion he helped transport silver from Mexico City, guard prisoners, and even, in 1741, collect tribute.[19] Moreover, Bertel was a man of recognized status in the Puebla community: an examined master woodworker, as well as a confectioner who was friendly with the urban elite. He was frequently called upon to appraise estates for the likes of the Guevara family.[20] While not necessarily as wealthy as those individuals, Bertel was respected and trusted enough to accurately assess their worth. If not a veritable member of Puebla's elite, he undoubtedly cultivated some of their habits and outlook. His writings reveal a man who conceived of the urban poor as the "plebe." In his capacity as the free-colored militia commander, he saw himself as playing the role of protector, keeping the better half of society safe from lower-class menaces.[21]

Despite his service record, wealth, connections, and numerous written pleas, Bertel managed to receive barely half of Almaraz's salary, and was given the post as interim colonel only. In addition to the arguments already forwarded regarding the perceived uniqueness of Almaraz's appointment, the reductions in authority and salary conveyed a sense of reserve on the part of administrators who were unsure of how an officer residing in Puebla would serve as leader of the free-colored militia. The distance from the capital, albeit short, might interfere with performance. The benefit of having the free-colored colonel situated in Mexico City was the obvious proximity to the highest officials in the colony's chain of command. Symptomatic of Bertel's reduced authority was the situation that developed in 1742, when two free-colored companies from Puebla were sent for garrison duty in Veracruz. Rather than commanding the soldiers himself, Bertel simply provided materiel, furnishing 108 men with weapons at the great personal expense of seven thousand pesos.[22] As in the years before the incorporation of the colonelcy, free-colored captains on this expedition were subjugated to the full authority of white officers.[23]

In 1748, Nicolas Bertel was succeeded to the post by his son Manuel Joseph Bertel. This time, the full colonelcy was conferred. While the documents do not speak specifically to the fact, the full appointment implies that a measure of good faith was now being placed in Puebla as the home base of free-colored militia operations. The trial period was over. Succession from father to son also reveals a large degree of trust placed in the abilities of the Bertel family to serve as the militia's supreme leaders. The appointment further restored some of the old luster to the post. Like Almaraz before him, Manuel Bertel was granted the equivalent salary of a Spanish infantry captain, along with special use of a royal medal engraved with a portrait of the king.[24] In an attempt to secure the full authority of his predecessor, Manuel took the initiative to write a letter to the viceregal staff in Mexico City, requesting a commission to conduct a colonywide inspection of the free-colored troops:

Since according to your wishes my command extends throughout New Spain, I have a special desire to reform all the other companies in the colony, bringing into them the many individuals who are *pardos*, but who refuse to recognize the flags of the [*pardo*] barracks, in their desire to enjoy the privilege of being whites, which they are not; and putting [my desire] into practice, it would serve His Excellency to intercede with his superior protection, commanding all members of the *justicia* of the places where I shall need to conduct reforms, not to place before me any impediment, under a penalty which you shall issue to them.[25]

Manuel was keenly aware of the history of the free-colored militia's evolution. His letter uses some of the same language found in Almaraz's original commission to tour the colony in 1726. However, the key difference was that Manuel had to press the viceroy into granting the inspection, rather than having it bestowed automatically. Unfortunately, illness struck before Manuel could carry out the task. Rather than lose the commission altogether, however, he requested that Francisco Manuel Suarez, the colonel *agregado* in Mexico City, be charged with the responsibility. The move marked the beginning of the decline in Puebla's influence over the free-colored militia. The new *agregado* rank had come about with Suarez's arrival to the colony in 1750, and for a time the existence of two colonels created some competition, despite the fact that Suarez was technically lower in rank.[26] But Manuel Bertel's deference in the inspection matter sealed the beginning of a process that witnessed the increased accumulation of power under Suarez's command in Mexico City. By the late 1750s and early 1760s, Suarez had risen quickly to the status of full colonel. He remained in place as the colony's only free-colored colonel until 1792–93, when most of the free-colored companies of the independent type were eliminated in Mexico.

The fact that the colonelcy was a featured part of the command staffs only in Mexico City and Puebla indicates another structural characteristic of the forces in which free-coloreds served. Cities were prone to having a larger and more diverse range of officer grades, including captain *comandantes*, *sargentos mayores*, *ayudantes*, and grenadier commandants. Rural areas rarely incorporated anyone above the rank of captain, regardless of whether the units were racially mixed or of the independent type. However, one aspect common to both urban and rural companies was that many of the junior posts were left unfilled. In the early 1750s, out of the sixteen racially integrated militia companies along the Barlovento coast of Veracruz, there were supposed to be forty-eight officers commanding the 2,257 militiamen of the region. But militia inspections found only thirty serving officers. Similarly, the provinces of Tuxpan, Tihuatlan, Tamiagua, and Tamapachi were supposed to possess a total of twelve officers but had only one *alférez* between them.[27] Farther south, the *pardo* cavalry company of Santiago Tuxtla had just one lieutenant commanding fifty-six troops during a review in 1759. The accompanying company of whites, with only eight men, was comparatively overstaffed with officers, possessing both a captain and a lieutenant.[28] The patterns observed along the Gulf coast were repeated in the Pacific provinces. In 1781, the racially integrated units of Tixtla, Chilpancingo, Chilapa, Atoyac, Teopan, and San Luis were found to have just twenty-eight officers in their companies out of an authorized fifty-eight posts.[29]

Officer staffs in Mexico City and Puebla were also found lacking. For the two-year stretch of 1774–75, over a quarter of Mexico City's officerships were vacant, while nearly half of the posts of Puebla were empty.[30] The situation was not, however, always so chaotic. In the 1740s, Puebla's command group was fully staffed, and in Mexico City only three posts out of twenty-seven were vacant in 1768.[31] In the city of Veracruz, officer staffs were also maintained at capacity from 1767 to 1770.[32]

Variation in the rate of vacancies was mostly a result of the process of officer recruitment. Depending on rank, the process took time and could be hotly contested. NCOs were conferred their positions directly by company captains. All procedures were handled internally, and the selection process often reflected the influence of military patronage, as a captain's favorites and friends were promoted to sergeants and corporals. While vacancies existed even at these upper enlisted ranks, it was less common, assisted by the fact that the entry requirements, both in terms of social and military standing, were fewer than for the commissioned posts.[33] Internal nomination procedures also tended to hasten the pace of filling choice NCO openings.

On the other hand, junior and senior officers acquired rank through application, promotion, or by direct appointment from municipal and royal officials. Application was the most common method for filling vacancies at the ranks of captain *comandante* and above during the late seventeenth and early eighteenth centuries. Militiamen submitted their requests and service records directly to the viceroy for consideration. The process could take several months to complete, and delays of up to four years were not uncommon.[34]

Men who were already officers and sought further promotion to one of the upper junior posts had their requests handled by the highest ranking officer of their unit. In contrast to those soldiers who applied for senior officer positions, there was little outside influence in the promotion procedure, except during the final confirmation process.[35] As with all important posts, confirmation entailed submitting the new officer's name to the viceroy for approval. This was almost an automatic guarantee. To be installed, the militiaman would then pay the *media annata* to complete the appointment.

The reason why free-colored militiamen retained large measures of control over simple officer promotions was that colonial officials believed that the candidates had been sufficiently screened beforehand. No soldier could be promoted from an NCO to an officership without some measure of outside review. Also, if a militiaman first joined the corps as an officer, he normally could not enter the post without the consensus of crown representatives or municipal authorities. Hence, the initial screening of junior officers ensured that they were suitable officer material and could be promoted to other junior ranks without question.

The method of direct officer appointment was employed in situations in which new companies were erected and staffed by men who had never served before, or where the vacancies of already established companies were being filled by men who equally lacked military expertise. Direct officer appointments probably involved the most intensive forms of scrutiny. For starters, a list of three candidates was proposed to the viceroy for each available officer slot. Upon the recommendation of town councils and military inspectors, one of these men would be selected for each post. Prior to the 1760s, senior free-colored officers played an important, if not definitive, role in selecting the short list of candidates. This mainly held true for free-colored companies of the independent type in Mexico City and Puebla, but it was also the case in Michoacán.[36] Conversely, racially integrated units always seemed to have more outside involvement in their officer selection process. However, after the 1760s, the influence of white military inspectors, town councils, *alcaldes mayores*, and governors increased in preparing the slate of candidates for free-colored companies of all types.[37]

Eligible men were ranked sequentially according to their merits. Almost invariably, the first candidate on the list was eventually appointed to duty. The decisive factors determining a successful appointment included an individual's wealth, social status, robustness, age, and his ability to read and write. Men in good health and under the age of fifty were preferred. Ample personal wealth was important for those seeking the highest ranking junior posts because officers, especially captains in rural areas, were responsible for outfitting their companies with supplies during times of emergency. Given this situation, it was not uncommon to find a young captain in his twenties commanding officers twenty years his senior.[38] For *tenientes* and *subtenientes*, wealth criteria still mattered but could be offset by a person's family ties, military experience, and political connections. Particularly, the sons of officers and personal friends of the *alcaldes mayores* found easy access into these positions. On the one hand, this resulted from the common belief among royal officials that the progeny of an established military legacy possessed a natural inclination for command. On the other hand, lackeys of the *alcaldes mayores* and *justicias*, especially in rural towns, were muscled into junior officer posts to provide provincial administrators with added measures of control over the populace.

Direct officer appointments also occurred to militia units that were being reformed or brought under new military regulations. Since these companies were not entirely new, more experienced candidates could be selected to fill the officer posts than under ordinary circumstances. Oftentimes, considerations of past military performance, health, and age meant that long-time militia officers were stricken from their previous positions. After 1760, stiffer implementation of literacy and wealth requirements, as well as concerns over whitening the officer corps, resulted in substantial loss of free-colored officers in the integrated units of the Gulf and Pacific coasts. We have already seen some of the effects of these policies in the previous chapter, examining the integrated companies of Papantla, Tampico, Pánuco, and Huexutla. Less commonly, whites were proposed to serve as officers in units designated specifically for free-coloreds. This did not occur in the major cities of service, but in smaller provincial towns. In San Andres Tuxtla, the company of *pardos* was reorganized between 1775 and 1776. Twelve candidates were proposed for the four open officer positions, of whom half were white. Ultimately, two *españoles* were given the highest posts of *captain* and *teniente*. Affluence loomed large in the final decision, as both finalists possessed assets amounting to more than twelve thousand pesos, matching the wealth of the ranking officers in the white company. It was also no coincidence that both men were born in Galicia, Spain, and had served for over thirteen years in the white militia. Notwithstanding, their prior military experience was relatively undistinguished: they had been mere foot soldiers in the white corps. But that did not prevent them from edging out the town's leading free-coloreds for the top officerships. Those few *pardos* who were "able to maintain themselves with dignity," although not to the extent of the whites, were relegated to the company's lower junior posts.[39]

In this instance, and in the majority of cases in which free-colored companies underwent reformation, the officer appointment process was thoroughly controlled by white military inspectors and town councils, with minimal input from free-coloreds themselves. Some reformers manipulated the appointments, finding ways to increase the means of bestowing high commissions on wealthy whites. For that reason, many whites were nominated for posts in the free-colored company of San Andres Tuxtla. For instance, Don Blas Antonio Perez, who eventually became the captain of *pardos*, had also been nominated in the second spot for the captaincy in the white company. Instead of giving him a lower position in the white unit, it was resolved that he would be given the next best thing to a white captaincy—command over the free-colored corps.

Since the officer recruitment process involved a great deal of screening, and seeing that free-colored officerships were only selectively filled throughout the colony, did those blacks who were appointed to these posts tend to fit a certain profile? Were there significant regional differences? A study of 199 service records taken between 1766 and 1784 offers insight into their background and careers.[40] Table 11 examines the amount of time spent by officers as NCOs and examines their tenure in the junior and senior ranks. The sample incorporates areas from the Pacific and Gulf coasts as well as the interior.[41] Table 12 gives information on conduct, military abilities, and valor for free-colored officers in Mexico City, Veracruz, Tuxtla, Tehuantepec, New Galicia, and Michoacán. Table 13 examines the ages of the militia officers in those regions, while Table 14 looks at their place of origin. Complete information was not available in every category, accounting for some numerical discrepancies. In all cases except for Xicayán, the soldiers appearing in the tables were in militia units that were either recently reformed or were on the brink of being reformed.

TABLE 11

Average Number of Years Spent by Free-Colored Officers in the Militia, 1766–84

Location of companies	Average years as soldier	Average years as corporal	Average years as sergeant	Average years as officers	Average years in militia	Total Number of Officers
Veracruz	8.5	2.3	3.8	6.2	22.1	10
Tuxtla	10.3	.3	.6	15.3	26.6	3
Mexico City	5.6	0	1.1	5.2	12.1	23
Michoacán[a]	0	.4	2.4	2	5.3	9
New Galicia[b]	.5	.1	.4	9	9.3	46
Antequera	8.4	3.7	2.4	9.4	24	7
Tehuantepec[c]	0	0	0	5.5	5.5	19
Xicayán[d]	not known	not known	not known	not known	31.7	17

Source: AGN, I.G., vol. 252-B, exp. 7, Diego Joaquin Garabito, November 1772; AGN, I.G., vol. 9, fs. 17–47; 62–81; 196–206; AGN, I.G. 422-A, Expediente formado sobre la creación de un regimento de infanteria provincial para resguardo de la costa sur; AGN, 483-A, Francisco Marti to Dn. Francisco Antonio Crespo, carpeta 2, May 29, 1784, Oaxaca; and AGN, I.G. 33-B, Arreglo de las companias de milicias de Tuxtla, por el sargento mayor de la plaza de Veracruz, Dn. Antonio Saavedra, 1776.

[a]Includes only the cities of Patzcuaro and Valladolid.

[b]Includes the city of Guadalajara, and the towns and cities of Compostela, Tamazula, Tusacuesco, Quauatitlan, Tecolotlan, the Hacienda of Ahuacapan, Ahualulco, La Magdalena, and Izatlan.

[c]Includes the entire province of Tehuantepec.

[d]Includes the towns of Tutepec, Cuistla, Teotepeque, Juchatengo, Juauila, Guajolotitlan, Pinotepa del Rey, Cortijos, Estancia Grande, Tapestla, and Santo Domingo.

TABLE 12

Military Performance Reviews for Free-Colored Officers in Mexico City, Veracruz, Tuxtla, Tehuantepec, New Galicia, and Michoacán, 1766–84

Rating	Capacity	Valor	Application	Conduct
Unknown Performance	1	31	0	8
Poor Performance	1	0	8	10
Regular Performance	34	1	37	23
Good Performance	13	10	8	16
TOTAL SOLDIERS	49	42	53	57

Source: Same as Table 11.

The information presented in Table 11 reveals that free-colored officers were divisible into three broad categories: those with extensive prior experience as NCOs (over five years), those with minimal experience (under five years), and those having none at all. In part, the amount of NCO experience a soldier brought to the officer corps was a measure of the role merit played in the system of promotions in the free-colored militia. Officers having more background in the lower ranks were the most likely to have advanced on account of demonstrated talent and ability. Their tenure in the NCO grades had given their superiors the opportunity to scrutinize their aptitude for carrying

TABLE 13
Average Age of Free-Colored Officers by Rank, 1768–72

Location of Companies	Rank	Average Age	Total Soldiers
Veracruz	Captain	42	2
	Lieutenant	47	2
	2nd Lieutenant	36	2
Mexico City	Colonel	42	1
	Sergeant Major	45	1
	Captain	36	6
	Lieutenant	37	7
	2nd Lieutenant	29	7
New Galicia	Captain	45	14
	Lieutenant	46	15
	2nd Lieutenant	40	14
Michoacán	Captain	40	3
	Lieutenant	31	3
	2nd Lieutenant	29	3
Xicayán	Captain	60	8
	Lieutenant	51	9
	2nd Lieutenant	45	9
Tehuantepec	Captain	45	3
	Lieutenant	46	3
	2nd Lieutenant	46	3

Source: Same as Table 11.

TABLE 14
Geographical Place of Origin for Free-Colored Officers in New Spain

Location of Companies	Place of Origin	Number of Officers	Total Soldiers per Location
Veracruz	Veracruz	7	
	Havana	2	
	Guinea	1	10
Mexico City	Mexico City	12	
	Lima	1	
	Veracruz	1	
	Inp. de Mogol	1	
	Caracas	1	
	Istlaguaca	1	
	Puebla	1	
	Havana	2	
	Santa Fe	1	21
Michoacán	Michoacán	8	
	Lima	1	9
Tehuantepec	Tehuantepec	17	
	Teposcolula	1	
	Oaxaca	1	19
Xicayán	Xicayán	44	44

Source: Same as Table 11.

out greater militia tasks. They were recommended for promotion based on those grounds. Being completely familiar with the militia routine at the enlisted level also meant that their presence frequently translated into a seasoned officer corps, capable of effective NCO management. There were few militia functions that they had not been called upon to carry out themselves, providing them with insights into how to enhance company performance. Officers in half of the sampled locations revealed significant NCO experience. Indeed, sixty-one officers began their careers as enlisted men. Surprisingly, the table further demonstrates that in areas in which NCO tenure was prominent, most time was spent at the rank of foot soldier.

Implicit in this observation is that a great number of officers were drawn from the common stock. Antonio Terril, the free-colored *ayudante* in Mexico City during the early 1760s, hailed from such low origin that he was sold into indentured servitude to the *obraje* of La Palma for being unable to pay an outstanding debt of only six pesos.[42] Like him, there were other militia officers whose civilian professions were thoroughly undistinguished when compared with those of lesser soldiers of their units. In Mexico City, for instance, a number of captains and lieutenants were found employed as cooks, carpenters, cigar makers, confectioners, and weavers.[43] It is true that for some individuals, ascension through the military ranks accompanied added success in their civilian endeavors. Puebla's Captain Joseph de Santander was a master dyer (*tintorero*). His successful business enterprise allowed him to dress in stylish British capes before suiting up for duty. At home he ate off fine imported china and relaxed in the comfort of his study, where he read Marcus Aurelius and gazed upon paintings of the king, the Virgin Mary, and historic battle scenes from Flanders. At the time of his death, he was recorded as being worth over thirty-seven hundred pesos in cash and goods. His brother, Captain Juan de Santander, was even more prosperous. The free-colored merchant was rumored to be worth over seventy thousand pesos during his military tenure, more than enough to be considered a member of Puebla's elite in the 1720s and 1730s.[44] For the Santander brothers, their officer commissions both reflected and helped them to increase their civilian social standing. But for other soldiers, there was little concomitant rise in civilian status as a result of obtaining officer rank. Captain Gregorio Sedeño lacked the means to afford respectable lodging for his family even years after first becoming an officer. He and his wife slept in modest quarters at Mexico City's free-colored militia barracks.[45] The wide spectrum of social classes found in the free-colored militia's officer corps, particularly in units of the independent type, differed greatly from companies reserved for whites. In Valladolid during the early 1760s, the top positions in the white unit went to the city's leading merchants, hacienda owners, and miners.[46] In Puebla during the same period, status distinctions reached down into the enlisted ranks. White corporals and sergeants tended to be employed in the upper-status artisan trades of silversmith, barber-surgeon, and arms maker.[47] Their subordinates were overwhelmingly involved in the lesser textile professions. In light of these more rigidly imposed class boundaries, the opportunity for advancement on the sheer basis of merit seemed greater for free-coloreds serving in segregated companies of their own than for whites in similar units.

In our sample, the locations where merit played its greatest role in molding the officer corps was in Antequera and Veracruz.[48] Every officer in both those cities had once been a foot soldier. Unlike the situation in most other locations shown in Table 11, these men's career profiles also featured experience in the positions of corporal and sergeant, thereby signaling a progressive, ladderlike ascension into the junior posts. In Antequera, there was slightly more emphasis on tenure at the corporal level than in Veracruz, where sergeants remained on post for longer periods. But in both cities, free-coloreds arrived to the junior and senior officerships after having logged an average of fourteen years as NCO, the longest such span in all the regions appearing in the table. Again, it must be emphasized that the stints these officers spent in the middling NCO ranks is testimony to the importance that experience and ability played in their eventual positioning into the higher posts.

The military proficiency garnered from their experience was deemed a necessity, especially in Veracruz, arguably the most strategic site in New Spain. Unlike Antequera, Veracruz housed a permanent garrison of regular army infantrymen, as well as a corps of dragoons and additional units of cavalry.[49] The nearby island fortress of San Juan de Ulúa offered further front-line support. Only the defenses of Mérida and Campeche could compare with Veracruz in fighting ability and numbers. In terms of militia forces, the port was equally well provisioned. With more than sixteen hundred militiamen, only Mexico City had a greater concentration of militia troops during the period from 1766 to 1770. Furthermore, the Lancers of Veracruz, rumored to be one of the premier citizen forces in the colony, operated within the port's jurisdiction. While it is questionable whether these extensive preparations led to an adequate defense, the heavy military investment in Veracruz meant that there was a demonstrated interest in maintaining high military standards.[50]

The performance reviews and experience levels of the port's free-colored militia officers reflected these elevated military expectations. Table 12 reveals that on the whole, the free-colored officers sampled in our study received ordinary ratings for their military performance. Of course, one must always be careful when using this subjective data, since the prejudices of military inspectors factored heavily into their performance reviews. As a general rule, they reserved their most outstanding comments for members of the nobility, hidalgos, or other wealthy whites of high birth who were deemed exceptional soldiers largely on account of their social credentials. The castes were perceived as inherently inferior. Even Mexican-born whites of lower birth and means were considered naturally inclined to lesser military performance than

whites of European origin. In light of this context, the service records of the
Veracruz militia represent an anomaly. There were ten free-colored officers in
the city from 1766 to 1784. Their services were reviewed in favorable though far
from glowing terms, with singular instances of a brilliant career. All had
proven their valor in military combat, with "good" performances. Similarly,
in terms of military capacity and conduct, each of Veracruz's ten officers
scored marks that ranged between good and excellent, constituting the bulk of
the soldiers receiving such reviews in the table. Only in terms of their
"application to military service" did they begin to resemble their counterparts
elsewhere in the kingdom, receiving mainly "regular" reviews. In short, strategic circumstances, as best exhibited in Veracruz, created a situation for the
free-colored militia whereby proven merit, performance, and experience
closely correlated to rank and promotions. Even inspectors, normally reticent
about bestowing accolades upon the castes, recognized their accomplishments
in ways that were not seen elsewhere in the colony.

Situated in a temperate valley far from the coast, Antequera's free-colored
officers resided in an area of lesser strategic importance than those in Veracruz.[51] In 1766, there were no regular army detachments in the city, and militia
forces totaled under five hundred individuals.[52] One would naturally be inclined to believe that Antequera was a place where martial spirit ran low. Nevertheless, the high level of NCO experience tallied for free-colored officers reflected a commitment to rewarding talent, creating a modestly capable force.
Importantly, promotions through the ranks were enabled by a long tradition
of continuous militia service in the city. Like those of Veracruz, where active
free-colored militia duty had its roots from the middle of the sixteenth century, Antequera's forces logged consistent, almost uninterrupted service from
at least 1701. Since that time, the soldiers had been called into action with relative frequency, being employed to patrol city streets, to quell Indian disturbances, and even to serve as intermediaries in helping to resolve local land disputes. The soldiers also enjoyed an especially close rapport with Oaxaca's *corregidores* and *alcaldes mayores*, whom they defended from harm on several occasions. The continuity of service provided ample opportunities for militiamen to develop extensive résumés, making many of them attractive officer
candidates. As of 1766, free-colored Captain Diego Antonio Medrano had
served in the corps since 1721, while his counterpart, Captain Juan Antonio
Mattadamas, had logged continuous service since 1742.[53] Both men had participated in apprehending numerous criminals and quieting local disturbances. However, unlike Veracruz, military officer promotions in Antequera
were made with less frequency. Service records show that although the free-
colored militia had been active from the beginning of the eighteenth century,
promotions were clustered around certain years: 1744, 1750, 1756, and 1766. All
were moments of structural and general personnel changes to the city's units,
centered around reforms and potential threats from pirates and hostile armies.

Without external prodding, promotions appear to have been stagnant, regardless of a candidate's ability. Hence, without the influence of outside circumstances, there were limits to the reaches one could climb in Antequera on merit alone.

In contrast to both Veracruz and Antequera, a different officer service dynamic evolved where militia duty was more sporadic. In Michoacán and New Galicia, the creation of free-colored units came about in the 1740s. One company was raised in Valladolid and Patzcuaro during the war with England between 1740 and 1741.[54] In 1746, a larger effort to create militia units was initiated along the Pacific coast to defend the region of Motines from possible attack. Still more musters were raised in Guadalajara and Tancitaro (Michoacán) in 1747, when the sighting of an unidentified ship triggered new fears of British aggression.[55] The energy used to create militia units ebbed quickly. The suspicious ship sailing the Pacific was discovered to be a friendly Dutch vessel. The advent of peace with Britain left the push for military reforms in hiatus. Military inspections conducted in the 1750s revealed that many of the free-colored companies founded in these areas had been abandoned. A great number of the men listed on the active rosters had died years earlier. Strides were made to increase militia effectiveness and place it on stronger ground. New units were formed in New Galicia in 1753 and again from 1758 to 1762.[56] Reforms and changes were made to the militia of Michoacán in 1758 and in 1762.[57] However, the desired results were not achieved.

The repeated starts and reverses worked against smooth turnover in the ranks, based on a step-by-step progression through the corps, as seen in the classic example of Veracruz. Information on Michoacán, New Galicia, and even Tehuantepec in Table 11 directly reflects such staggered militia development. Free-colored officer appointments in these areas were always made by town councils and military inspectors in the context of reforms. But unlike Antequera, where reforms also triggered appointments, the lack of an established military tradition meant that the officer candidate pool possessed minimal NCO experience at best. As a result, the criteria for officer appointments weighed heavily on an individual's birth, level of literacy, wealth, and social standing.

Officer career trajectories in Mexico City and Tuxtla represent a middle course between those of the other regions examined in this study (see Table 11). The time these officers spent as foot soldiers both approached and exceeded the levels found in Veracruz and Antequera. The implication is that merit played a shaping role in officer appointments in both locations. However, the time spent in the middling NCO positions of corporal and sergeant resembled the spotty service records of New Galicia and Michoacán. Consequently, talent alone did not account for most promotions and appointments. The centrifugal pull of status also appears to have been influential in building officer careers.

A unique blend of circumstances created the situations found in Tuxtla and Mexico City. Strategically and administratively speaking, both sites were important and in need of adequate defenses. Mexico City was, of course, the capital of New Spain. Commensurate with that status went a force of royal guards and dragoons drawn from the regular army. In the 1760s, the city's militiamen numbered over twenty-seven hundred, representing the largest contingent in the colony prior to 1770.[58] In a sense, Mexico City approximated Veracruz in terms of the value placed on defense and security. But there was an important difference. Like Antequera, the immediacy of foreign attack was reduced because of the land buffer separating the viceregal capital from the coasts. This meant that the level of preparedness striven for in Veracruz was definitely lower.

Despite geo-strategic similarities to Antequera, Mexico City's free-colored officers did not match their level of NCO experience. Perhaps this can be credited to another feature of Mexico City's military institution. It did not focus upon suppressing internal rebellions and protests to the same extent as its western counterpart. While William Taylor has counted at least ninety-one instances of community rebellion in central Mexico from 1680 to 1811, including Mexico City's major grain riots of 1692, a case can be made that Antequera's forces were more oriented toward dealing with small-scale village insurrections that took place *outside* of the city limits. Although there were only thirty-two such outbreaks in the Oaxaca Valley during the eighteenth century, with none matching the size of the Mexico City grain riots, the limited information we have on Antequera suggests that these problems were frequently handled by militia forces summoned from the provincial capital.[59] By contrast, when Mexico City's companies were organized for duty outside of the city, it was mainly to provide reinforcements for Veracruz against possible foreign aggression. While no firm conclusion can be made on the matter, one can posit that in Antequera, the high levels of mobilization made to confront neighboring disturbances intensified the desire to ensure that seasoned officers, with significant NCO experience, were found among its militia ranks. The situation extended to the free-colored corps. In Mexico City, different circumstances lessened the need for similar levels of preparedness.

Tuxtla was more prone to direct attack than Mexico City. Positioned along the Gulf coast, the region's location had made it an important zone of militia duty. After being founded in 1703, Tuxtla's free-colored militia marched to Alvarado in 1748, providing clutch garrison duty. The march was one of the highlights of their militia history, alongside their regularly posted, coastal watch. But military planners readily conceded that the military threat to Tuxtla was secondary in comparison with Veracruz. Only the shores between Antigua Veracruz and Medellin were considered feasible for the beachhead landing of a large expeditionary force. Extreme heat, rampant disease, harsh blowing *nortes*, the poor condition of the bays, and the presence of swamps and thick forests militated against the chance of a coordinated strike elsewhere, including Tuxtla. Moreover, inroads made against pirate activity in the Gulf coast area during the seventeenth and early eighteenth centuries had seriously reduced depredations. In the 1760s, many top members of the colony's military command staff believed that the most aggressive action Tuxtla would see during a crisis would be an occasional raid aimed at finding provisions for a larger invading fleet.[60] Not all military planners, however, fully agreed that Tuxtla was a strategic and defensive back burner. While the zone was not as likely to be attacked as Veracruz, it still offered rearguard support. As had occurred in Alvarado in 1748, the soldiers could make a quick march to the port in times of emergency, being located about thirty-five leagues from Veracruz. Also, military operations could be coordinated between Tuxtla's militia and the Spanish fleet.[61]

Militia life in Tuxtla reflected the shifting debates over the perceived military threat. Military reforms were carried out in 1748, 1759, 1765, and 1775 in accord with alternating desires to strengthen and streamline the corps. As with Antequera, promotions to officerships were infrequent and largely restricted to those reform years. Promotions within the NCO ranks, however, were uncommon even during other periods. Given the rigidity of mobility within the corps, and seeing that militia service had been fairly continuous in Tuxtla from the 1740s, and possibly as far back as 1727, what developed was a two-course path of ascension to officer candidacy.[62]

Although only three service records could be found for Tuxtla's free-colored officers between the years 1766 and 1784, they still represent half of the officers that would have served in the region's two *pardo* companies during this period and yield enough information for us to highlight the salient features of the two-tier process of officer ascension. On one route were those officers who began their careers as ordinary foot soldiers and who entered the junior officer posts without having served intermediate time as corporals or sergeants. Such men were promoted because they had demonstrated their military ability and were literate, a rarity in the countryside. There was a limit to how far they could ascend. Normally, their ceiling was at the rank of first or second lieutenant. The hallmark example is the case of Domingo Figueroa. Having joined the militia as a twenty-two-year-old infantryman in 1727, he remained a foot soldier for twenty-one years. In the midst of the militia reforms of 1748, his ability to read and write, along with his military aptitude, impressed reformers enough that he secured a first lieutenant's post, which he held for another twenty-seven years. Finally, at the age of seventy, he was forcibly removed from the militia by a new group of reform officers. The Figueroa case shows how, for some, the long periods of time that passed between promotions created lopsided careers, heavily weighted toward both the lower and upper ranks.

The second path of duty was less based on merit and is exemplified by the career of Gregorio de Rosario. Having joined the militia much later, in 1763, the thirty-three-year-old Rosario spent just one year as a foot soldier, moving on quickly to the positions of corporal and sergeant. These posts tested his ability to command, but in limited fashion. In all, he served a total of four years as an NCO. In truth, these ranks were nothing more than a holding ground for him until higher positions became available. Upon the death of his father in 1767, Rosario assumed command of the free-colored company as its captain. His rapid leaps through the ranks were credited principally to his wealth, family ties, and social standing, although he was also literate. Interestingly, all but one of his promotions were carried out in nonreform years, meaning that his military credentials were not as scrutinized by outsiders as Figueroa's had been.[63]

Officer career patterns in Mexico City offer variations on the Tuxtla themes, although with considerably more examples. Several paths to officer ascension were identifiable. Connections and status played prevailing roles in many of them. To begin with, consider that whereas all of the officers in Veracruz, Tuxtla, and Antequera had once been NCOs, only seventeen out of the twenty-three officers in Mexico City could claim such in 1768. Of those, just eight had served in the post of sergeant and none as corporal.

The first path of service dealt with senior officers. None had advanced without having served as common infantrymen. There are some reasons for this. Direct crown intervention in their appointments was greater than for the junior posts. For example, Colonel Suarez appears to have been hand-picked by the crown for duty in 1750.[64] Royal administrators were less willing to bestow the militia's highest commissions on unseasoned upstarts. Moreover, the crown depended on these senior officers to set examples for the others in terms of service. Of the three soldiers in Mexico City's free-colored militia who received good performance reviews in their capacity for service, two were senior officers. Experience and ability did not necessarily mean that these individuals would live up to their billing, however. Despite their aptitude for duty, the services they rendered were described as deplorable. Two of the three senior officers exhibited little "application" for duty. In terms of conduct, theirs was the worst of all officers, critiqued with words such as *péssima* and *malíssima*. As always, some of the harshness in the inspector's reviews originated from ingrained prejudices. Also, many despised the ability of free-coloreds to occupy positions of high command, such as the ranks of colonel and *sargento mayor*. On the other hand, as testified in different contexts, the behavior of these senior-ranking militiamen was often quite lax.[65]

It was at the junior officer positions where the impact of status and connections was felt the greatest, marking a second path to officer service in the capital. Acquiring access to the junior ranks had come almost under the exclusive control of Mexico City's free-colored colonel by the 1760s. Quite illegally, he bestowed these positions to his favorites, and to those willing to pay a fee. A number of foot soldiers advanced directly into officer positions through this route. The colonel exercised similar, arbitrary authority in dismissing officers. To facilitate his activities, the colonel completely ignored military protocol by refusing to submit the names of any officer candidates to the viceroy for approval. In that way, at least for the years stretching from 1750 to 1768, he forged the corps into a privately run enterprise.[66]

Some of the most meteoric officer appointments were found in the positions of captain and first lieutenant. Five of the thirteen men in those posts had never served as foot soldiers; four never served as NCOs. Second lieutenants by and large possessed NCO experience. As in Tuxtla, a number of these individuals owed their rank to family ties and wealth. Joseph and Lazaro Escobar held the posts of captain and lieutenant, respectively, having never served as NCOs. Both were the progeny of a prominent military family that traced its roots back into the seventeenth century. During the grain riots of 1692, a certain *Alférez* Joseph Escobar had helped save valuable crown goods from perishing amid the blazing fires that raged in the Plaza Mayor.[67] For those and other exploits he was promoted to *sargento mayor* of the battalion, and ultimately to lieutenant colonel. His distinguished career provided opportunities for his son, also named Joseph Escobar, to rise quickly in rank. Prior to the time of his father's death, the younger Joseph Escobar served as *alférez*. After his father died in 1708, he jumped to the rank of captain. The Escobars maintained family members in the officer corps until the termination of *pardo* military service in Mexico City during the 1790s. In 1779, for instance, there were a total of five Escobars occupying junior officer posts.[68]

For the Escobars, military success was linked to financial strength, and vice versa. Joseph Escobar the elder was able to provide a 1,500-peso dowry for his daughter when she married Juan Segura in 1692, who himself was a *pardo alférez* in the city's free-colored militia.[69] He continued to assist the newlyweds in their early financial endeavors, furnishing Segura with a cash gift of 700 pesos in the early 1700s. The early Escobars made careers for themselves as enterprising merchants, a rare occupation for free-coloreds, since commerce was traditionally dominated by whites. By 1708, the family possessed an extensive credit network (see Appendix Table A11). Joseph Escobar the elder owed 5,030 pesos that year, but he had loaned out a total of 6,379 pesos to a variety of individuals, including a smattering of lower government officials, property owners, bureaucrats, master artisans, and ecclesiastical officials. These business acquaintances offer a look at the family's social world. Contact with professionals and middle-class residents situated the Escobars in an enviable position in society when compared with the majority of Mexico City's poorer residents. In all, more than forty individuals were in debt to Joseph Escobar. He owed money to only four.[70] The majority of the loans he made were valued at less than 100 pesos, taking the form of small purchases credited to an account, or small loans to individuals in need of quick sources of cash. There were a few significant issuances, however, such as that made to Don Benito de Castro for 1,230 pesos. In contrast to the small loans he extended, Escobar was able to secure sizable loans for himself, such as the 6,000-peso loan he acquired from Don Andres de Berno. Demonstrating excellent financial solvency, the loan was almost paid off in full by the time of his death in 1708.

The father and son team's successful dealings allowed them to purchase a 9,600-peso estate and *obraje* (textile mill) in the fashionable San Cosme section of Mexico City. Not all of the collateral came through honest transactions, however. As *sargento mayor* of the free-colored militia, Joseph Escobar the elder was entrusted with tribute collection in the city. His son had maneuvered himself into the position of maize collector for the Hospital Real.[71] Shrewdly, they used some of these funds to underwrite personal expenses, supporting an elevated, middle-class lifestyle for the family.[72] The San Cosme estate was splendid for the times. Although distant from the more elite downtown center, the property was well watered, had a lush fruit orchard, and was located conveniently near the convent and church of San Cosme. Not far from the scenic Alameda Park, San Cosme was regarded as a quiet retreat from the busier inner city. However, faced with financial difficulties and saddled with the responsibility to divide his father's holdings among the three surviving children and widow, the younger Joseph Escobar arranged to sell the estate to Doña Catharina de Erenchun in 1715 for 12,000 pesos.[73]

The father and son team were succeeded in their financial success by Pedro de Segura y Escobar, the child of the marriage between Juan Segura and Margarita Escobar. Like his uncle and grandfather before him, he continued the family's merchant interests.[74] The overall condition of the family estate was unclear in the 1760s and 1770s. What is certain is that the Escobar brothers lived much more modestly than their predecessors. Commerce had ceased to become the chief family enterprise. The two brothers were artisans, Lazaro employed as a carpenter and Joseph as a bookbinder.[75] Joseph Escobar, a militia captain in the 1770s, lived in the confines of a *cuarto* in a *vecindad*, which was little more than a simple room in a large apartment complex. This lifestyle typified the working class of lesser economic means, since the choice properties within a *vecindad* were the *viviendas* (penthouses) and *accessorias* (multiroom suites).[76] These were usually rented or owned by the more successful artisans and lower-level professionals. Joseph's marriage choice even reflected his diminished economic status. His wife, Maria de la Luz Reyes, was a habitual drunkard who had lived licentiously before marriage. Joseph married her with the hope of being able to change her ways. They lived in a perennial state of conflict. Arguments turned to physical abuse as he hit her and refused to give her money. She declared that he was actively dissolving their union with his brutish behavior. Escobar landed in jail on several occasions on account of domestic violence.[77]

Despite severe legal and economic hard times, two of the Escobar brothers were found listed as officers in the 1768 militia service records. The way in which they acquired rank intimates that their family history and past legacy of financial success loomed large in their selection. Lazaro Escobar had become an officer in the *pardo* militia at the young age of twenty-one. His brother, Joseph Escobar, entered the officer corps in 1761 at the age of twenty-seven. Only through influence and connections could men hope to acquire these posts so early.[78] Moreover, the brothers were not simply made officers but were both assigned to the second company of fusiliers, which was the third most prestigious unit in the battalion. That made the young Captain Joseph Escobar among the most influential junior officers in Mexico City. To underscore the measure of the brothers' accomplishments, their quick promotions at early ages differed greatly from the primarily merit-based career patterns found in Veracruz. Here, only one free-colored militiaman out of fourteen had managed to achieve officer's rank while still in his twenties. Even then, it was only after having served ten years as an NCO. By contrast, in Mexico City, eleven of the capital's twenty-three officers had advanced to the commissioned grades while still in their twenties. In Guadalajara, another location where status was a strong determinant in the rise to an officership, three of the four captains found serving in 1772 had been promoted to their posts before the age of twenty-three.

Another good example of family influence contributing toward the rise of Mexico City's free-colored soldiers is that of the Villaseca family. Gregorio Villaseca was a captain of the free-colored *forastero* militia unit in the 1740s and 1750s. His means were more modest than those of the Escobars, his income coming from his job as a tailor. In 1756, his relative, Eusebio Villaseca, entered the corps at the age of sixteen. Although the boy did not advance immediately to officer rank, Gregorio's influence helped position him for a second-lieutenant's post by the age of twenty-one. When his brother, Quirinio Villaseca, opted for a militia career, strides taken by both Eusebio and Gregorio helped push him into a lieutenancy. The same was done for Pedro Villaseca, another family member who appeared as a lieutenant of the seventh free-colored militia company in 1779. Quirinio and Eusebio proceeded to live fairly comfortable lives. Between 1782 and 1783, they each moved into a *vivienda* on Canoa street in the *vecindad* of Dn. Juan Jayme.[79]

Table 13 provides additional age information on the officer corps by rank and region. We see that the most common age for free-colored officers was between thirty and fifty. One might initially expect seniority to prevail in structuring the militia hierarchy, meaning that the eldest soldiers received the highest rank. Such trends were prevalent in the regular army forces of the New World.[80] But on the contrary, for New Spain's free-colored militia, seniority manifested itself in only a few locations, with Xicayán and Valladolid serving as the clearest examples. In all but three of these provinces' ten free-colored companies, the captain was the oldest soldier in the command staff.[81] But even here, while not completely reflected in the table, there were several instances where *alféreces* were older than the higher-ranking *tenientes* (see Appendix Table A12). From the cases in our sample, the most faithful adherence to a seniority-based system was found in militia companies in which individual families exerted significant control over the ranks. In La Magdalena, a small town in New Galicia, the Lopez clan held every important militia post, extending from captain through first sergeant. The family's age structure was superimposed onto the military command structure, so that Dn. Francisco Javier Lopez, the eldest, served as captain. The pattern was repeated in many other units, meaning that when family members served together, older men usually outranked their kin. In towns in which several families competed for limited officer space in militia companies, it was not uncommon to find the youngest relatives of each clan serving in the posts of first and second sergeant, waiting for their opportunity to advance.[82]

A fair number of free-colored officers originated from cities that were distant from their service posts in New Spain. This was particularly true of the more cosmopolitan centers, such as Veracruz and Mexico City. Of the 199 officers surveyed, 103 provided a place of origin (see Table 14). Fifteen of those soldiers were foreigners to their militia base. One of the striking aspects of these individuals was that they tended to occupy the highest-ranking positions in the free-colored battalions. One of the two captains in Veracruz was from Havana. In Valladolid, one of the two captains was from Lima. The entire senior command staff of the Mexico City battalion was composed of outsiders. Colonel Francisco Suarez was from Mogol, *Sargento Mayor* Ramon Barrales was from Veracruz, and Adjutant Matheo Tunco was from Havana.[83]

An important reason for including foreigners in New Spain's *pardo* militia was for their military experience. Many of these men were dispatched from their cities of origin specifically for service in Mexico. They brought signed documents from their superior officers that would facilitate their integration into their new militia home. Narcisso Sagarra left Lima as a corporal in 1766. Upon arriving in Mexico City, he presented his credentials and was immediately promoted to the rank of *subteniente*. Soon afterward, he was sent to help quell an Indian rebellion in San Luis Potosí.[84] Others boasted even more impressive military résumés. Pedro Aotequin, from Africa, arrived in New Spain after having served three years as a soldier in the free-colored battalion of Cadiz, and having garnered another four years of naval experience as an artillery officer in the Armada de Barlovento. Like Sagarra, shortly after arrival in Mexico City, he too readily assumed militia command as a *subteniente*.

It was hoped that the quality of the free-colored battalions would improve under the direction of these seasoned foreigners. Their successes and limitations at enhancing *pardo* military effectiveness are amply seen in the career of Francisco Manuel Suarez. As has been mentioned before, Suarez arrived in Mexico City in 1750 with a viceregal commission to assume the position of colonel *agregado*, one of the highest ranks in Mexico's free-colored militia. Like Sagarra and Aotequin, Suarez had seen considerable previous action as a soldier, having served in Porto Belo where he had been taken as a prisoner of war. He seemed determined to instill his vast military knowledge into the soldiers surrounding him in Mexico City. As Suarez reflected in a letter written later in his career, he had worked hard at preparing his units and "maintained one of the most illustrious and able regiments [in New Spain] by means of indefatigable zeal to observe discipline and the use of arms."[85] Suarez was a strong advocate of the letter of the law and aspired to run a textbook battalion. He did not hesitate to beat his troops and officers when he considered that they were veering from the straight and narrow path he had set for them. To expedite punishment, he toted a short bullwhip wherever he traveled. He spared nothing in his efforts to bring about disciplined training. On one occasion he held his troops prisoner in the militia barracks, denying them both food and water for a day. In the afternoon, from 2:00 P.M. until 9:00 P.M., he sallied them out into the adjacent plaza where they marched senselessly for hours. The goal, of course, was to maintain troop readiness.[86] The soldiers in his companies complained and felt that he was acting too harshly. Nevertheless, Suarez remained firm, understanding that his methods merely imitated the standard disciplining procedures of the day. Corporal punishment and demanding training routines were featured aspects of military life throughout Europe in the eighteenth century.[87]

Needless to say, Suarez made enemies quickly. In 1763, he was instructed by the crown to prepare his companies for a possible march to garrison Veracruz. Part of the preparations involved streamlining his units, getting rid of all men considered unfit for service, including the elderly and sick. Suarez strictly complied with the orders, much to the chagrin of his soldiers. As he went through each company eliminating men from duty, the soldiers cried foul. The purpose of the march was to protect the port from a possible British invasion. The militiamen noted, however, that Suarez had postponed reducing his troop roster until *after* the peace was signed with Britain. According to their arguments, since the immediate danger had passed and there was no need to fortify Veracruz, all soldiers deserved to remain untouched in their battalions as before. Personal interests were at stake. Many of the men whom Suarez was dismissing had been career soldiers in the militia. They feared that as civilians they would suddenly be held subject to tribute payments and would lose their *fueros*. But that was exactly what Suarez wanted, they claimed. They maintained that his personal dislike for particular individuals was what goaded him to dismiss them, not the presence of any debilities or ailments. The clamor continued. On July 1, 1763, upset soldiers chafed when Suarez dared to change the uniform used by the companies. The new one was more costly, and purchasing the new gear would be a source of serious hardship for the average free-colored militiaman.[88]

Suarez retaliated, providing detailed and convincing explanations as to why each man was removed. Some were simply too old, a few were physically handicapped, some were chronic alcoholics, while still others posed serious discipline problems. Pedro Guadalupe, described as "haughty," frequently disobeyed his superiors. At times, he did not bother to perform his duties. For instance, when he and a small contingent of his subordinates were scheduled to keep guard at the hospital, no one appeared. Suarez had to substitute other soldiers for the task.

In the face of Suarez's retaliatory efforts, two officers, Francisco Guadalupe Orduño and Marcos Irigoyen, made life extremely difficult for the colonel in 1763. Orduño had a long history of disorderly conduct, and his name appeared more than once in court records.[89] Because of a lack of suitable officers, Suarez temporarily promoted Orduño from corporal to *alferez interregnum*, on the grounds that if he improved his behavior and demonstrated himself worthy, the promotion might be a permanent move. But by late spring, Suarez had resolved to remove Orduño from the militia altogether. Allegedly, Orduño had abused the privileges of his new post, inciting other officers and soldiers to scheme against their colonel. Orduño had supposedly paid fellow militiamen two to four reales apiece to protest their dismissal from the companies. Others were paid to file complaints against their colonel's behavior and character, stating that he committed numerous excesses while on the job. This was not the first time that Orduño had challenged the colonel. In 1761, along with Marcos Irigoyen and the *ayudante* Antonio Terril, Orduño lodged a formal complaint of abuses to the viceroy. Twenty-five soldiers testified in that instance, causing Suarez to be admonished with a written reprimand.[90] But the colonel's severe practices continued. Finally, in 1763, when Suarez changed the look of the free-colored uniform, Orduño and his allies had borne enough. They protested vehemently by parading around the city in the uniforms used by the soldiers of the Royal Palace. Orduño's multiple plots succeeded in stifling Suarez's initial efforts at dismissing free-colored militiamen from their companies.

Suarez realized that to carry out his plans, he had to deal first with Orduño. In previous clashings, he had already sufficiently undermined Orduño's character before the viceregal authorities, stating that he was a third-rate soldier who often found himself in jail. Now, for several months, he focused renewed energy on removing Orduño from service. Once that goal was achieved, he began systematically eradicating other troublesome soldiers. When Marcos Irigoyen, one of Orduño's chief collaborators, was issued his dismissal in November, he responded in a fury. Until then, he had plotted against the colonel through formal channels, authoring letters of denouncement with other unhappy militiamen. But now he dared engage in a more direct approach. Storming from tavern to tavern, Irigoyen rallied supporters to his cause and marched into the Plaza Mayor, where he proceeded to publicly denounce Colonel Suarez for removing him from his post.[91]

It took two years for these issues to be settled legally. All those whom Suarez wanted to dismiss were eventually removed from duty. However, they were placated in the sense that they ultimately received lifetime immunity from tribute payments. In short, the events of 1763 proffer a peek into the stormy relationships that erupted between the foreign-born, free-colored officer and the soldiers in his units. In Suarez's constant effort to improve the corps and fulfill his military responsibilities, bitter fights ensued. While in this case serious violence did not occur, sometimes angry soldiers lashed back at their superior with blows.[92]

Perhaps there would have been less of a quarrel if Suarez himself had lived the impeccable life that he demanded of his soldiers. The reality was that Suarez infrequently visited the barracks, used the corps for extortion, was prone to drunkenness, and was a notorious gambler. Shortly after joining Mexico City's free-colored militia, Suarez began charging an entrance fee of four and a half reales for all new militiamen who enrolled in the corps. Whenever free-colored militiamen were apprehended by justices of the peace, Suarez was usually dilatory in coming to their aid. When he did make the effort to release his men from jail, it normally involved a charge. Suarez even attached monetary value to his signature. Anytime soldiers needed papers to be signed, whether for promotions or for replacing lost *filiación* (militia registration) papers, militiamen could count on paying between four and a half and eight and a half reales. Suarez did anything for money. He pimped out his services to the tribute collector. Although militiamen were legally exempt from tribute, Suarez found ways to make sure that each year a number of his men never secured the necessary paperwork to avoid the fee.[93] Additionally, Suarez and his *sargento mayor*, who was also a foreigner, ran a card game out of the colonel's house to which all free-colored officers were coercively invited. Cleverly, the game was arranged just after payday. On a typical night, the officers lost their entire militia paychecks at the betting table, while the *sargento mayor* and colonel reaped the benefits. Both men also masterminded a clothing extortion racket. The 1763 uniform change was but one in a series of switches made to the militiamen's dress. Through periodically changing the style of the uniforms, opportunities were created for Suarez to draw up new contracts for wholesale clothes purchases. Military inspectors had already fixed the price that militiamen were supposed to pay for their uniforms in published decrees. But by secretly changing the dress code himself and using material that was cheaper than the authorized fabrics, Suarez opened up a chance to make profits. The unsuspecting rank and file paid the difference. To increase the effectiveness of the racket, all officers were encouraged to participate. A full audit of the *pardo* militia companies conducted by the military inspector in 1768 revealed that the officer corps was indebted to the battalion by a total of 2,612 *pesos*. The *sargento mayor* and Colonel Suarez owed the most. *Sargento Mayor* Barrales had illegally taken 1,682 pesos, while Colonel Suarez owed 450 pesos, largely as a result of the uniform pricing scandal.[94]

Suarez's vices were compounded by arrogance. While he could be endearing to his favorites, the colonel talked down to the majority of the men under his command and did not flinch at verbally abusing civilians. Possessed of an inflated sense of self-importance, the colonel maintained a rotating detachment of soldiers to guard his house.[95] The practice mimicked the retinues of the provincial *alcaldes mayores* and even the viceroy, who possessed a private palace guard. Suarez styled himself a "Don," using the honorific noble title in most of his signed documents. This produced great discomfort for his white peers and superiors, who insisted that his background and racial origin forever hindered him from possessing the title.[96]

Arrogance and a fondness for liquor proved to be a potentially explosive combination in February of 1768. One night, in the midst of a drunken stupor, Suarez ordered an armed brigade of free-colored grenadiers to patrol the city with him. While conducting rounds he committed various excesses—harassing innocent civilians and flogging a mule with his bullwhip. Most disturbing was his tirade in front of the barracks of the Crown Battalion. Relations between those regular soldiers and the free-colored militia had been festering for some time. Insults between the two groups had been exchanged, resulting in a minor free-colored casualty. Suarez himself had been personally affronted, being described as unfit even to serve as the coachman for the officers of the regular army unit. Atop that, the regulars boasted that they had been issued orders to kill off all the *negros* and *mulatos* in the city's free-colored units.[97] Matters came to a head that night. Prior to Suarez's patrol, some members of the Crown Battalion had resisted arrest by a free-colored unit. These regulars were eventually apprehended and brought into the free-colored barracks. There Suarez whipped them while issuing a sharp reprimand for their resistance to *pardo* military authority. To make a further statement, that night he marched his armed detachment to the Crown Battalion's headquarters, where, among other gestures, he gave them a piece of his mind. It was uncommon for free-colored soldiers to patrol the streets with loaded rifles, but, under orders, they carried their cartridges with them that night. In the tense atmosphere, cooler heads thankfully prevailed, preventing the event from escalating into an armed exchange.[98]

Clearly, the success of using foreign free-colored officers to improve the quality of the militia depended largely upon the personalities of the individuals selected. The case of Suarez demonstrates that the results were poor in Mexico City, the premier battalion in the colony in terms of rank. With the advent of the Bourbon military reforms, there was another approach utilized toward controlling free-colored militia behavior and enhancing troop preparedness. This involved the inclusion of a cadre of white veteran soldiers into the free-colored companies. For the most part, the changes contested free-colored autonomy over their units, especially in companies of the independent type. It is worth pausing here to examine the cadre to see precisely how the Bourbon reforms structurally threatened the integrity of the free-colored forces.

The challenges to free-colored autonomy began at the highest level. The appointment of an inspector general to coordinate the colony's military affairs had the effect of limiting the influence of the colonelcy. No longer would he oversee and regularly review New Spain's free-colored companies, arranging them into battalions as he saw fit. These tasks would now be carried out by the inspector and his appointees. Hence, the colonel's influence became restricted to his immediate city of service. Even more important was that the inspector came to assume broad authority for all military legal cases, militia requests, and petitions. His presence complicated the military legal process. Before the reforms, free-colored soldiers sent their legal cases directly to the *auditor de guerra*. A robed *audiencia* member, the *auditor*, reviewed and adjudicated their cases, sending his decision to the viceroy for final judgment. The viceroy's ruling was merely a procedural gesture; invariably, he approved the *auditor's* decision. After the reforms, the contact between the *auditor* and the soldiers was layered with new intermediaries. The inspector could intervene in litigation and petitions, submitting his thoughts on the cases. Importantly, the inspector's opinion might weigh heavily on the final verdict. Unfortunately for the free-colored militiamen, they could not be sure if his disposition was a friendly one. Although a soldier himself, the inspector defined himself differently. Being a regular army officer, as opposed to a part-time soldier, and hailing from mainland Spain, an inspector frequently harbored biases about New World militiamen in general, whatever their caste. But for some, free-colored military service was deemed particularly loathsome, yet narrowly tolerated because recruits were needed in strategic areas with small white populations. On occasion their feelings were vented, as occurred in 1778 when Inspector Dn. Pasqual Cisneros wrote a letter to the viceroy protesting Suarez's attempt to secure a salary raise. The letter wasted no time in pondering weightier matters. Having also participated in reforming Cuba's militias, Cisneros related that he saw no utility in preserving the free-colored colonelcy in the Americas, much less issuing Suarez a raise. With the presence of professional, regular army training officers, retaining the free-colored colonel became a redundancy.[99] Cisneros's suggestion to eliminate the colonelcy was not taken at this time, but in the 1790s, Subinspector General Pedro de Gorostiza took matters a step further. His methodical arguments, examining the utility of the free-colored forces versus their costs, played an important role in eradicating *pardo* and *moreno* duty in the colony's interior provinces.[100]

While decisive on larger issues, the inspector's influence was not nearly as important in reducing autonomy within the militia companies as that of the officers assigned to each veteran cadre. Those officials included up to ten individuals, normally consisting of a subinspector, two or four adjutants, and three or four *garzones* per regiment. Subinspectors attached to the free-colored corps held the rank of at least a regular army lieutenant, while adjutants were lesser junior officers or upper-ranking NCOs. In addition to their regular army experience, these men were hired for their administrative skills. Adjutants and subinspectors were literate and capable of managing a regiment's vast paperwork. They were also frequently called upon to train their free-colored subordinates in performing similar administrative tasks. Occasionally, that entailed teaching the militiamen the fundamentals of reading and writing. The *garzones* were the lowest-ranking members of the cadre. They were drawn from the enlisted ranks of private, corporal, and second sergeant. Joining the free-colored militia offered them an instant promotion, since all *garzones* were considered the equivalent of a first sergeant. Particularly in the major cities, *garzones* had the most frequent contact with the militia's rank and file, being housed in the militia barracks. With the cadre in place, any orders issued by free-colored officers were suddenly rendered questionable by the veteran attachés. The cadre also assumed the responsibility of organizing local militia reviews, assemblies, and training sessions. Because they were white and held regular army commissions, members of the cadre often brought a certain haughtiness to their work that weakened internal accord.[101]

Within the cadre, subinspectors presented the greatest challenge to free-colored autonomy. These men assumed many of the functions of the free-colored *capitan comandantes, sargentos mayores,* and colonels. Indeed, the subinspector became the chief coordinator of soldiers at the local and regional levels, commanding their officers and responding to local authorities on matters of legal procedure. It was he who handled much of the bargaining and negotiations when soldiers were apprehended by municipal magistrates. He also helped determine when a militiaman was eligible to invoke the *fuero.* Typically, he was responsible for supervising all the *pardo* companies in a designated province or major city and had the power to contradict any command issued by subordinate officers. With specific regard to free-colored units of the independent type, only the inspector general superseded his authority in the military chain of command.

Cultivating a close relationship with the subinspector could yield enormous benefits. In Puebla, Ignacio Dominguez owed much of his career to the favor he found with Subinspector Pedro Camuñez. Dominguez joined the militia in 1774 as an ordinary soldier. By 1779 he had climbed to the rank of *alférez.* While in cantonment in Cordoba and Veracruz during the campaign of 1782, Dominguez served as the de facto commander of his company in the wake of the death of his captain, Luis Santander. He was promoted to full lieutenant in 1784 and continued to assume responsibility for his company. Shortly thereafter, Subinspector Camuñez appointed Dominguez as the top free-colored officer of Puebla's free-colored battalion by making him the acting *sargento mayor* for five years. Camuñez justified these rapid promotions on the grounds that Dominguez had carried out all responsibilities with "zeal" and "genuine love" for crown service.[102]

However, we must keep in mind the utility of the appointments. Subinspector Camuñez was a newcomer to Puebla, arriving in 1777. That was the year in which he completed the provincial reform of Puebla's companies. At the same time, he issued Dominguez his first promotion, a rapid move from foot soldier to *subteniente*. Seemingly, it appears that as the subinspector was installing the veteran cadre, he was identifying potential allies in the battalion who could serve as counterweights to the influence of *pardo* officers who had been in power prior to the Bourbon reforms. Dominguez was an agent in that process. Additionally, in the 1780s, the subinspector's reluctance to quickly replace deceased officers indicated a further attempt to hamper free-colored officer influence. Instead of making new full appointments, he merely continued to promote Dominguez and multiplied his responsibilities.

Apart from favorably influencing the path of individual careers, the presence of the subinspector and cadre could be constructive to the free-colored units in other ways. Occasionally, these white soldiers experienced some of the same ridicule and jeering borne by the free-colored militiamen. While not necessarily a source of common bonding, such situations could prompt the cadre to take strong stands in favor of the free-coloreds in the units they served. More often than not, their primary concern was to improve the external image of the free-colored militia so as to enhance the meaning of their own duty. Remember that as long as the free-colored corps was viewed as inherently inferior, the cadres' reputation suffered by mere association. Take, for example, the situation in 1781 and 1782, when free-colored units from Puebla and Mexico City were stationed in Veracruz. Several members of the two cities' veteran cadres wrote formal letters to the viceroy, denouncing instances of verbal harassment committed by white soldiers in other units. The embarrassment of constantly stepping last in marching order, as well as being issued commands by unauthorized officers, were additional sources of complaint.[103] The cadre requested nothing less than equal treatment for white and free-colored units. Charges brought by white veterans on such matters normally carried more weight in court circles than did the complaints of the free-colored militiamen alone.

Members of the cadre sometimes took a stand on more important issues. In order to expedite trial proceedings and enhance the quality of military justice, Subinspector Camuñez introduced a proposal in 1779 to hire a scribe and a legal advisor for Puebla's free-colored battalion. The value of the suggestion was immense. The battalion would become more independent in handling its legal affairs by not having to rely on civilian court notaries, who had proven dilatory in preparing case files. The scribe and legal aide would be available for use in both military and civilian-related disputes, adding to the battalion's ability to curb trial time and reduce abuses by the civil courts. In 1781, Camuñez also attempted to reduce trial expenses for free-colored militiamen by not having them held accountable for paying the costly mailing fees involved in sending documents to and from the higher courts. The proposal was primarily intended to underwrite the costs of litigation related to the production of illegal liquor.[104] All of Camuñez's requests were initially denied, but a few years later the request for a scribe was eventually granted.

Camuñez was more successful in bringing about other changes. Again in 1781, Camuñez rallied to the defense of the militiamen's privileges. This time he demanded that *fuero* law be reconceptualized in terms of its application in cases where militiamen had been caught conducting illegal business transactions. An ordinance had been published in 1778 prohibiting Puebla's artisans from selling their goods and wares in the main plaza after 6:00 P.M. The decree was based on sixteenth-century guild laws aimed at ensuring high-quality standards of merchandise and denying market access to artisans who were not guild members. Any militiaman caught conducting business after those hours was subject to losing his *fuero* and being held accountable to the *justicia ordinaria*.[105] Camuñez noted that in Puebla, Cordoba, and Atlixco, an inordinate amount of *fuero* loss had resulted from these laws. This was not the first time that Camuñez had brought such issues to the attention of the higher authorities. In 1777, he fought ardently to secure the release of free-colored militiamen who had been apprehended for illegally selling hats in the *baratillo* (thieves' market).[106] Camuñez argued then that there were too many soldiers being incarcerated on these charges, resulting in a depletion of free-colored militia manpower reserves. He reified similar arguments in his legal petition of 1781. Although he did not call for a complete repeal of the guild laws, his demands effectively amounted to such. He wanted all future infractions on these matters to be brought under his personal jurisdiction, rather than that of the civilian courts. With the support of the *auditor de guerra*, Camuñez was granted several of his requests. While not a resounding victory, he at least secured the authority to keep all prisoners involved in illegal business transactions under watch in the barracks. However, it was left unclear if the military judges, or the civil courts, were to deliberate on the soldiers' final fate.

Men like Camuñez put forth the effort to assist free-colored militiamen because of their own self-interests. Securing privileges for the soldiers added to their own rights. Defending the free-colored militiamen was an indirect means of protecting themselves. The cadre did not blindly support all free-colored militia causes. There were frequent splits. Rather, the veterans chose their battles with calculated measure, sometimes working against issues of importance to the soldiers, such as salary raises. Whatever benefits the free-colored corps managed to secure by means of the cadre, there was still a lucid realization that the veterans' presence brought about an overall loss of *pardo* and *moreno* control.[107]

Free-coloreds in some regions fared better than others in retaining militia autonomy. This was best evident in companies of the independent type found in the colony's smaller towns, such as those along the Pacific and Gulf coasts. Subinspectors, and even the lower-ranking members of the veteran cadre were often altogether absent in such rural settings. Several strategies were devised to compensate for the lack of military training personnel. On the one hand, efforts were made to make the best use of available human resources. When possible, veteran commanders of nearby integrated, white, and mestizo provincial forces simply doubled as heads of any existing *pardo* units. Similarly, white *sargentos mayores* attached to provincial units performed double duty in disciplining the free-colored corps.[108] That approach worked best for the *cabeceras* of each province where the commanders and *sargentos mayores* usually resided. But militia companies were typically dispersed among several towns and villages, complicating issues of management and control. It was impossible for these commanders to be present in all locations simultaneously. Moreover, just convening the men for training was often a challenge. In the jurisdiction of Tehuantepec, soldiers in the three companies of *mulatos* and *negros* were drawn from distances as far as thirty-four leagues outside of the *cabecera*. In 1777, attempts were made to recruit men from distances within only seven leagues of the *cabecera*; however, strategic circumstances dictated otherwise, as troops were needed to protect the bay of San Francisco del Mar. Upon realizing that providing instruction for soldiers at these outer limits would be difficult, arrangements were made to appoint an adjutant major in the province who could assist in maintaining the proper training. Finding a suitable candidate was difficult, given the lack of available veterans and whites. Strides were made to recruit a core group of competent and literate NCOs from the local *mulato* population who would work to preserve the military readiness of the towns. Hence, during the era of reforms in Tehuantepec, the lack of whites over a territory of great distance actually prompted a more pronounced use of local free-colored soldiers to serve as key militia organizers and administrators.[109]

So far in this chapter we have examined the structural organization of the free-colored militia and studied the workings of the officer corps. Closely related to these themes are the topics of militia finances and salaries. Officers, first sergeants, and drummers were the only soldiers in the free-colored militia to receive regular monthly pay. In a battalion of more than five hundred troops, which had become the standard for Mexico City, Puebla, and Campeche in the 1770s, that would amount to just over thirty men. Other soldiers, namely the lower grades of enlisted men, received salaries only when appearing for assembly or when on campaign. Salaries were paid directly from the royal treasury, or from local funds established for the purpose by municipal and town councils. These were sometimes supplemented by private contributions from prominent individuals. From the 1760s onward, free-colored militia salaries were modeled after those established for blacks in Cuba. Table 15 provides a comparative breakdown of free-colored militia salaries and those given to the veteran cadre.[110]

TABLE 15

Monthly Salary of Free-Colored Militiamen and the Veteran Cadre, 1777

Rank	Salary in pesos	Rank	Salary in pesos
Captain	15	Private, Corporal, 2nd	
Lieutenant	10	Sergeant	6
2nd Lieutenant	8	Veteran Subinspector	60
1st Sergeant	6	Veteran Adjutant	35
Drummer	4	Veteran Garzon	18

Source: AGN, I.G., vol. 28-B, Correspondencia con el battalon de pardos de Puebla, 1777, Pasqual Cisneros, October 4, 1777, Mexico City.

What is readily observable is that the money received by most free-colored officers was negligible in comparison to the white cadre. Even *garzones* received more per month than free-colored captains. Obviously, junior free-colored officers could not survive comfortably off their salaries alone. The bare subsistence minimum for a family of four during the eighteenth century was 270 pesos per year.[111] Except for the senior officers, none of the soldiers' military income approached those levels. Moreover, while treasury records stretching from October 1777 through July 1779 reveal that free-colored officers in Mexico City were paid in full each month without fault, there were instances where soldiers' salaries were withheld or left unpaid.[112] In this regard, their projected income was not always a true reflection of yearly earnings. Additionally, like those of regular soldiers, free-colored militiamen's salaries were docked by payments to the military pension plan, the death benefit allowance fund, and for medical and travel insurance policies. Unfortunately, being free-colored militiamen meant that these soldiers were not completely entitled to all the benefits of those plans. Angry free-colored officers in Mexico City protested their payments to policies that did not cover them. After heated debate, they were successful in securing a refund for their years of contributions to the pension fund. But they were still held accountable for the eight *maravedis* per month channeled into the medical plan.[113]

After every charge was deducted, captains were perched in the best financial position of all the members of the junior officer staff. Their annual income rivaled that of some master artisans in the lower-status trades, not that that was much to boast about. On average, master cotton weavers and calico printers in Puebla made nine pesos a month in the eighteenth century.[114] Slightly more prestigious trades, such as a "master of the table" in Mexico City's cigar factory, earned twenty-five pesos a month.[115] Captains were outpaced in income by these latter individuals, and clearly lagged behind Puebla's successful master hatmakers. In a good month, hatmakers could bring in eighty-five pesos, almost the yearly salary of a militia *subteniente*.[116]

Lower-ranking soldiers approached parity with the basic wages of the laboring classes. A common tobacco worker and a rural hacienda peon both earned between two and two-and-a-half reales a day.[117] Considering that the average workweek was six days, this translated into a maximum of seven and a half pesos per month. Of course, given that most laborers were unable to find steady employment, their real earnings were usually less than that amount. But assuming full employment, we see that free-colored militiamen of the grades above first sergeant brought in more than the standard eighteenth-century wage. Enlisted men, however, earned the equivalent of two reales a day or less, putting them on par with the earnings of the urban underclass.

What we must keep in mind is that militia salaries, while low, were normally supplemented by the militiamen's civilian incomes. Very few relied exclusively on their militia pay to make a living. In this sense, free-colored militia officers, even if employed in menial jobs like cook or confectioner, tended to fare better economically than their civilian counterparts. Sometimes the impact of their militia salary meant only eating more meat every month. Yet that was a real difference. Even for the more prosperous officers, whose civilian careers were thoroughly distinguished, the extra funds were always welcome. Although worth several hundred pesos, these more prosperous militiamen did not always have ready cash. Therefore their salaries offered them a slightly greater degree of liquidity, allowing them to invest more in their business enterprises, extend small loans, or purchase the basics needed for daily living.

Colonel Suarez represents a breach from the traditional officer model. His income was derived wholly from his military career.[118] At nearly eighty-three pesos per month, his earnings significantly superseded those of even the white subinspector. Placed in comparative terms, Suarez's earnings equaled those of a mid-level bureaucrat in late eighteenth-century Mexico City.[119] With this type of income, Suarez did not need additional employment, especially in light of his numerous extortion rings and embezzlement operations. However, in 1778, citing the need to support his large family, Suarez dared ask for a raise to sixteen hundred pesos per year, which would have placed him at almost the same pay scale as a regular army lieutenant colonel.[120] As we have seen, his petition was rebuffed. Indeed, after the 1760s, salaries stood largely frozen for all officers, regardless of race and regardless of militia or regular army status.

Within the larger network of free-colored militia finances, salary expenses were absorbing costs. In the 1770s, during times of peace, between 1,268 and 1,304 pesos were spent per month on the free-colored officers of Mexico City and Puebla. A nine-year estimated salary projection in Puebla alone totaled 68,472 pesos for the period 1773–82.[121] This excluded the cost of training maneuvers, mobilizations, and assemblies, during which all militiamen were paid. For instance, during the militia inspections of 1777, the one-month convening of Puebla's 712 free-colored soldiers cost 3,960 pesos, well above the

city's monthly norm of 634 pesos.[122] Also, when Puebla's free-colored battalion
was stationed in Veracruz from July through November of 1782, monthly salary expenses consistently ran to over 2,500 pesos.[123] Salaries were compounded
with a multitude of other military costs. An examination of Mexico City's militia account books reveals that from 1766 to 1768, the free-colored companies
in the capital spent more than 60,000 pesos on uniforms and related purchases.[124] In 1769, another 1,400 pesos were spent to raise the census used to
help complete the free-colored battalion's rosters. Still more was spent for
weapon repairs and the cost of barracks. More than 7,290 pesos were given to
several religious organizations, including members of the Jesuit college of San
Andres and the ecclesiastics of Belemitas, for renting the militia barracks during the years 1765–87.[125] Weapon repairs ran another 5,456 pesos for the same
period.[126]

Until the 1760s, the militiamen themselves usually bore the burden of paying many militia expenses, save the cost of salaries. Beginning in 1767, a series
of special taxes, known as the Nuevos Impuestos, were implemented to help
further underwrite the bills. Throughout the colony, but specifically in Mexico City, Puebla, and Veracruz, these taxes were levied both on imported cloth
and pulque at rates of six reales for each *quarteroon* of cloth, and one-half real
for each *carga* of pulque.[127] The Nuevos Impuestos were combined with a
number of taxes specific to each individual region of service. In Veracruz there
existed an additional one peso tax placed on each *fanega* of cacao brought into
the colony from Maracaibo, and in Puebla a flour tax of three-fourths real per
carga was implemented from the 1760s into the 1780s.[128] In Oaxaca during the
1780s, proposals for expanding a tax on *mezcal*, already in place in Acapulco,
were considered for footing growing militia costs.[129] Apart from Veracruz, the
exact amount of income retrieved from these regional collections was not
known to bureaucrats in Mexico City. When in 1787 officials from Mexico
City's Royal Customs Office tallied how much had been collected by the
Nuevos Impuestos over the previous twenty years, a total of 797,042 pesos was
recorded. Some 349,792 pesos and 4 reales came from the cloth and pulque ex-
tractions, while 447,245 pesos and 4 reales came from the cacao tax. No mention was made of other collections. The money had been distributed throughout the colony, with Mexico City being given first claim to the militia funds.
At the time of the calculations, some 81,089 pesos still remained in the chests.
Evidence revealed that Mexico City had overdrawn its designated amount,
with the municipal government having had to contribute 24,191 pesos of its
own for posting militia defense.[130] While money from the Nuevos Impuestos
was directed at underwriting all provincial militia expenses, the laws were of
specific importance to the free-colored militia because they provided much of
the financing needed to run and equip these units. This reduced the individual
monetary commitment of the soldiers themselves, specifically in units that
had been reformed along provincial lines. Keep in mind that prior to the

Bourbon reforms and the implementation of the Nuevos Impuestos, the fiscal responsibility of the corps weighed much more heavily on the free-colored militia's soldiers. However, in militia units that had not experienced reforms, *pardo* and *moreno* soldiers were still held accountable for a large portion of the militia's bill.

In this chapter we have extended our look at the development of the free-colored militia to assess matters of internal structural composition. Issues of design, in terms of *tercio*, regiment, and company have been discussed. The essential features of the officer corps have been detailed, leading to an in-depth analysis of career trajectories and regional differences among command staffs. The challenge to free-colored militia autonomy posed by the veteran cadre has been outlined. Lastly, an overview of salaries and finances has been presented.

A few general statements can be made from this analysis. First, the modifications in the free-colored militia design that took place during the early eighteenth century essentially worked to increase overall militia autonomy, most notably from the 1720s until 1740, but also into the late 1750s. Alterations to the command staff were perhaps most meaningful in enhancing free-colored militia power at the unit and regiment levels, particularly in urban locations, which came to possess the largest and most diverse range of officer grades. It is important to stress that the structural reorganization processes of the early eighteenth century were accompanied by increases in militia responsibilities, as was noted in the previous chapter. This combination not only made service more meaningful, but also, as we will see later, it facilitated the path for increases in corporate privileges. We have also observed how the invigorated free-colored officer corps of the early eighteenth century played a steering role in militia affairs until the implementation of the veteran cadre beginning in the 1760s. At that time, new structural readjustments in many locations began to reduce and modify the terms of free-colored autonomy. However, throughout the century, the officer corps continued to reflect the potential avenues for upward mobility within the institution, while at the same time serving as an emblematic status marker for free-coloreds who had already achieved an impressive degree of success outside of the militia establishment. Depending upon specific regional circumstances and factors of strategic defense, the officer corps of a select city, town, or province was staffed by a varying mixture of individuals, some of whom had risen steadily through the ranks on merit. In Veracruz, Mexico City, and Oaxaca, among others, there were outstanding instances of free-coloreds who had climbed from foot soldier to officer. But others had acquired their appointments largely as a result of social criteria, including wealth, family ties, and education, accounting for a number of individuals who leaped into junior officer positions in their early twenties. Whether the militia careers of these individuals further served as a mechanism toward significantly enhancing their social position in broader colonial society is another matter, which will be addressed in the next chapter. Here, we have seen how militia salaries tended to supplement incomes but not necessarily propel soldiers into higher income brackets. Certainly, the more creative and ambitious officers, such as members of the Escobar family and Colonel Suarez, found ways of manipulating militia power, networks, and office into handsome financial gains. But for others, movement through the ranks brought more modest changes to their lives.

In the following chapter, we will begin to look more closely at the social issues that arose in the militia context. A focused assessment of the theme of social mobility, as manifested through recruitment, marriage patterns, and occupations will begin to lay the groundwork for probing even larger issues: namely, understanding how race and privilege assumed greater social meaning through the workings of a corporate institution.

CHAPTER THREE

The Contours of Duty: Recruitment, Occupations, and Marriage

O NE OF THE important questions to ask about the militia is to what extent did military service distinguish free-colored soldiers as different from ordinary civilian blacks? Traditionally, the militia has been presented as a vehicle for social and even racial mobility among the darker castes.[1] In this context, the militia experience has been interpreted as essentially transformative, reorienting free-colored relationships and networks in an enhanced fashion, paving the way for status ascension. According to many of these studies, as militiamen acquired more status under military jurisdiction, the strictures of caste became less of a concern because the privileges they secured eliminated many of the legal barriers associated with their race. As a result, either a racially neutered population was brought into being, unaffected by and unconcerned with race, or the military engendered a population poised for and actively engaged in the process of social whitening. In nineteenth-century Argentina, for instance, militia success provided certain high-level, free-colored officers with the means to routinely register themselves, and their family members, in baptismal and marriage registers reserved exclusively for whites.[2] In Brazil, a popular nineteenth-century saying captured the essence of military-inspired social whitening: "Is the *Capitão-mor* [militia chief] a *mulato?*" The response: "He used to be but is no longer. . . . How could a *Capitão-mor* possibly be a *mulato?*"[3] In Cuba, black officers who started their careers from humble origins could be found sending their sons to the university, seeding them for entry into the prestigious liberal professions. It was not uncommon to encounter Cuban officers, such as Antonio Flores, petitioning the crown to remove color barriers that might inhibit their sons from receiving advanced educational and professional training.[4] Throughout the Spanish Americas, free-colored officers flaunted their status in their names, using the distinguished "Don" title, often accompanied by the aristocratic "de" in their surnames. Of medieval origin, the "Don" was the honorific label of hidalgo status, differentiating nobles from commoners. In the New World, it was used to distinguish well-to-do whites from the castes.[5] The fact that many free-colored officers aspired to the *hidalguía*, and were actually referred to as "Dons" in a number of public documents, serves as added testimony to the possibilities for social ascension and whitening through the military ranks.[6]

Making the military an avenue for free-colored social and racial mobility was not the desired objective of Spanish America's military planners. At best, they viewed free-colored military participation as a means to instill discipline upon castes that were inherently viewed as unruly. Most bureaucrats and military functionaries held the common stereotype that any person tainted with *negro* blood was inclined toward licentiousness and crime.[7] Such suspicions were not limited to the multiple permutations of black offspring, but extended to mestizos as well. Yet, it was those possessing traces of black bloodlines who were the most scorned and feared.[8] Men such as New Spain's Francisco de Crespo upheld the military regimen as a means of free-colored salvation from natural vice. Blacks would be imbued with the basic values needed to transform them into active contributors to society, rather than their saddling it continually with problems of vagrancy, crime, and poverty.[9] Instead of an institution for social advancement, Crespo and a host of other planners viewed the military as a tool for social control.

The evidence that scholars have presented to demonstrate that the militia did not serve as a restraining force for black social actions rests largely upon a small number of examples derived from the officer corps, and from an examination of military legal codes. However stunning those individual examples of officer careers may be toward showing the transcendence of racial boundaries, the picture is not complete without an accompanying study of the rank and file. Indeed, in the Spanish Americas, singular instances of tremendous free-colored achievement could be found in almost all the major professions.[10] But it is collective experiences that matter most in determining the overall impact of an institution. Similarly, while studies of militia legislation have helped in arriving at a larger view of how the militia and its privileges should have operated, what is lost is their functioning under real conditions. In brief, the existing militia portrait may be too idealistic, arriving too quickly at conclusions that the militia was a welcome presence in free-colored lives, favorably separating them from the lifestyles of their peers. Opportunities for advancement certainly existed, but they were perhaps tempered with other concerns that militated against the overall attractiveness of service.

A variety of sources will be used here to deal with these issues. Recruitment documents, combined with marriage and occupational information, will serve as the principal methodological tools. Recruitment information allows us to examine who entered the service, why, and how. By determining to what extent the recruitment process was racialized, we can begin to assess the degree to which free-coloredness became eliminated as an issue for soldiers who entered the corps. An understanding of the recruitment pool further informs us about the militiamen's relative uniqueness or similarity in relation to the rest of society. Marriage and occupational data provides us with a look at their social standing after entering the corps and the race of their spouses. Intermarriage offers additional insight into the strength of racial affiliations. The occupational overview yields an understanding of the limits of social mobility.

Unfortunately, the nature of the surviving evidence does not allow for continuous views of Mexico as a whole throughout the colonial period. The best that can be achieved are detailed glimpses from a select group of locations at particular moments in the eighteenth century. Mexico City and Puebla, New Spain's two largest cities during the period, provide the best information on free-colored militia companies in urban settings. The rural province of Igualapa, along the Pacific coast, is presented as typical of areas where militiamen served in zones dominated by Indian and free-colored populations. In all of these centers, excellent comparative information is available on civilian free-coloreds, allowing us to establish with some certainty whether the behavior and condition of the typical soldier veered from that of his civilian counterpart. To round out the view of New Spain's free-colored militias, limited information is included on recruits in the city of Orizaba, along with material from the provinces of Tampico, Michoacán, and Acayucan.

Let us begin with recruitment. Precisely who staffed the militia? Free-colored militia forces relied upon a core group of volunteers, supplemented by a number of drafted recruits. Free-colored officers tended to exaggerate the participation of volunteers to enhance the luster of the corps in crown eyes, and to strengthen the ties of their fealty. Royal officials seemed to respond more obligingly to militia petitions when presented in the light that the forces willingly sacrificed life and limb in the name of the king. But in reality, impressment was a far more prominent feature in the process of militia recruitment than its officers cared to admit. Impressment was most widespread in the interior cities, as opposed to rural coastal towns, where there were fewer problems in maintaining steady enrollment. Christon Archer's theory about militia recruitment for white and racially integrated provincial units apparently held true for various types of urban-based, free-colored forces as well: "As a rule, the larger the city and the less personal the relationships between the various groups in the community, the more difficult it was to raise militia forces."[11]

Take into consideration the cases of Mexico City and Puebla. Free-colored militia companies in both cities were chronically understaffed, most evidently during times of crisis. During the militia mobilization of 1710, a full 168 of Puebla's 593 free-colored soldiers were green recruits, impressed into service that year.[12] In a militia review of Mexico City's free-colored units in 1762, there were 150 men absent from a battalion of 400 soldiers. Forty-seven men had perished in the typhus and smallpox epidemic of 1761–62, the rest simply disappeared, changed residence, or failed to report for duty.[13] Troop rosters from the mid-eighteenth century depict the staffing problem in more detail (see Ta-

TABLE 16

Monthly Distribution of Provincial Militiamen in the
Pardo Companies of Mexico City and Puebla, 1768–75

Month/Year	Number of Militiamen in Mexico City	Rate of Change by Percentage	Number of Militiamen in Puebla	Rate of Change by Percentage
May 1768	507	0	n/a	n/a
June 1768	505	−.4	610	n/a
July 1768	507	+.4	n/a	n/a
August 1768	500	−1.4	538	n/a
October 1768	495	−1	474	−11.9
November 1768	494	−.3	433	−8.7
December 1768	486	−1.7	466	+7.6
January 1774	450	−7.5	311	−33.5
February 1774	450	0	323	+3.8
March 1774	450	0	326	+.9
April 1774	443	−1.6	350	+7.3
May 1774	443	0	352	+.5
June 1774	443	0	367	+4.2
July 1774	443	0	366	−.3
August 1774	443	0	366	0
September 1774	443	0	384	+4.9
October 1774	443	0	360	−6.3
November 1774	443	0	357	−.9
December 1774	443	0	367	+2.8
May 1775	443	0	324	−11.8
June 1775	443	0	318	−1.9
July 1775	443	0	351	+10.3
August 1775	443	0	344	−2
September 1775	443	0	378	+9.8
October 1775	443	0	337	−10.9
November 1775	443	0	335	−.6
December 1775	442	−3	303	−9.6

Source: AGN, I.G., vol. 231-B, Estados de fuerza, Regimento de infanteria provincial y de pardos, 1768, Mexico City; AGN, I.G., vol. 233-B, 1774–75, Mexico City, Puebla, unnumbered folios.

ble 16). It was around this period when, within the context of the Bourbon military reforms, stiffer militia laws were implemented prescribing guidelines as to what militia companies should look like and how many men they were to contain. In accord with the policy changes, militia inspections, audits, and troop levies were conducted in both cities from 1766 to 1768. In 1766–77, Mexico City's free-colored troop strength appears to have been set at 520 men, distributed into seven companies. For the same years, Puebla's peacetime force was 610 men, distributed into six companies.[14] These numbers were rarely reached. In Mexico City, the free-colored corps was at full muster only for a few months after the aggressive militia levy of 1766.[15] Prime strength was almost attained again during the inspections of May 1768. But the ebbing trend was renewed. A low point was reached in 1770, when the city's forces plummeted to 428 men, just over 80 percent of fighting capacity.[16]

Regardless of retention difficulties, Mexico City's free-colored militia was still on a more stable manpower base than its neighbor, especially when observed over a twenty-month stretch in 1774–75. Puebla's companies hit near bottom in 1766, with a scant 280 soldiers registered.[17] The recruitment effort of 1768 brought the companies to full strength, but within six months the units were found at 76 percent of fighting capacity. It is true that Puebla was battling bouts with smallpox, measles, and whooping cough during that year. Indeed, disease claimed a score of lives from 1762 to 1768. The city's health problems were compounded by a severe drought that delayed harvests, adding to the already declining nutritional conditions that existed in the city.[18] However, the demographic group hit hardest by disease was that of children up to age seven, not adult men of militia age. Likewise, similar drought and nutritional problems affected Mexico City during the same period, without producing equally sharp drops in militia enrollment.[19] Even more revealing is that Puebla's militia forces continued to decline during the period of recovery from the diseases. Militia enrollment in 1770 had slipped to 368 soldiers, and by 1775, the city's forces were at less than half of their projected capacity.[20] True, another smallpox outbreak occurred in 1774. But instead of stunting growth as might be expected, Puebla's forces actually *gained* recruits during that year, albeit only few.

What should be drawn from this information is that prior to the new troop levy of 1777, Puebla was a site of frequent militia turnover, with free-coloreds constantly entering and leaving service. The companies were always understaffed, more so than in Mexico City. There did seem to be a pattern in the troop decline as militia rosters took their greatest dips in the months of October and November. One might surmise that the agricultural cycle had something to do with the flight, since these were principal harvest months.[21] On the contrary, most militiamen in Puebla were artisans, little affected by the labor demands of the peak agricultural season. Generally speaking, the low numbers were partly attributable to disease but more to a simple aversion to militia service. Mexico City's staffing troubles resulted from the same problems.

These last statements need some clarification. There was always a core group of soldiers staunchly committed to service in all cities and towns. It was these individuals who composed the bulk of the militiamen who remained on call during the lean months that followed periods of intense recruitment. Invariably, militia officers constituted some of these stalwarts, given that their stake in the corps was highest. They were the only individuals to receive regular monthly salaries; their commissions endowed them with significant prestige. Any dissipation of the battalion placed the status of their own positions in jeopardy. The core forces in Mexico City appear to have included its officers alongside some four hundred foot soldiers, while in Puebla, there were around three hundred militiamen resolutely involved in militia service during the period 1767–75. Again, it was these men who diligently appeared for militia re-

views month after month, who participated in the militia patrols, who performed training exercises, and who attended public militia functions.

For others, duty was perceived as offering its fair share of hardships. On the
one hand, there were the special problems that mobilizations presented. When
militiamen were called into action, they were forced to leave their homes and
businesses. Lesser artisans and agricultural laborers could not afford to hire replacements to stand in their place; consequently, their businesses, farms, and
families were left in neglect. As if to emphasize the point, the militiamen's
wives and families beseeched the viceroy for clemency when mobilizations
occurred, hoping to spare them from being sent into active service.[22]

Still other recruits shunned the grim possibility of illness or death while in
uniform. Mobilizations increased the chance of injury. Cantonment in Veracruz saw scores of free-colored militiamen perish, even though by virtue of
their race they were supposedly considered "immune" to many of the harsh
diseases that gripped the port. When 681 militiamen were sent from Puebla to
fortify the port in July of 1782, within four months of service, almost a third of
the forces were either reported sick or had been restationed to nearby Jalapa
and Perote for rest and recovery.[23] In view of these conditions, for many, military service lost much of its appeal. Unsurprisingly, attracting recruits became
difficult, especially in urban-based companies. Among those enrolled, one
could not be sure how many would stay for long.

If volunteers could not adequately staff the militia, exactly how were others
brought into the ranks? There appear to have been two main methods of conscription. One was a passive approach, while the other was active. Each offers
additional insight about the type of soldiers brought into the corps, as well as
commentary on the role race played upon entry.

The passive approach came into common use after the 1760s and involved
drafting soldiers by the draw of a lottery (*sorteo*). Passive recruitment was
characterized by the fact that potential conscripts were summoned to enroll en
masse, rather than being independently sought out by recruitment officers.
Each *sorteo* was preceded by a general census count of a community's population. The resulting document was then used to identify all eligible non-Indian
men between the ages of sixteen and forty. Based on the census, specific units
for free-coloreds, whites, or mestizos were drawn. Racially integrated companies of provincial cavalry and infantry could also be raised. In either case, once
the census was tallied, the eligible men were subdivided into three categories.
The first comprised widowers and bachelors without children. The second
category was reserved for married men, also without children to support. The
third comprised widowers and married men with children. The *sorteo* was
weighted so that there would be a greater chance that men from the first two
categories would be selected for duty. On the appointed day, all potential recruits would be asked to appear at a prearranged meeting place, usually announced by public decree several days beforehand. The names of the men were

written on slips of paper that were placed into hollowed wooden tablets. These in turn were placed into an urn. Into another urn were placed additional slips of paper, some marked with the word "militiaman" and others left blank. Young boys would be called upon to draw ballots from each urn. The names from the first urn were read aloud to the anxious crowd, along with the results of the ballots drawn from the second urn. If the drawing of a person's name coincided with the ballot marked "militiaman," he had to enroll for duty. However, if a name were drawn along with a blank sheet of paper from the second urn, the person was exempted from service until the next *sorteo*.[24]

This rather formal lottery process was utilized mainly during moments when new companies were raised, or when significant reforms were made to pre-existing units. A high-ranking, regular army officer usually supervised the process under these circumstances. But more commonly, as far as free-colored forces were concerned, the extravagance of the formal lottery was avoided. For instance, in cases where militia rosters had fallen to a critical number and could not be quickly replenished with standing volunteers, a community's *pardos* and *morenos* were simply instructed to appear at one of the town plazas. Sometimes the summons would be prefaced with fanfare, as militia officers used musicians to announce the impending levy. Once everyone was gathered at the designated area, a head count would be taken, a quick assessment of their health conducted, and snap judgments would be made by the militia's own officers as to who was to be enrolled into the corps. No census was conducted beforehand and influence from officers outside of the militia's immediate ranks was minimal.[25] This less formal draft procedure was even more passive in its approach than the *sorteo*, since it was the responsibility of the free-coloreds themselves to self-identify their racial status and appear for recruitment at the appointed moment. Scare tactics were used to help ensure they would indeed appear. Public statements were made, warning that all free-coloreds who failed to show would be reprimanded with a light jail sentence.[26] However, unlike the *sorteo* and its accompanying census, there were fewer ways to account for those who were absent under this procedure, allowing free-coloreds to evade the less formal recruitment efforts with more ease.

Under all forms of passive recruitment there were no outright attempts to target a specific social niche for duty. Rather, race became the guiding criterion for entry, along with one's physical aptitude and level of family obligation. Despite the relatively low intensity coercion techniques used to compel free-coloreds to conform with the levies, the passive recruitment process could still spark racial tensions. In September of 1766, the white *sargento mayor* of Valladolid, Dn. Phelipe Neve, attempted to recruit members of the *mulato* and Indian population into the city's newly formed provincial units. He and a small entourage marched through the streets playing drums, calling for members of these racial groups to congregate at the main atrium of the cathedral. After a few hours, men began trickling into the area, but once they neared the main fountain, they began picking up stones to hurl at the recruitment party. Hearing the turmoil, the *alcalde mayor* rushed to the scene to calm matters, but soon found himself thrown into the fray. Over the next few days, the air in Valladolid was tense. Three instigators of the mayhem were jailed, but others lurked in the city. Rumor circulated of a planned attack on the tobacco and *polvora* buildings. A harried Neve called for reinforcements to place barricades around the key administrative and commercial complexes of the city.[27]

Little explanation was given as to why Valladolid's *mulatos* and Indians reacted so strongly to enrollment. By contrast, under the process of active recruitment, not only were the motives for resistance clearer, but the instances were more frequent, although less violent and encompassing in scale. In lieu of the mass gatherings so typical of the passive recruitment process, active recruitment involved free-colored officers literally hunting down potential recruits in their homes. This may have been the most commonly utilized means of conscription, since its aim was not a wholesale replenishing of heavily depleted forces. Instead, active recruitment principally served as a patchwork remedy for small losses sustained by casual desertions and deaths.[28] The procedure was conducted routinely, from month to month, frequently degenerating into racial tugs of war, seen vividly in the cities of Puebla, Atlixco, Cordoba, and Mexico City. What made active recruitment so racially contentious was that free-colored officers possessed extreme authority in defining their recruitment pool. This differed from the free-colored summonses frequently observed under passive recruitment.

With the active levy, the officer staff was essentially charged with making very personal and often very independent choices regarding who was, or who wasn't, free-colored. In other words, the free-colored officer corps became a veritable gatekeeper of the free-colored population, especially in the cities, making stern decisions as to who *they* best felt belonged. A variety of tools assisted them in making their judgments, including tribute registers, census documents, and baptismal records. In theory, the combination of these references offered a distanced and neutral guide to racial status. But these sources were far from objective from the recruit's point of view. In fact, for urban centers such as Puebla, Guadalajara, and Mexico City, the very free-colored officers who were seeking conscripts for their companies were the same individuals contracted by the colonial government to draft the tribute and census registers.[29] As a result, those sources of information were normally stacked against the racial claims of the recruits. If doubts lingered about a person's racial status, the officers then relied on the guides of phenotype and reputational race. Officers would consult one's neighbors to establish if an individual was *de pública voz y fama* viewed as *pardo*, *moreno*, or *mulato*.[30] When the preponderance of evidence weighed in the officers' favor, the unwilling soldier was impressed.

Part of the trick in the active recruitment process was to locate the potential recruits, not always an easy task. Friends of eligible free-colored men covered for them, claiming not to know their whereabouts, or testifying that the wanted individuals were of a different race. Once they were successfully tracked, however, the careening list of excuses began. Men over fifty and the sons of widows received a legitimate military pardon by law. So did master artisans, teachers, surgeons, barbers, doctors, and pharmacists. With the establishment of the tobacco monopoly in Bourbon New Spain, tobacco workers in some locations were given an automatic exemption, as were agriculturists and miners in areas where militia duty posed a serious threat to the economy.[31] Those not falling within these excluded categories sought escape by other means. In the 1740s and 1750s, Puebla was particularly rife with those wanting to secure false baptismal records that lied about their race and age. Suspiciously fresh documents were presented to recruitment officers as they approached free-coloreds for duty. Other draft dodgers cried poverty. Already poor, they presented intricate arguments as to how militia service would serve to bring them into an even more ruinous state. A number of potential recruits claimed sickness to support their evasions, faking limps, mania, and other ailments. Like the chronically poor, the supposedly sick spoke at length about how they and their families worked overtime to secure the most basic necessities. Thus encumbered, there was just not enough time for them to perform militia labors. If proper release forms from an examined medic could support their allegations, then they were freed from militia obligations.

A few free-coloreds took the high road to avoiding duty, relaying that since their brothers were exempted from service by studying in the *facultad de medicina*, or by serving as minor government officials, they too should enjoy the same militia exclusions. Still others appealed to their affiliations with the clergy and white secular authorities. All dependents, servants, and coachmen of priests, nuns, and municipal officials were relieved from militia responsibilities by law. Connections to the elite provided these individuals with many of the same benefits derived from militia duty, thereby making service less attractive in their eyes. For instance, servants of the clergy and secular authorities did not pay tribute. When in legal trouble, they called upon the patronage of their masters, whose social influence in most matters was strong enough to turn legal odds in their favor. As a result, in unwritten terms, they possessed legal protection equivalent to the *fuero militar*.[32]

The heavy-handed methods of active recruitment were prejudicial to the socially weak, who had neither the economic means to offer bribes nor the patronage networks to escape duty. Those were the individuals who found themselves drawn most quickly into the militia ranks. Periodically, enough protest over unfair impressment arose from within the free-colored battalions that inspections by outside authorities were performed to assess the integrity of the practices. In Mexico City, for instance, pleas by soldiers who claimed to be mestizos and whites led to a review conducted by Don Joseph Merino in

1771.[33] Yet even those appeals did not always produce accurate results. In Merino's case, his review merely consisted of gazing over the free-colored militia rosters and comparing them with documents he had at his immediate disposal regarding the city's white regiments. Some of his papers may have also included the same tribute registers that led to unfair impressment in the first place. Merino was indifferent. Although the impetus for the inspection came from soldiers concerned that their true racial condition be respected, Merino's main motive was only to determine if any whites had been illegally purged from their units into the free-colored corps. Even that was a half-hearted effort. An exhaustive inquiry into each soldier's racial status would have been too time consuming and not necessarily desirable. Merino realized that whites impressed as free-colored foot soldiers were normally drawn from the common lot. Their fate mattered little to such officials, who often felt that properly placing these men in white companies would work to debilitate those units anyway. Bureaucrats like Merino reserved their attention for assisting those of more elevated standing.

The case of Mariano Guillermo Villegas is representative of instances in which crown officials took a more active interest in the fate of individuals whose racial status was brought into question by free-colored recruitment officers. In the 1760s and early 1770s, the free-colored *sargento mayor* Manuel de Santander hounded Mariano to serve in the corps. There was reason to be suspicious about his racial origin. Mariano was an orphan, taken in by white strangers. Born to unknown parents, the infant was left exposed shortly after birth in front of the home of Dn. Diego Carranco de Villegas. Unable to care for the child himself, Diego sent the baby off to his relative, Anna Teresa Villegas, who raised and educated the young Mariano. By 1771, Mariano had become a master coachmaker and had carved a respectable niche for himself in Pueblan society. That same year, Santander attempted again to impress Mariano into the free-colored militia. In the subsequent testimony, we see that although Mariano never knew his real parents, he claimed to be exempt from free-colored duty by birthright, signaling that both his natural father and mother were nobles. As evidence, he stressed that shortly after birth he had been placed on the baptismal register reserved for *españoles*.

Santander was unimpressed and tenaciously challenged the claims on two separate occasions. In his estimation, Mariano was undoubtedly a *mulato*. It was the circumstances surrounding his upbringing that gave him away. According to Santander, since a single mother had raised Mariano, his racial origin must have been dubious at best. As with many *mulatos* that he knew, clandestine lineage pointed assuredly to a coverup, a desire to hide black origins. Fortunately, Mariano was able to produce three white witnesses to testify in his behalf, including the important Licenciado Juan Manuel Martinez de Uloa, a presbyter. Martinez testified that Mariano's father had been a prominent member of the high clergy and that his mother had renounced the infant in an effort to preserve her own modesty and decency. While it seems doubtful that the other two witnesses actually knew Mariano's parents, they corroborated Martinez's testimony, alleging that both parents were *españoles nobles*. In reality, even Martinez's story seemed suspect. But regardless of the facts, the social standing of Mariano's witnesses, particularly the status of Martinez, proved to be the trump card in the case. Moreover, given that Mariano generally associated with whites and was a master coachmaker, which was one of the most prestigious and heavily capitalized artisan trades, the Real Audiencia ruled that it would be damaging to his reputation if he were placed in the *pardo* units. He was to be immediately stricken from the rosters and freed from all future free-colored service and tribute obligations.[34] In short, patronage, social networks, and personal status could assist one in evading service in situations in which race was in doubt.

Even the prospect of acquiring commissions of high rank was insufficient to change the disposition of some potential recruits from avoiding service in the free-colored corps. In Puebla during 1763, the free-colored *sargento mayor* attempted to conscript several members of the Aguilar family into the city's *pardo* units. He offered Felipe Aguilar, the oldest of the prospects, a lieutenant's post. His son, Joseph, was to be made a captain. Felipe's brother was issued the rank of *alférez*. After making the assignments, the *sargento mayor* gave the family fifteen days to comply with his orders. The men were outraged. After hunting for their baptismal records and marriage documents, they appealed to the court, stating that they were the descendants of mestizos and whites: "[We] are all clean and free from that awful [*mulato*] race."[35] The Aguilars also claimed to be commissioners in the white unit of Capt. Don Joseph Velazquez de Lorca Merino. When that unit was mobilized and marched to Veracruz, the family had contributed uniforms, equipment, rations, and horses. Felipe Aguilar added in his statement that he and his brother were well over the age of fifty, the maximum age for which men could be considered for service.

The *sargento mayor* was dumbfounded. "It is common knowledge that they are *pardos* and the sons of *morenos*," he said in his testimony. In fact they were "famed to be *pardos*."[36] In this instance, public, or reputational race, was pitted against the allegations of the family members. The court hesitantly ruled in favor of the Aguilars. In their judgment, the family had proven themselves to at least be *castizos*.[37] The actual racial status of the Aguilars was never determined, but what stands clear is that for some, the privileges and prestige of a high-ranking, free-colored militia post was still not enough to override concerns about the stigma of color. Similar situations were found in Tlaxcala, where in the 1750s, Col. Manuel Bertel nominated three individuals for the posts of captain, lieutenant, and *alférez*. Here too, the men apparently were known free-coloreds, but unlike the situation of the Aguilars, Tlaxcala's militia commanders possessed documented proof of their *pardo* status. Still, the men managed to evade service. One claimed to be "a man of the cloth." Another had become a soldier in the white militia units, not to be removed. The third possessed a special *inhibitoria* that offered him exemption from military service altogether. Bertel was fined two hundred pesos by the courts for attempting to recruit the men, which he narrowly avoided, emphasizing that according to his records, each of these individuals was eligible for recruitment into his companies.[38]

Families such as the Aguilars were caught in the act of passing. Yet if militia duty supposedly provided a boost to one's efforts at social whitening, why did individuals avoid service in cases like these? Evidently, for some free-coloreds, the type of social whitening offered through *pardo* militia channels possessed an unwanted corollary: whitening and status ascension had to be done within the framework of acknowledging one's race. Militia-inspired social whitening was just that: it was not true whitening, nor physically "passing" for a lighter hue. Upon enrollment, everywhere the soldiers went they could be identified as belonging to the local *pardo* and *moreno* battalion. This somatic fact seeped down into each soldier's family. Mother, father, siblings—all were affected, hindering everyone's goal of "passing" as well. In some cities, soldiers were even required to wear special items of clothing to indicate their rank and color. Veracruz's free-colored troops sported red ribbons "of two fingers length with a bow" in their hats, advertising their status when dressed in civilian clothes.[39]

Such observations are significant, since many major cities, especially Mexico City and Puebla, provided occasions for remarkable color transformations.[40] For instance, Manuel Francisco de Villanueva, a *mulato* slave born in the 1690s, fled his master's sweatshop after years of servitude. Arriving in Puebla in 1724, Villanueva met members of the religious order of San Agustín. Surprisingly, Villanueva, a colored man, joined the religious order that same year and became a priest. In essence, he had passed from being a *mulato* to white, since the preponderance of priests were whites. Fearing possible detection, Villanueva then moved to Mexico City, where he could better hide his true identity. It was not until 1735, when an employee of his master spotted him in the capital city, that the true identity of Villanueva was discovered.[41]

As easily as Villanueva had slipped into the church hierarchy, other free-coloreds were finding their way into white military units. Seventeen percent of Puebla's white militia regiments of 1,044 men were discovered to be *pardos* in 1767.[42] These soldiers reckoned that if they were going to serve, it would be better to solidify their ties with the socially dominant white sector than to enter the free-colored corps. Interestingly, the men who skirted entry into the *pardo* forces because of their skin color sometimes looked strikingly like others who willingly joined these units. The Tapia brothers, Juan and Rafael, voluntarily registered in Puebla's free-colored battalion between 1782 and 1784, at the young ages of eighteen and nineteen, respectively. At the moment of their enrollment, Juan was described as being of *color trigueño claro*, meaning of light olive complexion, among the fairest possible shades in the free-colored spectrum. His brother was even lighter, being described simply as *claro* and having blonde hair and blue eyes.[43] If these men had not proclaimed themselves to be free-coloreds, there was little else to physically distinguish them from whites and mestizos, given that *filiación* papers of members of these two racial groups tended to be almost identical to those of the Tapia brothers.[44] Evidently, employing racial characteristics as the standard of entry into the free-colored corps became a tenuous and sometimes contentious matter, made more difficult by the wide range and ambiguity of phenotypes.

The fluidity of the free-colored racial categories—*pardo, moreno, mulato*—was exhibited in even more detail during 1792, when moves were made to abolish the free-colored militia in Puebla, Atlixco, and Cordoba. The termination of duty brought an abrupt end to many of the privileges the soldiers had traditionally enjoyed, particularly tribute exemption. To evade full exposure to tribute laws, some of the battalion's soldiers relocated their residence and joined the fixed, all-black militia regiment in the port of Veracruz. Between 38 and 47 men of Puebla's battalion of 451 soldiers chose this route.[45] Others opted to try a change in racial status. As evidenced by the 1792 militia census, taken shortly after news of the militia's demise had been publicized, many men who had been comfortably categorized for years as *pardo, moreno,* or *mulato* adeptly claimed that they were of the lighter castes (see Table 17). Some 30 percent of the corps took this approach, amounting to 131 men. By far the most numerous were the self-described mestizos. Phenotyically speaking, this category was easier to feign. A few soldiers claimed to be *indios,* invariably professing to be *caciques,* thereby tribute exempt. A sprinkling of whites and *castizos* were recorded as well. The census enumerator, Tomas Zotina, was privy to the former soldiers' designed attempts at wiggling free from the tribute burden. Indeed, he was commissioned to conduct the census in order to correctly identify the former militiamen and place them on the upcoming year's tribute registers. To curtail possible evasions, Zotina added a statement at the end of his summary sheet that was intended to compensate for anticipated racial forgery: "[A]ll of the castes who are not [registered here] as *mulatos* are considered in the figures of the columns as if they were."[46] In this way, Zotina bought the crown time. Until the former militiamen could prove their racial claims, they were all assumed to be free-coloreds. After further inquiry, some "*mulato*" soldiers were actually successful in pleading out of their racial condition. Whether these individuals were truly free-colored or not is questionable. But that is the point. The militia was filled with people who could straddle the racial divide. When the benefits of service seemed best, some chose to remain in the corps, donning the full baggage of being a free-colored militiaman. Others, who could skillfully maneuver in society without free-colored militia ties, or who were disillusioned by the privileges military service had to offer, exited the corps at the first opportunity, or stubbornly resisted entry. High turnover rates, understaffed companies, and difficulties in recruitment reflect these realities.

TABLE 17

Racial Breakdown of the Militiamen in Puebla's
Cuerpo de Pardos y Morenos, 1792

Professed Race	Number of Militiamen	Percentage
Mulatos	304	67
Indios	8	2
Mestizos	90	20
Castizos	18	4
Españoles	15	3
Absent	16	4
TOTAL	451	100

Source: BNAH, Archivo Judicial de Puebla, rollo 2, fs. 1–45v.

TABLE 18

Monthly Distribution of Provincial Militiamen
in the Pardo Company of Jalapa, 1774

Month/Year	Number of Militiamen in Jalapa	Rate of Change by Percentage
January 1774	79	n/a
February 1774	79	0
March 1774	79	0
April 1774	79	0
May 1774	79	0
June 1774	79	0
July 1774	79	0
August 1774	79	0
September 1774	79	0
October 1774	79	0
November 1774	79	0
December 1774	79	0

Source: AGN, I.G., vol. 233-B, 1774, Jalapa, unnumbered folios.

Up to this point, the focus of our discussion has been on recruitment issues and problems in the major urban-based militia companies. In smaller towns and rural areas, the recruitment picture seemed considerably better. Table 18 presents series data for Jalapa in 1774. Much smaller than Mexico City and Puebla, Jalapa's *pardo* militia company was manned by nearly half of the town's free-colored male population.[47] Although the sample runs for just twelve months, one is struck by the stability of the company's roster, and that it remained at its prescribed strength for the entire period. Tobacco cultivation, an important enterprise in the region that demanded year-long intensive labor and attention, did not seem to rupture the pattern of militia assemblies at all in 1774. The situation in Jalapa does not seem unusual for the lesser cities and rural sites. In fact, in rural communities with populations large enough to sustain sizable militia contingents, there were reports of overstaffing, as free-coloreds crammed into the corps. This was best visible along the Pacific and Gulf coasts. It is important to note that overstaffing became a problem only after the 1760s. Prior to that time, relaxed militia regulations and guidelines prevailed, keeping crown officials relatively unconcerned with the dimensions of the corps. But in the era of Bourbon military reforms, with its emphasis on increasing overall militia efficacy and standardizing the terms of service throughout the colony, closer attention was paid to the composition of the units.[48]

Differences in enrollment patterns between the larger cities and rural areas had much to do with the dynamics of militia costs versus benefits. The average soldier in the countryside probably got more out of his militia affiliation for less participation than his urban counterpart. Despite attempts to centralize areas of duty in the mid-eighteenth century and to reduce the distances soldiers had to travel in order to reach their headquarters towns, many militiamen in rural zones continued to live too far away from their points of service to be effective soldiers. Even in light of the increasing volume of militia responsibilities in the seventeenth and eighteenth centuries, militiamen residing in isolated surroundings were prone to sloth and inactivity. Often their captains encouraged enrollment without duty. In places like Tuxtla, where, among other obligations, the militia was responsible for posting a coastal watch known as the *vigía*, captains made no amends for their efforts to recruit as many men as possible under the loosest of service conditions. *Vigía* duty was supposed to rotate among all the men in a coastal militia company. But in practice, only a fraction of their number were involved, normally between two and twenty men in any given unit. This was completely acceptable to the militia captains. Quality and breadth of service ran secondary to concerns over padding a special military coffer, known as the *vigía* fund, which was established to underwrite the expenses of the coastal watch.

In actuality, almost all free-coloreds living along the coasts were required to pay the fee prior to the 1770s, regardless of militia status. The payment rate usually ran half a peso per year for bachelors and widowers between the ages of sixteen and fifty, and one peso for married couples.[49] Exceptions were made only for the physically handicapped, militia officers above the rank of corporal, and for the soldiers actually commissioned to perform the watch.[50] The reason why local militia captains were so keen on trying to increase militia enrollment was that they were able to secure added control over *vigía* collections in this manner. In general, all of the contributions made by militiamen were taken exclusively by their captains and his legates. The *vigía* contributions of civilians were normally collected by the local *justicias*.[51] Consequently, by having larger militia companies to draw from, militia captains subsequently expanded the tax base that fell under their jurisdictions.

Justicias customarily withdrew a 5 percent commission from their *vigía* collections, sanctioned by law. Free-colored officers were legally prevented from keeping any portion of the *vigía* fund for themselves. After taking collections, the officers were to make arrangements for the prompt transfer of funds to a strongbox located in the *cabecera*, or at the home of the provincial militia's commander. Three keys were then issued, one to the commander himself and two to the most senior officers in the vicinity. These were the only men with authorized access to the chest. They were to supervise *vigía* spending so that the money went solely toward paying the overhead for the *vigía* watch. Any excess was either to be saved for years of scarcity or used to underwrite repairs to weapons, barracks expenses, and the cost of munitions. At least those were the cited objectives. In practice, captains and officers in outlying rural areas often delayed transferring the money to the *cabecera*. Although collections were normally taken during Holy Week, or in two equal installments during the months of September and April, it might be months before the money reached the hands of the provincial commander. In the meantime, it was not uncommon for militia officers to quietly whittle away any excess funds, using the money as a personal expense account. Again, that explains some of the eagerness with which officers tried to persuade free-coloreds to enroll for service, even to the point of routinely releasing them from duty after inscription. A glimpse of such graft can be seen in Acayucan from 1761 to 1762. Militia lieutenant Juan Domingo Ramos allegedly spent 33 pesos of his company's 100 peso *vigía* contribution on untraceable expenses, although he insisted that the discrepancy reflected the reduced amount of money that he had been able to acquire from his men that year. Other account sheets for the same period recorded that only 40 pesos of *vigía* income were collected for Acayucan's five hundred free-colored soldiers. Conservative estimates would have placed their anticipated *vigía* contribution at 375 pesos. Subtracting 182 pesos for the costs of maintaining the coastal watch, this left 153 pesos unaccounted for. In the wake of the missing money, all fingers pointed at Lt. Domingo Ramos.[52]

While officers were interested in expanding their rosters for the purposes of increasing the *vigía* fund, potential recruits did not have to comply. However, there were additional incentives that made enrollment attractive to them. In Tuxtla, *vigía* contributions that were routed through the hands of free-colored officers were sometimes used to underwrite certain legal expenses that the region's *pardos* and mestizos had pending before the Real Audiencia.[53] Along the Pacific coast, *pardo* militiamen in the 1770s attempted to use the military as a vehicle to secure farmland from the crown's *tierras realengas*.[54] In both instances, monetary contributions made to the militia were visibly rechanneled back for community benefit. In places like these, there was a concrete perception among residents that the military served as a benefactor, providing important tribute immunities and legal leverage for individuals on a personal level, while serving as a potential legal and political voice on the community level. This is an important point. Although there was the tendency for high-level bureaucrats to view free-coloreds in blanket, homogenous terms, they rarely conceived of them as being able to act on their own behalf as a coordinated, political entity. By contrast, bureaucrats did hold such a perception of Indians, thanks in no small measure to the distinct, relatively autonomous governmental structures they possessed in their *pueblos de indios* and the way in which Indians often collectively presented their demands and petitions. The militia, therefore, substituted as a mouthpiece for the group concerns of free-coloreds in the largely hispanicized villages of the rural coasts.

To highlight this situation, let's closely examine the militia-based appeals for the use of crown lands (*tierras realengas*) along the Pacific coast during the 1770s. In their petitions, *pardo* soldiers from Zihuatanejo, Ixtapa, Papanoa, and Petacalco, explicitly stated that they were presenting themselves to the royal courts as a *república*, or community. Although the men were dispersed over several villages in the province of Zacatula, theirs was a unified community formed *conceptually*, bonding over one thousand black households through the common militia link. Seeing that crown policy favored issuing land grants to "communities" over private individuals, the soldiers felt that their arguments virtually entitled them to acquiring special farmlands for their sustenance. If given the land, the community could then be actualized, as militiamen from various villages would relocate to form a distinct physical community of *pardo* soldiers. Any intruders on their space would be forcibly removed, thereby preserving the coherence of a *pardo* military settlement.

In reality, there were some problems with their proposals. The amount of land in question was vast, stretching for an indeterminate length of coastline and extending nearly two leagues inland. Residential atomization, rather than residential coherence, would probably have resulted if the project were to have been successfully realized. In some cases, *pardo* soldiers would have remained close to their original towns without leaving, simply expanding onto adjacent crown farmland according to their needs. Keep in mind that the militiamen were appealing for the right to select for themselves what property from the *tierras realengas* best fit their purposes.

Fears, jealousy, and infighting brought the land grant proposal to a halt. The local *justicias*, some of whom had settled the lands illegally themselves, managed to scare some militiamen into believing that the crown would bring harsh retribution for their brash efforts to annex the territory. They used a combination of delay tactics and bluffs to buy time that could be used to disable the free-colored litigation. Equally subverting were schemes aimed at undermining the credibility of the militiamen's hired legal aides. Enough militiamen were convinced that their *apoderado* was seeking to advance his own interests in the affair that there was a petition for him to return the money they had spent to contract his services.[55]

Despite the outcome, the case demonstrates the manner in which militia participation could be perceived as desirable for the collective free-colored good. Moreover, these sentiments were brewed in a context of militia service that seemed typical of the rural coasts. Zacatula's forces manned a *vigía* and fulfilled the labor requests of the *justicias*. Additionally, the soldiers assisted in matters of defense, protecting the region from pirates and natural predators such as mountain lions and alligators. But on the whole, service appeared un-regimented in comparison with the larger cities. Zacatula's militia was wholly volunteer-based, and the laissez faire style of command helped keep the ranks full. According to the militia's own officers, there were no recorded instances of desertion in the corps, given the way in which the companies were man-aged. The generally positive impression held by free-coloreds of the militia extended into the effort to expand its influence in more politically, and even racially, charged matters.

What are we to draw from the analysis of military recruitment? First and foremost, the recruitment process of free-colored forces was in large part arbitrary. Soldiers were picked up by lottery or by head counts; they were randomly sought out in their homes; they were volunteers. Especially in cities, militiamen were viewed by recruitment officers as little more than warm bodies filling vacant posts, instead of individuals fitting a specific, desired social profile. Hence the recruitment net was cast out wide across the social spectrum, attempting to ensnare the poor, the well-to-do, and anything in between. One might be inclined to believe that this would produce an in-stitution that was fairly representative of the social background of the free-colored population in the areas of service. Two main factors militated against that eventuality. On the one hand, there was the fundamental issue of race itself. The phenotypic markers utilized by recruitment officers could be as arbitrary as their recruitment methods. Without a clear, normative definition existing for the free-colored population, conflicts over phenotype erupted, most evidently in the active recruitment efforts. In matters of racial doubt, families and individuals with access to resources and connections were able to free themselves from duty, whether they were truly white/mestizo or simply attempting to "pass." Men of equally nebulous origins, but of lesser means, were less fortunate. That seemed to bias militia duty toward the middle and lower classes. In short, given how racial criteria contributed to the recruitment process, the free-colored militia stood the strongest chance of being both racially and socially representative of its parent population in areas where so-matic issues were less contentious, and where distinctions of phenotype were clearest.

The second factor that militated against the representativeness of the insti-tution dealt with the special military exclusions that some enjoyed. Servants and domestics, teachers and pharmacists, master artisans and barbers—that is, many of the high and low occupations—were legally exempt from duty. As individuals exercised their right to exemption, particularly in areas where service was often disdained, the militia came increasingly to encompass the middling occupational sectors. Conversely, in areas where the militia possessed a more positive community image, one might see a greater inclusion of these legally excluded sectors into the corps, and consequently a more representative free-colored militia. Based on what we have already seen regarding fluctuations in troop rosters, we might expect the militia to have been less inclusive and representative in the larger urban settings than in smaller rural ones. These ideas will be tested shortly.

On a final note, comparing the level of volunteers versus conscripts in the free-colored militia provides commentary on the theme of racial identity. It is unfortunate that the historical record on recruitment is weighted toward complaints and arguments over racial status. While this evidence yields enormous insight into the sometimes fractured, internal racial dynamics of the corps, what is lost is detailed information on the volunteers for whom militia service was an affirmation of race. Keep in mind that while places like Puebla and Mexico City had their fair share of enrollment problems, there was always a solid core group active in the service. In Puebla, even at the moment when the free-colored militia was dismantled and some men maneuvered to alter their racial status, the vast majority of the soldiers continued to willingly record themselves as *mulatos* and free-coloreds. As seen with the Tapia brothers, not all of them were unquestionably of African descent in a physical sense. Yet they still claimed free-colored affinities. We are led to conjecture that there were multiple avenues of racial expression within the militia framework, and layered degrees of attachment to free-colored identity. Recruitment represented a two-way street. Through volunteering for duty, a large number of individuals seemed committed to articulating their lives within the framework of a free-colored racial status. Meanwhile, another contingent of soldiers, mainly conscripts, negotiated their race with more stealth. Apparently, the former were more prevalent in the rural coastal areas, while the latter were found mainly in the cities.

In building further upon our assessment of the distinctiveness of the free-colored militia, military census documents provide us with a closer view of the soldiers' occupational status, allowing for firmer statements to be made about their employment condition in relation to that of free-colored civilians. As has been mentioned, the data for New Spain is sparse and difficult to find in series. Consequently, a multiregional, holistic view of their occupational behavior, decade by decade, is impossible to obtain. What has been done here is to provide an in-depth look at the soldiers' occupational situation at certain moments during the eighteenth century. The sources used include several military censuses raised in the context of militia reforms. Information from these documents is then compared with data on free-coloreds from already published demographic studies. To supplement those works, additional material on free-colored civilians has been consulted—namely, the parish, tribute, and census registers for Puebla and Igualapa.

Unfortunately, there have been few efforts to standardize much of the published secondary source material on occupational status. This poses a potential problem for the kind of broad-based analysis conducted here. There are still numerous unresolved debates over the status of certain jobs, and whether those could, or indeed should be, regrouped into larger categories. Indicative of some of the problems are the classic questions: did the agricultural occupation of *labrador* refer to an independent landowner or a mere sharecropper? Similarly, did a person labeled as a *sastre* (tailor) run a heavily capitalized workshop that serviced the elite, or was he a small-time artisan who dealt mainly with hoi polloi? In an effort to compensate for possible inconsistencies, and to facilitate comparisons with a wide range of occupational literature, I have organized jobs in two ways. The first breakdown delineates professions according to economic sectors. That is to say that all persons whose professions could be grouped under textile production, woodworking, services, and so forth have been arranged according to their type of employment.[56] Such a breakdown highlights the areas of the economy into which population groups were channeled. In an attempt to deal with basic differences in employment status, the delineation of occupations according to "classes" has been deemed best, as opposed to groupings based on skill levels.[57] Stratification by class is said to reduce the margin of error that a skill-based approach would generate, since in the latter, the documents alone do not necessarily reveal if specific trades involved more training and knowledge than others. Additionally, skill is not always a good guide to status. For example, a highly skilled master shoemaker rarely enjoyed the same prestige as a journeyman goldsmith. The use of class is employed here primarily to distinguish between two tiers of occupational status: the lower/middle status professions versus the upper status trades. The principal guides in developing both the "economic sector" and "class-based" methodologies have been the studies of Guy Thomson; Patricia Seed; and John K. Chance and William B. Taylor.[58]

Mexico City is an excellent starting point for analysis. Using the 1767 militia census, the soldiers' civilian occupations are detailed (see Table 19). The 1753 municipal census, as analyzed by Seed and Castro Gutiérrez, provides data on the general free-colored population (see Table 20).[59] What immediately surfaces is that the militiamen were mainly concentrated into the textile and clothing industries, with a secondary concentration in leatherworking and a tertiary involvement in metals. The two most numerically important professions were those of the tailors (*sastres*) and shoemakers (*zapateros*), accounting for over a third of all militia occupations.[60] Unsurprisingly, with such heavy emphasis in the production of textiles and leather goods, artisans surfaced as the primary occupational category. However, the bulk of these artisans were involved in the lower and middle status crafts. Only thirteen militiamen qualified as members of the upper social classes, including an *encomendero*, a wholesale merchant, a sacristan, and a master hatter.

TABLE 19

Occupational Structure of the Free-Colored Militiamen in Mexico City, 1767

	Number of Militiamen	Percentage
Breakdown by Economic Sector		
Transport and Services	25	6
Construction and Building	26	6
Metalwork	40	10
Clothing and Textiles	147	37
Commerce and Trade	18	4
Woodwork	16	4
Leatherwork	79	20
Food and Drink	16	4
Mining	1	0
Arts and Entertainment	3	1
Administrative, Professional, Church, Military	1	0
Agricultural/Pastoral	0	0
Cigar Workers	18	4
Other Industry	11	3
TOTAL[b]	401	99
Breakdown by Class		
Lower-Status (Labor and Services)	26	6
Lower/Middle-Status (Artisans)	346	86
Upper-Status (Artisans)	10	3
Middle/Upper-Status (Non-Artisans)[a]	19	5
TOTAL[b]	401	100

Source: AGN, I.G. 497-A, Pie de lista de los oficiales, sargentos, tambores, cabos, y soldados de expresada compañia [Mexico City] con distinción de sus nombres, estatura, edad, estado, y oficio, 1767.
[a]Note that this category includes merchants, managers, shop-owners, and sacristans.
[b]Not all percentage totals may equal 100% because of rounding.

TABLE 20

Occupational Structure of Free-Colored Men in Mexico City, 1753

Breakdown by Class	Percentage of Free-*Mulatos* (N=1089)	Percentage of Free-Blacks (N=27)
Lower-Status (Labor and Services)	53	89
Artisans	44	7
Middle/Upper-Status (Non-Artisans)[a]	4	4
TOTAL[b]	101	100

Source: Seed, "Social Dimensions of Race," 580.
[a]Note that this category includes merchants, managers, and shop-owners.
[b]Not all percentage totals may equal 100% because of rounding.

The militia employment breakdown represents a stark contrast with free-colored occupational information revealed in the 1753 census. While almost 90 percent of the militiamen were artisans in 1767, less than half of Mexico City's adult, free-*mulato* and free-black men were artisans in 1753. During this earlier period, the service sector surfaced as their primary employer. Given that occupational patterns changed slowly in colonial New Spain, it is almost certain that service-related employment continued to play a prominent role in most free-colored lives into the 1760s. Admittedly, the 1753 sample is biased in that it recorded inhabitants only in the central area of the city, where we would expect to find a greater number of domestics residing near, or inside, the households of the urban elite. But it is unlikely that the pattern would have changed radically even if complete figures were available. It is safe to posit that the artisan professions were overrepresented among free-colored militiamen when compared with other free-coloreds in Mexico City. On the other hand, service professions were underrepresented. Indicative of the situation is that there were only nine militiamen categorized as servants, as opposed to more than 570 free-colored servants recorded in the 1753 census. In the managerial-related and commercial professions, free-colored militiamen also appear to have been slightly more visible than the average free-colored resident. However, militia participation in these positions tended to be extremely small in relation to their presence in the labor market on the whole, and even smaller when compared with creole whites and peninsular Spaniards who were similarly employed.[61]

Despite the fact that the militiamen were more significantly represented in the artisan professions than their racial peers, their heavy distribution into the textile and leather industries appears normative for free-colored artisans during the middle of the eighteenth century. Castro Gutiérrez's study of guilds in 1753 demonstrates that regardless of militia status, *sastres* and *zapateros* were the two principal employment areas for the city's black and *mulato* artisans.[62] As is also traceable for the militiamen, he finds that metalwork constituted a distinguishable tertiary employment sector, with *herreros* surfacing as the third most numerous black artisan profession. One should not be surprised that textiles served as a primary employment sector for free-colored artisans. The low capital outlay needed to begin a simple tailor's practice made the profession attractive to a wide range of individuals. Indeed, the 1788 guild records reveal that *sastres* were among the leading artisan trades in Mexico City, employing large numbers of whites and mestizos as well. At this time there were 1,215 *sastres*, second in number only to masons (*albañiles*) and primary school teachers. Since teaching was more closely affiliated with the liberal professions than with the craft trades, and since there were only 16 examined master teachers, as opposed to 1,327 apprentices, we can assert with confidence that tailors actually constituted the second most numerous artisan profession in the city during late colonial times.[63] Textile-related trades continued to dominate all guild professions into the 1840s.[64] Hence, it is fair to say that the large number of free-colored textile workers found in the 1767 militia census, particularly *sastres*, reflected broader, citywide occupational patterns.[65]

It would be erroneous to assume that because there were a large number of free-coloreds involved in tailoring, it was necessarily an artisan trade of lower status. In actuality, despite the low capital outlay needed to start the practice, it was, in vertical terms, atop all other stages in the process of cloth production.[66] In this sense, along with the *bordadores*, tailoring was considered to be among the most desirable jobs within the textile industry. The profession also placed its artisans in fairly direct contact with the consumer market—that is, the final product did not need to enter any additional finishing stages before reaching the hands of the customer. Tailoring was deemed respectable in the eyes of urban residents because of this contact, but more so because the clientele were people who could afford to purchase clothes: buyers of shirts, blouses, capes, pants, and skirts. There were many urban dwellers lacking these means. By all accounts, one's wardrobe was a taxing expense in urban Mexico City, compounded by the high prices needed to acquire even more basic necessities, such as food. Many opted to purchase semifinished textiles from weavers rather than pay the minimum twelve to twenty-four pesos needed to buy the type of clothing a *sastre* could provide. As a result, many people roamed the streets in half-finished fabrics, while others sported second-hand apparel, "rented" wear, or soiled outfits from freshly exhumed graves. Still others walked about half-naked, as has been consistently cited in the literature about lower-class urban populations.[67] While there were gradations in the amount of prestige *sastres* enjoyed, by and large the profession was respectable because it distanced the artisan from the commoners.

The leatherworking craft of the *zapateros*, another popular trade among the militiamen, presents a different picture. Compared with *sastres*, the *zapatero* was held in lower esteem, even though both crafts enjoyed direct contact with the consumer market. As Angulo Aguirre has made clear in his study, a cobbler's products were considered practical and principally made for mass consumption, whereas the design touch of a tailor could be more valued for its aesthetic appeal.[68] Part of what made shoes accessible to the lower ranks was that the materials used to make them came largely from within the colony itself, whereas certain necessities for tailors had to be imported from abroad. Despite these considerations, it must be stated that as a profession *zapateros* were gaining popularity in late eighteenth-century Mexico City, if not slight prestige. In 1794, *zapatero* guild membership more than doubled from its 1788 numbers, and by 1811, census records reveal that an equally large number of individuals practiced the craft outside of the formal guild structure.[69] These gains seemingly marked more entry into the profession by Indians and whites. However, the craft persisted in being dominated by free-coloreds and mestizos. If the number of militia shoemakers tallied in 1767 persisted until the

TABLE 21

Occupational Structure of the Free-Colored Militiamen in Puebla, 1710

	Number of Militiamen	Percentage
Breakdown by Economic Sector		
Transport and Services	32	6
Construction and Building	1	0
Metalwork	48	9
Clothing and Textiles	226	43
Commerce and Trade	27	5
Woodwork	23	4
Leatherwork	109	20
Food and Drink	25	5
Mining	0	0
Arts and Entertainment	14	3
Administrative, Professional, Church,		
Military	4	1
Agricultural/Pastoral	5	1
Cigar Workers	0	0
Other Industry	12	2
TOTAL[b]	526	99
Breakdown by Class		
Lower-Status (Labor, Agriculture, and		
Services)	49	9
Lower/Middle-Status (Artisans)	432	82
Upper-Status (Artisans)	14	3
Middle/Upper-Status (Non-Artisans)[a]	31	6
TOTAL	526	100

Source: AHAP, legajo 1255, fs. 74v–77.

[a]Note that this category includes merchants, managers, and shop-owners.

[b]Not all percentage totals may equal 100% because of rounding.

1780s, then free-colored soldiers alone may have accounted for up to a quarter of the city's formally registered *zapateros*. Again, while it is wrong to assert that shoemaking was a trade of lower status because it employed large numbers of free-coloreds, it is undoubtedly true that free-coloreds found a distinct occupational niche in this craft because of its reduced social status.

Puebla's militia occupational breakdown was highly similar to that of Mexico City (see Tables 21 and 22). The richness of Puebla's census materials allows us to examine two separate periods, one at the outset of the eighteenth century and the other near the end of the century. The militia census of 1710 reveals that free-colored soldiers were concentrated into textile production, leatherworking, and smithing, at roughly the same proportions as in Mexico City during the 1760s. Indeed, except for construction work and the arts, there was little appreciable difference in the militia's occupational structure between the two cities. Over the course of the eighteenth century, the distribution of Puebla's free-colored militiamen in the city's economy changed slightly, but the basic structures found earlier remained in place. Textiles and leatherwork over-

TABLE 22

Occupational Structure of the Free-Colored Militiamen in Puebla, 1792

	Number of Militiamen	Percentage
Breakdown by Economic Sector		
Transport and Services	7	2
Construction and Building	16	4
Metalwork	26	6
Clothing and Textiles	191	47
Commerce and Trade	5	1
Woodwork	21	5
Leatherwork	58	14
Food and Drink	31	8
Mining	0	0
Arts and Entertainment	7	2
Administrative, Professional, Church, Military	0	0
Agricultural/Pastoral	2	0
Cigar Workers	27	7
Other Industry	20	5
TOTAL[b]	411	101
Breakdown by Class		
Lower-Status (Labor, Agriculture, and Services)	7	2
Lower/Middle-Status (Artisans)	385	94
Upper-Status (Artisans)	12	3
Middle/Upper-Status (Non-Artisans)[a]	7	2
TOTAL	411	101

Source: BNAH, Archivo Judicial de Puebla, rollo 2, fs. 1–45v.
[a]Note that this category includes merchants, managers, and shop-owners.
[b]Not all percentage totals may equal 100% because of rounding.

whelmingly remained the two most prominent economic sectors of their involvement. Textile workers even increased their presence in 1792, but that was counterbalanced by distinguishable ebbs in the proportion of *zapateros* and metalworkers. In fact, one of the greatest changes to occur over the century was the gradual displacement of metals as the tertiary area of militia employment. Perhaps not too much should be made of this. Metalwork, as in Mexico City, always occupied a tenuous back seat to textiles and leatherwork, pacing just a few percentage points ahead of its nearest numerical competitor.

Other noticeable changes in Puebla included gains made in the construction and food industries. Also, participation in the royal tobacco monopoly opened a new realm of employment, providing work for several individuals in the royal tobacco factory. There was a sharp decline in the already small number of individuals involved in commerce. By the end of the century, there were no free-colored *tratantes*, or petty dealers, which had been an important profession for militiamen in earlier decades. Additionally, within the textile industry itself, certain changes were traced in terms of select profes-

TABLE 23

Occupational Structure of the Free-Colored Men in Puebla, 1720

	Number of Men	Percentage
Breakdown by Economic Sector		
Transport and Services	32	26
Construction and Building	0	0
Metalwork	6	5
Clothing and Textiles	42	34
Commerce and Trade	9	7
Woodwork	9	7
Leatherwork	16	13
Food and Drink	1	1
Mining	0	0
Arts and Entertainment	2	2
Administrative, Professional, Church, Military	5	4
Agricultural/Pastoral	0	0
Cigar Workers	0	0
Other Industry	0	0
TOTAL[b]	122	99
Breakdown by Class		
Lower-Status (Labor, Agriculture, and Services)	32	26
Lower/Middle-Status (Artisans)	72	59
Upper-Status (Artisans)	4	3
Middle/Upper-Status (Non-Artisans)[a]	14	12
TOTAL[b]	122	100

Source: AHAP, legajo 1384, fs. 1–66v.

[a]Note that this category includes merchants, managers, and shop-owners.

[b]Not all percentage totals may equal 100% because of rounding.

sions. Whereas most free-colored militiamen were tailors in 1710, by the end of the century a greater proportion of soldiers were weavers. The meaning of this shift is somewhat difficult to explain. Earlier in the century, Puebla's weavers appeared to have enjoyed a higher status than tailors. Their guild was highly respected throughout the city, and even a significant number of whites hailed weaving as a choice profession. As the century progressed, there was a serious decline in the craft's prestige. Although the job continued to be reasonably well situated within the process of textile manufacture, the daily wage of a weaver had dropped to a pittance, less than two reales a day, the pay of an agricultural peon, and, by most accounts, just under the subsistence level for the eighteenth and nineteenth centuries.[70] Consequently, what might initially appear as an upward social move in light of the 1710 occupational evidence was essentially a lateral move. Free-coloreds were routed from tailoring into weaving at a moment when the status of weaving was on the decline. As a re-

TABLE 24

Occupational Structure of the Free-Colored Men in Puebla, Tribute Census of 1794

	Number of Men	Percentage
Breakdown by Economic Sector		
Transport and Services	79	16
Construction and Building	15	3
Metalwork	36	7
Clothing and Textiles	175	36
Commerce and Trade	4	1
Woodwork	17	4
Leatherwork	44	9
Food and Drink	27	6
Mining	0	0
Arts and Entertainment	1	0
Administrative, Professional, Church, Military	1	0
Agricultural/Pastoral	4	1
Cigar Workers	68	14
Other Industry	13	3
TOTAL[b]	484	100
Breakdown by Class		
Lower-Status (Labor, Agriculture, and Services)	79	16
Lower/Middle-Status (Artisans)	389	80
Upper-Status (Artisans)	10	2
Middle/Upper-Status (Non-Artisans)[a]	6	1
TOTAL	484	99

Source: BNAH, Archivo Judicial de Puebla, rollos 43–44, Tributos, Expediente formado en virtud de las exigencias hechas por los alcaldes ordinarios al gobernador intendente Don Manuel de Flon con el fin de cobrar tributos de negros y *mulatos*, Puebla, 1795.

[a]Note that this category includes merchants, managers, and shop-owners.
[b]Not all percentage totals may equal 100% because of rounding.

sult, weaving did not enjoy any more social prestige than tailoring did at the beginning of the eighteenth century, and probably less.

Seen in retrospect, nearly all of the major free-colored militia occupations in Puebla carried approximately the same amount of social weight throughout the century. None of them were particularly noteworthy employment opportunities. From the white elite perspective, every artisan job that the free-colored militiamen performed was menial, since they were all "mechanical" in nature, not employing a sufficient amount of raw intellectual power to qualify the soldiers for membership into the upper levels of society. *Zapateros, sastres,* and *tejedores* were singled out specifically for such criticism.[71]

Yet, as in Mexico City, Puebla's free-colored militiamen were greatly underrepresented in the least prestigious service-related jobs. A combination of sources have been used here to highlight the employment patterns of the free-

TABLE 25

Occupational Structure of the Free-Colored Men in Puebla, Parish Census of 1790–92

	Number of Men	Percentage
Breakdown by Economic Sector		
Transport and Services	39	22
Construction and Building	0	0
Metalwork	10	6
Clothing and Textiles	72	40
Commerce and Trade	5	3
Woodwork	6	3
Leatherwork	11	6
Food and Drink	10	6
Mining	0	0
Arts and Entertainment	1	1
Administrative, Professional, Church, Military	6	3
Agricultural/Pastoral	3	2
Cigar Workers	7	4
Other Industry	10	6
TOTAL[b]	180	102
Breakdown by Class		
Lower-Status (Labor, Agriculture, and Services)	45	25
Lower/Middle-Status (Artisans)	126	70
Upper-Status (Artisans)	1	1
Middle/Upper-Status (Non-Artisans)[a]	8	4
TOTAL[b]	180	100

Source: AHAP, legajo 1385, fs. 69–103v; AHAP, legajo 1387, fs. 136–77v; AHAP, legajo, 1388, fs. 178–237v; AHAP, legajo 1389, fs. 238–326; and AHAP, lejago 1390, fs. 2–99v.
[a]Note that this category includes merchants, managers, and shop-owners.
[b]Not all percentage totals may equal 100% because of rounding.

colored urban masses. An incomplete but useful census from 1720 offers a look at urban occupations in the downtown section of the city, allowing for comparisons with the 1710 militia census data. A tribute census taken for Puebla's free-colored residents from 1793 to 1794, combined with parish census information from 1790 to 1792, allow for views at the close of the century (see Tables 23–25).[72] Using these sources, we observe that at various moments during the eighteenth century, the service sector employed between 16 percent and 27 percent of the working, free-colored male population. By contrast, free-colored militiamen worked in the services at rates of just 6 percent in 1710, and under 2 percent in the 1790s. Interestingly, while representing an important source of free-colored income, Puebla's service sector was not their dominant employer, as in mid-eighteenth century Mexico City. Artisan professions occupied more than 60 percent of free-colored residents toward the beginning of the century, and upward of 71 to 82 percent on the eve of the nineteenth century. For those free-colored civilians who were artisans, textiles and dress were

TABLE 26

Occupational Structure of the Free-Colored Militiamen in Orizaba, 1769

	Number of Militiamen	Percentage
Breakdown by Economic Sector		
Transport and Services	16	15
Construction and Building	0	0
Metalwork	7	6
Clothing and Textiles	15	14
Commerce and Trade	0	0
Woodwork	5	5
Leatherwork	21	19
Food and Drink	1	1
Mining	0	0
Arts and Entertainment	1	1
Administrative, Professional, Church, Military	0	0
Agricultural/Pastoral/Tobacco Workers	39	36
Other Industry	4	4
TOTAL	109	101
Breakdown by Class		
Lower-Status (Labor, Agriculture, and Services)	55	50
Lower/Middle-Status (Artisans)	53	49
Upper-Status (Artisans)	1	1
Middle/Upper-Status (Non-Artisans)[a]	0	0
TOTAL[b]	109	100

Source: AGN, I.G., vol. 232-B, Dionisio Surtado, August 14, 1769, Orizaba.
[a]Note that this category includes merchants, managers, and shop-owners.
[b]Not all percentage totals may equal 100% because of rounding.

the industries of choice, accounting for more than 40 percent of their number. That is not surprising, given Puebla's reputation during the colonial period as Mexico's chief textile producing center. But on the whole, free-coloreds occupied a middle position between whites and mestizos in the late eighteenth century with regard to the percentage of their population that was employed in textile-related industries. Mestizos were directed into these jobs at rates of 50 percent of their population, while whites were employed at rates of 30 percent.[73]

For our purposes, it is important to stress that the major similarities between free-colored militiamen and civilian artisans ended at the level of textiles. In the 1793–94 tribute census, which is perhaps the most reliable of the census counts reviewed here, the important militia craft of leatherworking was not as significant to civilians as cigar making in the late eighteenth century. The lesser importance of leatherwork among the general free-colored population is confirmed by the parish census materials, although cigar workers are much less prominent than in the tribute registers.[74] Regarding tertiary eco-

TABLE 27

Occupational Structure of the Free-Colored Militiamen in Patzcuaro, 1762

	Number of Militiamen	Percentage
Breakdown by Economic Sector		
Transport and Services	3	5
Construction and Building	6	9
Metalwork	7	11
Clothing and Textiles	13	20
Commerce and Trade	0	0
Woodwork	4	6
Leatherwork	9	14
Food and Drink	1	2
Mining	0	0
Arts and Entertainment	0	0
Administrative, Professional, Church, Military	2	3
Cigar Workers	1	2
Agricultural/Pastoral	16	25
Other Industry	2	3
TOTAL	64	100
Breakdown by Class		
Lower-Status (Labor, Agriculture, and Services)	18	28
Lower/Middle-Status (Artisans)	39	61
Upper-Status (Artisans)	5	8
Middle/Upper-Status (Non-Artisans)[a]	2	3
TOTAL	64	100

Source: AGN, I.G. 296-B, unnumbered pages, Valladolid and Patzcuaro, 1759–62.
[a]Note that this category includes merchants, managers, and shop-owners.

nomic sector involvement, it is always hard to pass firm judgment, but as with the militiamen, there were slim numerical differences distinguishing the civilian professions falling into this tier. The proportion of individuals in these jobs was always small, usually well under 10 percent per category. Taking into account the small number of individuals involved in the various professions, there were numerous similarities between militia and civilian occupations at this level. Nevertheless, civilian free-colored professions rarely paired neatly with the militiamen's involvement in the tertiary economic sectors (compare Tables 21–25).

In lesser cities and towns, such as Pátzcuaro, Valladolid, and Orizaba, the patterns observed in Mexico City and Puebla continued to hold (see Tables 26–28). Militiamen in all three centers were involved in the artisan crafts above all others, with special emphasis on the textile and leatherworking industries. One is led to believe from the evidence that almost regardless of the location of a town or city, free-coloreds found an economic niche in these professions. Even in major mining centers such as Guanajuato, the proportion of free-

TABLE 28

Occupational Structure of the Free-Colored Militiamen in Valladolid, 1762

	Number of Militiamen	Percentage
Breakdown by Economic Sector		
Transport and Services	6	10
Construction and Building	0	0
Metalwork	2	3
Clothing and Textiles	34	56
Commerce and Trade	3	5
Woodwork	4	7
Leatherwork	6	10
Food and Drink	2	3
Mining	0	0
Arts and Entertainment	1	2
Administrative, Professional, Church, Military	1	2
Cigar Workers	1	2
Agricultural/Pastoral	1	2
Other Industry	0	0
TOTAL[b]	61	102
Breakdown by Class		
Lower-Status (Labor, Agriculture, and Services)	2	3
Lower/Middle-Status (Artisans)	52	85
Upper Status (Artisans)	3	5
Middle/Upper-Status (Non-Artisans)[a]	4	7
TOTAL[b]	61	100

Source: Same as Table 27.
[a]Note that this category includes merchants, managers, and shop-owners.
[b]Not all percentage totals may equal 100% because of rounding.

coloreds in these fields could be high. There, although free-coloreds were overwhelmingly channeled into mining-related fields, the number of shoe-makers was considerable during the late colonial period. With a little more difficulty, free-coloreds found their way into the profession of tailoring.[75] Oaxaca reports similar trends in the eighteenth century. The cochineal and textile industries, which had taken root in the 1740s, assumed new life with the loosening of the Cádiz trade monopoly in the mid-eighteenth century. As a consequence, weaving became more important, and by 1792, the profession occupied more than a quarter of the non-Indian population.[76] Free-coloreds found a comfortable space in this area of the work force.[77]

Despite what seems to have been a generalized presence of free-coloreds, and particularly militiamen, in the textile and leatherworking trades, unique features of an area's local economy were usually reflected in the militia occupational breakdowns of smaller urban centers and rural towns. In Orizaba, which was a noted center for the cultivation of tobacco and which possessed its own tobacco factory in the late colonial period, a significant portion of free-colored militiamen were described as *tabaqueros*, or tobacco workers (see Table 26).[78] Given the town's location along the Mexico-Veracruz highway, transportation and commerce professions formed another numerically important employment category.[79] But the impact of these economic endeavors on the free-colored militia was limited, especially given the reduced opportunities for free-colored access to the commercial sector. In fact, none of the militiamen registered were involved in commerce. There were a few militiamen involved in transport, but at levels disproportional to the importance of the transportation professions to the local economy. However, considering that many transport jobs were secondary in social status to artisan trades, the militiamen's professions in Orizaba, *tabaqueros* included, appear to have once again stood the middle ground in terms of overall social prestige. The soldiers were overrepresented neither in the high-status commercial jobs nor in the lower-status occupations. At the same time Orizaba's militia reflected the unique orientation of the city's economy toward tobacco.

As in Orizaba, Pátzcuaro's militia forces mirrored the important presence that agricultural professions played in the local economy (see Table 27). At the same time, there was a gravitation toward artisanry, observed in the high number of militia textile and leatherworkers found in the city.[80] In the more urbane Valladolid, the seat of Michoacán's administrative apparatus in the late eighteenth century, agricultural professions played an even smaller role in the militia (see Table 28). That is despite evidence for strong income derived from wheat and maize cultivation.[81] Apparently, the impressive number of looms recorded in Valladolid during the late eighteenth century signaled the presence of a vibrant textile industry, with added opportunities for tailoring and weaving.[82] These opportunities clearly resonated in the free-colored militia. Except for Puebla, artisans did not so thoroughly dominate the free-colored militia's ranks anywhere as in Valladolid. Nowhere was there a greater proportion of *sastres* in the corps: they represented more than half of all militia occupations in the city. Based solely on an examination of militia records, one is inclined to believe that free-coloreds held a virtual monopoly on the tailoring profession. There were only nine *sastres* recorded in the city's mestizo and white militia units. But such observations present a demarcated break from the traditional image of Valladolid's black occupational habits. Previous scholarship has maintained that the service industry employed more blacks than any other sector.[83] Although not based on hard evidence, if the interpretation is true, then the situation in Valladolid provides yet another example of the militia emerging as an institution that represented individuals who were a cut above the ordinary, free-colored rank and file.

Whatever status the soldiers enjoyed, it is important to keep in mind that their occupations were typically socially inferior when compared with men in white militia units. In Valladolid during the early 1760s, more than half of the white militia company of 125 men was composed of merchants, government administrators, estate owners, and shopkeepers.[84] Free-colored militiamen who were comparably employed numbered only four men (7 percent). So many influential people sought duty in white units because in Michoacán, the militia could be manipulated by the elite to solidify their position, expand their patronage, negotiate attractive business deals, and acquire crown favor.[85] *Cabildo* members, being influential in the process of granting officer commissions, often selected themselves for these posts. By combining both municipal and military authority they could offset the political influence of the church. While there were many whites who actively avoided enrollment, enough socially important members were attracted to service in Michoacán that they shaped the overall standing of the institution.[86]

Similar statements can be made about Puebla. The sheer size of the city may have reduced the level of intimacy between the elite and the militia. Fewer men of the economic stature found in Valladolid dared don an NCO's uniform in Puebla. But the officer corps was always staffed by luminaries.[87] Militia rosters from 1710 provide an excellent picture of the six white companies that operated in Puebla. More than a quarter of the muster of 1,039 men were merchants, shopkeepers, or silversmiths. By contrast, well under a tenth of Puebla's free-colored companies boasted militiamen in similar positions. Over time, there was a small decline in the occupational prestige of Puebla's white militiamen. Shopkeeping, which was the second most common profession earlier in the century, did not occupy a prominent standing in the top three trades by mid-century. Some of the status changes coincided with a slackening of racial standards for entry into the white regiment. Whereas in 1710 virtually all of the men were whites, by 1767 a quarter of the soldiers registered in the twelve companies were categorized as mestizos or free-coloreds.[88] Even with the new racial influx, the basic distribution of militiamen into the artisan crafts remained the same, and despite a lesser representation in the commercial sector, white soldiers were perceived as occupying a higher social standing than members of the free-colored corps.

Although the free-colored militiamen's occupational profile may have never approached that of the white units, in the rural countryside their professions tended to resemble those of their civilian brethren to a stronger degree than in the larger urban centers. A contributing factor to the greater parity in employment status resulted from a less diverse range of job choices. Indicative of the situation was the province of Igualapa, situated along the Pacific coast in what is today known as the Costa Chica. Agriculture thoroughly dominated the lives of the province's residents in colonial times. Sixteenth-century experimentation in raising commercial livestock and cash crops, such as cacao, contributed to the steady growth of the African-based populations of the province. Slaves were initially brought in to work these enterprises, and through gradual processes of emancipation the number of free-coloreds expanded. Additionally, free-coloreds who were already working in nearby

TABLE 29

Occupational Structure of the Free-Colored Men in Igualapa, 1791

	Number of Men	Percentage
Breakdown by Economic Sector		
Transport and Services	31	2
Construction and Building	1	0
Clothing and Textiles	6	0
Woodwork	1	0
Professional	1	0
Agricultural/Pastoral	1,277	97
TOTAL[b]	1,317	99
Breakdown by Class		
Lower-Status (Labor, Agriculture, and Services)	1,296	98
Lower/Middle-Status (Artisans)	8	1
Upper-Status (Artisans)	0	0
Middle/Upper-Status (Non-Artisans)[a]	13	1
TOTAL[b]	1,317	100

Source: AGN, Padrones, vol. 18, fs. 209–305v.
[a]Note that this category includes estate managers and overseers.
[b]Not all percentage totals may equal 100% because of rounding.

provinces as ranchers, muleteers, gold panners, fishermen, and cane-cutters were attracted to settle in the area. By the late eighteenth century, free-coloreds had almost matched, if not surpassed, the indigenous population in terms of overall demographic size and importance in Igualapa.[89] In the meantime, the province's large-scale commercial agricultural endeavors became concentrated on the property of two grand haciendas, one mill, five *ranchos*, and four estancias, all operating in full stride by the time of the 1791 census.[90]

Notwithstanding, subsistence plots remained the norm. The occupational breakdown of the province's free-colored residents reflected this reality (see Table 29). Regardless of their heavy numerical presence, Igualapa's free-coloreds were employed in only thirteen types of jobs.[91] Of these the *labrador*, or farmer, was the most heavily represented, with 93 percent (1,229) of all free-colored men occupied in the profession. Coupled with the pastoral occupation of the *baquero* (cowboy) and the *sirvientes* (servants), some 98 percent of the region's free-colored male population was accounted for in just three professions, none of which were artisan related.

Igualapa's artisan community was minuscule, regardless of race. It would be unfair to judge the impact of free-coloreds on the artisan crafts by simply examining how many of their number were routed into those professions. One must first consider the overall composition of the artisan trades. In 1791 there were just twenty-one artisans in the province, out of a working, non-Indian male population of 1,538. In view of the small numbers, the presence of

TABLE 30

Occupational Structure of the Free-Colored Militiamen in Igualapa, 1791

	Number of Militiamen	Percentage
Breakdown by Economic Sector		
Transport and Services	10	1
Construction and Building	0	0
Clothing and Textiles	3	0
Woodwork	1	0
Professional	0	0
Agricultural/Pastoral	813	98
TOTAL[b]	827	99
Breakdown by Class		
Lower-Status (Labor, Agriculture, and Services)	821	99
Lower/Middle-Status (Artisans)	4	1
Upper-Status (Artisans)	0	0
Middle/Upper-Status (Non-Artisans)[a]	2	0
TOTAL[b]	827	100

Source: Same as Table 29.
[a]Note that this category includes estate managers and overseers.
[b]Not all percentage totals may equal 100% because of rounding.

free-coloreds in the artisan crafts was considerable, since eight of the twenty-two artisans were *mulatos*. However, considering the free-colored share of the labor pool, which was 85 percent, their number of artisans was not proportional to their greater numerical presence; they represented just 36 percent of the artisans. Consistent with our previous observations about the impact of free-coloreds in the textile industry, we see that half of the province's *sastres* were *mulatos*, as well as the province's only hatter. Consequently, the trends observed in Puebla, Mexico City, and Valladolid hold true in the rural countryside, if on a considerably reduced scale. Unlike the major cities, leatherwork and metals were not arenas of free-colored employment in Igualapa. Still, most jobs falling in these categories remained beneath the status of most resident Spaniards. Indians and mestizos composed the entirety of the *herreros* and *zapateros* in Igualapa.[92]

How did the free-colored militiamen of Igualapa compare with the general free-colored population? To begin with, militiamen accounted for 63 percent of working men (see Table 30). A full 98 percent were agriculturists, meaning that free-colored soldiers were overrepresented in that department. Consistent with what we have seen in the urban setting is that militiamen, even in rural Igualapa, continued to be underrepresented in the service sector. A scant seven servants were found among their number. In terms of artisans, there was more evenness between soldiers and civilians than was observed in either Puebla or Mexico City. Igualapa's militia accounted for exactly half of the province's

TABLE 31

Occupational Structure of the Free-Colored Militiamen in Acayucan, 1793–94

	Number of Militiamen	Percentage
Breakdown by Economic Sector		
Transport and Services	9	3
Metalwork	6	2
Commerce and Trade	3	1
Woodwork	2	1
Leatherwork	4	2
Agricultural/Pastoral/Fishing	243	91
TOTAL[b]	267	100
Breakdown by Class		
Lower-Status (Labor, Agriculture, and Services)	252	94
Lower/Middle-Status (Artisans)	11	4
Upper-Status (Artisans)	1	0
Middle/Upper-Status (Non-Artisans)[a]	3	1
TOTAL[b]	267	99

Source: AGN, I.G., vol. 416-A, unnumbered pages, Acayucan, 1795.
[a]Note that this category includes merchants, estate managers, and shopkeepers.
[b]Not all percentage totals may equal 100% because of rounding.

small contingent of free-colored artisans. With respect to the militiamen's presence in the highest-status free-colored occupations, such as professionals and estate managers, the numbers were surprisingly much smaller than for the civilians. This was most likely a result of two factors. First of all, militia ties were neither determining elements nor prerequisites for occupational success. While they could enhance employment chances for some, significant achievements were frequently made outside of the militia framework. Secondly, although all of the militia officers were *labradores* (fifty-three officers), probably not all were lowly farmers. Unfortunately, the census does not provide further information about the size of their holdings, nor insight into whether they were sharecroppers or independent planters. Nevertheless, the census is quite useful. On the whole, we can conclude that while differences existed between the militiamen and their peers, especially with respect to the service sector, by and large, the status gap that separated a soldier's profession from that of an ordinary civilian was much smaller in the rural environment than in urban centers. Igualapa's situation probably held true for free-colored units in similar areas throughout the colony. Keep in mind that an important contributor to the greater equilibrium in the coastal countryside stemmed from the fact that a larger percentage of free-colored men were militarized. Nearly seven out of every ten free-colored adult men were registered in the corps in Igualapa. It is unlikely that the same could be said for a Puebla or Mexico City.[93] Moreover, as Igualapa also demonstrates, the higher ratio of

TABLE 32

Occupational Structure of the Free-Colored Militiamen in Tampico, 1780

	Number of Militiamen	Percentage
Breakdown by Economic Sector		
Transport	36	4
Dress and Textiles	1	0
Commerce and Trade	5	1
Woodwork	2	0
Leatherwork	5	1
Agricultural/Pastoral/Fishing	812	94
TOTAL	861	100
Breakdown by Class		
Lower-Status (Labor, Agriculture, and Transport)	848	98
Lower/Middle-Status (Artisans)	8	1
Upper-Status (Artisans)	0	0
Middle/Upper-Status (Non-Artisans)[a]	5	1
TOTAL	861	100

Source: AGN, I.G., vol. 53-A, Thomas Serrada, August 16, 1780, Tampico.
  [a]Note that this category includes merchants, managers, and shop-owners.

militarization took place in a context in which there was lesser occupational diversity to start with.

An examination of free-colored militia forces in the provinces of Tampico and Acayucan serves to underscore the major occupational trajectories traced above for soldiers in the rural sphere (see Tables 31–32).[94] Each of these provinces occupied vast spaces along the Gulf coast in what is today the state of Veracruz. In 1781, Acayucan was described as possessing 2,730 Indians, 1,031 free-coloreds, and 134 whites dispersed among twenty towns and thirty-five haciendas. The province was primarily agricultural, with maize and beans constituting the main subsistence crops. Cotton was also harvested on plantations, and the haciendas were dedicated to raising *ganado mayor*, with special emphasis on cattle and horses. To a lesser extent *filastica* was gathered, and wood was logged in the province.[95] As in Acayucan, the inhabitants of Tampico were heavily involved in raising livestock, so much so that observers noticed that most other foodstuffs were not sown. Jerked beef became a staple in the diet of Tampico's non-Indian residents, as was fish caught along the bountiful coasts. Butter, ham, wine, and flour were generally imported. Although maize was grown, its limited cultivation brought periods of scarcity.[96]

A lack of comparative census information prevents us from viewing militia occupations alongside those of civilian free-coloreds, as was done with Igualapa. However, we see that in each province, agricultural, fishing, and pastoral tasks occupied most militiamen roughly to the same extent as in Igualapa (see Tables 31–32). As elsewhere, few militiamen worked in the service industry.

Indeed, none of Tampico's soldiers worked in that sector. Unlike their counterparts along the Pacific coast, a small number of militiamen managed to enter into commerce, and a significant number of militiamen, particularly in
Tampico, also transported goods to market. Lastly, in Acayucan, while the artisan trades were few, the primary free-colored crafts were related to metal-
working. From this analysis we can conjecture that, by and large, free-colored
militia occupations in the countryside tended to be homogeneously directed
into the agricultural, fishing, and pastoral professions. Slight differences in the
orientation of independent local economies accounted for the small participation of free-coloreds into the crafts, commercial sector, and transport industries, but, by and large, there seems to have been great occupational uniformity in New Spain's free-colored militia units along the rural coasts.

By way of summary, the employment evidence taken from various cities and
provinces throughout Mexico allows us to establish that the soldiers were more
socially distinct from their racial peers in urban settings than in the colony's rural towns. What mainly differentiated these militiamen from civilians was the
high proportion of artisans among their number. Yet, despite being distinguished by a higher level of artisans, the types of craft jobs held by most urban
soldiers were not notably prestigious. Free-colored militia artisans in New
Spain's cities were heavily involved in the textile and leatherworking industries.
In other words, instead of nucleating in the upper-status trades, the soldiers entered professions that typified the civilian free-colored artisan class. It is true
that the colony's free-coloreds probably possessed an independent social
structure that was different from that of whites and mestizos, causing them to
rank the worth of occupations differently. Similar to the case of slaves, in which
domestics and low-level artisans enjoyed much greater esteem than common
field hands, so too did the militia's many *sastres* and *zapateros* possess an elevated value in free-colored eyes. Nevertheless, there were still discernible limits
to the militiamen's social prestige—their artisan jobs were not exceptionally
privileged in greater society. The occupational status ceiling fell even further on
the liberal professions and merchant enterprises. Here, civilians and militiamen
alike held only a few positions. In short, while the average militiaman in the urban environment generally enjoyed a better social image than the masses of free-
colored civilians employed in the service sector, on the whole his overall social
position occupied the middle ground in the colonial world. Instead of providing a vehicle for social whitening through dramatic class ascension, for the majority of soldiers, the urban militia experience stood the best chance of increasing one's standing *within* the free-colored social realm. In the countryside, a
more constrained set of occupational choices brought still less room for differentiation. Apart from some very minor exceptions, employment homogeneity
was the rule: militia status did not necessarily lead to any appreciable difference
in class standing.

TABLE 33

Marriage Structure of Free-Colored Militiamen and Civilians in Puebla, 1720–92

	Race of Bride %						
Free-Colored Husbands	Mulatas	Mestizas	Castizas	Indias	Españolas	Unknown	N = 100%
Militiamen, 1792	17	43	5	8	27	0	143
Civilians, 1790–92	36	35	6	6	13	4	161
Civilians, 1720	36	28	3	0	2	31	95

Source: AHAP, legajo 1385, fs. 69–103v; AHAP, legajo 1387, fs. 136–77v; AHAP, legajo, 1388, fs. 178–237v; AHAP, legajo 1389, fs. 238–326; AHAP, lejago 1390, fs. 2–99v, AHAP, legajo 1384, fs. 1–66v; and BNAH, Archivo Judicial de Puebla, rollo 2, fs. 1–45v.

TABLE 34

Marriage Structure of Igualapa, 1791

	Race of Bride %					
Husbands	Mulatas	Mestizas	Castizas	Indias	Españolas	N = 100%
Free Colored Militiamen	94	4	0	2	0	623
Free-Colored Civilians	91	6	0	3	0	213
Mestizos	39	45	0	6	10	88
Españoles	11	20	0	5	64	61

Source: AGN, Padrones, vol. 18, fs. 209–305v.

Let us now turn away from the analysis of the militiamen's occupational status to observe their marriage behavior. Did the same dichotomy that existed between rural and urban occupational profiles persist with the militiamen's spousal choices? To what extent did militia marriage patterns resemble those of free-colored civilians? Does marriage evidence provide further clues as to social status? Tables 33 and 34 compare free-colored militia and civilian marriage patterns in two areas where the most complete information is available, the city of Puebla and the rural province of Igualapa.[97] The Puebla military census of 1792–93 reveals that free-colored (*mulato*) endogamy in the companies was very low (see Table 33). Most militiamen had mestiza brides, and even white women were brought to the altar more frequently than *mulattas*. Intermarriage was least common with *castizas* and Indians. Puebla's parish registers from 1790 to 1792 allow us to compare the militia marriage patterns with those of civilian free-coloreds. For additional analysis, the municipal census of 1720 has been included as well. From these records, we see that free-colored endogamy represented roughly a third of the marriages sampled at various moments during the century. There is little change from the 1720 data and the material taken in the 1790s, suggesting that endogamy rates, with some fluctuations, were probably fairly consistent throughout the century.

In light of even the lowest endogamy figures for the general free-colored population, militia marriage endogamy was exceptionally low. The soldiers

tended to marry outside of their race at much greater rates than their peers.
The fact that militiamen married so frequently with mestizas is not surprising.
These women were prime spousal partners for *mulatos* and *pardos* throughout
the colony. Puebla was no exception. The census and parish registers record
that despite wide fluctuations in the proportion of mestizas married by the
general free-colored population, these brides always ranked as either the first
or second choice for nuptials. On the other hand, wedlock to Indian women
was low for civilians and militiamen alike. This may come as a surprise, given
that Indians were important spousal choices for free-coloreds in places like
Guanajauto, San Luis Potosí, Charcas, Jalapa, and San Luis de la Paz.[98] There
was certainly no lack of available Indian brides in Puebla. Indians composed
the single largest racial group in the city.[99] However, their endogamy rates were
the highest of all groups, and when they did intermarry, Indian women chose
mestizo husbands first, then whites.[100]

White women were notably overrepresented as militia spousal partners. In
fact, Puebla's free-colored militiamen intermarried with white women at significantly greater proportions than did mestizo men in the 1790s. Only 20 percent of mestizo marriages were with whites.[101] Hence, the data suggest that
free-colored militiamen possessed an advantage in the marriage market with
respect to white women that even transcended traditional caste boundaries.
The advantage improved with rank. Of the nine married free-colored junior
officers, six had white wives, two had *mulatta* wives, and only one married a
mestiza. From this evidence alone it is hard to determine if the soldiers' greater
intermarriage with white women was helped mainly by their military status,
or by the status of their nonmilitia careers. We have already discussed how,
occupationally speaking, the militiamen generally tended to occupy the middle ground in Mexico's cities. While not in notably prestigious professions,
the high number of militiamen who were artisans undoubtedly provided
some added exposure and standing in the marriage market over those civilians
who worked in service-oriented occupations. And for a select few free-colored
soldiers, their occupations brought true status indeed. Four of the city's officers, for example, were found employed as master artisans, painters, and merchants. For leading militia families such as the Bertels and Santanders, their
wealth alone would have made them attractive grooms for anyone but the best
white families. In all likelihood, the improved opportunities for militiamen to
marry outside of their race emanated from a combination of both militia and
occupational status.[102] Additionally, while the sample does not allow us to
make definitive conclusions, we can also speculate that those white women
who were selected as brides were of a low enough socioeconomic position to
be accessible to the militia's blacks.

Matters were different in rural Igualapa. To begin with, the marriage market was of a different complexion. Free-coloreds and Indians dominated the
province, with small numbers of whites and mestizos. In this marriage envi-

ronment, none of the free-colored men intermarried with white women, nor even with the fair-complexioned *castizas* (see Table 34). These precious few women were concentrated in the hands of mestizo and white men. But given the overall dearth of white and mestiza women in Igualapa, endogamy was hard to maintain among the lighter castes. Mestizos were the least endogamous group, with over half of their marriages taking place outside of the race. Unlike elsewhere in New Spain, the preferred interracial brides for mestizos were not Indians or whites but free-colored women.[103] White marriage behavior was equally atypical for the colony. While most of their marriages were endogamous, they were barely so. The proportion of exogamous unions was inordinately high, representing just over a third of all nuptial ties. Interestingly, white cases of endogamy tended to fit a specific profile. A great number of *españoles* in the province were foreigners, sojourning to fill bureaucratic positions, engage in commerce, or to minister a spiritual message. These whites traveled in retinue, accompanied by siblings, relatives, and dependents. Typically, they arrived brides in hand, accounting for almost three-fourths of the province's white, endogamous marriages. For those who came to Igualapa under different conditions, or were born there, endogamy was a much more difficult enterprise. White men in that situation married available *castizas*, mestizas, or *mulattas* according to their social station and profession, with the more affluent favoring the lightest brides.

Endogamy among free-colored men and women ran high, over 90 percent. Men outmarried at slightly greater rates than women. Although the rates of male intermarriage with mestizas, *castizas*, and whites was small, it should be mentioned that free-colored men married nearly as many mestizas as the mestizo men did. In other words, despite the small numbers, free-colored men had a profound impact on the mestizo marriage market. Their impact also made it necessary for some white suitors to explore other marriage options. Interestingly, occupational success was not an apparent reason for the mestiza/free-colored marriages, since only a fraction of the already small number of free-colored artisans and professionals married mestizas. Most of the grooms were simple farmers and servants. One can conclude that there must have been different tiers of status and marital eligibility operating in the province that did not correlate neatly with race or occupation. If the caste system had been replicated in practice, or if a class-based marriage hierarchy were firmly in place, then all mestiza women would have been wedded by their racial peers, or at least by the province's most successful free-coloreds. Given what we have seen, the social structure in Igualapa was such that the province's most elite individuals were all white and involved in endogamous unions. Under them was a small strata of moderately well-to-do whites and mestizos, who also tended to exhibit endogamy but frequently intermarried with each other. Alongside them were a handful of successful free-coloreds who intermarried occasionally with mestizas but mainly sought *mulatta* wives. Then there were the poorer masses, predominantly free-coloreds and Indians, but with a small strata of mestizos and whites. As with the elites, endogamy was the norm among the lower groups. Of course, miscegenation was present, but to a small degree. In sum, miscegenation and exogamy were most characteristic of Igualapa's non-free-colored and non-Indian groups, and then only among the middle and lower social sectors.

Perhaps the most surprising aspect of the Igualapa marriage market was that Indian brides were not taken with significant frequency by any racial group. High levels of indigenous endogamy were nothing rare in New Spain; in fact, it is what scholars have come to expect. But the paucity of Indians who married interracially in a province so heavily populated by free-coloreds is noteworthy, especially since in other areas they married free-coloreds, and even mestizos, in greater numbers. Of the 1,036 married men who were categorized as mestizo, white, or free-colored in Igualapa, just 24 had an Indian mate. Free-colored intermarriage with Indians was the lowest, at 2 percent. Certainly the physical distance that separated many Indians from towns housing a mixture of races played a role in reducing Indian intermarriage rates.[104] Indigenous populations tended to live in their own pueblos, where they managed their own affairs and consequently preserved a measure of social distance from non-Indians. However, as studies of rural Morelos reveal, towns and villages of predominantly mixed race, such as the ones listed in Igualapa, often contained a significant number of Indians nonetheless.[105]

Unfortunately, the nature of the 1791 census does not offer a full look at the distribution of the indigenous population in Igualapa, but we can surmise that in each of the locations cataloged, Indians probably represented at least 15 percent of the total number of residents.[106] One would be inclined to believe that low Indian/free-colored intermarriage rates were a result of a cultural divide as much as the physical separation between racial groups. While the hypothesis must remain speculative, one can conjecture that particularly in Igualapa's racially mixed towns, where an important Indian presence was registered, there was a reluctance on the part of both free-coloreds and Indians to wed the other.

How did the free-colored militiamen fare in this constrained marriage market? Soldiers constituted 70 percent of the free-colored spouses in Igualapa but represented only 66 percent of free-colored interracial marriages. Therefore, free-colored militiamen demonstrated a slightly lower tendency toward exogamous marriages than the province's free-colored population on the whole. Indeed, Table 34 shows that civilian exogamy was slightly greater than that of the militiamen, both with Indians and mestizas. Even when calculated by rank, there was no substantial increase in militia exogamy. Out of the eighty-one soldiers holding the rank of sergeant or above, just six contracted marriages outside of their race. In a reverse scenario from Puebla, the highest ranking officers in Igualapa were more endogamous than their subordinates.

Only one captain out of sixteen took a mestiza bride. Clearly, rank alone did not necessarily equate to success in attracting spouses outside of the race. But when class is factored into the equation, militiamen fared a little better, since only two soldiers who were artisans married outside of the race. In short, the militiamen's marriage patterns, as with their occupations, tended to reflect the behavior of the broader free-colored population.

A further word is needed about the nature of marriage evidence and the scope of its implications. Unlike employment data, which principally yields insight into social position and class standing, marriage-related documents can also provide information about racial affiliations and bonds. Marriage registers have been a commonly used tool for examining the difficult issue of racial identity. For instance, high endogamy rates have been associated with cultural continuity and racial consciousness. Significant degrees of exogamy have been upheld as indicators of assimilation, as subordinate racial groups sought to improve their social lot in a caste-rigid society through a whitening strategy.[107] Numerous studies have maintained that blacks and free-coloreds, more so than Indians and mestizos, were the most avid pursuers of exogamous relationships. According to the logic, marrying a lighter-skinned spouse offered one's children better chances for social advancement, since they were placed at an additional step's distance from the restraining taints of African bloodlines. In terms of the marriage's immediate impact, the darker partner was said to improve his or her personal "passing" efforts, be it through opening up a new and phenotypically lighter world of social contacts and professional ties, or just by having the bragging rights of marriage to a spouse of supposedly superior genetic stock.

Recent research on free-colored intermarriage has confirmed that Afro-Mexicans were New Spain's most exogamous racial group, despite the fact that endogamous unions were the norm for all races during the colonial period.[108] Scholarship has also periodized free-colored marriage patterns. *Pardo*, *moreno*, and *mulato* exogamy was lowest during the sixteenth and seventeenth centuries, when the black population was invigorated by steady shipments of slaves.[109] Exogamy increased after 1650, picking up tempo considerably in the eighteenth century. The new marriage scene was affected greatly by declining slave imports in the eighteenth century.[110] With substantial decreases in slave arrivals, the black population found it hard to sustain links with ethnic Africans, both in terms of marriage and culture. Miscegenation increased and the colony's black population grew lighter in phenotype, becoming principally *mulato* and *pardo* in composition.[111]

Another major advance forwarded by research has been a detailed understanding of the types of partners that free-coloreds selected most frequently. Rarely were nuptials contracted between *morenos* (pure blacks) and whites, which represented a tremendous leap along the caste system's somatic scale. Instead, smaller racial hops were more commonplace. A notable number of intermarriages took place within ethnic categories.[112] Blacks frequently inter-married with *mulatos*, and *pardos* with Indians and *mulatos*. Outside of the framework of ethnic-based marriages, the most significant interracial contact took place along what has been labeled the "mestizo/*mulato* boundary," with a large number of exogamous unions occurring between those two racial groups.[113] Finally, as has been previously mentioned, in places such as Jalapa, Guanajuato, Charcas, and San Luis Potosí, scholars have found that Indian spouses were statistically important marriage partners for all shades of free-coloreds. In most of these centers, the Indians' low social position placed them in easy reach for Afro-Mexicans.[114]

I have provided this information to demonstrate that much of the recent scholarship on free-colored exogamy has tended to undermine the thesis that whitening, or "passing," was the primary objective of intermarriage. In a study based on late seventeenth- and early eighteenth-century Mexico City, Douglas Cope has argued that worries over race were mostly an elite affair. Free-coloreds, who fell mainly within the category of plebeians, saw little material benefit from marriage to a mestizo, white, or *castizo* who lived in the same squalid conditions as they did.[115] Interracial marriages, when they occurred among plebeians, most likely resulted from casual contacts and relations be-tween individuals, rather than from strategic jockeying for racial ascension. Cope adds that the task of passing involved intense psychological effort, ac-companied by a complete reorientation of social networks. The exertion and strain were greatest for those making significant racial leaps—for instance, from being *mulato* to being white. Attempting the transition was not for ev-eryone. In part, he asserts that these considerations were why so many exoga-mous unions took place within ethnic boundaries, or between *mulatos* and mestizos. Marriages of these types involved less estrangement. Even at the mestizo/*mulato* boundary, where nuptials between both groups entailed a crossover from one ethnic divide to another, there was less alienation. Com-monalties shared by each racial group facilitated the transition. *Mulatos* were neither too rooted in an African-based heritage, nor mestizos too tied to their Indian roots, for the transition to be marked in a cultural sense. Indeed, both races occupied their position in the *sociedad de castas* because they had already whitened to some degree, be it by bloodline or, as is mainly exhibited in the mestizo case, by the adaptation of Spanish mannerisms and habits.[116] Unde-niably, whatever forms of free-colored exogamy were most prevalent, interra-cial unions could eventually culminate into passing for white. However, recent scholarship emphasizes that the progression was done incrementally, follow-ing the somatic scale prescribed by the *sociedad de castas*. Devoid of its ur-gency, whitening, as much as it was a conscious plan of free-colored families, was at best a multigenerational objective. There were few immediate ramifications for the married couple.[117]

How does this discussion relate to our analysis of the free-colored militia? Generally speaking, scholarship has taken quite a different view of the militiamen's marriage patterns. Although lacking hard statistical evidence, some have posited that the militiamen's privileges, rank, and social standing dramatically increased the soldiers' attractiveness on the marriage market. Whereas civilian free-coloreds had fewer opportunities to court fair-skinned brides, as militiamen they were believed to possess an added advantage.[118] As the soldiers exercised their attractiveness through inordinately high rates of intermarriage, they were believed to demonstrate a greater interest in whitening than was ordinarily seen in civilian society.

What we have seen in Tables 33 and 34 speaks directly to these issues. Vigorous rates of militia exogamy in Puebla, especially with whites, appear to initially confirm the above hypothesis, suggesting that many of the city's militiamen were concerned with racial ascension. On the other hand, the whitening process involved an array of factors that cannot be detected solely from marriage data. To accurately assess the soldiers' commitment to racial mobility one would need to compare marriage registers with a host of other public and private records, carefully examining both how the militiamen referred to themselves and how they were discussed by others in racial terms. That would have to be done for each individual who contracted an exogamous marriage, with particular focus on those militiamen who chose *españolas* for brides. The most we can say from the information presented in Table 33 is that if a free-colored bachelor in Puebla sought to diversify his range of potential brides, joining the militia was undoubtedly a smart choice. If whitening was his ulterior motive, then the very fact of his militia status limited the ascent of his racial climb. Keep in mind what we observed earlier in the analysis of free-colored militia recruitment procedures. A considerable number of individuals evaded duty because they realized that serving in the corps actually accentuated the badge of color. Therefore, even if soldiers took white spouses, their prospects for whitening were counterbalanced by the high visibility of being a *pardo* soldier in the local free-colored battalion.

In Igualapa, joining the corps had even fewer positive effects for those who hoped to use their militia affiliation as a vehicle for whitening. The militiamen's pool of marriage partners virtually mirrored that of the civilian population, and in terms of attracting lighter brides, the militiamen's chances were actually reduced by entering the corps. Free-colored endogamy proved to be the overwhelming marriage choice among soldiers. Did that insinuate the existence of a greater racial consciousness for provincial-based militiamen than for those in Puebla? Again, using just the evidence in Table 34, it would be hard to draw a concrete conclusion. But we can definitely posit that whitening appeared more difficult, and was probably a less attractive endeavor, for soldiers in the countryside.

Throughout this chapter I have argued that militiamen in rural areas were less likely to be distinguishable from free-colored civilians, both in terms of their marriage patterns and their nonmilitary careers. Urban settings simply yielded greater possibilities for differentiation. With respect to occupations, the middle social strata of artisans, more so than the lower-status service professions, were brought into duty. A sprinkling of free-colored elites were attracted as well, though others kept their distance, often out of concerns for passing and fears related to mobilizations. While many urban-based militiamen had more desirable occupations than their civilian counterparts, arguably it was not the militia affiliation that improved the job opportunities for most. Therefore, the militia was not necessarily a direct source of occupationally related class mobility. Rather, the selection process involved in recruitment played a pivotal role in defining the type of individuals who eventually enrolled, attracting artisans over other groups.

Urban-based militiamen were again differentiated from their civilian brethren through intermarriage. In Puebla, there was a greater degree of exogamy in the militiamen's nuptials than in rural Igualapa, where there was a close correlation between militia and civilian marriage choices. Substantial intermarriage with whites suggests that if soldiers sought whitening in Puebla, then some strides were possible within the militia framework. But it is unclear how consciously the militiamen turned to exogamy as a whitening strategy. For soldiers concerned with such matters, social whitening in the militia, as manifested through marriage and even through occupational advancement, had to be at least a two-step process that initially involved an affirmation of the soldiers' race. Participation in free-colored companies, notably of the independent type, was not race-neutral. Subsequent privileges, opportunities, and advancement—that is, the status mobility of the soldier, became centered around the military corporate institution in racialized form. Even units of the integrated type, when heavily staffed by free-coloreds, became affected. While some individual soldiers may have preferred to have their militia-imbued privileges viewed in isolation from caste concerns, members of colonial society often denied them that opportunity by seeing their militia corporate affiliation through racial lenses—the men were ultimately *milicianos pardos* or *morenos*. But as the free-colored militiamen worked to secure privileges for themselves, they reworked the meaning of race at the same time. Asserting oneself as a *pardo* or *moreno* could be done more confidently when the person possessed a militia affiliation, because being free-colored no longer carried the full legal and social baggage traditionally associated with race. Rather than whitening, the effect produced was a definitional alteration of free-coloredness through militia corporate privilege. Sometimes the benefits the soldiers garnered had an impact on civilian free-coloreds as well, affecting their racial perspective. Again, of course not all free-coloreds rushed to embrace a *pardo/mulato/moreno* racial identity, even if they had some say in its design. The militia's own recruitment difficulties, often centered around issues of race, reveal tensions in that regard. However, enough individuals were swayed by the militia's role in the racial formation process that its influence cannot be ignored. In the following chapters I will expand on this discussion, examining the links between corporate privilege, militiamen, civilians, and race. An overview of the tribute establishment and its connection with the free-colored militia will be offered, and an investigation into *fuero* rights will be presented. Finally, the role of race will be assessed through a variety of interactions that took place between the soldiers themselves, and with various colonial authorities.

CHAPTER FOUR

The Loathed Tax

I N   C O M P A R I S O N   T O   what is known about Indian tribute practices, free-colored tribute has been a relatively unexplored topic in colonial Latin American historiography. Part of the lack of attention stems from the great inconsistencies that existed throughout the New World regarding free-colored tribute collection procedures and exemption requirements. Scholars have been inclined toward taking exemptions at face value, dismissing tribute's greater relevance by not delving completely into the processes that initially led to relief, nor observing the political discussions triggered by the free-colored tax.[1] The military establishment offered Spanish America's black populations one means of exemption. In New Spain, securing tribute exclusion through the militia was a contested and debated affair, ultimately presenting insights on how corporate privilege could be reinterpreted as racial privilege. The goal of this chapter is threefold. Beginning with an overview of the way the tribute establishment functioned, the chapter proceeds to examine the steps by which free-colored militiamen garnered tribute relief in colonial Mexico, while assessing the avenues for how this unique military privilege became upheld as a broader civilian exclusion. Finally, the challenges of the Bourbon military reforms to the tribute relief structure will be analyzed.

Tribute was a responsibility of free-coloreds throughout the Spanish Americas. In its earliest manifestation, free-colored tribute policy resulted from debates over whether the offspring of marital unions between blacks and Indians should be held liable for payment. Already by the mid-sixteenth century, collection among the indigenous population had begun to take mature form, being superimposed upon preconquest tribute structures.[2] While the crown felt little need to explain its actions, some royal officials justified their stance toward Indian tribute on the grounds that these were conquered peoples who had customarily paid some form of coerced tax under the Aztec and Inca regimes. Moreover, Indian villages (*pueblos de indios*) enjoyed special land-holding privileges under Spanish rule, including select agricultural benefits, communal land rights, and villagewide legal protections. Over time, administrators perceived these distinct privileges as fundamental motives for holding Indians accountable for payment.[3]

Although free-coloreds were not congregated into such collective living circumstances, the crown determined on May 18, 1572, that the children of black and Indian unions should be subjected to tribute as well. The proposition was ratified in May of 1573.[4] Both decisions emanated from an overall reassessment of tribute policy that began in the middle of the sixteenth century. As the crown grappled to take greater control over its colonies' fiscal resources from the hands of the *encomenderos*, and feeling the impact of severe Indian population decline, royal bureaucrats began to implement new tribute methods to compensate for projected losses in revenue.[5] Gradually, free-coloreds were factored into these new schemes. However, the 1572–73 legislation reveals that royal administrators were initially hesitant about taxing blacks. Both laws enacted during these years are best interpreted as extensions of Indian tribute policies, since they applied exclusively to the *pardo* and *zambo* castes, each of which possessed blood ties to Indian ethnic groups. Indeed, the original 1572 decree was issued in large measure to curb the rate of promiscuity among Indian women who felt that they could exclude their children from the tax if they were fathered by non-Indians.[6] In short, these early laws represent the crown's exploratory efforts at redefining the scope of the Indian community for tax purposes.

In April of 1574, all previous cautions about maintaining tribute solely among Indians or Indian-related castes were abandoned, as free-*mulatos*, *negros*, and the full spectrum of black hues were called upon to bear the tribute burden. According to royal reasoning, since *negros* possessed a long tradition of paying tribute in their native African kingdoms, surely the same should be requested of blacks living under the Spanish domain. We should recognize these sentiments as echoing the rhetoric of colonial administrators who used native preconquest practices as the grounds for their Indian levies. But for free-coloreds, Spanish authorities further added that tribute was a fair price to pay in exchange for the status of freedom and the privilege of living peacefully on royal soil. Final versions of free-colored tribute policy were drafted between 1577 and 1591. It was decided that it would be at each viceroy's discretion to determine the exact amount to be collected per head, adjusted to the economic means of the black population in their regions. Accurate census counts, providing each viceroyalty with a complete understanding of the geographical distribution of its free-colored population, would be implemented to facilitate collection. The crown anticipated difficulties. Whereas Indians were mainly organized into *pueblos de indios*, which provided fairly stable, rooted populations that were easily tallied, placed on tribute rosters, and subject to collection, the free-colored population was considerably more mobile, drifting where economic opportunities seemed best. This complicated the collection process, since extra effort was needed to locate free-coloreds. Lack of residential stability also meant that there could be significant variation in a region's black population from one year to the next, rendering tribute registers useless. Royal authorities attempted to reduce the potential fiscal mayhem by ordering free-coloreds to live with *amos conocidos*, or masters of known reputation. It was decreed that blacks could not leave these men without a signed pass from the local justices. In the event that someone managed to escape without permission, the authorities would be notified, a search conducted, and, once found, the subject was to be briefly jailed. After completing his sentence, the free-colored worker would be returned to his master. These same masters were to act as tribute overseers, ensuring that all taxes were paid from their workers' salaries.[7] These clauses in the tribute code strongly suggest that an ulterior motive of free-colored tribute policy was to force blacks into the wage-labor economy by making their services more available to estate owners.[8] Their enterprises were struggling to find workers in the 1570s and 1580s as the Indian population dwindled because of disease.

Attempting to place strict demands on a free population was met with open hostility. There is little evidence that the master/worker system ever took hold, and tribute collection among free-coloreds persisted as a difficult challenge. In colonial Peru in the 1570s, viceroy Toledo, who initially embraced the tribute policy, shied away from its full implementation in later years. Into the seventeenth century, collections there were haphazard at best.[9] In Chile in the late 1690s, lackadaisical tribute payments pushed the *audiencia* of Santiago to write a law of re-enslavement for those refusing to pay. In Venezuela, tribute collection attempts were met with flight into isolated communities and *cumbes*, while in Guatemala, futile tribute efforts brought an end to the levy in 1769.[10]

Tribute collection in New Spain met with similar difficulties. Free-coloreds thoroughly despised the tax, claiming that it presented a severe economic burden, especially in isolated rural communities where specie was hard to obtain and where subsistence farming was the primary means of existence. All adult men between the ages of eighteen and fifty were accountable. From the 1670s until the mid-eighteenth century, the cost for a full tributary fluctuated between twelve and sixteen reales per year.[11] That generally kept pace with tribute rates for Indians, who in the seventeenth and eighteenth centuries paid eight reales and a half-*fanega* of maize in tribute. The maize contribution was worth about four and a half reales. In addition to straight tribute, Indians paid a score of other fees, including money for judicial salaries, a contribution to their community treasuries, *alcabala* (sales tax), Indian hospital charges, and a royal service contribution (*servicio real*). Established in 1592, the *servicio real* was a four real tax designed to underwrite unspecified monarchical expenses.[12] Excluding *alcabala*, the combined sum of these taxes approximated seventeen and a half reales per year in the eighteenth century.[13] Free-coloreds also paid *al-*

cabala and the *servicio real*. As with tribute, these additional sums were paid reluctantly.

In the late eighteenth century, there were moves to increase tribute rates for Indians and free-coloreds. Documents from the Yucatan in 1788 reveal an effort by the provincial governor to raise the free-colored, full-tributary fees to twenty-four reales a year, outpacing the proposed Indian rates, which were to be set at sixteen reales.[14] Along the Pacific coast, in the Intendencies of Oaxaca and Puebla, rates reached twenty reales per year by 1793 for full tributaries. Half-tributaries paid twelve reales.[15] When compared with agricultural wages in the eighteenth century, the tribute burden was heavy. Reports from rural Veracruz revealed wages to be two reales a day, with at least one real needed for food.[16] These hacienda pay scales had remained largely unchanged since the 1630s.[17] Although tribute was not collected from women, they were still considered to be tributaries. When a free-colored man married a woman of tributary status, he then assumed her burden and became responsible for the full tribute rate. Until marriage, men over age eighteen paid only half-tribute. Widowers were also half-tributaries. Excluded from payment altogether were those individuals who worked as servants for ecclesiastical and high secular authorities.[18] With the implementation of the tobacco monopoly in the Bourbon reform period, tobacco workers were exempted as well. A number of free-coloreds feigned sickness when tax collectors arrived. But only legitimate, long-term illnesses and infirmities were accepted as excuses. Even then, the subject had to present a signed document from a commissioner that detailed the nature of the illness. Other free-coloreds attempted to evade tribute by conveniently taking business trips when tax time arrived, claiming that matters outside of town needed urgent attention. Tribute collectors continued to hold these individuals liable upon their return. Tributaries were considered truly absent if missing from their place of residence for more than ten years. Even at that point, efforts were made to locate the lost to ensure that they were paying tribute in their new place of residence.[19]

Free-colored tribute collection procedures followed the general guidelines used for Indians. The first step involved preparing the tribute register (*matrícula*). Specially appointed commissioners (*comisionados de matrícula*) assisted district governors and their subordinates (*alcaldes mayores* and *tenientes de justicia*) in obtaining accurate counts of the tributary population based upon the census records of head towns (*cabeceras*) and their subordinate villages (*sujetos*).[20] Census documents were supplemented by ecclesiastical and hacienda records, providing updates on the most recent baptisms, marriages, and deaths. Tribute registers were normally created every five years. The efficiency and accuracy of the *matrícula* process improved dramatically after the middle of the eighteenth century.[21] The commissioners could produce up to four tribute lists in all: one for Indians living in *pueblos de indios*; one for *indios laboríos*, or those working as day laborers on rural estates; another for tributaries known as *vagos*; and the last for free-coloreds. The *vagos* category referred to individuals without a fixed place of residence, or living in remote *ranchos* distant from village centers. Although primarily intended to refer to Indians, the list could include free-coloreds (*mulatos vagos*) and even mestizos, who were occasionally called upon to pay tribute in some regions.[22] Late eighteenth-century legislators claimed that the goal of preparing the *vagos* list was to identify the dimensions of a region's idle population so as to redirect them into meaningful employment. As seen with the early development of free-colored tribute policy, the *vagos* enumeration effort was a tactic used primarily to increase the hacienda labor pool, while also ensuring that tribute payments would be regularly met.

Each type of register was supposed to include detailed information on the tributaries, including their occupation, marital status, race, age, family size, and wife's racial status.[23] While the aim was to have specific *matrículas* for Indians and blacks, in practice, free-coloreds were found in all register types. A number of blacks resided in *pueblos de indios*, where they seem to have been welcomed. Although there are several cases in the historical record where blacks illegally muscled their way into positions of power in these *pueblos*, there is also evidence that Indians allowed free-coloreds to reside in their communities so as to share village expenses, thereby easing some of their financial burdens.[24] In more extreme circumstances, communities populated almost wholly by blacks were recorded as *pueblos de indios*. For example, the town of Santa Ana Tepetitlán, founded by former slaves in the sixteenth century to defend Guadalajara, was designated a *pueblo de indios* in late eighteenth-century official documents. This was despite the fact that the site continued to be inhabited largely by blacks. These circumstances have caused William Taylor to speculate that in the late colonial period being "Indian mainly meant village tributary."[25] Consequently, the jumbling of free-coloreds in the various *matrícula* types seems partially symptomatic of a fluid conception of race on the part of certain regional administrators, as well as the actual physical relocation of blacks into Indian communities.

Tribute was collected every four months in the sixteenth and seventeenth centuries. In the late eighteenth century, payments were made twice a year, half in midsummer and the rest during the Christmas season.[26] Just as with payment rates, tribute schedules might vary according to region. For blacks living in *pueblos de indios*, payments were submitted to local Indian officials, who in turn handed the money to their *gobernadores*. Eventually the funds reached the *alcalde mayor* or *subdelegado* of the region. Free-coloreds living on isolated ranchos, or in largely mestizo/Spanish towns, tended to have their money collected directly by the subordinates of the *alcaldes mayores*. Given difficulties in tracking free-colored tributaries, *alcaldes mayores* often found it convenient to employ free-colored militia officers to make collections.[27]

From what is known about the tribute collection process, there was room for considerable graft. The crown tried to institute measures to ensure that each region submitted the amount of tribute owed. At the beginning of an *alcalde mayor*'s term he had to place bond on the estimated tribute to be collected in his region.[28] This was done with the help of a *fiador*, or bondsman. Penalties for not paying the predetermined amount could result in the jailing of an *alcalde mayor*.[29] Not all areas in colonial Mexico strictly adhered to this practice, and in places such as Nueva Vizcaya, Sonora, and Sinaloa, some *alcaldes mayores* assumed office without posting the deposit. Apart from the bonds, the crown did little else to deter illegal collection practices. Indian governors, *alcaldes mayores*, *tenientes de justicia*, and other tribute officers unabashedly overcollected from the local population without reporting the excess. Men appointed to the post of *alcalde mayor* had often paid dearly for their offices and sought to recoup their losses through tribute exploitation.[30] Their subordinates followed the example. Collection was taken from white and mestizo men married to Indian and free-colored women, although clearly forbidden by law.[31] In the eighteenth century, local officials received one real per Indian tributary placed on their registers. This inspired more corruption as officials submitted inflated calculations of their population's size in order to line their own pockets.[32]

Despite the prevailing abuses, Indians deemed tribute payments bearable at least because they saw concrete benefits in exchange for their contributions. As has been previously mentioned, tribute underwrote their community privileges and gave their *pueblos* a distinct legal status. Some have observed that tribute constituted an important element of Indian sociopolitical identity: it was an expression both of their citizenship in their communities and their vassalage to the crown.[33] Indians used the fact that they paid tribute as a bargaining point in their negotiations with royal officials. Invariably, the beginning of their petitions would contain the words *indios tributarios*, emphasizing that they had done the crown the favor of regularly submitting payments, and now they expected something in return.[34] On the other hand, free-coloreds rarely saw any tangible recompense to their tribute payments, making the fee even more cumbersome in their eyes. Nor did free-coloreds consider tribute a particularly strong source of legal leverage in their crown dealings. *Alcabala* payments were perceived to be more useful in that regard. Blacks in Tamiagua, for example, recounted how they faithfully paid sales taxes on their fishing enterprises, even though fishing was not listed as a taxable activity in the *alcabala* code.[35] They hoped that by stressing their *alcabala* payments, they could free themselves from tribute.

Another factor that tarnished tribute payments was that they were seen as a social stigma, something not to be paid by decent people (*gente de razón*). In the largely Spanish and mestizo towns were many free-coloreds lived, tribute payment added difference to their lives, widening the social divide between the races. Consequently, certain segments of the free-colored population balked when commissioners tried to place them on their tribute registers. This held particularly true of the *mulatos blancos*, whose fathers were white.[36] Tribute law actually produced a gray area with regard to this segment of the population. When a black woman married a white man or a mestizo, neither husband nor wife was legally responsible for tribute. Yet little was stated in the *bandos* about the status of their adult children.[37] Perhaps because of their fathers, these *mulatos blancos* appear to have enjoyed special status inside their own communities, being regularly incorporated into white militia units or receiving other privileged treatment and recognition over darker blacks.[38] But in the minds of tribute collectors they were viewed indifferently, seen simply as another part of the larger, homogeneous free-colored mass, and liable to taxation.

Notwithstanding the multiple aversions free-coloreds had toward paying tribute, high-level bureaucrats in colonial Mexico seem to have been committed to making the institution work, perhaps more so than elsewhere in the Spanish Americas. In 1587, the viceroy declared that anyone resisting payment would be punished with one hundred lashes and one year's service in an *obraje*. In 1598, the penalty was stiffened to two hundred lashes.[39] Recent publication of the royal account records from New Spain's twenty-three *reales cajas* allows us to analyze in detail the actual ability of the crown to extract tribute from free-coloreds, as well as to offer a partial reconstruction of how the levy functioned in the colony.[40] It must be stressed that while the figures presented accurately depict the summary sheets of the fiscal officers (*cartas de cuentas*), at the same time they do not provide us with a complete overview of free-colored tribute in the colonial period. This has much to do with the categories employed by treasury officers in presenting their figures in final form. Most notably in the eighteenth century, there was a tendency to lump free-colored tribute contributions alongside those of the *indios vagos* or *indios laboríos*.[41] That trend coincided with a colonywide increase in Indian hacienda workers, and probably reflected the crown's interest in simplifying account-keeping by using broader categories for grouping populations whose economic behavior was similar, regardless of race. With the use of a sole entry, all of the tribute-paying, floating population could be accounted for. As a result, entries in account books from several regions in the eighteenth century refer to free-coloreds under long titles such as *tributos de negros* and *mulatos y indios laboríos*. In Guadalajara from 1757 to 1787, tribute categories were generalized to the extent that summary sheets had only two categories, one entitled tribute from New Galicia and the other entitled tribute from New Spain, neither of which made any specific racial designations. In Michoacán, account records from 1792–97 reveal that although tribute was collected from *mulatos* during those years, the final summary sheets make mention only of *tributos reales de indios*.[42] One can follow the paper trail to examine how free-coloreds disappeared in the process of simplification. Initially, revenues from free-coloreds in various towns in Michoacán were collected by local officials under the rubric of *tributarios mulatos*. These tributaries had been identified from the special free-colored *matrículas*. Their money was then remitted to the regional administrative center of Valladolid. Records show that there, *mulato* tribute contributions were grouped with those of the *indios laboríos* in the account books. In 1792 and 1793, their money was collectively known as simply that of the *vagos*. Lastly, in the final summary stage, *vago* tribute contributions passed into the category of Indian tribute (*tributos de indios*). Such practices in the late eighteenth century seem to have been the norm rather than the exception.[43] In short, changes in the administrative language used by the fiscal bureaucracy create some lacunae in our knowledge about free-colored tribute contributions. But in contrast with areas like Guatemala, policies from high royal administrators demonstrate that fairly consistent efforts to collect tribute from free-coloreds persisted until the end of the colonial period.

The sixteenth and seventeenth centuries offer the most complete impression of free-colored tribute patterns, given that several *cajas* reported revenues in racially precise terms. There were only thirteen functioning *cajas* in New Spain by the end of the seventeenth century, six of whom reported collection of free-colored revenues. Not all of the taxes recorded in the summary sheets were straight tribute collections. The account books include payments of the *servicio real*, as well as payments of back tributes.

Colonial Mexico's three major administrative seats of Guadalajara, Mexico City, and Mérida, as well as the important mining center of Zacatecas, provide the best series data. The other two *cajas*, in Tabasco and Veracruz, offer very small glimpses into free-colored tribute. The Tabasco fiscal series runs barely the span of a decade, from 1605 until 1612. The Veracruz *caja* reports collection from only two years, 1605–6 and 1608–9. It is not clear whether free-colored tribute payments stopped completely in those areas afterward, or if they were regrouped under different categories. We do know that after the 1670s, the impact of militia tribute exclusions seriously altered the dynamics of the collection process in both locations. By far the most complete record is that of Guadalajara, running almost without interruption from 1581 to 1752. Unfortunately, the Guadalajara series begins to combine free-colored tribute contributions with those of the *indios laboríos* in 1663. This prevents us from isolating and analyzing free-colored payments after that year. The series offering the best understanding of free-colored tribute revenues comes from the all-important *caja* of Mexico City, with accounts logged from 1576 to 1697. Mention of blacks disappears from these records altogether in the eighteenth century. Since many towns and cities throughout New Spain remitted their revenues here prior to further redistribution, the Mexico City *caja* not only provides insight into the fiscal lives of free-coloreds in central Mexico but also is suggestive of trends that might have occurred elsewhere in the colony.

TABLE 35

Tribute Revenues Submitted to the Caja de Mexico during
the Sixteenth and Seventeenth Centuries

Year	Tribute in pesos	Servicios de Negros in pesos	Total Revenue Contributions	Annual Rate of Change by Percentage	Percentage of Total Revenue Taken in Tribute Arrears
1576–86	14,664		14,664		0
1586–96	16,746	1,477	18,223	+24	0
1596–1606	18,081	4,889	22,970	+26	0
1606–16	12,319	4,913	17,232	−25	14.1
1616–26	15,416	5,268	20,684	+20	24.2
1626–32	12,515	3,910	16,425	−21	64.7
1636–46	21,613	7,297	28,910	+76	6.3
1646–56	18,104	6,352	24,456	−15	0
1656–66	20,704	8,823	29,527	+20	11.3
1666–76	26,157	10,805	36,962	+25	0
1676–84	44,063	2,946	47,009	+27	0
1684–93	41,766		41,766	−11	0
1695–97	11,485		11,485	−72	0
TOTAL REVENUE			330,313		

Source: TePaske and Klein, Ingresos y egresos.

Combining all information from the *reales cajas*, we observe that total free-colored tribute revenues reached 351,581 pesos for the years 1576–1697. Of this, 330,313 pesos were reported from the Mexico City *caja* alone. If we include the figures aggregating payments of both *indios laboríos* and free-coloreds, the total revenues collected from 1576 to 1752 reaches 519,731 pesos. The bulk of the *mulato/laborío* payments came from Guadalajara and Mérida (165,670 pesos). It must be stressed again that these statistics represent the minimum amount of tribute collected during the colonial period, and that the actual figures were probably much higher. Nevertheless, when compared with tribute revenues collected from Indians, the free-colored numbers are small. For example, for the single year of 1770, indigenous contributions just to the *caja* of Mexico City were 844,257 pesos. In fact, the annual tribute revenues to this *caja* from Indians averaged over 200,000 pesos per annum for the entire eighteenth century. Seventeenth-century contributions were much lower, but consistently over 10,000 pesos per year, a decline from the peak recorded sixteenth-century figure of 459,323 pesos, paid in 1586–87.

As stated earlier, an analysis of the Mexico City *caja* affords the best look at free-colored tribute patterns in sixteenth and seventeenth centuries (see Table 35). Since treasury officials sometimes recorded information in haphazard fashion, at times clustering the revenues of several years into a single entry, the table breaks down the fiscal data into approximately ten-year groupings. The major exceptions are 1626–32 and 1676–97, for which insufficient information prevents an analysis of ten-year time frames. There are other gaps in the series, but those are relatively minor in comparison.[44] The revenues have been separated into the categories of tribute and service taxes (*servicio real*), to allow for comparisons between these two types of collections. No service taxes were extracted from 1576 to 1596. But from 1678 to 1697, treasury officials combined all service and tribute revenues into the same entry. The column with figures regarding total revenue contributions combine both the service and tribute levies for all years so as to provide for better comparisons. Finally, the last two columns give the relative fluctuation in total revenues per decade in terms of percentages, as well as demonstrating the proportion of total payments collected in the form of back taxes.

Excluding the years 1626–46 and 1695–97, we observe that total tribute revenues tended to increase per decade at rates of about 20 percent or higher, with three periods of decline in revenue collection. The declines may be credited to a variety of factors. Sometimes natural disasters caused ruptures in agricultural production, spurring economic hardship. There were twenty-five droughts recorded in New Spain between 1600 and 1699, and in Mexico City from 1604 to 1629 there were six major floods, the last one being so severe that it took until 1634 for the waters to recede.[45] Moreover, in the area of Mexico City, the entire decade preceding the great flood of 1629 had been particularly dry, resulting in several bad harvests.[46] Perhaps some of these difficulties contributed to the recessions observed by Klein and Tepaske in the overall income of eleven of New Spain's *cajas* between 1610 and 1630, in the 1640s, and again around 1670.[47] During such lean years, Spanish authorities frequently suspended tribute payments temporarily, yielding occasional sharp rises and declines in the annual tribute records as taxes were alternately forgiven and then collected at higher rates.[48]

The periods of decline may also indicate irregularities in the tribute collection process, and even some level of mismanagement. Some insight into these possibilities comes from examining the collection of back taxes. Arrears point to a breakdown in collection efforts caused by an inability to pay, tax evasion, or corruption. We observe that the first period of decline coincides with initial efforts by royal officials to collect overdue tribute. This was followed by a sustained intensification in the collection of unpaid taxes stretching into 1632. There is no coincidence that emphasis on recovering arrears came at this time. The period from 1621 to 1640 witnessed the administration of three successive viceroys who implemented severe austerity measures in the colony. Their efforts were a response to demands from the Spanish monarchy to raise more revenues to underwrite heavy crown expenditures during the Thirty Years' War.[49] *Alcabala* rates jumped from 2 to 4 percent as a result of the Union of Arms agreement of 1627, which slapped a 250,000-peso annual burden on New Spain for fifteen years. This was followed by crown demands that the

colony contribute heavily toward the provisioning of the Armada de Barlovento, a battle squadron designed to significantly improve naval defense in the
Caribbean.[50] Alongside stricter trade legislation, policies to reduce graft and
wasteful expenditures were implemented to help meet the fiscal challenge.
Consequently, the period from 1621 to 1640 is best interpreted as a time of fiscal readjustment, as the colonial administrative apparatus streamlined the tax
structure and corrected past imbalances. Redoubled strides in the collection of
free-colored arrears were part of this process. Although agricultural hardship
in central Mexico during these same years compounded tribute collection
problems, officials insisted on trying to maintain a stable income.

It should be noted that Indian arrears were collected more frequently than
those of free-coloreds during the colonial period. This would suggest that
when overdue taxes were collected from free-coloreds, it marked a dramatic
fiscal policy shift. Indeed, after 1640, the only other recorded collection of free-
colored arrears came from 1658 to 1660, during the viceregal administration of
the younger duke of Albuquerque.[51] His ambitious fiscal program resembled
the zeal of his predecessors in the 1620s. Upon assuming his post in 1653, he
sternly criticized the previous administration for neglecting their responsibilities, most notably in terms of tax collection. Our information on the *caja* of
Mexico confirms his assessment, recording a decline in free-colored revenues
from 1646 to 1656. To remedy the problems, Albuquerque sent out teams of
commissioners to review tax-collection procedures in the provinces and to
make appropriate arrangements for collecting arrears. In Mexico City, Albuquerque began his reforms by purging his own administration and arresting
the *regidor* Felipe Moran, just months after assuming the vice-regency.

Albuquerque's reform policies were particularly aimed at free-coloreds,
who he felt had been afforded too much license in the past. He stiffened ordinances concerning their access to *pulque*, as well as laws regarding their bearing of arms. Whereas other viceroys may have loosely interpreted the king's
decrees pertaining to blacks, Albuquerque preferred strict, literal interpretations of the laws.[52] The overall increases in free-colored tribute at mid-century
are credited, in part, to the policies of Albuquerque.[53]

If the summary sheets are to be trusted, after 1656 the tribute collection
process generally stabilized, and there was a period of sustained growth with
only minor aberrations until the eighteenth century. The difference in the
amount of tribute collected during the peak period from 1676 to 1684, and the
amount collected during the first decade, from 1576 to 1586, is impressive: a
more than threefold rise in revenues over a century. Although the decade-by-
decade rate of revenue increase remained under 30 percent after 1656, the table
does not accurately reveal the suddenness of the surge in income during the
brief eighteen-year stretch from 1679 to 1697. That period alone accounted for
29.5 percent of the total revenue collected during the 121-year series. Part of the
increase in tribute can be credited to the rising number of free-coloreds

populating New Spain over the course of the seventeenth century. Detailed, colonywide studies of the demographic situation for blacks during the period remain to be conducted. Several regional studies have begun to appear, as well as the ambitious effort of Colin Palmer to trace the contours of the Mexican slave trade prior to 1650. However, full information focused on free-coloreds is lacking. The best existing work on the subject is still that of Aguirre Beltrán.[54] He calculates the Afro-Mexican population in 1570 at 23,004, most of which were African slaves.[55] His estimates are based upon a variety of census projections, including those of Viceroy Dn. Luis Velasco and Gérman Latorre. Combining African slave import figures with extrapolation from his 1570 and 1742 estimates, Beltrán calculates that by 1646 the black population had risen to 151,618, at that time being largely free-colored in composition (116,529). Using the commissioned census count of Villaseñor, Beltrán puts the Afro-Mexican population of 1742 at 286,327 persons.

Beltrán's figures are problematic as exact calculations, since there is a great deal of supposition and assumption in his methodology.[56] But as indicators of general trends, he seems accurate. He points to a gradual *mestizaje* of the black population in the seventeenth century, yielding a plethora of free-colored castes by the mid-eighteenth century. Applying Beltrán's generalities toward our understanding of the tribute picture, we note that the tribute burden was probably felt most strongly during the early period of taxation, when there was a smaller free-colored population base to draw upon. The majority of blacks were slaves from 1576 to 1600. As the free-colored population increased in the early 1600s, it did so at a time when there appears to have been problems in the tribute-collection process. This is indicated by periods of decline in total revenues, as well as strong moves to collect arrears during the first half of the seventeenth century. The viceroys attempted to compensate for these problems and maintain steady tribute pressure. But given that actual total tribute revenues did not differ appreciably from those recorded between 1596 and 1606 until after the 1650s, the overall tribute burden on the expanding black population may have been lighter until after mid-century. This leads to the interpretation of the early seventeenth century as a time of relative stasis with regard to tribute revenues and pressure. After the 1650s, serious, sustained gains were made in revenue collections, capped off by a sudden burst toward the end of the century. In short, the tribute burden may have been heaviest toward the end of the sixteenth and seventeenth centuries.

Militia service offered a means by which free-coloreds could escape the dreaded tribute burden. Although there is evidence that free-colored militiamen in Campeche secured exemption in the 1630s, and that Mérida may have enjoyed relief by 1644, the majority of New Spain's *pardo* and *moreno* militiamen did not acquire the privilege until after 1677, precisely when information from the *caja* of Mexico City reveals that tribute pressure was rising.[57] While the nature of the tribute documentation does not allow for detailed discussion of the matter, the new collection pressures may have been a motive behind free-colored moves to seek avenues for relief. The mysterious disappearance of blacks from the account sheets of Mexico City's *caja* at the beginning of the eighteenth century may have had as much to do with the general expansion of militia tribute immunities throughout the colony, which increased significantly at the close of the seventeenth century, as with procedural changes in the bureaucratic labeling of tributaries. Furthermore, in Mexico City itself, the development of certain complications in the way that the tribute process was administered may have erased some free-coloreds from the tribute record. Hence, the lack of eighteenth-century references to the tribute collection of blacks indicates, to some extent, a successful series of challenges to the tribute establishment.

Contrary to popular belief, tribute dispensation was not a privilege that was simply doled out by royal officials to soldiers as a prearranged benefit in a planned militia structure, nor does militia service itself seem to have been a mere substitute for paying tribute.[58] Militia organization was loosely structured prior to the Bourbon reform era of the 1760s. Benefits were accrued through trial and error, rather than under the aegis of a larger master plan. Moreover, with regard to tribute exemption, Mexican viceroys and high administrators wanted to retain this tax over as much of the free-colored population as possible. It was mainly because of fears over pirate incursions and potential invasion that the crown was willing to negotiate on the issue.[59]

In 1676, captains Agustín Torres and Manuel Fernandez Morgado, of the *pardo* and *moreno* militia units in Veracruz, requested tribute exemption as compensation for their military duties. In the arguments they presented to the Real Audiencia, the two officers stressed that free-colored military services were rendered voluntarily and without pay. They had consistently performed sentinel duty and manned the fortress of San Juan de Ulúa. Furthermore, the men in their units furnished their own weapons and uniforms, making the militia financially independent of the royal treasury. All these costs weighed heavily on the soldiers, who were said to be poor. Moreover, being located in the port of Veracruz advantageously placed them in frequent contact with sailors who kept them abreast of happenings throughout the Atlantic World. Thanks to this news, the captains added that they were well aware of the fact that free-colored militiamen in Santo Domingo, Havana, Campeche, and Guatemala had already been granted tribute exemption. The militiamen's pleas prodded an investigation by the Consejo Real de Indias. On June 15, 1676, it was confirmed that blacks in several port cities in the Spanish Americas were relieved from tribute. In fact, in many areas, such as Cuba, there was no prior record of tribute having ever been collected. Investigators observed that the racial status of the militiamen in Veracruz was the same as that of the soldiers in the port cities that already enjoyed the exclusion—all were *pardos* and *morenos*. A supplementary document from the *corregidor* of Veracruz added that the soldiers under his jurisdiction had always served with promptness in the face of enemy threats. Captain Torres had recently outfitted a boat at his own expense to attack pirate positions along the Alvarado River. The investigation further noted that there had been crown precedent in upholding the rights of free-colored soldiers, specifically in the royal decrees of July 21, 1623, and March 19, 1625. Here, it was explicitly mentioned that whatever *preminencias* (privileges) had been previously bestowed upon *pardo* and *moreno* militiamen by royal officials were to be protected by subsequent administrations. Governors, viceroys, and captains-generals were to respect the fact that the free-colored militiamen, many of whom were simple agricultural laborers, had risked their lives in the name of the crown. In a related decree, investigators from the Consejo Real discovered that Indians living on the Chichimec frontier had been exempted from tribute because of their role in providing military defense. All of the findings prompted the decision to terminate the tribute obligation for free-colored militiamen in the port of Veracruz. A *real cédula* was drafted to this effect in March of 1677. Minor finalities still had to be worked out before the law took hold. Lost documents had to be located and information on tribute burdens elsewhere in the Americas had to be reconfirmed. The free-colored soldiers of Veracruz hired a *procurador* (legal representative) to continue pleading their case before the Real Audiencia. Finally, on July 10, 1679, Viceroy Fray Payo authorized the exemption.[60]

The successful bid for tribute exemption in Veracruz sparked a tide of requests for similar exclusions throughout the Gulf coast region. First were the petitions of soldiers in Acayucan, representing the province of Guazacualco. Although some documents point to 1670 as the date when this area secured an initial form of exemption, in actuality it appears that the process was fully formalized after 1678.[61] These exemptions were followed by those from the province of Guachinango (1679), Papantla (1688), Tabasco (1691), and eventually the town of Jalapa (1697) among others. By the end of the seventeenth century, exemptions had been granted to select locations along the Pacific coast.[62] What characterizes all of the petitions, and what is important for understanding future rulings on tribute matters, is that every successful request took the form of individual contracts between the crown and the free-colored inhabitants of a specific town or region.[63] Royal officials preferred handling matters in piecemeal fashion, reviewing situations case by case, and granting exclusions on the merits of each request. Often, the initial appeal for exemption would originate from a *cabecera* (head town) and then be applicable to several locations within a province. In the majority of cases, the exclusions were said to last indefinitely, although there are some instances in which contracts lasted for just a few years.[64] Likewise, there were regional differences as to who was included in the exemption. But in almost every case, over time, the militiamen's wives and children were eventually relieved.

In a few instances, as in Zacatula (Guerrero), black militiamen tried to ob-

tain dispensation from *alcabala* (sales tax) payments along with tribute remis-
sion.[65] These requests were usually denied. Crown income derived from the *alcabala* normally amounted to more than tribute payments, and the royal government wanted to avoid losing this important source of revenue. In the 1780s,
free-coloreds in Acayucan customarily paid between four and sixteen pesos of
sales tax per year on their cattle and cotton harvests, representing at least double the amount paid by a full tributary.[66] To be eligible for *alcabala* relief, the
soldiers' petitions had to prove that their crops and livestock were raised purely for subsistence purposes. In essence, royal authorities viewed the *alcabala* as
a different type of charge from tribute, tightly linked to regional economies
and business transactions, rather than being a simple head tax. This caused
them to be less willing to negotiate the fee in exchange for militia services. The
alcabala was cherished to such an extent that some military planners actually
favored abolishing tribute in order to stimulate sales tax revenues. Lieutenant
Colonel Dn. Benito Pérez wrote in the 1790s that freedom from tribute offered
blacks in Xicayan more opportunities to concentrate on their agricultural activities. Therefore, tribute exemption coverage should continue and even be
expanded in the province. This should be accompanied by changes in free-
colored residency and land-holding patterns, so as to boost production and
maximize the use of regional resources. On the other hand, Pérez staunchly
advocated that the *alcabala* be maintained so that the royal treasury could reap
the full benefits of the invigorated economy. Over time, he predicted that by
employing his recommended course of action, more money would be generated in *alcabala* and *rentas reales* receipts than could have ever been expected
from tribute.[67]

Successful petitions for tribute exemption did follow an unspoken set of
guidelines in their lines of argument, modeled after the appeals made by Captain Torres and Captain Morgado in Veracruz. In all instances the crown was
approached with great humility. The soldiers emphasized their poverty to underscore the oppressiveness of the tribute burden. Highlighting the predicament of poverty appears to have been a standard legal strategy used in appeals
to the crown, employed in other contexts by women and Indians to demonstrate the need for royal protection.[68] As an added touch, the militiamen discussed the plight of their families and how the trials of militia service diverted
them from fulfilling pressing domestic obligations. Then soldiers related a list
of past services. This included local feats and engagements with pirates, supplemented by geographical details that would convey the sense of danger to
their provinces. For example, the soldiers of Guazacuálco discussed how pirate threats were greatest in their area, given the many bays along the coast that
could anchor a fleet and provide entry into the interior. Moreover, the Guazacuálco River was a principal artery deep enough to support large enemy vessels, and long enough to give access to regions as distant as Tehuantepec and
Guatemala.[69] Militiamen in Guachinango relayed that pirate activity was more

pronounced in their province than in Guazacuálco, given the location of the lagoon of Tamiagua.[70] Still, Tabasco's soldiers claimed the same of their province, stating that their coast was in the most danger, and so forth. In almost all cases the vision of the soldiers was local. The services they rendered and the dangers expressed in their exemption requests dealt with the circumstances of their provincial worlds. Helpful in their petitions was a discussion of militia cost effectiveness, always a welcome argument to a parsimonious crown. The soldiers stressed that their services were bought on the cheap, and that royal authorities should view tribute exemption in light of salaries spent on soldiers of the regular army. If the crown were to field a force of veterans in the same areas where the militiamen operated, the expense would run one real a day per soldier. The cost of granting tribute exemption paled in comparison. For only two pesos (sixteen reales—that is, the annual cost for a full tributary), the crown obtained a free-colored militiaman for an entire year. That same amount would employ a veteran for less than three weeks.[71] Free-colored militiamen even stressed that they could outperform regular units on the field, since they were born and raised in their provinces, making them well adjusted to the harsh climate. This reduced the risk of death caused by yellow fever and other unexpected illnesses that consumed veteran forces along the coasts of the Americas.[72]

Invariably in their pleas, free-colored soldiers, especially along the coasts, highlighted their watch duties, the *vigía*. The *vigía* was a high-priority issue on the crown agenda, and when faithfully maintained, *vigía* service is what in large part secured an exemption request.[73] In the previous chapter we discussed the finances of the *vigía* watch. The duty itself consisted of a rotating guard of militiamen kept at strategic points along the coast, preferably near bays and river openings deep enough to sustain large ships. It closely resembled the system of civilian watchtowers that had been instituted to help defend the coasts of Spain.[74] Along the Mexican Gulf coast, the *vigía* was suspended from November to January, given that violent winds, called *nortes*, discouraged sailing. During wartime, however, the *vigía* was preserved year round. Each *vigía* rotation lasted between one and two weeks, with men returning home on Sunday mornings before 10:00 A.M. In the late eighteenth century, watch was normally kept by two men, supported by errand boys usually drawn from nearby Indian populations.[75] These youths supplied the soldiers with extra food rations. Sometimes they provided canoes and other equipment needed to get the watchmen to and from their posts. Ordinances outlining the responsibilities of the *vigía* dictated that the watch be kept for twenty-four hours, with the men alternating their responsibilities every three to four hours. The distance of the *vigía* from a militia base town could be great, in excess of five leagues. Some watch points were located in extreme isolation, hidden in thick brush or hoisted high on hills. A system of signals, sometimes involving lanterns or sending the second watchman to alert the closest settlement, was devised. Depending on the distribution of militia companies in a given region, a single militia unit could be responsible for manning several *vigía* sites simultaneously. In the early years of the *vigía*, the services seem to have been rendered without recompense. But unlike normal militia responsibilities, such as patrol duty, the *vigía* eventually developed into a salaried militia post.[76]

Although the majority of tribute exemption requests involved direct interactions between militiamen, their hired legal assistants, and high crown officials, there were exceptions to that model when the opinions of local functionaries and elites were opposed to the idea. In Tabasco, for instance, the governing elite intervened in the negotiating process and attempted to shape the terms of free-colored tribute exclusion. The initial petition for exemption began in classic form. In 1691, free-colored militia sergeant Juan Esteban journeyed to Mexico City to present his case to the viceroy in the name of all the "*morenos* and *indios laboríos*" who had rendered military services in the province. Investigations ensued. These triggered several *juntas* (assemblies) at the provincial level. The opinions of the *alcalde mayor*, as well as his subordinate administrator of the coastal region, Captain Bernardo Lizarriaga, were consulted. Both men maintained that tribute exclusion should be granted solely under the provision that all free-coloreds and *indio laboríos* seeking the privilege be relocated to Villahermosa, the former capital of the province. According to these officials, Villahermosa was one of the most strategic points in the region, centrally located to thwart enemy advances into the interior. However, in the 1660s, the city sustained heavy damage from pirate raids, causing the majority of the Spanish population to flee the site for more security farther inland. In truth, much of the Tabasco coastline was firmly under pirate control—namely, that of British corsairs who sallied forth freely throughout the province, gathering supplies, stealing cacao, capturing slaves, and plundering villages. Tabasco's proximity to the Island of Tris (also known as Isla del Carmen) worsened the situation. In addition to being a pirate headquarters, the entire Laguna de Términos region had become a camp for British lumberjacks who collected various dyewoods in the interior. Their presence added to the sense of danger in Tabasco.[77]

The two provincial officials were interested in repopulating Villahermosa and increasing the depleted militia strength of the city in order to improve the defenses of local Spanish economic interests and settlements. They believed it would be impossible to attract residents to the city without exerting pressure. Sergeant Esteban responded to their terms in a letter to the viceroy. He saw no need to abide by the conditions outlined by the *alcalde mayor*. Just five leagues outside of Villahermosa, in the area of Chontalpa, resided 150 blacks and *indios laboríos* who rendered continuous military service, manning six *vigías* and defending the sandbars of Chiltepeque, Santa Anna, and Dos Bocas. Moving these militiamen to Villahermosa would leave Chontalpa defenseless, exposing numerous river openings in the process. According to Esteban, the militiamen of Chontalpa, and others, would best benefit the colony by remaining in their current residences.

The viceroy's final decision supported the soldiers' point of view. Although the arguments made by the *alcalde mayor* and Captain Lizarriaga gained considerable support from local notables, it was ultimately the *vigía* services rendered by militiamen that prevailed in their case. The provincial officials wanted to reorganize the region's defenses to sustain their own narrow interests, at the expense of opening various inroads into the colony. These were unacceptable terms to members of the high bureaucracy, who had the greater strategic concerns of the kingdom in mind. Tribute exemptions in Tabasco were granted to the militiamen unconditionally.[78]

What the pattern of exemption requests reveals is that prior to the Bourbon military reforms, there were no sweeping, multiregional tribute dispensations issued for the militia at large. The closest approximation to that was a trend in crown policy whereby, prior to the 1740s, successful requests were granted almost exclusively to "frontier" locations. Such areas were defined as places that were frequently exposed to enemy attack, either by hostile Indians or pirates. Port cities, border towns, and coastal villages all qualified. According to the crown, the character of militia service was different in these settings than in the interior, where relative calm did not demand such a frequent call to arms. It should be stressed, however, that these frontier units were not being rewarded because of any superior military abilities. Rather, prior to the 1760s, rewards for militia service were based more on the sheer fact of strategic location than on proven military effectiveness. The policy of preference to frontier units was articulated in a number of *bandos* and *cédulas*, written in the early eighteenth century. Perhaps the most comprehensive decree was that of May 20, 1724, wherein it was decided that *fuero* privileges would be extended to militiamen in port cities.[79] Yet even in this promulgation, no encompassing statements were made with respect to tribute, leaving it to the individual initiative of the soldiers to actually secure exemption.

Free-colored tribute exemption cases raised by militiamen in Puebla and Mexico City provide important counterexamples to the situation outlined above. Those cities, located at the heart of the colony, were not frontier settings. Nonetheless, militiamen who served there felt that their services qualified them for dispensation. In the early 1740s, the ranking officer of Puebla's free-colored companies, Nicolas Bertel, argued that while units along the coasts were given exemption for services performed locally, the companies of Puebla had frequently marched great distances in the name of duty. Puebla's militiamen defended the port of Veracruz on three separate occasions during the eighteenth century, without receiving any remuneration. The latest instance was in 1742, to protect the port from British aggression that had already brought assaults to Portobello and Cartagena.[80] Bertel and his fellow captains paid for the expedition personally, furnishing a hundred lances, swords, and *bericues*, as well as the salaries for 108 soldiers.[81] In addition to Veracruz, Puebla's units had been stationed in Campeche and Mexico City at various moments during the seventeenth and eighteenth centuries, all at their own expense. These missions were conducted alongside their home responsibilities in Puebla.

In granting tribute exemption to Puebla's free-colored militiamen, the crown seemingly took a step away from its traditional policy of favoring the frontiers. However, it must be emphasized that it was not the local services of the Puebla units that most impressed royal authorities into issuing the dispensation. It was their supplementary roles as reinforcements to militiamen already stationed at the *puertos fronterizos* that garnered relief. In short, while the crown occasionally offered exemption to units located in the interior, it did so largely in terms of the responsibilities those companies performed on the frontier.

Upon hearing word of the successful move in Puebla to obtain tribute relief, free-colored militiamen in Mexico City quickly followed suit with a case of their own. Presented in 1743, their arguments were almost identical to those of their neighboring counterparts. They underscored their trips to Veracruz, despite the fact that their most recent march had taken place at the beginning of the eighteenth century. They also recounted their local services, highlighting their role in quelling the Mexico City grain riots of 1692 and their duties as an auxiliary police force. As with Puebla, these home services were important in altering the crown's perception of danger in the interior but were not decisive in securing exemption. Instead, tribute relief was granted in 1744 on the grounds that the militiamen were disposed to travel to Veracruz when necessary.[82] Unlike the majority of other exemption cases, royal officials placed restrictions on Mexico City's free-colored companies in exchange for the dispensation. If the privilege were to be enjoyed, then there would have to be a cap placed on the number of soldiers allowed into the militia. At the time, Mexico City possessed eight free-colored companies, totaling approximately four hundred men. While that constituted a proper battalion, there were no set limits regarding the maximum number of companies the city could employ. Theoretically, all adult men could enroll, forming several free-colored battalions. Although Mexico City's free-colored militia forces had experienced their share of staffing problems in the past, treasury officers envisioned a scenario in which there would be a sudden rush to join just to obtain the tribute exemption. They stipulated that from that date onward, Mexico City would be limited to eight companies of fifty men apiece. In their estimation, that would provide more than a sufficient number of troops to conduct the units' policing duties. Royal officials added that they would try to implement additional control measures to ensure that the new tribute benefit was not counterproductive, somehow impeding the militiamen's obligation to patrol the city's streets.[83]

If not in Mexico City, the fears of the treasury officials were rightly justi-fied, as evidenced elsewhere in the colony. Especially in rural coastal commu-nities, when tribute exemptions were announced men enrolled as never be-fore, even if they lived too distant from militia base towns to possibly render effective service.[84] The general increase in militia participation was the first step in a series of processes by which blacks began to reinterpret the military exemption as applying to all free-coloreds, including those of nonmilitia status. Free-colored efforts at taking full advantage of military benefits were helped by the vagueness and paucity of militia legislation. There were few military ordinances issued for the New World in the seventeenth and eight-eenth centuries. The contours of militia duty still rested upon the old decrees of 1540 and 1590, which were, in turn, modified versions of medieval Castilian legal codes. These laws loosely stipulated that military service was to be ren-dered by all residents of the Indies, with the actual organization of militia companies to be handled by town councils.[85] Some later clarifications were made regarding the status of Indian and free-colored soldiers, but generally speaking, the decrees did not place restrictions on the number of militia com-panies that could exist in a given region. Mexico City after 1744 was an anom-aly. Elsewhere, the flexibility in the militia structure allowed free-coloreds to broaden the coverage of tribute exemption by creating space for unlimited numbers to join. Militia participation reached such a point in New Spain's lowland coastal communities that local officials complained that tribute could not be collected from blacks because all claimed the military exclusion.[86] More precision regarding the terms of militia duty came after the publication of the military ordinances of 1734.[87] At that time, racial distinctions for cavalry and infantry units were implemented in the Americas. Even stricter reforms came about from the 1760s to the 1780s, as Bourbon military planners downsized the militia forces of many communities to inspire greater discipline and effective-ness. Nevertheless, a high proportion of free-coloreds remained under arms. The case of Igualapa seems typical for the coastal lowlands. One year prior to the military reforms of 1792, out of 1,272 adult, free-colored men over the age of eighteen, some 66 percent were enrolled in the militia. Another 2 percent were militia "promissaries," meaning that they were slated to enroll in the near future. Combined with the 3 percent who were infirm and unfit for military service, more than 70 percent of free-colored, adult men in Igualapa could claim tribute relief, the majority thanks to their militia status.[88] Surprisingly, this high percentage of free-colored militiamen was in place even after two decades of Bourbon military reform had already taken effect in the region.

Bourbon military planners also had a clear understanding of the type of soldier deemed ideally suited for service. Unmarried, adult men standing 1.5 meters tall and between the ages of sixteen and thirty-six or eighteen and forty were considered most desirable.[89] Yet married men and those in their forties were also considered acceptable.[90] Strides were made by Bourbon military reformers to stock the militia with men fitting those criteria.[91] But the 1791 census of Igualapa demonstrates that great liberty was taken with the requirements, with mere children taking up arms and service lasting late in life, often right until death. Some 42 (14 percent) of Igualapa's 299 free-colored youth between the ages of ten and seventeen were on the active militia rosters, with many more categorized as promissaries. Above the age of fifty there were fifty-seven soldiers, or 7 percent of the adult militia fighting force. One man, a *mayordomo de estancia*, still carried arms at the age of ninety-six.[92] Evidence from other areas in Mexico reveals that Igualapa was not exceptional. In the province of Xicayan, a full 34 percent of the men holding the rank of second sergeant and above were over the age of fifty.[93] Elsewhere, commonly reported ages for service ran from ten to sixty.[94] Of course, free-coloreds understood that by extending the age of service the number of individuals covered under the umbrella of military benefits increased as well.

Another tactic used by free-coloreds to broaden the coverage of tribute relief involved joining the militia and then quickly leaving its ranks, claiming to tax collectors that they had once been soldiers. The frequency of such turnover in units along the Gulf and Pacific coasts reached a critical point in the 1770s. Local officials complained that although some towns had companies of only fifty men, up to three hundred would be excluded from tribute on the grounds that they had once served.[95] Blacks further expanded militia benefits by redefining the scope of military privilege. Initial tribute exemptions were intended exclusively for the militiaman, his wife, and children. After the 1760s, Bourbon reformers eliminated the privilege for children.[96] But in practice, entire kinship networks—including parents, siblings, nephews, and grandchildren—would successfully claim exclusion on the basis that one of their family members was a soldier.[97] In one interesting circumstance, nine soldiers in the provincial regiment of Toluca who actually had enrolled as mestizos were discovered to be *mulatos* and *pardos* after fourteen years of duty. During the time of their service, the militiamen's parents and siblings, whose racial status was nebulous at best, had all enjoyed tribute exemption on the basis of having a militiaman in the family.[98]

In the province of Nayarit, along the northeastern fringe of New Galicia, free-coloreds also claimed exemption on account of dubious affiliations with the militia. A company of free-colored auxiliaries had been brought from Paramita to buttress the defenses of the presidios of Nayarit sometime in the early eighteenth century. While stationed inside the presidios, free-coloreds were legally exempted from tribute. But over the years, many ventured forth to live permanently in the small communities that were taking root in the region. No longer sanctioned soldiers, and living outside of the immediate jurisdiction of the presidial commanders, these free-coloreds still claimed exemption in the 1720s. They argued that regardless of their militia status, they had not hesitated in past years to respond when called upon for military service. For example, they had assisted the Jesuits in smashing pagan idols in the province. In the partidos of Rosario and Corapa, they had participated in expeditions against hostile Indian communities.[99] In return for their constant state of readiness, they refused to pay tribute. Although their claims were not legitimated until 1753, only a fraction of the population paid tribute during the intervening years.

Important to the process of expanding tribute privileges beyond the circle of soldiers were the actions of local officials. These included the *alcaldes mayores* and their subordinates. Sometimes newly installed officials confessed a complete lack of knowledge regarding who should be charged tribute, given doubts about the extent of coverage of militia privileges.[100] As they wrote to their superiors to clarify matters, tribute for all blacks might remain uncollected. Even when members of the high bureaucracy handed down their final decisions, laws were open to different interpretations, resulting in more delays.[101] Debates over administrative jurisdiction proved another avenue that provided temporary exemption for blacks who lacked military ties. For example, in the 1780s, tribute collection reached a state of paralysis in the Naval Department of San Blas in New Galicia.[102] Confusion ensued, as no one wanted to assume the responsibility for collecting tribute. In 1784, the *alcalde mayor* of Tepic was charged with the task. He complained that San Blas, being located more than twenty leagues from his own *cabecera*, was too far away for him to oversee tribute collection. Moreover, he detailed that the people listed on San Blas's tribute rosters did not all live in the department but were dispersed over several regions. He pointed out that a good number of the tributaries were sailors, spending most of the year in transit to and from Manila and the Californias. The most effective way to acquire tribute from this seaborne population would be to collect when everyone had returned to the home port, normally at year's end. Again, he noted that this would be too much to ask of him. As a result, free-coloreds do not seem to have paid tribute in San Blas during 1784.

A proposal was made for the *alcalde mayor* of nearby Sentispac, José Maria Dávalos, to perform the task. He assumed this responsibility in 1785, after logging only eleven days as *alcalde mayor*. Dávalos began his assignment dutifully, appointing a number of subordinates to assist him. Soon, however, they encountered problems. Complaints regarding administrative jurisdiction persisted, albeit in altered form. Whereas the *alcalde mayor* of Tepic had protested that collecting tribute in San Blas fell beyond the scope of his office, the challenges Dávalos now faced were internal ones, launched by San Blas's own municipal authorities and naval officers. As soon as Dávalos's team attempted to take up collection, sailors and soldiers cried foul. Dávalos's subordinates tossed several protesters in jail in order to emphasize that tribute collection was being taken seriously. That just sparked further outrage. Tensions reached a point where a white naval officer violently threw his cane at one of the col-

lectors, trying to dissuade him from collecting free-colored tribute. Such out-
bursts could not be contained, however, since, much to Dávalos's chagrin, local authorities were not cooperating with his collection team. In fact, San
Blas's chief civilian administrator (*comisario*) had sided with the sailors and
soldiers on the issue of tribute exemptions. Eventually, a higher investigation
into the problems in San Blas was conducted. It revealed that tribute laws had
been revised by viceregal decree in 1781 and 1784, stipulating that all free-
colored and Indian men in the navy were liable to tribute. Nevertheless, the
seamen and *comisario* maintained that special crown ordinances drafted specifically for the armada continued to preserve their *fuero* rights and tribute exclusions. Apparently, the simultaneous existence of several contradictory laws
yielded the opportunity for conflict. From the point of view of the soldiers,
while viceregal policies regarding tribute may have changed, higher crown law
overrode those decisions, allowing them to retain their privileges.

In San Blas, the problems over administrative jurisdiction became intertwined with vying interpretations of tribute laws, bringing free-colored tribute collection to a deadlock. A frustrated Dávalos managed to gather only some
four hundred pesos of tribute in 1785, before renouncing his commission as
collector. In 1786, the duty fell again upon the unwilling *alcalde mayor* of
Tepic. As late as 1788, tribute was collected partially at best for the free-colored
population of the region.[103]

The predicament in San Blas, while not common, was not unusual. High-
ranking military officers sometimes intervened to support free-colored tribute
exemption demands in the late eighteenth century.[104] On occasion, these officers were themselves colonial administrators, as the Bourbon reform era
witnessed an increase in the appointment of Spanish-born military men as *alcaldes mayores*, *subdelegados*, and *gobernadores*.[105] In one exceptional circumstance, the governor of Tabasco, a former military captain in the Regiment of
Lisboa, stood firmly against a set of proposed tribute changes that would have
negatively affected the black soldiers in his province.[106] As a general rule, white
military officers interceded when tribute policies endangered the benefits enjoyed by free-colored militia units along the Gulf and Pacific coasts, areas perceived as vital for the colony's security. Surely, not all officers shared the view
that a militia stocked with blacks, and lacking proper military training, was
actually an effective fighting force.[107] Indeed, biases and prejudices could lead
to antagonistic behavior toward free-colored soldiers.[108] But for those that did
see utility in their duties, there was a consensus that militia privileges, like
tribute exemption, fostered a certain esprit de corps that added quality to militia service and ensured that blacks would defend the colony willingly.[109] As
the San Blas case demonstrates, their collective actions could stall the tribute
process to a point where even collection for nonsoldiers was affected.

Apart from petty jurisdictional struggles, confusion over the applicability
of tribute laws, and direct intervention by military officers there is evidence

that many provincial authorities actually accommodated free-colored civilians in their pursuit of tribute relief. *Alcaldes mayores* and *tenientes de justicias,* while complaining about difficulties in collecting tribute, did not always stiffly challenge free-colored claims to exemption, especially prior to the Bourbon reforms. Such allegations seem to contradict everything we currently know about the character of these officials, their profit-driven behavior, and the nature of their offices. Presumably, they would have wanted to incorporate as many people as possible under tribute coverage to expand opportunities for graft. Yet it is important to keep in mind that our present understanding of the tribute practices of the *alcaldes mayores* comes mainly from research on Indian communities, where the majority of the work on colonial tribute policy has been done. Tribute collection among free-coloreds abided by a different set of rules, especially from those that functioned among Indians residing in *pueblos de indios.* Militia service played a crucial role in modifying the free-colored tribute arrangement. For instance, provincial administrators were sometimes nervous that if tribute exemption laws were interpreted too narrowly, free-coloreds would not provide military duties, especially the *vigía,* leaving important regions defenseless and exposed to attack. Fears of sparking civil unrest and rebellion in their jurisdictions was another concern. In Acayucan during the 1780s, there was a real anxiety that since so many men were militiamen, any tinkering with the tax structure could trigger an uprising that would be difficult to subdue.[110] Additionally, members of the *justicia* and various *alcaldes mayores* did not want to compromise the important functions that the militiamen performed, such as armed escort services, prison guard duty, night patrols, and other auxiliary tasks. Tribute matters had to be dealt with delicately to keep the forces loyal and to coax them into performing the whims of local functionaries. Requesting tribute of militiamen's close relatives, or demanding payment from communities during times of economic difficulty, held the potential of damaging an already fragile relationship. Obviously, each provincial official possessed a distinct personality and perspective on how he was to conduct the affairs of his office. But all of the above were prevalent concerns, affecting an administrator's disposition toward enacting free-colored tribute.

Laxity in applying tribute to free-coloreds stemmed greatest from worries over securing rural labor. The decline of slavery in colonial Mexico after 1650 placed an added emphasis on seeking new workers for sugar and cotton plantations, haciendas, *ranchos,* and so forth. Some of these estates belonged to the *alcaldes mayores* themselves, who boasted diverse portfolios in their attempts to maximize profits during their short tenure. The partial recovery of the indigenous population in the late seventeenth and eighteenth centuries, alongside emigrations from the *pueblos de indios,* offered solutions to growing labor needs, but not adequately for all regions. In Morelos, the labor challenge was met by incorporating greater numbers of free-coloreds as wage-earners on sugar haciendas. Cheryl English Martin's study of the resident populations of twelve haciendas in Cuautla, Xochitepec, and Eastern Morelos records blacks as dominant in all but one location.[111] Similar trends occurred in Igualapa. While the military census of 1791 does not allow a complete view of the Indian population, the emphasis on free-colored labor was marked, as blacks outnumbered whites and mestizos on haciendas, *ranchos*, sugar mills, and *estancias*.[112] Observations from officials in Xicayan and Tabasco confirm these patterns.[113] Studies of Veracruz yield the same, albeit with some variations, since slave labor continued to play an important role on rural estates into the late eighteenth century.[114]

Alcaldes mayores could be relentless in their quest for labor. In the province of Xicayan, Dn. Joseph de Ayala Matamoros allegedly impressed members of the nine free-colored militia units to do his personal bidding. They worked as supplementary field hands and transported his goods to market as muleteers. Others performed minor tasks, all under coercion and without pay.[115] In regions like Papantla, white estate owners sought military officer posts over free-coloreds for similar reasons, namely to force them into working their lands and fisheries.[116] These tactics underscore the fact that actually securing free-colored labor was a difficult task, exacerbated by the residential mobility of this population group. Several schemes were devised to try to keep free-coloreds in particular regions. Discussions continued over forcing residency on haciendas, where blacks could be closely watched and controlled.[117] Propositions for establishing separate *pueblos de negros* were forwarded. They were to be patterned after the *pueblos de indios*, with blacks holding common lands and being encouraged either to cultivate a cash crop or raise cattle for metropolitan centers such as Antequera or Mexico City. For administrators, the benefits of such settlements included easy access to blacks for tribute. Even parish priests favored the idea as a means to provide a solid spiritual ministry.[118] Unsurprisingly, none of these plans ever took hold. Enforcement of any such scheme was too difficult. Blacks continued to live as they pleased, sometimes virtually alone or in remote *ranchos*, occasionally in *pueblos de indios*, at other times in racially mixed towns.

Considering these realities, many *alcaldes mayores* understood that the best means of attracting and retaining the free-colored population in their provinces was by being flexible with privileges. If free-coloreds were being charged tribute with zeal in one jurisdiction but not the next, experience taught that there would be mass migration to escape the region imposing the burden. Eventually, a mosaic-like system of regional privileges evolved in colonial Mexico. In areas where free-coloreds figured prominently into the rural population and where they composed an esteemed source of labor, local officials were often more lenient in the application of colonial tribute laws that prejudiced blacks. A few examples include Chicontepec, Guachinango, Xicayan, Pánuco, Tampico, Papantla, and Tehuantepec.[119] Tribute leniency involved extending exemption to free-colored civilians by winking at their false claims of being soldiers. During the Bourbon reform era, leniency also included maintaining relaxed standards for entry into the militia so as to maximize the number who could enjoy exclusion. Ironically, it was the supposedly exclusive militia benefits that served as a primary tool for provincial administrators, assisting them in providing tribute clemency for all free-coloreds living under their jurisdiction. This was because militia exemptions offered administrators an additional excuse to present to higher authorities concerning missing tribute payments. Keep in mind that at the outset of their administrations, *alcaldes mayores* were expected to hand over a predetermined amount of tribute for blacks and Indians, under stiff penalties if they failed to fulfill this obligation. Repeatedly, these officials completely liberated themselves from submitting the free-colored portion by recounting problems in the collection process, especially on account of the widespread extent of military exclusions. It is true that free-coloreds actually increased their enrollment in the militia, but some of the claims of the *alcaldes mayores* were exaggerated. The tribute charade would be performed as long as it benefited the *alcalde mayor*, ensured an adequate labor supply for his province's estates, and did not jeopardize his post in the process.

A number of colonial administrators jealously guarded against proposed changes to the tribute exemption patterns that had taken shape in their provinces. When Tabasco's governor pleaded to the viceroy in the late 1780s for the free-colored soldiers under his jurisdiction to remain exempt, he expressed concern that any changes in tribute policy would radically alter the balance of privileges in the Gulf coast region, placing his domain at a comparative disadvantage. All of his neighbors, including the jurisdictions of Yucatan, Chiapas, Tuxtla, and Acayucan, had tribute exemption laws in place. If Tabasco veered from this pattern, the ensuing free-colored flight from the province would be disastrous for an already depressed economy.[120] Other administrators preferred subtler approaches in preserving customary tribute practices. When pressed by superiors to enact collections, they did so half-heartedly for perhaps a year or two, soon returning to their old routine.[121] In a handful of rare instances, *alcaldes mayores* took the extra step of absorbing tribute payments themselves rather than to disturb the balance of privileges in their areas.[122]

The situations described applied mainly to rural coastal settings, namely in colonial Tabasco, Veracruz, New Galicia, and Oaxaca. In the urban environment, free-coloreds did not rush to join the militia to seek exemption in the same ways seen in the countryside. Tribute exemption leniency evolved differently. For urban administrators, securing estate labor was of less concern, as was the risk of jeopardizing the important military duties performed by the soldiers. If Mexico City is indicative of urban trends, then leniency resulted from the confluence of racial and class diversity in the urban environment, a paternalistic approach toward governance by municipal authorities, and jurisdictional disputes.

Mexico City's free-colored population, although confined to a smaller area than provincial dwellers, could be equally difficult to track during tribute time, as witnessed by evasions during census counts.[123] Some escaped tribute by "passing," which seemed more possible amid the greater anonymity of the cities.[124] Others had help from friends. Poverty in the urban setting had an equalizing effect, diminishing the social distance between blacks and the poor of other castes. As a survival strategy, the urban poor assisted each other, regardless of race, to escape the hands of the law in instances of robbery, illicit sexual activity, brawling, and other criminal proceedings.[125] This type of cooperation was likely to have extended to tribute dodgers as well. Another factor to consider in the development of tribute leniency in the urban setting was the laissez-faire style of governance by city officials. At least in Mexico City, municipal authorities governed less to control the behavior of the urban masses than to contain their illegal activities to the plebeian sector. Even high levels of minor crime were accepted as long as the larger social fabric was not threatened.[126] Tolerance extended to tribute. In 1673, the Marqués de Mancera wrote that tribute was to be exacted "with a light hand" from blacks and *mulatos*. Policies of tribute leniency were implemented to depict the municipal government as a benevolent and paternalistic entity, inspiring the poor to respect and trust urban administrators as caring for their interests.[127]

Jurisdictional problems, which persisted throughout the eighteenth century, further frustrated efforts at regularizing tribute exaction in Mexico City. At the beginning of the 1700s, there were several misunderstandings between the *contador general de tributos* and the *corregidor* regarding who was responsible for conducting collections. After years of debate, the *contador general* decided to farm out tribute collection to private individuals, many of whom were free-colored militia officers themselves. In 1781, the crown called forth an investigation into the matter, feeling that it had lost hundreds of thousands of pesos in irregular collections stretching back to 1694. The inquiry produced a *reglamento* specifying that all future free-colored tribute was to be taken by the *alcaldes ordinarios*. But by 1783, the special investigative commissioner examining the case had lost his authority to deliberate. Tribute collection reverted back to a nebulous state, being handled haphazardly by the *alcaldes de barrio*. In 1790, a new series of investigations were initiated, with proposals forwarded to end the caste-based tribute system entirely. In its place, class considerations were to be marked as the principal criterion used to determine if a person would be subject to payment. Anyone found aimlessly walking the streets *desnudo* ("naked") was to be taxed in order to compel him to find a job. After much discussion, the class-based scheme was ultimately considered unfeasible in New Spain. As debates continued, tribute collections in the city remained erratic, persisting into the first decade of the nineteenth century.[128]

Over time, leniency in the application of tribute laws in select urban and rural locations caused tribute exemption to be viewed by black civilians as a genuine legal right, institutionalized by custom if not by written law.[129] This was expressed most vividly in coastal communities where the lax application of militia exemption codes had provided fairly continuous civilian tribute relief since the late seventeenth century. When reforms threatened to change tribute policies in Tepic and Sentispac during the late 1770s, civilian free-coloreds asserted to the courts that they should continue to remain exempt, as they had since ancient times (*en lo antiguo*). Here, the tradition of militia-based exemptions was not nearly as old as in places such as Tabasco or Guazacualco. Free-colored companies had not been formed in the region until 1753. Only in 1762 did crown officials formally consider expanding tribute amnesty to civilian free-coloreds, mainly out of fear that the hostilities of the war with Britain might reach the northern coast of New Galicia, thereby endangering the port of San Blas. In exchange for sentinel duties, royal officials proposed exempting all 360 *tributarios vagos* in the area until the war's conclusion, regardless of militia status.[130] After additional debate, the administrators quickly rescinded their original offer, stating now that tribute would be relieved solely if civilians were mobilized to counter an attack. But in the minds of the free-colored populace, the stricter laws never took hold. Free-colored civilians only occasionally paid tribute after 1762. By the early 1780s, civilian blacks were found claiming exemption simply because of the fact that they were *pardos* and *morenos* who inhabited the coast. The original deal, that is, exclusion in exchange for emergency sentinel duty, was wholly forgotten. The result was an interesting twist; civilians were claiming relief *because they were free-coloreds*, whereas the crown held them accountable for tribute on those same grounds. In their writings the civilians saw no difference between themselves and the free-colored militiamen, whom they described as "just the same."[131] From their perspective, formal militia duty became a secondary criterion for tribute exemption. They lived in the same communities as the militiamen, were of the same caste, and contributed indirectly to the safety of the region. In their estimation, as elsewhere in the coastal areas of Mexico, these had become sufficient terms for free-colored civilians to advocate exclusion.

We can only speculate as to why blacks were given greater leniency than Indians living in *pueblos de indios* with regard to tribute payments. An important consideration is that Spanish colonial administrators perceived Indian settlements to be remarkably cohesive.[132] This contrasted with their understanding of the free-colored population, which was considered vagrant and undisciplined.[133] Corporate life for Indians in the pueblos added to the overall impression of unity. Participation in confraternities and village fiestas, collective labor enterprises, *compadrazgo*, communal land-holding—all of these elements were believed to instill a territorial rootedness in the mentality of the Indian population.[134] An enduring network of village officials was also important in preserving the veneer of continuity and stability.[135] The institutional apparatus of town government that took shape in the sixteenth century re-

mained virtually intact throughout the colonial period, despite political in-
trigues and internal discord.[136] The overriding sense of unity and control
within the *pueblos de indios* led royal administrators to conclude that tribute
collection did not threaten the basic structural integrity of Indian villages, although excessive tribute and labor demands could bring about protests, rebellions, and evasions.[137] In the minds of the administrators, tribute was a pressure that Indian communities were prepared to meet, collectively and under
compulsion if necessary.[138] As has been previously mentioned, villagers ultimately understood the important role that tribute played as a leverage mechanism in their legal disputes, making them more willing to pay. Moreover, successful extraction was facilitated by Indian officers who knew their local
populations well. Combined, these factors reduced the danger of massive emigration from the pueblos because of tribute.[139]

When emigration did occur, unlike with blacks, Indian resettlement did
not fully undermine the tribute process. Extreme measures were taken to track
dislocated Indians. If they moved to other pueblos, where they became known
as *forasteros*, they were still held accountable for their outstanding debts and
labor obligations if caught. They were simply placed on the tax rolls of their
newly chosen homes. If they resettled on the smaller *ranchos* the same rules
applied.[140] Also unlike free-coloreds, the threat of labor loss because of emigration was reduced by the formal mechanisms used for acquiring Indian workers. *Encomienda, repartimiento*, and labor drafts were firmly in place during
the sixteenth and early seventeenth centuries, giving way to various illegal but
effective coercive measures in the eighteenth century. Additionally, patterns of
Indian migration often favored the haciendas. Population increases in certain
pueblos created a pinch on village lands, driving some Indians straight to the
estates. This was the case in colonial Jalisco, where the expanding regional
economy prodded Indians to play increasingly variegated roles outside of village life.[141] In other cases, the aggressive territorial encroachment of estates
onto pueblo-held lands forced Indians into the life of wage laborers and tenant
farmers.[142] Even in central and southern Mexico, a harmonious coexistence
was achieved between haciendas and pueblos.[143] Neither structure was completely compromised by the existence of the other. Since estate labor demands
were seasonal in these sections of the colony, Indian peasants left their towns
for the haciendas only during the months when they were most needed. In
return, their labor services provided them with the cash they required to fulfill
tax and tribute obligations. They resided in their towns during the rest of the
year. Of course, this model did not apply everywhere in New Spain, but it
shows that in some regions, labor accommodations were worked out to the
mutual benefit of the pueblos and haciendas, thereby preserving the basic
structural cohesiveness of the pueblos.

In summary, the malleability of the *pueblos de indios* in the face of change,
combined with the relatively mild effects of Indian emigration on regional la-

bor patterns, created a different situation for colonial administrators than what has been observed for free-coloreds. Tribute privileges did not have to be negotiated in the same manner for Indian pueblo inhabitants. If they did, the crown stood more to lose given that tribute revenues generated by the indigenous population significantly outnumbered free-colored revenues because of the larger population base. It was a situation that royal officials sought eagerly to avoid.

Not all Indians resided in *pueblos de indios*, however, and not all *pueblos de indios* fit the cohesive descriptions described above.[144] Colonial administrators were aware of the variances and treated Indians living as *vagos* and *laboríos* with more care. Records from Tabasco in the 1780s reveal that *indios laboríos* had been excluded from paying tribute since 1691.[145] This paralleled the exemptions granted to free-coloreds during the same time period. Like free-coloreds, *indios laboríos* in Tabasco served as militiamen. Although there is little documentation detailing their participation in the service, it appears that a general *laborío* tribute exclusion developed alongside that of the free-coloreds. Step by step, tribute exclusion became more inclusive for both racial groups, as eventually not only militiamen but also all Indians of *laborío* status and free-coloreds were exempted in the province. Yet a clear separation of privilege divided *laboríos* from the Indians living in *pueblos de indios*, who were still subject to tribute. In the eyes of the colonial authorities, the lifestyle of the *laboríos* more closely resembled that of free-coloreds and mestizos. As if to emphasize the point, the *subdelegado* of Tabasco called for grouping *indios laboríos, pardos*, and mestizos under a single category on census lists taken after 1788.[146] In short, depending on the region, so-called rootless Indians were treated more like free-coloreds in New Spain, whom they were depicted as resembling by provincial administrators. This extended to matters of tribute. Outside of Tabasco, evidence reveals that while the tribute of these free-roaming Indians may not have been entirely forgiven by provincial authorities, the tax was voluntarily incurred by hacienda and estate owners who sought the labor of *indios vagos* and *laboríos*.[147] Despite these trends, the residents of the *pueblos de indios*, who were more numerous than their counterparts, continued to be held accountable for payment.

The Bourbon reforms of the mid-eighteenth century inspired crown administrators to re-examine the tolerant tribute policies of previous decades. Not only were the exclusions granted to free-colored civilians brought into question, but the basic tribute exemption afforded to militiamen was reassessed as well. Two factors accounted for the increased scrutiny. On the one hand, there was greater interest in fiscal overhaul to underwrite increasing expenses for the massive, imperial-wide defense program. Mexico's treasury functioned as an important *situado* (royal subsidy) that financed the operation of the crown's holdings throughout the New World, especially in the Caribbean. Evidence reveals that after the 1760s, there were sharp rises in remittances from Mexico to the Caribbean, with Cuba receiving the majority of the funds.[148] Bureaucrats sought to maximize income from every available resource so as to provide this subsidy, as well as to increase remittances to Spain, while still meeting the overhead costs needed to run Mexico's own civil, administrative, and military apparatus. Declines in tribute returns, brought on by a combination of lax policies and epidemics, were identified as areas where revenues could be increased. Viceroy Amarillas had already recognized the need for wholesale tribute reform in the 1750s. But it wasn't until the early 1760s when serious actions were taken to improve collections. A royal proviso circulated in several provinces demanding tougher collection practices for free-colored and *laborío* "vagabonds who roam[ed] their respective jurisdictions without any destination [or] employment."[149] Some *alcaldes mayores*, like those of Acayucan, Zacatula, and Tabasco, responded to the decree by attempting collection from free-colored militiamen, who in turn countered their moves by obtaining special viceregal dispensations.[150] These struggles were difficult ones. In Zacatula, militiamen who were pressured into paying tribute tried to petition the crown for continued relief but found themselves bullied by the *alcalde mayor* for their attempts. He confiscated their possessions and threatened them with whippings of two hundred lashes apiece. Despite such feuds, fiscal overhaul continued. On December 14, 1763, a *real cédula* was issued, formally calling for ordinances to be drafted that would improve tribute efficiency. An assembly convened to handle the matter, and in 1765 a new tribute code was completed, being approved by the king in July of 1770.[151] Much of the energy behind fiscal reforms in the 1760s came from the appointment of José de Gálvez as visitor-general to New Spain in 1765. Under his direction, and that of the *contador general*, additional adjustments to tribute policy were made in 1769–70. Their work laid the foundation for invigorated tribute revenues. From 1770 to 1780, a reported 7,882,610 pesos were collected, a more than 30 percent increase from the previous decade.[152] After Gálvez's visitation ended in 1772, a network of fiscal committees continued to supervise reforms into the nineteenth century.[153] For free-colored soldiers, the result of these changes meant a critical review of the militia exemption, and a predisposition by fiscal ministers to abolish the benefit.

Alongside greater interest in fiscal austerity, the other major factor contributing to a close evaluation of past tribute policies involved the implementation of the Bourbon military reforms. The transition to the provincial militia system created status distinctions among militia companies. Supposedly being better organized, disciplined, and trained, the new provincial forces were considered by early Bourbon military planners to be the only units eligible for full militia privileges. Meanwhile, pre-existing companies that had not been placed on a provincial footing would have to lose their benefits, although their militiamen would still be called upon to perform the same services as before.

The end result was to be a contraction of tribute coverage, reduced to include only the free-colored militiamen serving in provincial units.

The military reform process was fraught with problems that created difficulties for military planners wishing to relegate privileges exclusively to provincial companies. The fact that the provincial system was implemented in New Spain in piecemeal fashion, rather than simultaneously in all regions, meant that there was a frequent need to update laws addressing military privileges.[154] In addition, the design of the colony's militia plan was constantly changing, since the king allowed considerable discretion among New World officials to tailor the number of units employed in Mexico as they saw fit. From the 1760s until 1810, viceroys and military inspectors continually debated whether it was best to increase the number of regular troops or militia forces in the colony.[155] The result was a perennial state of flux, as no one was sure if the number of provincial units called for during one viceregal administration would carry over into the next. Problems were compounded when reforms were left incomplete in some regions, casting doubt on whether the companies raised in these areas were truly provincial.[156] Some reformed units completely lacked the characteristic veteran cadre. Others had veteran attachés but remained poorly trained. Even laws outlining militia privileges proved unclear and sometimes contradictory. Two important edicts were issued regarding the provincial forces, the first on May 3, 1766, and the second on December 24, 1767. Under the first decree, Viceroy Cruillas granted white militiamen access to the *fuero* privilege in both civil and criminal cases. Meanwhile, the decree restricted free-coloreds to enjoying full *fuero* rights only in cases involving military matters.[157] The 1766 decree also detailed numerous tax exemptions, including tribute relief, for *pardo* and *moreno* provincial soldiers. The second edict made some changes to the set of free-colored benefits. Here it was announced that the *pardo* battalions of Puebla and Mexico City were to enjoy the same complete *fuero* rights as whites, in addition to tribute exemption.[158] Mexico City and Puebla were singled out for mention because as of 1767, those were the only locations with free-colored units arranged along provincial lines. Having their privileges clarified in writing so early significantly reduced the number of tribute-related complaints lodged by these battalions.

But reforms were taking place elsewhere in New Spain. Access to privileges in these areas was less concretely defined. In the province of Tantoyucan (northern Veracruz), changes had redesignated many of the older free-colored companies as *sueltas*, or untrained reserve units. Neither the 1766 nor 1767 decrees explicitly addressed the tribute situation of this unit type. Also excluded from mention were those units that were neither provincials nor *sueltas*, but which possessed special *cédulas* conferred in the early 1760s that had provided them with tribute exclusion. Were their old privileges to continue to be recognized? What about free-coloreds who served in racially integrated provincial forces? What exactly were their rights? Given the multiple ambiguities produced by the reform process and its accompanying legislation, militiamen took the opportunity to interpret both decrees in the broadest possible manner. For example, in Tantoyucan, a contingent of free-colored soldiers deciphered the 1766 decree as granting them full tribute immunity. The *alcalde mayor* supported them in their efforts. In Queretaro, a host of free-colored militiamen who were not actually enrolled in any of the city's provincial units, claimed that even in light of the 1767 decree, their units remained both tribute exempt and entitled to the *fuero* of white militiamen.[159]

Complaints and requests for clarifications piled into the office of the viceroy from throughout the kingdom. Inquiries from the coasts were the most numerous, seeing that these were areas where tribute leniency had been felt the greatest during the eighteenth century. In response to the queries, between November 21 and 22, 1770, Viceroy Marques de Croix, under the influence of Visitor-General Gálvez, issued a decree that explicitly determined that only provincial cavalry and infantry units were to be excluded from tribute. All other companies would be considered urban in status, and thus, liable to payment.[160] These included the *sueltas*. Problems persisted despite these clarifications. The new legislation was not widely circulated among district governors and military commanders, thereby leaving many regions ignorant of any policy change. Furthermore, when Croix's successor, Antonio María de Bucareli, assumed office in 1771, he backtracked on the decree. Gálvez tried to persuade Bucareli that it was in the colony's best interest to publish the document as a *bando* for wider distribution. Instead, the viceroy called for a thorough investigation into tribute matters. The rationale behind his reluctance to publish the 1770 decree is unclear, but McAlister has suggested that the viceroy did not want to rush into bestowing any militia privileges until he had first reorganized the militia himself, customizing it to his own liking. Only after reaching a complete understanding of how many provincial units, as opposed to urban units, he wanted to exist in New Spain would it then be appropriate to afford privileges.[161] In the meantime, throughout the colony there were conflicting opinions on how to proceed with free-colored tribute. Some administrators collected the tax in their jurisdictions from militiamen and civilians alike. Others remained reluctant. Free-coloreds continued to present their cases for exemption before the viceregal court.

When tribute was collected, the ensuing complaints could incorporate a broad cross-section of society. Sometimes there were regional implications to the protests. Tribute exemption, unlike other militia benefits such as the *fuero*, was a type of privilege that had been enjoyed in uniform fashion by all free-colored soldiers. As we have seen, it was also commonly extended to civilians. Any dramatic shift in tribute policy instantly affected everyone alike, be they captains, soldiers, or civilians.

Generally speaking, free-colored appeals for tribute relief after 1760 were reminiscent in structure and content to the initial requests for dispensation made during the late seventeenth and early eighteenth centuries. Since many communities possessed some form of local archives, free-coloreds consulted these repositories when writing their petitions, perhaps believing that by employing arguments similar to those presented for past exemptions, they could once again sway the crown to their favor. Their appeals were supplemented with a record of military deeds performed throughout the eighteenth century. Unlike tribute cases presented by Indians, free-colored appeals were bolder in their challenges to the crown. As Taylor has observed, Indian legal proceedings typically assumed the form of protests against tax innovations. Either complaints were made against increases in old tax levels, or against the introduction of completely new charges. Protests never questioned the state's right to impose tax, labor, or tribute demands.[162] Since the premises of crown law were never directly disputed, the weight of the accusations fell on the implementers of royal will; select *alcaldes mayores* and *tenientes* found to be engaging in excessive practices were the targets of Indian anger.[163] Free-colored tribute appeals were very different. Military service had altered the financial obligations traditionally assigned to blacks, even to the extent that civilians were affected. In some areas, regardless of militia status, being *pardo* or *moreno* had evolved into an analogue for being tribute-exempt. Although in case testimonies individual *alcaldes mayores* were identified as being abusive by exacting tribute, what was being questioned was not innovation in the levels of the tax but actually the crown's right to collect tribute from blacks in the first place. Importantly, free-coloreds, militiamen, and civilian alike were not averse to describing the situation concretely in these terms, displaying levels of racial confidence and awareness that were rarely matched in other types of colonial documentation. The century-long effort to acquire tribute exemption, and the abrupt challenge to exclusion status, prompted the solidification of a shared, free-colored racial understanding around a specific corporate privilege.

With that said, militiamen more commonly raised tribute exclusion cases than civilians did. A committee of high-ranking, free-colored officers would either travel to their *cabecera* to petition the *alcalde mayor* directly, or hire an *apoderado* (legal representative) to present their cause to the authorities in Mexico City. Oftentimes, both approaches were utilized. Whatever the circumstances, there was almost always the impression of racial unity, as free-colored officers claimed to speak on behalf of all the *milicianos pardos y morenos* of their respective towns and provinces. However, mention of exclusions for free-colored civilians was kept to a minimum. Evidently, either militiamen were mainly concerned about their own privileges in these writings, or they may have tacitly understood that any tribute benefits secured would eventually extend to civilians as well, as had transpired in past years. Never-

theless, militiamen from certain towns might still be enticed to claim that all
adult, free-colored men in their communities served as soldiers, so as to ensure
that coverage was extended to civilians.

Another reason why civilians were routinely excluded from mention in
tribute cases may have resulted from the advice of the *apoderados*. Case files
that ultimately reached Mexico City almost always had some input by these legal advisors. They understood that the most successful arguments were those
narrowly related to soldiers. This was because cases were then sent through
military channels, where the review process involved a ruling made by the
military *auditor*. The viceroy invariably supported his decision. The advantage of having tribute cases heard by the *auditor de guerra* was that he reviewed
the appeals conscientiously, on the basis of military merit, analyzing such
factors as training, the overall utility of the units, and their strategic location.
He juggled the ambitions of the soldiers with the larger aims of the Bourbon
military reforms. Furthermore, his corporate affiliation to the military favored
free-colored militiamen. Although a trained lawyer, he understood their roles
as military defenders more than other bureaucratic officials. The *auditor*'s influence counterbalanced attacks made by royal treasury officers, who cared less
about the militiamen's military responsibilities than they did for increasing
crown revenues.[164]

Appeals for exemption could take other forms. In Guajolotitlan (Oaxaca),
when the *alcalde mayor* attempted to charge tribute in the 1780s, free-colored
civilians and militiamen were united in protest under the influence of Lieutenant Policarpio de los Santos. Here, a lone, free-colored militia officer worked
virtually independently to organize an entire town to resist payment. His notorious reputation as a bruiser intimidated coy and reluctant villagers to follow his lead.[165] In another situation in Acayucan, incensed free-coloreds con-
spired with neighbors in the provinces of Tuxtla and Cozamaloapa to plan a
regional resistance to payment in 1781. Fortunately for colonial administrators,
the secret correspondence of the multiregional plot was uncovered and the
event was foiled.[166] While certainly not the norm, heavy-handed instances of
collective free-colored defiance, on the level seen in both Guajolotitlan and
Acayucan, certainly existed elsewhere in New Spain. Notwithstanding these,
there were other situations where the press for tribute exemption involved a
more diverse cast of individuals, including whites. The jurisdiction of Xicayan
in the 1760s and 1770s presents an insightful example of how local politics
could intervene to expand the range of players.

Xicayan's militia was reformed between 1765 and 1767, when regular army
colonel Dn. Carlos Sarrio raised fifteen companies in the region. Six of these
were labeled *español* dragoons, while the remaining nine units were designated as free-colored cavalry/infantry companies. Given the shortage of whites
in the region, the dragoons of *españoles* actually incorporated large numbers of
mestizos, *mulatos*, and *mulatos blancos*. There seemed to be an effort to sepa-

rate lighter-skinned blacks from the darker hues, as *pardos, morenos,* and *negros* formed the bulk of the nine free-colored companies. Unlike elsewhere in the kingdom, the reforms enacted by Sarrio did not include a veteran cadre. Consequently, the two senior military officers in Xicayan continued to be the *alcalde mayor,* who held the rank of *capitain aguerra,* and the *sargento mayor,* Dn. Phelipe Izusquiza, a Spaniard who had held the post since 1760. Their immediate subordinates were the captains *comandantes* of the fifteen companies. When the 1767 decree was issued, free-colored soldiers in Xicayan interpreted the law as granting them full tribute exemption, since they served in key roles as coastal guardians. But Visitor-General Gálvez later determined that the units of Xicayan were useless for the defense of the colony and should be subjected to tribute. As with units elsewhere along the Pacific coast, he surmised that military reforms here had not improved the overall quality of the companies. In 1771, when the *apoderado fisco,* Dn. Fernando Sánchez Pareja, was sent to Xicayan to assist the *alcalde mayor* in creating the new tribute *matrícula,* he ordered the *alcalde mayor* to place all free-colored militiamen on the registers.

The soldiers were alarmed. They submitted intricate information to the viceroy regarding their services. Apart from their regular duties as auxiliaries to the *justicia,* they stressed their maintenance of the *vigía,* their assistance in transporting mail, silver, and even the *rentas reales* across the adjacent cordillera. In light of their services, Bucareli decided on February 1, 1773, that the militiamen of Xicayan could retain their exemption, but only those enlisted in the nine free-colored companies. *Mulato* militiamen enrolled with the *españoles* were not included in the tribute dispensation because they performed the most limited of duties, occasionally congregating in their companies for training, or to meet sporadic military crises.

Despite Bucareli's decision, the *alcalde mayor* feared that charging tribute would present problems for his administration. After the *apoderado* left Xicayan, the *alcalde mayor* opted to pay tribute for all liable free-coloreds from his own pockets in order to avoid complications. The practice was continued during the opening years of the administration of his successor, Dn. Joseph de Ayala Matamoros. However, in 1777, another *apoderado fisco* visited the region to update tribute registers. He proceeded to acknowledge the exemption of the soldiers in the nine free-colored companies but remained steadfast in holding all other blacks subject to payment, including the *mulatos blancos* enlisted as white dragoons.

Ayala seized the opportunity of the *apoderado*'s visit to make a political statement. According to rumor, Ayala had been attempting to run Xicayan as his private fief. He had managed to bring the soldiers of the free-colored militia under his influence, compelling them to perform labor services and to sell him their agricultural goods at greatly devalued prices. But he did not exercise similar control over the white units. On more than one occasion the *alcalde mayor* had expressed a desire to extinguish their companies. Now, supported with the evidence collected during the *apoderado*'s tribute investigation, Ayala proceeded to charge tribute from the more than two hundred *mulatos* in these units, collecting some 127 pesos by force. All who resisted were jailed. Another 1,400 pesos were seized from the militia's common fund, which had been established in 1748 to defray emergency military expenses. There was general outrage among the *mulatos* enrolled in the white dragoon regiments. Some forcibly demanded the return of their money. Others challenged the *alcalde mayor*'s authority, stating that even as *capitan aguerra*, he was not their supreme commander. Many more soldiers simply abandoned the ranks.

Sargento mayor Izusquiza intervened on the soldiers' behalf, presenting their complaints personally to viceregal representatives in Mexico City. Other white officers, particularly Captain Zamorategui, supported him. Mudslinging continued as the *alcalde mayor* described Izusquiza as a *muerto de hambre* (pauper) who did not even live near the soldiers, and whose main preoccupation was stirring trouble in Xicayan. Each man accused the other of overstepping the bounds of his authority. Meanwhile, *mulatos* in the dragoon companies supported a proposal to eliminate the nine free-colored companies. In their stead, the dragoons, whites included, would assume all the responsibilities previously carried out by the free-colored units. A backlog of cases in Mexico City and the misplacement of documents protracted a final decision on the tribute status of the *mulatos blancos*. After three years of intrigue, the *mulatos blancos* drafted a letter:

And this Sir? Why must the militias of Xicayan be perceived as useless, and looked upon with disdain by the alcaldes mayores every five years that an apoderado of the real fisco visits to impose tribute? And why must the blacks and mulatos in the companies of Spaniards be looked down upon as well? Are we not coastal guardians? Do not the battalions of pardos in Tampico, Pánuco, Huexutla, Tantoyucan, Santa Maria Usuluama, Alvarado, Tacotalpa, and the Costa del Norte (the Atlantic coast) enjoy privileges and tribute exemption? And in the Costa Sur (Pacific Coast), do not the towns of Teguantepeque . . . Igualapan, Acapulco, the coast of Atoyaque . . . and those which follow, do they not enjoy tribute exemption? What is the reason that we in the companies of Xicayan do not enjoy the same privileges?[167]

As a counterweight to the oppressive authority of the *alcalde mayor*, the *mulatos blancos* urgently requested that a veteran cadre be added to their units. Ordinarily, in places like Mexico City and Puebla, free-colored soldiers saw the cadre as an anathema to their right of self-governance. But in Xicayan, their inclusion was seen by the *mulato* dragoons as the best possible way to avoid further grievances, since the authority of the cadre would theoretically supersede that of the *alcalde mayor*. The militiamen perhaps believed that the men of the cadre, being soldiers more than administrators, might be enticed to view the tribute dilemma from their perspective. Additionally, the cadre's presence would work to stabilize military benefits and provide continuity in local military decision-making, since these veterans would supposedly reside in the province for longer periods than the transient *alcaldes mayores*. Lastly, the inclusion of the veteran cadre was deemed more palatable to the *mulato* dragoons because, unlike their darker counterparts in specifically free-colored units, these *mulatos* enjoyed less access to the officer ranks. Therefore, the cadre's presence did not pose a challenge to their commanding authority, since they had very little to begin with.

The *mulato* dragoons found a ready ally in the military inspector, Dn. Pasqual Cisneros. While confessing to know little about the particular situation of Xicayan's companies, he agreed that they should enjoy privileges similar to those that were currently being granted to soldiers near Veracruz, since units on both coasts essentially performed the same functions. He also shared the *mulatos'* opinion that the nine free-colored units could be abolished entirely, since they were rumored to be little more than puppets of the *alcalde mayor*. Cisneros argued that their elimination would benefit the royal treasury with increased tribute revenues. Perhaps unaware of the double jeopardy of his statements, he forwarded his decision to the *auditor de guerra*, who was more cautious in his deliberations.

In 1780, Auditor Valcarcel determined that no innovations were to be made to the current militia structure. In that way he hoped to quell any potential disturbances that might arise from men being involuntarily removed from their companies. Second, he noted that the *sargento mayor*'s actions in this matter had indeed transgressed the authority of his command. He ruled that Izusquiza should refrain from further seditious activities. But with regard to tribute exemption, the actual heart of the disputes, no final decision was made. Instead, the case file was shuffled back to the desk of the military inspector for further review.[168]

Many aspects of this case were unique to Xicayan, but others reflected the general situation encountered with tribute appeals throughout the colony. In terms of generalities, we see that the case was deliberated upon by the *auditor de guerra*, with input from the military inspector. The final decisions here, as with others in New Spain, were often slow in coming. The *auditor*'s careful review led to inconclusive results, contributing to renewed problems at the provincial level from year to year. Nearly four years of legal proceedings produced nothing concrete in Xicayan for the *mulatos blancos*. The Xicayan case is unique in that *mulatos blancos* were found pitted against other black militiamen in direct competition for benefits. Although there are numerous instances of divisions among blacks in the historical record, normally the nature of tribute inquiries witnessed free-colored unanimity, at least on the surface. Xicayan actually exhibited this model in 1771–73, during the legal maneuvering in which the nine free-colored companies managed to secure their tribute exemption status from Viceroy Bucareli. But the model broke down in 1777. On the one hand, Bucareli's decision in 1773 to exclude some soldiers from paying tribute, but not others, brought forth disunion. On the other hand, the interference of local politics increased the divide. Rifts were brought into full relief as the *alcalde mayor* worked to exercise supreme control in the region. This united both *mulato* and white dragoons in closer alliance. Although Xicayan was not unique in having free-colored soldiers stationed in white regiments, their tight relationship was atypical, and credited in large part to Ayala's actions. In regions where the *alcalde mayor* played a lesser role in trying to control militia companies, and where blacks were predominantly placed in the ranks of free-colored units of the independent type, there was more racial unity on tribute matters.

In the 1780s, additional legislation was drafted to clear lingering ambiguities regarding the privileges of various kinds of militia units. On May 30, 1781, and March 15, 1782, Viceroy Martin Mayorga finally declared in concrete terms which companies were provincial, and therefore exempt from tribute. With regard to infantry, the units of San Carlos (San Luis Potosí), the two Legiones del Principe (Guanajuato), the *pardo* battalions of Mexico City and Puebla, as well as the companies of Cordoba, Tlaxcala, Toluca, and Oaxaca were determined to be on the provincial footing. In terms of cavalry and dragoons, the regiments of Queretaro and Puebla were considered provincial.[169] Many of these units were not separated into specifically designated *pardo* and *español* companies, but it was understood that free-coloreds serving in any of them were tribute exempt.[170] A special provision was added to include militia units broadly defined as occupying the coasts of Veracruz. There, tribute exemption was extended to companies that had enjoyed exclusion prior to the Bourbon military reforms, regardless of whether they were provincial, *suelta*, or urban. On May 8, 1782, a similar decree followed for free-coloreds in Acapulco.[171]

Mayorga felt pressured into granting these exemptions, seeing as Spain was at war with Great Britain (1779–83). He was supported in his reasoning by the king.[172] Additionally, Mayorga was completely dismayed with the state of military readiness in the kingdom, and perhaps believed that by extending the tribute grace, along with *fuero* rights, he would ensure the loyalty of these coastal forces in case of emergency. As further incentive, he added that upon the war's conclusion he would consider renewing the privileges for Veracruz, provided that the militiamen had rendered exemplary service. Unfortunately, the immediate postwar years were ones of administrative confusion in New Spain, as two viceroys died in quick succession. This produced relative negligence on militia reforms at the highest levels of the bureaucracy, leading to inactivity on the renewal of the Veracruz exemption. Seeking new sources of revenue, on March 21, 1787, the *fiscal* of the Real Hacienda wrote to the viceregal court requesting to resubject Veracruz's free-colored militiamen to tribute. But on September 1, 1787, the incoming viceroy reconfirmed the militia exclusion and expanded its scope to include all units along the coast, whether they had enjoyed tribute benefits in past years or not. Between 1788 and 1790, news of the expanded exemption was published widely in towns along the Veracruz coastline.[173]

Mayorga's concession of tribute exemption in Veracruz and Acapulco pointed to weaknesses in the crown's ability to govern Mexico's coastal, free-colored population in times of crisis without resorting to some form of compromise agreement that would coax them into military duty. The concessions were a tacit confession of the failure of the Bourbon military reforms to establish a set of privileges that were tied solely to the implementation of the provincial military system. The efforts to increase the quality of the militia, and to exclusively reward those units that met the new standards, simply did not work in all areas of the colony. As royal officials came to terms with difficulties in raising provincial forces, many took a second look at the role of urban and *suelta* units. Indeed, although the provincial system was incorporated to improve militia effectiveness by creating units in which men would be obligated to serve outside of their local communities, the crown's intent was never to totally eliminate the urban and *suelta* companies.[174] Major Pedro de Gorostiza announced in his plan of 1776 that these were the most important militia units in the colony, since provincials had proven to be a mere fiction. For the defense of New Spain he recommended heavy reliance on urban and *suelta* companies, alongside an expanded number of regular troops. The Crespo plan of the late 1780s also featured *sueltas* and urban companies as key defensive components. Likewise, Crespo's successors, Flórez and Mendinueta, attached great importance to both militia types but called for the *sueltas* to incorporate a regular training regimen.[175] At the local level, military commanders involved in raising provincial units often expressed the superiority of utilizing *sueltas* and urban companies.[176]

From the point of view of the free-coloreds that manned many of these units, if the colony were to continue to rely on their numbers for defense, Bourbon military planners would have to alter their view on disbursing military privileges. Principally, this entailed adjusting Bourbon military defense schemes to encompass the benefits that were in place before the reform effort, including some civilian exclusions. Tribute exemption had evolved as a regional privilege over the course of the eighteenth century, and this fact surfaced again in the tribute debates that took place between the crown and free-coloreds after 1760. In cases presented to the viceroy, militiamen stressed the importance of their location as the essential aspect that gave meaning to their services. In Xicayan, for instance, the *mulatos blancos* were not just militiamen, they were also "coastal guardians" protecting the colony's frontier. Similarly, soldiers in places such as Tamiagua, Zacatula, Jalapa, and San Blas all argued that the extension of privileges should be based on locational criteria rather than on reforms—that is, the placement of watchtowers, *vigía* points, key access roads, rivers, and bays.[177] Viceroys were also reminded that the late seventeenth and early eighteenth century contracts drawn between soldiers and the crown took the form of agreements with towns, cities, and provinces. With the notable exceptions of Mexico City and Puebla, these contracts offered privileges in exchange for soldiers serving *in their localities*.[178] Seeing as these were ancient rights, the militiamen maintained that regionally based tribute exemptions could not be stripped on the whim of bringing about military reform.

Even members of the treasury reluctantly understood the message. In April 1781, under the pressures of war, the *fiscal* of the Real Hacienda, Dn. Ramon de Posada, wrote that although free-colored militiamen had caused great losses to the treasury in past years, soldiers in areas such as Tepic and San Blas would have their tribute appeals considered on a regional basis. However, only those towns and provinces that "according to custom and tolerance" had enjoyed past exclusions would be reviewed.[179] Locations standing the best chance of success were those able to produce a *real cédula* to support their cause, as well as a coherent argument as to why tribute exemptions were granted in the past. Mayorga upheld this policy, which served as the basis for granting exemptions along the coasts of Veracruz.

By the early 1790s, the distribution of military tribute privileges that were in place throughout the colony greatly resembled the pattern that existed prior to the Bourbon reforms. A few more provincial units had been created after 1780, bringing tribute immunity and *fuero* rights to the Battalion of San Blas, the Regiment of Guadalajara, the Battalion of Valladolid, and the Dragoons of Michoacán.[180] By 1791, Tabasco's urban and *suelta* units secured official tribute exemption as well, under the general dispensation in effect for soldiers in Veracruz. Even along the coasts of colonial Oaxaca, where tribute exemption issues had proven more contentious than in Veracruz, urban and *suelta* companies that were raised prior to the reforms tended to enjoy relief by the mid-1780s.[181] Reversals to their rights began to take effect shortly after 1790, but in limited fashion.[182] Consequently, the Bourbon military reform effort of the 1760s through the 1780s, while bringing new challenges to the older militia system, did not displace its privileges. It would ultimately take the draconian measures instituted by Viceroy Revillagigedo in eliminating free-colored service to finally undermine the pattern of tribute benefits that had evolved over the course of the century.

CHAPTER FIVE

The *Fuero* Privilege

T HE FUERO MILITAR, or military legal exemption, has been critically examined by previous scholarship as a privilege with the potential to
subvert the legal structure of the colony by granting scores of residents access
to a parallel judicial apparatus that deliberated on criminal matters differently
than the ordinary courts.[1] The *fuero* was certainly nothing new to the colonial
world. Since the sixteenth century, *fueros* were among the most coveted elements that defined corporate life. The *fuero* is what separated a group from
ordinary civil jurisdiction, since with it an organization not only possessed its
own self-governing body but also the ability to independently adjudicate its
members. In New Spain there were at least thirty-four identifiable corporate
entities with their own tribunals.[2] Members of the elite, such as clergymen,
merchants, and miners, while not a corporate group themselves, normally enjoyed some form of *fuero* by means of their occupations.[3] The military *fuero*
was seen as problematic because of its increasingly extensive social reach. Prior
to the Bourbon military reforms of the 1760s, the *fuero militar* had been
granted jealously, almost completely restricted to the officer corps. In this way,
even within a corporate institution, the privilege was graduated such that it
worked to preserve the basic status distinctions between the *plebe* (commoners), and the *gente decente* (respectable folk). However, the urgent need to improve the colony's military design brought radical change to the distribution
of the privilege. After mid-century, common foot soldiers were given un-
precedented access to the *fuero* at increasing rates.

Cruillas's provincial militia decree of May 3, 1766, outlined the essential
features of *fuero* coverage as follows: soldiers would no longer need to be on
active duty to receive coverage, and during mobilizations the scope of their
privileges would increase. When inactive, NCOs were given immunity from
criminal courts. When mobilized, enlisted men enjoyed the civil and criminal
fuero. Officers retained the civil and criminal exemption regardless of mobilization status. NCOs and officers alike were granted the *fuero pasivo* on uncon-

ditional terms, meaning that they possessed the immunity as defendants in litigation. By contrast, the *fuero activo*, or plaintiff's immunity, was still reserved as a guarded right for the most prominent militia officers. In addition to the *fuero*, both the commissioned and enlisted grades were granted a series of supplementary legal privileges known as *preeminencias*. Included among these were exemptions from the payment of *servicios*, which were imposed monetary contributions regularly demanded by the crown. Moreover, militiamen could not be taken to debtor's prison, nor could their possessions be forcibly seized to pay outstanding debts unless owed to the royal treasury. Militiamen could forgo serving in a municipal office. Upon retirement, soldiers who had served with honor and had logged a minimum of twenty years of duty in the militia received special documents entitling them to lifetime use of the *fuero* and their military uniforms. The same applied to soldiers who retired after fifteen years on account of serious injury or illness. Militiamen could also utilize the military jurisdiction to assist them in preparing their wills and testaments, as well as in settling matters regarding their estates.[4] As the number of provincial forces increased in New Spain, so did *fuero* and *preeminencia* coverage. By the late 1780s, more than seventeen thousand soldiers possessed these expanded military privileges.[5] The sweep of coverage extended even further when it is considered that members of the militiamen's families were frequently included under the privileges as well.[6]

As with tribute exemptions, the new *fuero* benefits implemented in the 1760s were supposed to apply solely to the newly created provincial militia forces. In their original form, the laws excluded free-coloreds from coverage, be they in provincial or urban units. However, Croix's decree of December 24, 1767, laid the fundamental groundwork for broadening the *fuero* to include *pardos* and *morenos*, by providing the provincial battalions of Mexico City and Puebla with access to the privilege equal to that of whites. Yet, as seen with tribute legislation, the 1767 decree lacked clarity, giving leeway to a multitude of vying interpretations over its codes.[7] Although the law was designed to apply to only two cities, soon free-coloreds in provincial units throughout the colony claimed equally comprehensive *fuero* privileges. Shortly thereafter, blacks in urban and *suelta* companies joined into the fray by clamoring for rights that more vividly transcended the original intentions of the law.

For example, in Cozamaloapa and Papantla, free-colored militiamen not only demanded full *fuero* coverage for urban and *suelta* units but also claimed title to the *fuero activo* and *pasivo* for all troops.[8] Needless to say, the free-colored militiamen's interpretation of their privileges clashed with that of the provincial authorities, who sought to curtail their courtroom immunities. An almost comedic competition ensued as military officers and provincial governors bickered over matters of legal jurisdiction. The *alcalde mayor* of Cozamaluapa tightly adhered to his presumed authority to adjudicate civilians and militiamen alike in his province, regardless of *fuero* rights. Meanwhile, militia captains asserted an exaggerated sense of judicial authority over their subordinates. As a result, when militiamen committed crimes, they were often tried twice for the same infraction, once by the *alcalde* and again by the militia.

Equally stammering to the locution of justice in Papantla and Cozamaluapa was the open competition for prisoners between military and provincial authorities. By means of the *fuero*, it was customary for militia captains in rural areas to use their homes as a jailhouse for militiamen. House arrest was often a light affair. Although shackled, the soldiers might frequently be released to enjoy dinner, conversation, and wine. During the 1760s and 1770s, a captain's ability to hold prisoners was brought into question as there were outright struggles between provincial authorities and militia officers over matters of custody.

Throughout the colony, the conflicting liberties that both soldiers and magistrates took toward interpreting the free-colored militiamen's *fuero* rights led to regional variations in the application of military legal justice in New Spain. There were also regional differences that evolved regarding the number of free-coloreds who were to be covered under *fuero* law. In the port of Veracruz, free-colored *fuero* privileges appeared severely constrained. Until 1784, *fueros* were granted only to active-duty militiamen enrolled in one of the disciplined companies, the elite lancer companies, or in the provincial regiments.[9] This excluded several hundred soldiers from coverage. By contrast, in Tantoyucan, which included the jurisdictions of Tampico and Pánuco, *fuero* was extended to all free-colored companies indiscriminately.[10] In Mexico City, Puebla, Cordoba, and Atlixco, only free-colored militiamen in provincial units appear to have enjoyed the privilege. But unlike Veracruz, *fuero* was granted without need for active duty or mobilization.[11] In Querétaro, confusion over the exact meaning of *fuero* law led to a relaxed interpretation of the legislators' intentions. Throughout the 1770s, free-colored militiamen in the city's *pardo* cavalry companies behaved as if their *fuero* were equal to that of whites, without any particular stipulations.[12]

In 1784, a decree was issued to eliminate free-colored *fuero* privileges altogether in Veracruz. This was followed in 1787 by legislation intended to eliminate free-colored *fuero* rights everywhere in the colony.[13] These policy initiatives did not, however, take root. By the late 1780s, *fuero* had become an institutionalized fact of life for free-colored militiamen throughout New Spain, regardless of local differences in the level of *pardo* and *moreno* inclusiveness under *fuero* law. Additionally, there were numerous independent regional agreements that had been privately signed between the militiamen and crown authorities that counterbalanced any attempts to reduce their privileges. Such was the case in Tabasco, where despite animated feuds between members of the military jurisdiction and the provincial authorities, the free-colored militiamen's private contract stood as a thorn against all moves to undermine their *fuero* rights.[14]

Matters took a different course in the 1790s, when free-colored military service suffered a serious decline at the hands of Viceroy Revillagigedo. The aggressive disbanding of free-colored units forced scores of *pardos* and *morenos* to lose their immunities. Yet even amid the changes, *fuero* rights remained in place for the limited number of soldiers who continued to serve in the corps. This was because after Revillagigedo's downsizing reforms took effect, he declared that any remaining free-colored militiamen would proceed to enjoy the same corporate benefits as their white counterparts in the provincial forces. Consequently, courtroom exclusions were brought to full parity, regardless of color. The policy was maintained by Viceroy Branciforte into the latter years of the eighteenth century.[15]

From this brief legislative overview, we can conclude that despite the multiple policy shifts and ambiguities regarding the coverage of *fuero* privilege, it remained an important benefit for free-colored militiamen throughout the second half of the eighteenth century. The major question concerning us here is, What were the implications of the privilege? Did it offer social mobility as has often been claimed?[16] Did it alter the militiamen's position within the caste system?

Some have proposed that the *fuero* worked to diminish the role of race in the militiamen's legal affairs. Such claims intimate that when soldiers were called to appear in the military courts, their social and racial origins played less of a factor in the deliberative process than under ordinary methods of adjudication. Therefore the crown's efforts at using race as a means of social control were rendered less effective.[17] Certainly, the militiamen's contemporaries noted that free-coloreds were aware of their new legal leverage. Allegedly, fear and respect for municipal authority were abandoned as they repeatedly ignored the warnings of civilian magistrates. Apparently, some even used their *fuero* to intimidate fellow citizens. There are accounts of free-colored militiamen boasting that they were granted authority by the king to kill people indiscriminately. In this way they proceeded to cow others into doing their personal bidding.[18]

Most of the claims scholars have made about free-colored militiamen with respect to the *fuero* are based on circumstantial evidence. Here, a more in-depth assessment of the *fuero* is attempted through an analysis of several types of cases to which it applied. The objective is not to offer a holistic overview of the military *fuero*. Such a study could stand alone as a monograph in itself. Rather, the idea is to present representative examples that detail how the *fuero* worked for free-colored militiamen, and ultimately, to assess its relationship to race.

When a free-colored militiaman was caught in the act of a crime by civilian authorities, rarely was he immediately identified as belonging to a militia company, particularly in major urban areas such as Puebla and Mexico City.

Even in smaller towns, where there was a greater chance that the apprehending official might know the soldier personally, the first act of arrest almost always involved taking him into custody under normal, civilian jurisdiction. There were strict laws as to how the justices were to proceed from that point. After the soldier identified himself and his company captain, *fuero* law dictated that the *justicia ordinaria* was to secure proof of the soldier's status. Word of his capture was to be given to his superior officer so that a copy of his *filiación* papers, or enrollment documents, could be released. In the meantime, civilian judicial officials could proceed in limited fashion with the *sumaria*—that is, the preliminary investigative procedure in which witness testimony was taken and charges filed.[19] Once the fact of the soldier's status had been established, copies of all case depositions and charges were to be handed over to his regiment's senior officer for review. This officer would then make a decision as to whether the case belonged under military jurisdiction. There were a number of circumstances, known as *desafuero*, that caused soldiers to lose their civilian legal immunities. For example, if the litigation had been initiated before the soldier had enrolled in the militia, he was barred from exemption. Similarly, resisting arrest or participating in riots, prohibited gambling, treasury fraud, disrespect for civil authorities, and certain property suits all qualified for *desafuero*.[20] Civilian authorities would retain custody of the soldiers in those situations. But if a case fell properly under military domain, then the prisoner was to be released to his regiment without delay. Time was of the essence. Until the matter of proper jurisdiction had been resolved, militiamen were not to be mistreated, punished, insulted, or charged fines while housed in civilian jails.

Once it was determined that a case was to proceed through military channels, the soldier was transferred to his barracks, or to the home of his captain, for detention. After further investigation into the crime, all relevant paperwork would be forwarded to Mexico City and examined by the *auditor de guerra*, the military's supreme legal authority. He would make a ruling on the matter. There were, however, some exceptions. If an infraction was specifically of a military nature, then the soldier's senior military officer was authorized to deliberate and merely pass his decision on to the *auditor* for approval. But in most situations, the *auditor* adjudicated based on the presented evidence. His decision would be handed to the viceroy and an appropriate punishment would be meted out.[21]

Such was the ideal manner in which the military judicial system was to operate. In practice, the *fuero* privilege rarely functioned so smoothly. The main problem was that there were just too many opportunities open for civilian authorities to impose their will. When they chose to take advantage of these chances, the process of military justice could not unfold as planned. Additionally, when captured soldiers made mention of their militia immunity, law enforcement agents felt slighted and often acted more arbitrarily. In the case of

Martín Carrasco, a soldier in Mexico City's *pardo* battalion, he was beaten repeatedly with the flat end of a municipal official's sword when he was caught
amid a crowd of gamblers on the night of September 7, 1778. A scribe noted
that the beating was initiated when Carrasco claimed: "The *justicia* does not
have jurisdiction over me because I have a [military] superior who handles my
cases."[22] As the arresting official flogged Carrasco, he boasted that he would
prove once and for all how he had a greater authority to punish soldiers than
the officers of their units.

Most of the initial stages of *fuero* abuse took place at times like these, just
after capture. These were the moments when militiamen were most vulnerable. Until military authorities were notified of custody, the soldiers remained
at the full mercy of their captors, incarcerated, alone, and with few allies. The
fact of their militia status was left to prove, and civilian law enforcement agents
did their best to delay notifying the soldiers' military superiors. Even after the
military jurisdiction had been properly informed of the event and a soldier's
filiación papers had been secured, civilian authorities still found ways to stall.
A militiaman might remain in jail several months before being transferred to
his barracks. Sluggish legal procedures did not help matters. The operation of
colonial justice could be notoriously slow, partly given the great attention to
minute detail.[23] As documents were shuffled around from different offices,
soldiers remained in captivity, regardless of the nature of the crime, and regardless of whether they were innocent or guilty.[24]

Some additional situations serve to further illustrate the militiamen's predicament. On the night of February 20, 1780, Francisco Patiño, a *mulato* soldier in the free-colored battalion of Mexico City, was brought to the *Acordada*
jail for having used a knife to stab a fellow militiaman. The conflict took place
in the context of a jealous rage. Patiño had been living in consensual union
with Maria Sabina de León, a *mulatta*, for nearly fifteen years. At eight in the
evening she left their house to buy bread but was casually diverted by Joseph
Thomas, a militiaman from Patiño's battalion. The two began talking, when
suddenly Patiño, who had been searching for her at home, approached them.
Patiño called her a *cochina* ("pig") and asked what she was doing speaking
with Joseph. He smacked her with a closed fist and drew his knife, slashing Joseph.

Three officials from the *Acordada* were nearby and chased down the assail-
ant. Almost immediately after apprehension, Patiño claimed *fuero* immunity,
but the *Acordada*'s scribes deliberately left the invocation out of his testimony.
It was not long after his capture that members of Patiño's company began to
receive word of the fracas. But the news reached them by hearsay rather than
by proper notification from the civilian authorities. That same night, Patiño's
second sergeant appeared at the *Acordada* jail to confirm his colleague's militia
status and to submit his *filiación* papers. He was rebuffed. Tribunal officials

readily dismissed the evidence, stating that Patiño was just a lowly musician in the free-colored corps, not a true, rifle-bearing soldier. In their eyes, his menial military role, along with his race, demoted his legal standing. He was not entitled to the *fuero*. But in truth, they had no say in the matter. Only military authorities could establish *desafuero*.

Over the next few days, others testified to Patiño's militia status. Among them was José Molina, the standard bearer of Patiño's unit. He approached the tribunal officials after spying his comrade in a holding cell during a brief visit to the *Acordada* jail. However, like that of the rest, his testimony had little effect. After more than two months in captivity, an angry Patiño managed to draft a letter to his subinspector. He noted that due process entitled him to confinement in his barracks, at least until the matter of culpability was resolved. Moreover, in his mind the alleged crime was not serious. He had gotten word that Joseph Thomas had made a complete recovery from his knife wound just eight days after the event. Spurred by the letter, by April 25, 1780, the *auditor de guerra* was notified of the situation and a full military investigation was instigated. In the meantime, the *Acordada* proceeded with its own ruling. By May 17, its ministers had resolved to sentence Patiño to two hundred lashes and eight years of hard labor in the artillery unit of Havana. They wasted no time in issuing the punishment. Patiño was whipped publicly in the streets of Mexico City that same day. In the meantime, the military inquiry was en route for consideration by the viceroy.

Military authorities were outraged when they learned of the *Acordada*'s actions. Subinspector Benito Tineo and the *auditor de guerra* had not even finished deliberating as to whether the case belonged under civil or military jurisdiction. Furthermore, they alleged that Patiño had successfully established his militia affiliation and should have been released to his barracks in late February. In the end, the machinations of the subinspector and *auditor* managed to free Patiño, but only after protracted debate with *Acordada* ministers. Patiño spent an additional month in jail before going home.[25]

The case is characteristic in many ways. First of all, shortly after apprehension, the details of the crime quickly became afterthought. All of the people involved in the dispute, including the victims and aggressor, were free-coloreds. The combination of their low social status and race weighed heavily in the final outcome, in that it was not Joseph's violent actions that were the core issues of justice for the *Acordada*, but rather that Patiño had dared walk the streets with a prohibited weapon. The larger implications of this event were more important than the event itself. Since Patiño was a *mulato*, a race deemed naturally inclined toward aggressive criminal behavior, the courts resolved that something had to be done before similar actions threatened to harm others who were not of his same class and caste. Weapons in the hands of such people endangered the lives of wealthy whites as well as the free-colored poor.

Therefore, the *Acordada*'s stiff punishment was designed to send a message aimed at limiting the context of future danger, rather than dealing a punishment appropriate to the particulars of the case at hand.

The ordeal was recast in a different light once the military inquiry was underway, this time as a struggle over procedure and jurisdiction. In Subinspector Tineo's letter to the viceroy, he mentioned that Patiño, like countless militiamen before him, was victim of an abuse of rights. Again, the specificity of the case became lost in the larger questions of rights and privilege. Patiño's situation became merely another statistic in the military's ongoing struggles with civil authorities. It is unsurprising that the subinspector and *auditor de guerra* became personally involved in the issue. The soldier's race and class became subsumed under the consideration of corporate privilege. It was corporate privilege that defined the place these military authorities enjoyed in society. Any reduction in its value, even if launched against a free-colored soldier, had a direct impact on the prestige of the posts these white officers enjoyed. In this sense, these officials approached the matter with racial blinders on. Corporate, not racial, privilege was at stake.

Patiño's ordeal underscores the fact that while free-colored *fuero* coverage may have encompassed a much broader range of individuals after 1767, its impact was limited because the privilege did not always work. There were many more men like Patiño, some languishing in jail for having committed no crime at all. In 1778, Subinspector Benito Tineo recorded that thirty-two soldiers had officially complained about violations of their *fuero* rights by ministers of the *Acordada* and *Real Sala de Crimen*.[26] Widespread *fuero* transgressions dampened troop morale. In Mexico City during the late 1770s, only one-third the number of militiamen that had regularly attended military exercises in previous years continued to do so. When confronted by their captains about their absences, many conveyed that they were dismayed by the constant infringement upon their legal rights. Since being a militiaman seemed to invite trouble, they believed that they were better off simply being ordinary citizens.[27] The soldiers had a point. The ease with which militiamen were apprehended and charged in Mexico City meant that in practice, militia status did not significantly distinguish them from the social ranks whence they were drawn. Particularly in the larger urban centers, lower-status artisans—not to mention unskilled workers and the unemployed—were almost powerless against arrest. Gabriel Haslip's study of urban crime in Mexico City reveals that in 1796, 48 percent of apprehended criminals in Mexico City were lower-status artisans, while another 30 percent were unskilled or unemployed. The elite and middle classes were rarely apprehended, representing just 4 percent of jailings.[28] Most of Mexico City's free-colored militiamen were lower-level artisans, the group most prone to arrest. Although a statistical study has yet to be performed for the instances of military *fuero* violations, based on the evidence reviewed here, the pattern of easy jailing among artisans does not appear to have been seriously interrupted by the possession of *fuero* privileges.

Not all free-colored soldiers received equal *fuero* support. We have already mentioned that there were distinctions in terms of the extent of *fuero* coverage according to rank. Rank also tempered the sentencing of cases as well. In 1788, when Lieutenant Ignacio Domínguez murdered Joseph del Campo in self-defense, he was sentenced to eight years exile at a distance of twenty leagues from his hometown of Puebla. Other homicides performed by lower-ranking militiamen received much stiffer penalties. Soldiers Joseph Ignacio Corbello and Joseph Francisco Castillo were executed in 1792 for committing murder and robbery.[29] José Anzures, an infantryman in Mexico City, was sentenced to ten years' hard labor in the *presidio* of Havana for accidentally stabbing Vicente Ramierez on the night of June 14, 1787. The sentence was reduced to ten years' light labor at San Juan de Ulua after Anzures was diagnosed with tuberculosis while awaiting the final decision of his case in the *Acordada* jail.[30] In Puebla, two militia foot soldiers were sentenced to exile for homicides they committed in the late 1770s. These sentences were upgraded to two and three years' hard labor at San Juan de Ulua in Veracruz.[31] In contrast to the relative comfort of involuntary exile, *presidio* labor sentences were exceptionally harsh. If the assignment were distant from one's place of residence, the initial journey to the site was rife with difficulties, as convicts were routinely beaten and scorned by their escorts. Upon arrival, the workers were faced with poor dietary and living conditions. Rations were insufficient. Clothing was often sold for tobacco or alcohol, resulting in a considerable degree of "nakedness" among the laborers. Cramped living spaces often saw slave laborers locked away indiscriminately with the accused criminals, their status being virtually indistinguishable within the compound.[32]

Avoiding harsh punishment via the *fuero* was not only a function of rank, but also of connections. Convicted murderer Lieutenant Ignacio Domínguez did not begin serving his exile sentence until after 1790, more than two years after the judge's ruling. Prior to that time, he managed to avoid punishment through cultivating a close relationship with the militia's subinspector. He even used his friendship to negotiate having his place of exile moved to nearby Atlixco, just four leagues outside of Puebla. There, he would still be able to retain his militia officer commission, since the free-colored companies of Atlixco were considered part of Puebla's battalion. Domínguez's good fortune stemmed from the fact that Subinspector Camuñez had been able to reroute the case file into the hands of his friends during the years 1788 to 1789, ignoring standard military protocol. But Camuñez died suddenly in 1789, leaving Domínguez without the protection of his primary military patron. Camuñez's interim replacement was not so forgiving of Domínguez's crime, and upon hearing the details of the case, he promptly called for the lieutenant to be placed under military arrest. News of Domínguez's delayed punishment was passed to the *auditor de guerra* and viceroy. After a surprisingly quick deliberation, Domínguez lost his militia commission and was immediately banished from the province.[33]

Military connections could also include family ties. *Pardo* soldier Ignacio Rosario, the son of Captain Gregorio Rosario, went on a thieving spree in Tuxtla during 1791. He stole two mules, a chair, some reins, and several pigs from various individuals around town. Upset residents denounced him to his company's superior officer, Captain Diego de Palma, who also happened to be Tuxtla's *juez político* and the *teniente de justicia*. Palma proceeded to capture Ignacio and pressed charges. The details of the case were then forwarded to Tuxtla's supreme military commander; however, the whole ordeal was handled half-heartedly. Ignacio spent just twenty-six days in jail before being set free.

That was not done without criticism. Both Tuxtla's commander and the *auditor de guerra* preferred a stiffer punishment and ruled that if Ignacio were found guilty of the crimes, he should be sent to the public works projects at the *presidio* of Havana. But the decisions of these high military authorities did not take a firm hold in Tuxtla. Distance from the colony's principal bureaucratic centers provided the town's legal authorities, namely Palma, with more operating room to act independently. Moreover, Palma occupied an incredibly influential position in the town. Being both a prominent military authority as well as the chief civilian authority, he was in an advantageous position to customize the law as he saw fit. His actions reflect his split loyalties. On the one hand, acting as a conscientious *teniente de justicia*, he felt obliged to hold Ignacio in detention for the sake of his public image in the town. He even placed Ignacio in chains for emphasis. As an added touch, he managed to procure a small monetary retribution for the aggrieved parties, thereby conveying the sense that he was fulfilling his responsibilities. But on the other hand, Palma was not uninfluenced by the status of Ignacio's father, as well as his own militia ties. As pressures mounted for him to increase the sentence against Ignacio, even from the military's own representatives, Palma opted to set the prisoner free, using a combination of authority derived from both his military and civilian legal jurisdictions.[34]

Lower-ranking soldiers whose militia connections were weak and who could not rely on the power of family ties were the most exposed to the abrogation of their *fuero* privileges. When the *mulato* soldier José Ignacio Pantoja raped a young woman in the summer of 1781, he remained in jail for almost three months before military authorities finally came to his assistance. He was ignored because, according to his superiors, he was a soldier in name only. He had virtually abandoned his units, almost never appearing when called to duty. Nor did he participate in training exercises or inspections. As if to emphasize the weakness of his corporate bond, it was a sergeant who eventually took up his case, rather than the customary commissioned officer. When word finally reached the subinspector that Pantoja's proceedings were already being handled by the civilian justices, his reaction was detached and unemotional, quite a contrast to many of the other cases he had handled that year. As a matter of routine, he notified the *auditor de guerra*, who proceeded to delegate full judicial authority to the civilian courts. In the end, the independent clamoring of Pantoja's mother may have had more to do with his eventual release than did his militia status.[35]

Could the *fuero* serve as a springboard for racial identity among the militiamen? Apparently, there were a number of factors that militated against that possibility. Quite simply, the majority of *fuero*-related crimes were highly personal. They were sex crimes, robberies, instances of domestic violence, homicides, gambling, illegal business transactions, and so forth. Almost all were transgressions of established social norms that were supposed to be adhered to by every colonist, regardless of race. When a soldier was captured in one of these acts, he invoked the *fuero* essentially to save himself from harmful prosecution. Invoking the *fuero* was an appeal to an established corporate right that happened to be conceded to free-colored companies. Being free-colored was not the determinant of the privilege. Consequently, the majority of *fuero* cases, as far as they transcended being personal matters, naturally lent themselves to easier interpretation within the context of jurisdictional feuds, rather than racial conflicts.

In our discussion of tribute exemption, there was a fundamental difference. The corporate right became extended to the larger community through practices of tribute exemption leniency. Therefore, what was originally just a corporate privilege became reinterpreted as racial privilege. An infraction regarding one free-colored, be he a militiaman or civilian, held ramifications for the whole. For the *fuero* to have meaning beyond the personal or even the corporate military realm, an appropriate context had to exist. Specifically, if the *fuero* was to assume a distinct racial meaning, then crimes had to be racially charged, or able to galvanize racial sensibilities. Flagrant abuses of the soldiers' *fuero* rights by nonmilitary authorities were more likely to trigger these concerns, rather than simple crimes performed by the soldiers themselves.

A hallmark feature of militia duty, the night patrols, produced one type of situation where issues of race became intertwined with the militiamen's duties and *fuero* privileges. Attacks on the soldiers came in various forms. There was outright racial slander, widespread public jeering, conflicts with white regular soldiers, exchanges of insults with civilians, and confrontations with municipal officials. In the larger cities, these were almost daily happenings. The affronts worked to unite the free-colored militiamen, solidifying a basic sense of difference between themselves and their critics. In situations like those that took place in Mexico during February of 1760, racial polarization was precipitated. Free-colored militiamen were repeatedly teased by soldiers from the

Crown Regiment that they had orders to kill off every *negro* and *mulato* in the free-colored battalion.[36]

Sometimes the accusations, taunts, and attacks leveled by colonial residents were wholly warranted. In Puebla during the 1720s, citizens perhaps rightly accused the militiamen of abusing their own authority while on patrol. Their allegations detailed freewheeling extortion, as free-colored militiamen apprehended the innocent, seized their belongings, and freed them only after a "contribution" of several reales. Many acts of resistance to free-colored authority and subsequent *fuero* violations stemmed from these concerns. However, in numerous other instances, such claims were conscious exaggerations launched by those who winced at the thought of free-coloreds occupying positions of power. The night, which had been legislated for so long as a restricted time for black activities, was becoming a time when they roamed freely, unmonitored, and with weapons. Early eighteenth-century Puebla grew to be a hotbed of intense rivalries between community elites, municipal authorities, and free-colored militiamen. Racial biases became intertwined with their jurisdictional and *fuero* disputes.

A 1720s incident involving Isidrio Herrera serves to demonstrate how the conflicts were manifested. At around 9:00 P.M. on September 19, 1725, Herrera, a shoemaker and militiaman in one of Puebla's free-colored companies, left his job to begin patrolling the city streets on the local night watch. Not having the proper arms with him, he took his *tranchete* on the beat, a small tool normally used for repairing shoes but extremely dangerous when used as a weapon. An hour later, Herrera ran into Captain Don Miguel Bermudez, a minor city official and an officer in the white militia corps. Apparently Bermudez had been tracking Herrera, having asked several people in the neighborhood as to his whereabouts. Immediately, Bermudez began interrogating Herrera, asking him angrily why he carried a *tranchete* instead of his halberd. Then he asked why Herrera wasn't wearing the proper insignia for the night watch. While Herrera fumbled for answers, Bermudez motioned for his assistant to seize him. Full of spite, Bermudez repeatedly called Herrera a dog. On the way to jail, Bermudez gave him one hundred lashes. Once they were in front of the jailhouse, Herrera was whipped again, this time to the sound of a trumpet and with a public pronouncement of his "crimes." After spending a miserable night in jail, Herrera was set free the following morning.[37]

The minor infraction of wielding the *tranchete* would have been resolved quickly under ordinary circumstances, perhaps with a verbal reprimand and a conversation with Herrera's superior officer. But race magnified the situation into a much larger affair. First, it is important to stress that the event was not a chance happening, but a premeditated action on the part of the city official. In his testimony of September 22, 1725, he admitted that what caused him to seek out Herrera were the actions and behavior of free-colored militiamen at large, rather than the simple transgressions of a single soldier. Often, he stated, when walking the streets of Puebla, coloreds could be found carrying illegal small arms, such as the *tranchete*. When asked what they were doing, these free-coloreds responded acerbically that they were "on patrol." This impertinence must have constantly grated on Bermudez. He further claimed that these "patrols" led to a great deal of crime and violence. When he had captured militiamen on these grounds in the past, they were quickly let free with the assistance of the *teniente* of the *alcalde mayor*. It was with that in mind that he resolved to make an example of Herrera.

Everything about the event emphasized theatricality, with the audience being the Puebla community at large. The loud exchange between Herrera and Bermudez served to attract attention. The words spoken by Bermudez rang with an air of authority: "Where is your insignia, why aren't you carrying your authorized weapons?" He was clearly trying to undermine Herrera on legal grounds, taking away his authority to be on the beat. Once that was accomplished, he gloated in victory, using some of the standard language of barroom bravado of the day, calling Herrera a dog. This action served to dehumanize the free-colored soldier. Then there was the quick recourse to corporal punishment. He could have inflicted a lesser sentence. He could have chosen other places to beat Herrera, perhaps behind the closed doors of the jail, as was more customary in similar instances in Mexico City.[38] But for Bermudez, the whipping was for public display—the first series of lashings being administered on the street for all to see. Then, at the jailhouse, he awakened the surrounding neighborhood at 11:30 P.M. with trumpet blares and a public speech, treating the chance, white elite onlooker to a taste of colonial styled justice. Once Bermudez's actor had played out his role and recuperated in jail, he was set free, again re-emphasizing that the punishment and crime were not as much at issue for Bermudez as was the public show.

Although we have already seen a few instances in which corporal punishment was inflicted, it must be stressed that whippings were not a common form of discipline in colonial Mexico. Convict labor sentences were far more frequent, and in such a minor matter as this, brief confinement would have been the maximum penalty.[39] But as was discovered in later testimony, Bermudez inflicted the whippings more as a means of exhibiting the social distance that existed between himself and the free-colored militiamen. He detailed in his deposition how he fully understood that when *mulatos, negros,* mestizos, *sambingos,* and *lobos* were found publicly carrying small arms, they were to have their weapons seized after the first offense. A second offense would incur a ten-day jail sentence. Third-time offenders would receive one hundred lashes, *if they were slaves.* Free-coloreds, on the other hand, were to be perpetually banished from the province upon their third transgression. Bermudez's sentence clearly exceeded these terms, essentially equating Herrera's first-time infraction with the seriousness of a third-time slave violation. This was the point. Bermudez was demonstrating himself to be above the law, able to inflict whatever punishment he desired. By contrast, he held free-coloreds accountable to the strictest possible interpretation of the law. He read the legal code literally when it forbade blacks from using small arms, and cast a blind eye at the special legal protections that were afforded to militiamen, despite the fact that under the militia provisions, Herrera actually had a valid case in wielding his *tranchete* on patrol. When questioned about his extreme behavior, Bermudez intimated that Herrera's flogging was done as symbolic atonement for the collective breach of arms laws by free-coloreds in Puebla.

Gossip travels fast. Witnesses to the event passed the information on quickly, so that soon much of Puebla was informed of the news. The free-colored militiamen wasted no time in pressing legal charges. By September 22, 1725, just three days after the event, the *sargento mayor* and all the captains of the free-colored companies presented a case for the viceroy's consideration. Through the eloquent wording of their lawyer, they argued that their military privileges were being violated. The subsequent case testimony provides a kind of cross-section of the observers, and begins to demonstrate how the event affected and reflected the thinking of some of the townspeople. On one side, there were the supporters of Herrera. These witnesses included two whites, one of whom had known Herrera since he was fourteen, the other being just a casual observer of events. Another batch of Herrera's supporters included free-coloreds, many of whom were militiamen. On the defense were witnesses who had prior histories of confrontation with Puebla's colored militiamen. What is interesting about all the witness testimonies, particularly in Herrera's behalf, is the uniformity of the arguments and facts presented. Some testimonies are identical, line per line. This causes us to question whether the witnesses actually saw the events they described, whether they were influenced by gossip, or if they were well coached before giving testimony.

The courts were pressed with reaching a decision. Free-colored militiamen sought Bermudez's immediate punishment for the abuse of *fuero* rights. Bermudez sought the abolition of militia rounds and further curtailment of free-colored military privileges. Opting to tread neutral ground, the courts ruled that the night patrols were to continue but stipulated that a small white contingent would have to be incorporated into the patrolling units, in hope of taming some of the militiamen's allegedly belligerent behavior.[40]

In some aspects, the Herrera incident resembles the earlier *fuero* infraction we observed regarding Francisco Patiño. Both cases dealt with prohibited weapons. But in Patiño's situation, the crime of bearing the knife outweighed the issue of race in the minds of *Acordada* officials. The proceedings of the case were handled in almost race-neutral terms. In the Herrera affair, race definitely assumed stronger overtones, both in the events surrounding the *fuero* violation and in the ensuing litigation. Interestingly, race was seen as more of a biting issue in the eyes of the municipal authorities than for the militiamen. After all, it was Bermudez who had difficulty reconciling militia duties with the free-colored castes and who wheeled in race as an aspect of the case. From the soldiers' perspective, their militia privileges were the salient matter at hand, which was reflected in the types of arguments they conveyed to the courts. This did not mean that they were left unaffected by Bermudez's race-based assaults. Indeed, Bermudez's quick infliction of corporal punishment and his perspective of viewing free-colored soldiers in the same legal category as slaves produced instant shocks in the corps. In fact, the use of corporal punishment in this case probably hurt more than ordinary *fuero* abuses, precisely because it was aimed at reminding the soldiers of their links to slavery's chains. However, the men understood that their best tactic in curbing future race-based slights was to keep the legal focus of their confrontation based on matters of corporate privilege.

To an extent, the plan worked. While not achieving a resounding victory over Bermudez, the soldiers did not lose, either. It was only because Bermudez had successfully managed to recontextualize the case, bringing into evidence matters that extended beyond Herrera's immediate actions, that the crown was able to find fault with both parties. The courts may not have been a perfect environment for free-colored militiamen to deal with outsiders' challenges to their privileges. As seen here and elsewhere, royal adjudicators were predisposed toward obliging the concerns of the colonial elite before that of the free-colored soldiers. But in hindsight, the militiamen were still able to subdue their critics in the courts to the extent that the basic structure of their rights was preserved. Importantly, the legacy of their military services came into play in their arguments, adding weight to their position. Bermudez's attempt to play the race card did not work, because the royal officials who deliberated on the case were prodded to see beyond the concerns of race, contemplating the overall usefulness of free-colored militia services. Such an outlook from crown officials offered the militiamen sufficient maneuvering room to negotiate their status in society, allowing them to use their position as soldiers to alter the effects of local opinions regarding race.

More so than the night patrols in New Spain's urban centers, it was the colony's rural villages, particularly those possessing large free-colored populations, that proved to be the most fertile ground for the escalation of *fuero* abuses into wider racial issues. Oftentimes, a high percentage of the free-colored male population were militiamen in these towns, giving *pardoness*, or free-coloredness, a direct correlation with military law and privilege. In such an atmosphere, there was a concrete understanding that free-coloreds possessed a grounded legal status that could differ from laws traditionally assigned to the black population. When violated, the rights of soldiers could become interpreted as an abrogation of the rights of the free-colored populace in general. Abuses to high-ranking individuals might generate a quick free-colored response. Usually, their high community and militia standing placed them in a special position for reprieve. Abuses to lower-ranking individuals normally had to be of greater magnitude, and with wider implications to the free-colored population, in order to produce a race-based community or militia response.

Events in Acayucan present us with a sample scenario. Free-coloreds constituted the second most numerous racial group in the province, numbering just over a quarter of the population in the late eighteenth century.[41] Militiamen represented anywhere between 38 and 48 percent of the entire free-colored population.[42] On April 11, 1762, Francisco Salomon, a *pardo* soldier in the militia unit of Lieutenant Juan Domingo Ramos, was dragged into jail for threatening to punch the *teniente general* of the province. The ordeal was precipitated as Salomon was resisting arrest for "living badly with his wife."[43] Rumor had it that the incensed *teniente*, Don Antonio Guerrero, was preparing to retaliate for the feint by issuing a severe sentence of one hundred to two hundred lashes. At this point, the crime escalated into a *fuero* abuse, as the *teniente* was going to inflict punishment independently, without prior consultation with the proper military authorities. When Lieutenant Domingo Ramos got word of the news from his wife the following day, he responded in an uproar. "Never before in Acayucan has a *pardo* been whipped," he exclaimed in later testimony.[44] He felt an obligation to act immediately.

So far, the event was unfolding like countless others in the colonial archives. A free-colored soldier had been rudely tossed into jail under the threat of corporal punishment. Issues of *fuero* underlay the jailing. There was a quick response by a militia leader upon his hearing rumors of the event. However, what happened next begins to distinguish the case from the rest. At 11:00 A.M. on Easter Sunday morning, Domingo Ramos began visiting some of the homes of his fellow soldiers, calling them together for a secret assembly. Holy Week was an opportune time for militia mobilizations, since all the soldiers from disparate parts of the province were united in the *cabecera* for the observance of religious festivities. The militia had also been performing special patrol duty during those days, striving to keep order amid the drunken revelry. Shortly after Passover, however, Acayucan's *teniente* had disbanded the militia, inasmuch as they had fulfilled their protective responsibilities. Therefore, it was without the sanctioned authority of command that Lieutenant Domingo Ramos was summoning his soldiers. He made nine house calls in all. With considerable discretion, he asked the men to convene privately at his house under the cover of night. The subsequent details of the case are cloudy. While languishing in jail, the lieutenant claimed that his summons was an innocent one. He merely wanted to assemble the men in order to pay a visit to the jailhouse, where the group would kindly request Salomon's release. But other testimony contradicted the supposedly benign nature of Domingo Ramos's intentions. One militiaman confessed that the soldiers were asked to bring their weapons with them in order to attempt a jailbreak. This would not have been the first time that Domingo Ramos had tried such a maneuver, having assisted the town's priest in liberating a friend during the previous decade. Unfortunately for the plotters, word of the scheme leaked out. Two whites overheard discussions of the affair and denounced the soldiers forthwith to the *teniente*. Domingo Ramos was called to answer to charges of conspiracy. After getting into an armed struggle with the *teniente* himself, Domingo Ramos was arrested.[45]

Rich with anecdote, drama, and action, Domingo Ramos's case file provides unique insights into free-colored militia affairs. But for our purposes, just a few major points need to be highlighted. The first is that Domingo Ramos's behavior demonstrates that on occasion, the free-colored militia could be used as an instrument to protect the greater rights of the *pardo* population as a whole. Importantly, Domingo Ramos viewed the situation in these terms himself. Although Salomon was a member of his militia company, what most irked Domingo Ramos about the ordeal was not simply the violation of military *fuero*, but that the prospect of whippings could lead to greater arbitrary abuses by the *teniente* for all free-coloreds in Acayucan.[46] To reiterate: "Never before in Acayucan has a *pardo* been whipped," he exclaimed. As with Bermudez in Puebla, the possibility of witnessing a free-colored endure corporal punishment jeopardized overall *pardo* community status, debasing them to the level of common slaves. The *teniente*'s wanton threats of punishment had to be contained. The testimony provided by white witnesses corroborates that other free-colored soldiers shared Domingo Ramos's viewpoint. The conversations the *españoles* allegedly overheard bespoke of the militiamen boasting that they were ready and willing to take up arms against the *justicia* to prevent the flogging. According to the soldiers' knowledge, whipping any free *pardo*, not just a militiaman, was against the law. The town's women had already acted to prevent an instance of corporal punishment years earlier, staging a jailbreak to release a man slated for punishment. Now it was the militia's turn to stand in defense of *pardo* rights.[47]

Whether Domingo Ramos was planning an attack on the jailhouse or not, what we see from the affair is that the militia provided him with a crown-endorsed framework within which to present his views and to act. His position as head of his company granted him the power of command over troops, although he stretched the terms of his authority during these events. His uniform, his insignia, and his sword were additional symbols of authority that he flaunted at various moments during his seditious activities. When called upon to answer to the *teniente general* for charges of conspiracy, Domingo Ramos took the time to change from his field clothes into full military uniform, an act that thoroughly irritated the *teniente*. Domingo Ramos understood that in military dress he ceased to be a mere subordinate citizen, but was a soldier with his own privileges and jurisdiction. Costumed as a soldier, he could negotiate or retaliate with the provincial government, possessing symbolic crown backing. As if to emphasize the act of demoting Domingo Ramos to commoner status, one of the first acts his captors performed when he was apprehended was to strip him of his militia insignia. The symbolic support Domingo Ramos conveyed in uniform finally materialized seven months later, when the military *auditor* exonerated him from blame in the case and asked that all seized possessions be returned to his custody. He was even to be reinstated to his militia post without restrictions.

Perhaps because the plot was discovered, free-colored testimonies showed serious rifts of opinion regarding the attempt to free Salomon. None of the militiamen questioned ever admitted to supporting Domingo Ramos's cause. Some claimed to have been drunk when their lieutenant initially approached them. In a stupor, they allegedly misunderstood his beckon, or could not recall his request for their assistance. Others said that while they heard out Domingo Ramos's appeal, they never intended to comply with his wishes. All professed complete obedience and primary allegiance to the *justicia*, being submissive to their militia leader only in secondary fashion. One can completely understand the soldiers' testimony. They sought to distance themselves from Domingo Ramos at any cost. At the time they were being interviewed, Domingo Ramos was sitting in a jail cell, stricken with cholera. The militiamen sought every means to avoid a like fate. But perhaps their actions speak more loudly than their testimonies. It is telling that none of the free-colored soldiers who so adamantly expressed their allegiance to the *teniente* ever denounced Domingo Ramos to the authorities during the hours preceding their lieutenant's capture. In a town that seemed rather racially divided, one can only suspect that if whites had not uncovered the plot, the situation might have played out differently.

While the Domingo Ramos episode is a good one for demonstrating how a specific *fuero* case could become a larger racial issue with communitywide implications, the details of the case file leave out many of the processes involved in understanding the development of racial identity. Just how did the town's free-coloreds come to view themselves as such? What was the full nature of the relationship between the military and race? How did *fuero* rights tap into these larger racial themes?

Perhaps another example, fleshed out in careful historical detail, can clarify some of these deeper questions. In rural coastal towns, there were many forces that helped to construct a free-colored identity. Militia participation was but one of these. Political, economic, and social relationships combined to create a sense of *pardoness* or *mulatoness*. Consider the jurisdiction of Tamiagua, located along the northern coastal area of the intendancy of Veracruz.[48] As in Acayucan, the free-colored presence was marked. As late as 1791, there were 4,344 *pardos* and *mulatos* in residence, as opposed to 336 *españoles*, 58 *castizos*, and 95 mestizos. Over half of the free-colored population lived in either the head town of Tamiagua or in the surrounding haciendas and *ranchos* located within five leagues of the *cabecera*. Aside from Tamiagua proper, there were

three other major towns in the jurisdiction: Tuxpan, Tihuatlan, and Tema-
pache. All were situated within twelve leagues of Tamiagua. In terms of military participation, a substantial portion of the adult male population was under arms. Before military reforms took effect between 1763 and 1781, there were
between 500 and 800 *pardo* men enrolled in the jurisdiction's militia, with
more than 400 consistently registered in the town of Tamiagua.[49] After the reforms of 1781, the units were downsized, so that there were 663 men of all races
in the militia.[50] In 1793, the forces were reduced again, so that there were only
four provincial companies, with 448 men.[51] Nevertheless, the coverage of
military privilege and *fuero* remained high until this period, mostly in Tamiagua itself, which continued to retain the greatest number of companies.

The economy of the region was primarily dedicated to agriculture. The
secondary towns cultivated pepper, sugar cane, maize, beans, and cotton. Livestock, both *ganado mayor* and *menor*, was raised in Tihuatlan and on the vast
estate of the Marqués de Uluapa. There was some light industry, namely the
production of wax, jugs, and wooden items. Most of these products were fab-
ricated in Tuxpan. However, despite the apparent variety of economic endeavors, the jurisdiction's reputation was built on fishing, especially in the
cabecera. Residents there made excellent use of their location near the lake and
rivers of Tamiagua to reap excellent catches. Shrimping became a regional spe-
cialty. For improved fishing opportunities, some chose to construct homes on
a large island, the Isla de Lobo, situated in the lake. From there, they could easily sally forth in canoes to make their catches.[52] Estimates from the 1780s conveyed that the fishermen gathered between thirty thousand and forty thousand
arrobas of fish per year, fish that was later distributed to major markets such as
Mexico City.[53]

To fully understand the development of racial identity in Tamiagua, one
must inevitably understand the relationship of the people to their economy.
Long before the militia became an important bearer of privilege in the jurisdiction, the region's inhabitants were involved in struggles over fishing rights,
access to fishing equipment, and land claims. The way in which these disputes
unfolded provided opportunities for an articulation of racial difference. *Pardoness, mulatoness,* and whiteness came to have distinct meaning in economic
and political contexts, as racial groups positioned themselves to garner added
fishing benefits from the crown and provincial authorities. At a later point,
militia privilege served to solidify the process of racial differentiation that had
already been underway. Therefore, before examining the subject of *fuero* violations, it is important to trace the evolution of how race came to play an important role in Tamiagua's economy and politics. The clearest manifestations
of racial difference were found in the *cabecera*.

For nearly a century after the conquest, free-coloreds, Indians, and whites
coexisted in the town of Tamiagua without major discord. Demographic decline caused by illness and disease struck the indigenous population hard,

virtually destroying a thriving pre-Hispanic commercial area that was controlled by the Nahuas but populated by Huastecos.[54] In the wake of the demographic decline, families of whites, mestizos, and free-coloreds began migrat-
ing to the territory with increasing frequency. By 1601, signs of conflict arose.
The dwindling indigenous population felt that their fishing privileges were in
jeopardy from whites seeking to restrict their access to Tamiagua's rivers and
sandbars. A case was brought before the *Real Audiencia* that year in an attempt
to secure Indian fishing rights. In 1603, it was resolved that the two groups
were to have equal use of the main river and lake, and that neither was to im-
pede the other's endeavors. Matters were complicated by the fact that not only
were fishing rights at stake in the legislation, but access to equipment as well.
Traditionally, there had been community-wide access to boats, *jacales* (shacks),
fishing nets, and other instruments of the trade. Of special regard were the
large and expensive shrimp nets. Prior to 1603, whites seem to have paid the
town government a small fee for the use of these materials. Indians were excluded from payment. Apparently, this arrangement was to be maintained after the 1603 decree.

New problems arose in 1644. That year, the *vecinos* of Tamiagua made an
attempt to secure an official land title (*composición*) for use and ownership of
the river.[55] On April 4, 1644, the title was granted at the price of two thousand
pesos, but under strict provisions. Although whites had largely footed the bill,
the deed's issuance was not to preclude any racial group from having access to
fishing rights or the communally shared fishing equipment.[56] In fact, Indians
were to be given first preference in selecting fishing locations and gear. These
preferential rights did not bother the Spaniards, since Indian numbers had
fallen to the point that their presence was almost insignificant in Tamiagua.
But the number of free-coloreds had begun to soar. Although free-coloreds
had always been a part of the pueblo from the time of its Spanish refounda-
tion, between the years 1644 and 1645, they outnumbered whites by a ratio of
three to one.[57] Whites were stingy when it came to extending benefits to this
large population group. In effect, 1644 signaled a shift in how the traditional
debates over fishing rights were to be played out in the future. Whereas the
sixteenth- and early seventeenth-century debates centered around Indians and
whites, the latter half of the seventeenth century and the early eighteenth century witnessed the growing prominence of free-coloreds in the discussions.

Shortly after the 1644 land title was issued, free-colored representatives
Francisco Alejandro, Christobal Sánchez, and Manuel de la Cruz wrote a letter
to the viceroy stating that prejudice was being displayed against members of
their race by whites. The *mulatos* of the Tamiagua had contributed a full 650
pesos toward the *composición* but were not being given the same fishing rights
as other residents. In their estimation, the problem emanated from those responsible for implementing the terms of the decree, as well as those in charge
of distributing the town's fishing equipment. In both cases, these men were

white *vecinos* who had personally paid handsome sums toward the *composición*. Two men, Antonio González Rollette and Antonio González Leiton, were singled out for special reproach. Both were Portuguese immigrants who served the town in the capacity of *jueces comisarios*. When fishing nets were distributed, these two made sure that the nine best nets were always reserved for white use, while the six worst were given to the *mulatos*.

The *mulatos* argued that they were not to be treated in this manner. Not only did their financial contribution make them equally as deserving of fishing privileges as whites, but in addition they were *hijos de naturales del pueblo*, meaning that they were born to long-time residents of the town. This longevity was a lot more than many recent white immigrants could claim.[58] But the *mulatos'* statement was full of double-entendre. *Natural* was a synonym for "Indian" in the colonial period. Hence, free-coloreds shrewdly played upon their parental links to the indigenous community in their arguments, being completely aware that these connections might allow them to partake of the highly privileged fishing rights that the Indians enjoyed. For those who lacked direct ancestral bloodlines, the free-colored representatives argued that a great many of their number had taken Indian brides and were thus tied to Tamiagua's indigenous population through marital links.

Part of the experience of being free-colored was that one's racial status was at once clear and ambiguous. Clarity stemmed from the fact that *mulatos* and *pardos* were not white, black, or Indian. Ambiguity stemmed from the possibility that free-coloreds could be affiliated with any one of these racial groups. Consequently, free-coloreds could manipulate the expression of their race to fit any of the parent racial categories, while at the same time claiming to be a unique group of their own. In Tamiagua, that was certainly the exercise free-coloreds engaged in during the mid-seventeenth century. In the same breath that the free-colored spokesmen bannered their indigenous heritage, they also dispelled notions lodged by white *vecinos* that free-coloreds failed to constitute a distinct *vecindad*, or community. The basis for enjoying preferential access to fishing rights depended upon internal community cohesion, which Tamiagua's whites systematically denied the free-coloreds displayed but which the free-coloreds tried hard to sustain.

The free-colored spokesmen continued their letter. To strengthen their eligibility for fishing privileges, they noted that free-coloreds had served the town well as exemplary soldiers. Tamiagua was open prey to pirate raids and hostile Chichimec incursions. More so than whites, free-colored militiamen claimed to have provided punctual and useful services in His Majesty's name. By adding the element of military duty to their arguments, the free-coloreds sought additional leverage in their negotiations. Before closing their letter, they took another snipe at Tamiagua's whites. Those most responsible for restricting free-colored fishing access were the Portuguese residents of the town. Free-coloreds had learned that the crown had published a *cédula* that legally prevented people of Portuguese origin from residing in ports. Since Tamiagua was located along the Gulf coast, the free-coloreds insinuated that the law demanded a prompt relocation of the worrisome Portuguese inhabitants.[59]

The crown resolved that free-coloreds and whites were to have equal fishing privileges. The decisive argument in the decision was that free-coloreds had paid a fair share of the *composición*. On these grounds, any local justices or *jueces* found violating their rights could be fined five hundred pesos per infraction. Except for the suggestion to deport Tamiagua's Portuguese residents, crown officials essentially adopted the proposals forwarded by the free-colored spokesmen in terms of how to proceed with distributing fishing equipment. Their letter requested that the best fishing nets be distributed among the races in fourths, and the worst ones in thirds.[60]

The decision took effect on paper only. In 1661, *pardos* and *mulatos* were found once again leveling the same complaints of previous decades to the viceregal authorities. The men responsible for distributing fishing equipment continued to be biased in how they issued the nets and boats. Safeguards against these practices had supposedly been instituted. Each year's distributors were to be publicly elected from a lot of disinterested candidates. But the *alcalde mayor*, in direct violation of the law, thoroughly influenced the voting process and helped fix the slate of candidates, thereby ensuring that his cronies acquired the posts. Then he arranged for the best equipment to be given to his favorites. In the face of these ploys, free-coloreds continued pressing their arguments of old. They stressed that white turnover in Tamiagua was high, meaning that most whites benefiting from the illegal practices were recent arrivals. These were not true *vecinos*. Simply on account of seniority, free-coloreds argued that they were entitled to the most comprehensive fishing privileges.[61]

Free-colored arguments shifted gears in the late seventeenth and early eighteenth centuries as a combination of added legal experience and failed petitions gave *pardos* and *mulatos* more political savvy. Instead of emphasizing their links to the indigenous community, which had gained limited results, free-coloreds tried buttressing their ties to their white forefathers. A new history of the town emerged to support their arguments. In 1732, various testimonies taken by Tamiagua's free-colored elders brought the salient features of the story into full relief. There were several phases in the revised local history. Shortly after the town was refounded by Spaniards, whites were forced to seek black and *mulatta* wives, given the dearth of available Spanish women. Realizing the ample opportunities for fishing and shrimping, whites and free-coloreds founded a thriving fishing industry, and together they purchased the deed to the Tamiagua River. Over time these white ancestors died off, leaving their *mulato* children to replace them. The *mulatos* proceeded to become part of the larger, expanding *pardo* community (*vecindad*). In this very fluid conception of race and time, *whites passed into being free-colored* over the course of the seventeenth century. Because of this, although the original deed to the river specified that the *composición* had been paid by both whites and blacks, in the eighteenth century there were no whites to speak of in Tamiagua whose forefathers had been around at the moment of the deed's purchase. All pure whites were relative newcomers, thereby excluded from having rightful access to the river and the community's fishing equipment. Additionally, a great number of whites who fished in the town were residents of distant *ranchos* who appeared periodically only to exploit Tamiagua's rich fishing resources.[62]

Of course, Tamiagua's resident whites opposed this interpretation of the town's history and responded with their own vision of events.[63] Understandably, from their perspective, privileges were more concretely attached to race and were not transferable over time. Their arguments pointed to the legal documents of 1644–45, stressing that privileges garnered by whites in one era applied to whites in later periods, regardless of their place of origin. To uphold their static view of race and privilege, they stressed that when the town's whites initially gave their monetary contribution for the *composición*, they did so as a pueblo, meaning that they did so as a specific racial group. The implicit understanding was that future pueblos of whites in Tamiagua would be entitled to the same benefits. Since these early whites also footed a full three-fourths of the *composición*'s costs, eighteenth-century whites argued that they, like their "forefathers," should be granted primary access to choice fishing locations and equipment. At the very least, all fishing materials should be equally divided in thirds among the town's three races.[64]

While seemingly equitable on the surface, white pleas for an equal distribution of fishing equipment and river access would have seriously prejudiced the much larger free-colored population. According to rumor, there were only four whites who physically lived in the town, and just thirty Indian families. By contrast, there were at least four hundred free-coloreds in residence.[65] Matters finally achieved a measure of conclusion in 1732–33 as free-colored efforts and arguments to secure exclusive hold over the river prevailed. Viceregal authorities issued an *amparo de possessión*, which officially passed all fishing and river rights over to the *pardos*.[66] The town's racial divide, already sharp, was now cut deeper, as threats were loudly exchanged between the races to burn each other's homes to ashes.[67]

At the same time that struggles over fishing rights managed to congeal Tamiagua's free-coloreds into an identifiable community, replete with a political agenda, even tighter cohesion was provided by militia ties. Documents from early eighteenth-century Tamiagua frequently refer to the town's free-coloreds in a type of terminology seldom seen elsewhere in the colony. In places such as Puebla, Mexico City, and Veracruz, free-coloreds were most commonly discussed in documents simply as *pardos libres*, *morenos*, or *mulatos*. In Tamiagua, free-coloreds were consistently referred to as the *vecindad de pardos libres militares*—literally, the community of free-*pardo* soldiers.[68] The terminology was used both by crown officials and free-colored representatives. One can interpret the greater significance of the reference to indicate that military service became an integral part of what it meant to be free-colored in the town, regardless of whether all free-coloreds served in the militia or not. The military bond also became part of how the free-coloreds presented themselves to the state, and how they hoped they would be dealt with in terms of their petitions and privileges. Indeed, it is noteworthy that when they secured the *amparo de posesión* in 1732, their military affiliation and activities played an important role in bolstering their image, despite white attempts to mar their services.[69] In the language of some documents, they received the *amparo* as militiamen, not just as free-coloreds.[70]

Since being *pardo* was virtually indistinguishable from being a militiaman, when free-coloreds were wronged, the full weight of the militia might come to their aid. Such a situation occurred in 1710, when Joseph Alexandre was accosted by the local justices for owing a white merchant ten pesos. Unable to bring him to jail, the authorities seized his pavilion and chair. In mosquito-ridden country, pavilions were a necessary protection for people who spent a considerable amount of time outdoors. The act of confiscation upset several members of the free-colored community, particularly Nicolas Alexandre, the free-colored militia captain. Along with a small group of soldiers, he approached the *teniente de justicia* about the matter. The encounter became intense and two shots were fired, wounding the *teniente* in his rear.[71] Whites who were present on the scene quickly apprehended Nicolas and members of his party, violating Nicolas's *fuero*. Joseph Alexandre's wife was soon sought out and incarcerated as well. Two days passed before further action was taken. Meanwhile, Joseph retreated into hiding in an area known as El Limón, where he gathered together a host of *mulato* troops. On the third day, he commanded this group, over two hundred strong, in battle formation. The armed contingent marched to the jailhouse and intimidated the *teniente de justicia* into releasing all of the prisoners. After the incident, the militiamen set up camp on the other side of the Tamiagua River, anticipating a white reprisal. Several visits were made by high-level officials, including the *alcalde mayor* and the *teniente* of the neighboring jurisdiction of Techicontepec. The viceroy had issued a dispatch for the rebellious *mulatos* to be rounded up and turned in to the greater provincial authorities. However, the free-coloreds managed to stave off capture by paying a bribe of one thousand pesos. According to successive justice officials and provincial administrators, the *mulatos* and *pardos* were never the same after the event, becoming ever more bold in their resistance to authority. In the testimony of Tamiagua's white militia captain, Don Bartholome Gil, "[M]ulato pride has reached such proportions that they voice the ability to kill any *teniente*, and for one thousand pesos they will be set free, just as they did after wounding Don Eugenio Normate y Galarreta."[72]

This rather lengthy example has been provided to show how the militia bond was linked in an interconnected fashion with other forces toward establishing a racial identity. The explosive *fuero* event involving the Alexandres cannot be completely understood in isolation, but as part of the processes of free-colored land disputes, in which militia duty became a leverage mechanism. As *pardoness* and *mulatoness* assumed meaning in the town's political and economic struggles, the militia evolved, literally, into a definitional aspect of race—the *vecindad de pardos militares*. It was as a community of free-colored militiamen that benefits could be best secured. The interlocking bonds of race, family ties, and militia affiliations produced a situation whereby what might seem like a minor *fuero* violation could be intensely magnified by the militia call. The Alexandre affair was quite distinct from the situation in Acayucan. There, the threatened abuse of *fuero*, specifically the whippings, became seen as a violation of racial privilege, serving as the clarion call to drastic action. In Tamiagua, it took less to escalate the *fuero* abuse into a community-wide matter. One can postulate that this was because the militia link enveloped the town's free-coloreds almost completely. Nicolas Alexandre's rank and wide personal influence may have also played a factor in the militia rally. Hence, there was no need for further racial incentives to motivate a vigorous, free-colored response.

By way of summary, the free-colored *fuero*, as with the *fuero* of whites, assumed its greatest influence in the second half of the eighteenth century, alongside the new expansive thrusts of privilege launched by the Bourbon military reforms. *Fuero* was not a completely reliable benefit and resulted in many hardships and abuses for the men involved. The privilege was not enjoyed evenly by all troops. Rank, family ties, and internal militia relationships all affected how *fuero* worked. In its everyday, common application, *fuero* invocation held little ramification for precipitating race-based responses from the corps, or even inspiring grand, community-level action. The privilege was highly personal, centered on matters of intimate interest to the parties immediately involved. However, when civil officials violated free-colored *fuero* privileges, there was a better chance that a more comprehensive cast of characters would become involved in the case. Yet even in these instances, the preservation of corporate privileges tended to be the overriding concern of those who supported the aggrieved militiamen. It took special contexts or extraordinary instances of abuse to provoke matters into heightened racialized events.

In light of these considerations, it is unlikely that *fuero* alone presented a serious threat to the strictures of the caste system. On the other hand, it should not be dismissed as a "minor privilege."[73] The importance of the *fuero* rested in offering a framework within which colonial law could be critically questioned, even if unsuccessfully on many counts. For the militiamen, there were some cases in which courtroom battles tempered the malignant racial behavior of some municipal officials. In this fashion, the soldiers could alter their status in local society in limited ways. On even a smaller number of occasions, *fuero* provided opportunities, particularly in communities with a significant number of free-colored soldiers, to give a crown-sanctioned spin to bold free-colored claims of privilege for militiamen and civilians alike.

CHAPTER SIX

The Meaning of Race

THE PREVIOUS CHAPTERS have described the free-colored militia as an institution, examined the social profiles of its participants, and discussed the two most fundamental privileges associated with free-colored service. Throughout the analysis, the relationship between race and duty has been explored. The purpose here is to isolate the discussion on race to arrive at a better understanding of how it factored into free-colored militia relationships and translated into their larger self-image.

In analyzing how race functioned in the free-colored militia, it is important to provide an overview of the way that racial language was used. Understanding how and when terms like *pardo*, *moreno*, and *mulato* were utilized helps establish if there was a particular commitment by the crown, or by free-coloreds, to favor specific forms of racial references. Likewise, we can determine if there were significant similarities or differences between the crown's racial perspective and that of the militiamen. Table 36 provides a sample of 107 racial references taken from documents discussing free-colored militia affairs in Mexico City and Puebla. References by kings, viceroys, scribes, municipal authorities, and military auditors fall under the category of "Crown Officials." References by the militiamen themselves fall under the category of "Free-Colored Militiamen." The time span covered includes the years 1703–41, with the bulk of the references (45) coming from 1722–26. This time frame was selected because it represents a period when the militia experienced dramatic structural changes in each city. The implementation of added responsibilities, notably in the form of night patrols, altered the level of militia duty. Militia corporate bonds were affected in the process, and serious internal disputes arose regarding rank and privilege. All of the cases come from civil court records, which provide the most complete understanding of the early militia in both cities, given that military files from the Indiferentes de Guerra branch of the National Archives tend to concentrate on the post-1760s era. Furthermore, civil records provide great diversity in

TABLE 36

Racial References to Free-Colored Militia in Civil Documents, 1703–41

Type of Racial Reference	Crown Officials	Free-Colored Militiamen	Total
"Units of *Pardos* and *Morenos*"	38	22	60
"Units of *Mulatos* and *Negros*"	3	2	5
"Units of *Pardos* and *Negros*"	0	1	1
"Units of *Pardos*"	15	5	20
"Units of *Morenos*"	2	4	6
"Units of *Mulatos*"	7	0	7
Militia Reference without Racial Specification	2	6	8
TOTAL	67	40	107

Source: AGN, Civil, vol. 224, exp. 152; AGN, Civil, vol. 130, pt. 2, exp. 480; AGN, Civil, vol. 158, pt. 7, exp. 16; AGN, Civil, vol. 87, pt. 2, exp. 5; AGN, Civil, vol. 130, pt. 3b, exp. 29; AGN, Civil, vol. 130, pt. 2, unnumbered *expedientes*.

terms of information, making possible a look at relations between the militia and society.

The table reveals that the term "*pardos* and *morenos*" was the most common expression used to refer to free-colored militiamen, being employed frequently by both crown officials and free-colored soldiers. The category was among the more racially inclusive of those encountered in the civil records, accounting for so-called pure blacks, or *morenos*, and those who were racially mixed, that is, *pardos*. In the technically precise language of the caste system, *pardos* actually referred to the offspring of blacks and Indians, but in practice, the word developed into a synonym for *mulato*. "*Pardos*" and "*morenos*" were among the most euphemistic terms available in the caste nomenclature for free-coloreds. *Mulato*, for instance, was derived from the word "mule," and *negro* had an equally derogatory effect.[1] It is of little surprise that free-colored militiamen were prone to using the more favorable references to discuss themselves, but it is initially surprising that crown officials followed suit. In surveying the legislation pertaining to blacks in the Recopilación de Leyes (1681), one sees that the crown frequently resorted to discussing free-coloreds in the pejorative *mulato* and *negro* terminology. But there was a pattern to the usage. When blacks were discussed in belligerent contexts, when regulations for punishments or fines were outlined, and when laws expressly restricted their behavior, the crown tended to use more depreciative racial language. However, in legislative measures pertaining to black military services, and in legal codes in which blacks were described as leading peaceful lives, the racial labels changed, favoring the word *moreno*.[2] While it is difficult to make strong conclusions on the matter, in light of the evidence from both civil records and the Recopilación de Leyes, it appears that military service altered the crown's impression of free-coloreds to the extent that they were more commonly referred to under the most favorable terms afforded to blacks under the caste system. Free-colored militiamen themselves adhered to the same racial framework in most of their references.

Although the common use of the term "*pardos* and *morenos*" suggests similarities in labeling patterns between the crown and the soldiers, matters diverged in the use of other racial categories. This reflected different racial outlooks. The second most frequently used category in the civil documents was simply that of *pardos*. Again, euphemism was important in the decision to use this label, as well as that of *morenos*. Nevertheless, there were important differences in the way crown officials applied these categories and the way free-coloreds used them. In crown writings there was a tendency to jumble various types of racial references. In the same document, an official might refer to the free-colored companies as units of *pardos*, units of *mulatos*, and units of *pardos* and *morenos*. In 1703, the viceroy spoke of the free-colored militiamen of Mexico City as being both units of *pardos* and *morenos*, as well as units of *mulatos* and *negros*.[3] On the other hand, free-coloreds tended to be more consistent in their approach, using a single type of nomenclature throughout their documents. On those occasions in which they did mix terminology, there was a definite method to it. For example, if a free-colored soldier identified himself as a *moreno*, there was a proclivity to describe his companies as *moreno* units. The same occurred with *pardos*. In one instance, a soldier described as a *negro* referred to the free-colored militia of Mexico City as units of "*pardos* and *negros*."[4] In a similar vein, *moreno* militiamen were apt to describe the militia units as companies of "*morenos* and *pardos*," an inversion of the traditional pattern of "*pardos* and *morenos*." The inversion placed primary emphasis on the soldiers' own race. Hence, the use of racial labels, and the choices made by the soldiers to describe their companies as "*pardo* units" or "*moreno* units," revolved around matters of racial specificity. Each racial term had relevance, and the color of the men who described the militia factored into their choice of language. For crown officials, these same labels did not have the same meaning. While royal administrators did demonstrate the desire to depict free-colored militiamen euphemistically, there was a competing tendency to view blacks homogeneously. The indiscriminate mixing of racial categories, sometimes resulting in the use of various types of racial descriptions in the same sentence, reflected that perspective.

The occasionally chaotic racial designations applied by crown officials were not completely without their own internal logic, however. High-ranking royal administrators in Mexico City handled a variety of cases from all over the viceroyalty. A single military *auditor* dealt with militia petitions from Oaxaca, Veracruz, Acayucan, Puebla, Papantla, Mexico City, and so forth. The documents he would receive from each location incorporated a racial language that was particular to each region. For example, the term *mulatos blancos* was in vogue in certain areas of the Pacific coast in the eighteenth century to describe light-skinned free-coloreds, whereas in the port of Veracruz, the label *mulato* was often favored over *pardos* until the 1760s.[5] Even when racial labels were the same over several regions, the people being referred to might be different. *Pardos* in Tabasco may have had a different phenotypic description than those in New Galicia. When reading case files, royal administrators in Mexico City picked up on the cues of "racial-speak" in each region. In the civil records analyzed here, it was clear that high-ranking royal administrators made some effort at copying the style of the racial language submitted to them by the militiamen of both Puebla and Mexico City. Much of this is credited to the physical structure of the documents. For example, when militiamen sent their cases to the *auditor de guerra*, he would usually write his comments, case summaries, and decisions directly in the margins of the original pages sent by the soldiers. As a result, his writings were affected by the immediacy of being able to see the militiamen's paperwork in front of him. The same occurred when files were forwarded to fiscal auditors and the viceroy. In an interesting twist, one might surmise from this process that the soldiers' racial perspective, as manifested in their writings, influenced that of the crown, rather than vice versa. Of course, one can certainly argue the limits to which the militiamen's racial view actually shaped that of royal administrators. The rote practice of writing reams of documents a day probably militated against the development of any coherent sense of racial labeling. Once again, the multiplicity of regions sending militia petitions inevitably led to an additional blurring of racial conceptions. Partly on account of these reasons, while we do see crown efforts at faithfully incorporating racial localisms in its correspondence, we also observe that in crown documents that were not written in the margins of the original militia petitions, there was a loss of racial precision in the language. The racial homogenization of free-colored companies by royal officials was greatest at those moments.

Ironically, these initial observations convey that it was the free-colored militiamen themselves who most attached meaning to color distinctions, although it was the crown that authored the caste system as a mechanism of social control. Can these impressions be supported with concrete examples? How did the soldiers' racial perspective manifest itself in practice? Internal militia relations offer a superb means of studying these questions. Competition for militia privileges sparked the greatest racial quarrels, occasionally unveiling the reality of free-colored disunity based on shades of color. The post-1683 period, with its added privileges and responsibilities, emerges in the historical record as the critical time for these types of debates. Militia companies of the independent type, namely in Mexico City, Veracruz, and Puebla, are the best documented cases. The heavy bent on subtle racial divides in urban-based companies should not be taken to mean that race was unimportant in shaping militia relations in the rural sphere. Rather, rural companies experienced a different dynamic. Since so many units were of the racially integrated type, the competition for rank and privilege was cast over a wider color spectrum. As a result, whereas competition for an illustrious captaincy within the segregated companies of Mexico City might be narrowed down to a *negro* versus a *mulato*, in a town like Tamapachi, that same post might be contested by a mestizo or a white as well. In this context, the emphasis of distinction between a *negro* and a *mulato* was reduced, though not completely irrelevant.[6] Another important factor to consider is that the free-colored companies in cities possessed a greater range of command posts and honors. The privileges and status of positions such as captain *comandante,* colonel, or *sargento mayor* paled in comparison to anything available in the rural towns. In short, there were more privileges and distinctions at stake in the cities, being distributed amid a more selective pool of candidates. For these reasons, while there was certainly racial scrambling in the integrated units of the countryside, the nuances of color *among blacks* came into starker relief in the segregated companies of the cities.

The changes of 1683 brought about greater distinctions among soldiers in Mexico City. The oldest unit was placed under the auspices of the captain *comandante,* with his soldiers becoming the city's most esteemed forces. By 1711, that company alone had grown to a strength of 225 men, including an attachment of 25 elite grenadiers. When the reins of *comandante* power passed from Ambrosio de Pino to Gregorio Albis in about 1700, the other free-colored officers protested vociferously.[7] They argued that the *comandante* arrangement threatened the harmony of military operations, since one unit held undue precedence over the others, complicating marching unity. They also planted the idea that since a major mobilization had not taken place for some time, the *comandante*'s authority had not been exercised recently and was therefore no longer needed. They called for the distinction to be wholly abolished, thereby placing all captains and companies on an equal footing, subject only to the command of their sergeant major. Their moves met with failure: Albis's *comandante* post was confirmed in 1703.

In November 1711, Albis made a move to increase the number of grenadiers in his unit to 50. In his proposal he requested that the men be trained by Lieutenant Pedro de San Joseph, described as the *moreno mas antiguo* of his company, and who had prior experience in commanding grenadiers.[8] Permission for the augmentation was granted, but it was not implemented until September of 1718. Albis's enemies retaliated immediately when the changes were enacted. They claimed that Albis had augmented the grenadiers illegally, without obtaining the necessary royal documents of approval. Captain Andrés de Peña spearheaded the attacks, proposing to create a new company of his own, which was actually a loosely veiled plot to weaken Albis's authority and remove the illustrious grenadier units from his jurisdiction. Of all Mexico City's foot soldiers at the time, the grenadiers were the most distinguished, wearing a special blue viceregal insignia, having added access to the viceroy, and performing special exercises during festivities and royal gatherings. Intrigue throughout the year saw Peña illegally inviting members of Albis's grenadiers to join his new, still unauthorized company. Eventually the crown granted Peña the right to found a separate grenadier unit, but that did not halt the scheming. While allowing Peña to raise his own company of grenadiers, the crown had not called for the eradication of those already under Albis's command. Nor had the crown diminished any of the privileges granted to the *comandante* unit, which was Peña's ulterior motive. In actuality the crown had exacerbated the problems, inciting Peña to step up his efforts to steal and remove the grenadiers under Albis's command. A frustrated crown was consulted to mediate the debates once more. Royal officials, tired of having their desks backlogged with militia quibbles, demanded a quick end to the messy affair, relating that if Peña stirred up any more trouble he was to be sentenced to six years of hard labor in a *presidio* of the viceroy's choosing.

When Albis finally retired in the early 1720s, after having been promoted to the position of sergeant major, he left the privileges of the *comandante* company largely intact, but at the same time under fire. Albis's subordinate, Lieutenant Pedro de San Joseph, applied for the vacated *comandante* post in 1724, after having logged a twenty-six-year career. In his request he recounted how he had risen steadily through the ranks, having started from the lowly position of foot-soldier. Opposed to his promotion was Colonel Sebastian de Almaraz, who as a captain had challenged Albis's status in earlier years. Almaraz had just recently been promoted to the post of colonel, and he desired to eradicate the *comandante* position, or at least to stack it with his friends in order to increase his own personal authority. The *comandante* had evolved into the third-ranking office in the colony's militia, allowing its holder to substitute for Almaraz in his absence and that of the lieutenant colonel.[9] The *comandante* also had a notably strong voice in local militia affairs. Among Almaraz's strategies to hinder San Joseph's appointment was the proposal to separate the companies into specifically *pardo* and *moreno* units. Already the militia was divided according to residency. Those described as *forasteros* or *extravagantes* served in their own company. These included most foreigners and those who did not possess a fixed residence in the city. Almaraz's proposal for race-based divisions were modeled upon the companies of Veracruz, which had possessed specific *pardo* and *moreno* units from early in the seventeenth century. Even Puebla had briefly experimented with *pardo* and *moreno* segregation in the opening decade of the eighteenth century.[10]

Although Almaraz was supported by a corps of ambitious free-colored officers in this move, Pedro de San Joseph responded in an uproar. Never had there been such distinctions beforehand in Mexico City. He, as a *moreno*, would definitely suffer from the division, since the split would remove him from the *comandante* company. More important, the changes would largely erase the primacy of the city's oldest unit. New requirements would need to be met for a soldier to become captain *comandante*, if the post were still to remain available under the new order. All previous *comandantes* in the capital had been racially categorized as *negro/moreno*. If Almaraz's idea were to be realized, future *comandantes* would come from the *pardo* or *mulato* groups.

After investigation into the matter, Almaraz's scheme was denied by the crown, leaving the previous structure of the units in place. But the colonel did not give up easily. He challenged San Joseph's appointment to the *comandante* position by questioning his credentials. Too young, undistinguished, lacking in merits—the colonel was scathing in his observations. Almaraz proceeded to support a second candidate for the post, one whose service record was actually quite similar to San Joseph's, except for the important fact that the new candidate was the colonel's personal friend.

Almaraz's new move sparked a frenzy. Soon, other would-be captains scrambled for the post. The feuding officers created a temporary state of confusion, and by November of 1724, several men were found signing documents as the captain *comandante*, with no one actually having been appointed to the post. In the end, the viceroy issued the title to Pedro de San Joseph.[11]

The entire ordeal emphasizes the role that prestige and privilege played in designing the internal relations of these companies, including their racial identity. To gain a little bit more status some men were not averse to playing the race card, disrupting the structural harmony of the companies. Whereas before the bickering the soldiers served in mixed units of *pardos* and *morenos*, once the possibilities for becoming *comandante* opened, militiamen could suddenly become divisible as *moreno* or *pardo*. In other words, questions about privilege spurred some soldiers, like Almaraz, to use the hierarchical arrangement of the caste system to their personal advantage. It is interesting that the crown, the creator of the *sociedad de castas*, did not buy into the argument in this case. The former military structure prevailed instead. Despite strong challenges, high-level royal officials recognized the merits of San Joseph's service and would not allow him to be dislodged, nor denied the post of *comandante*. By the end of the dispute, even Almaraz himself began to support San Joseph. Race presented the possibility of undermining the situation in Mexico City during this ordeal, but the merits of service kept the potential divisiveness of color in check.

Fine gradations of race proved equally divisive, if not more so, for free-colored militiamen in Veracruz. As mentioned, free-colored soldiers had always been separated there into *pardo* and *moreno* companies, creating a structurally induced competitiveness between the races. Even the *mulato* category had become a distinguishable group among the soldiers. By 1741, four free-colored companies operated in the port, two of *morenos* and two of *mulatos*, with *pardos* being incorporated into the *mulato* units.[12] Matters were made more complex in that a substantial number of the port's militiamen hailed from abroad, namely from "Guinea." These soldiers were recognized by Spaniards as a crack fighting force, many having been seasoned beforehand as defenders in the peninsular port of Cadiz. The contingent of African blacks was incorporated mainly into Veracruz's *moreno* militia units. Issues of color and birthplace rapidly surfaced as contentious matters. With legislation passed in 1714, the crown attempted to ameliorate some of the conflicts that revolved around place of origin. It was decreed that African-born blacks were to enjoy equal status in parades and other public functions. Their captains were not to cause trouble, nor were other free-colored officers to engage them in petty disputes. African-born blacks were even given the right to occupy illustrious posts, such as that of the *comandante*.

The 1714 legislation was heeded in name only. Whereas in Mexico City, dark-skinned *morenos* had held the *comandante* position from 1683 through the early 1720s, in Veracruz their appointment to the post persisted as a relative novelty, regardless of whether they came from Mexico or Africa. Consequently, in 1739 the appointment of *moreno* Captain Pedro Mathias as *comandante* proved particularly irksome to the city's *pardo* and *mulato* militiamen. According to Mathias, these two racial groups had always enjoyed numerical superiority in the militia and had attempted to steamroll everyone else into subordination. They expressed anger at the mere possibility that *morenos* might one day come to dictate their companies' responsibilities. If *pardos* and *mulatos* had any say in the matter, Mathias believed that they would conspire to eradicate *morenos* from militia duty altogether. In fact, in protest of Mathias's appointment as *comandante*, secret gatherings took place in 1741 at the home of an unidentified *mulato* captain. Groups of *pardo* and *mulato* men and women plotted their course of action. Public denouncements were made. Broadsides ridiculing the *moreno* militiamen were posted on street corners and above the doors of private homes. To give their arguments the moral high ground, the *pardo* and *mulato* militiamen added in their attacks that it was they, rather than the *morenos*, who were the first to demonstrate their devout, spiritual piety through formal recognition of the "santa religion." They were the first who advocated and founded Veracruz's free-colored militia confraternity.

The weight of their denunciations was aimed at reversing the tide of the *comandante* appointment.[13] But as in Mexico City, once word of the difficulties reached the governor of Veracruz, he immediately silenced the stirrings. Mathias remained on post, being seen as the best man for the job. Royal interest in upholding the standards of military service, and in preserving law and order, kept the divisiveness of race in check once more. Despite continued internal grumbling, the *pardos*, *mulatos*, and *morenos* were forced to find common ground and continue their militia duties under the direction of the *moreno comandante*.

In internal struggles, issues of race could prove dangerously divisive for free-colored militia cohesion, particularly when layered with competition for privileges. However, free-colored militia interactions were not limited to relations among themselves. In the last chapter we saw how the soldiers responded to outside threats of *fuero* violations. Before that, we observed free-colored rallies to threats of eradicating their tribute exemption benefits. For the most part, in circumstances in which the free-colored militiamen's rights were threatened by outsiders, more racial unity occurred. The same took place in more everyday events, such as the racial snubs endured during militia night patrols, or taunts borne while conducting constabulary tasks for the provincial *tenientes de justicia*. The militiamen's assailants in these situations viewed all free-coloreds, not just the darker-skinned hues, with suspicious scorn. Therefore, it became difficult to isolate and finely distinguish the derogatory experience of a *mulato* from that of a *moreno* or *pardo*. As a result, race-based aggression performed by outsiders against any one of the militiamen had implications for the entire corps.

Atop this was the corporate bond. While it may have been deemed perfectly acceptable for the soldiers to bicker among themselves about the nuances of race, the same commotion took a different meaning when roused from without. Under such circumstances, the men's corporate affiliation was a mediator, the force that engineered the militiamen's unity. The basic privileges and integrity of their institution were in jeopardy; racial differences had to be subsumed in order successfully to confront the danger. The supreme outside challenge to the free-colored militia came in the context of the Bourbon reforms, with its accompanying threats to reshape and ultimately abolish the corps. An examination of the militiamen's responses when faced with the possible extinction of service speaks importantly to their racial outlook and its correlation with military privilege.

In Veracruz, the transition to the provincial militia system in the 1760s meant that the all-black company of grenadiers was slated for removal. Each of its members was to be placed in the new, racially integrated companies of fusiliers. Free-coloreds promptly protested the change. The grenadiers had enjoyed an elite status within the militia order. Losing the company amounted to relinquishing a measure of prestige. The loss also meant relinquishing a number of important officerships. Most junior grades would go to whites in the newly formed integrated units. But if the grenadiers could be retained, then free-coloreds would continue to maintain an expanded number of opportunities for advancing into the commissioned ranks. Unfortunately, their initial protests to preserve the unit were unsuccessful. The free-colored grenadier company was abolished shortly after 1764.

In 1769, Joseph Antonio Soto, a former *moreno* lieutenant in the grenadier unit, along with Joseph Morantes and Francisco Javier Buenvecino, began an independent effort to re-establish the company.[14] The trio wrote directly to the inspector general explaining in detail the great value not just of their old unit but also of the colony's free-colored militia as a whole. They highlighted the militia's services in assisting the Armada de Barlovento during the critical years of 1743–46. To calm the traditional fears of free-colored rebellion, they carefully outlined how the militiamen lived peaceful civilian lives. Along with their observations, they submitted a list of sixty-five men who had already expressed a desire to staff the company. Importantly, Soto added that he would personally cover all of the expenses of the unit, paying for uniforms, munitions, and weapons. He asked only that he be compensated with the title of captain and be allowed to select subordinate officers of his own choosing.

The terms of the agreement were favorable to the inspector, who authorized the re-creation of the unit. In his mind, a cost-free unit of seasoned militiamen was a welcome addition to the port's defenses. Veracruz's *cabildo* was not so enthralled. The drain of free-coloreds into Soto's unit would mean that there would be fewer men available to fill the other provincial companies. Seeing that the proposed company of grenadiers had no strict limits as to its size, the *cabildo* imposed a cap of fifty-six men. Soto was outraged. That would mean a loss of some of his soldiers. Appearing before the *cabildo* himself, he proposed that they reconsider their actions. If they were to restrict his company in that fashion, then at least they should allow the men forced to leave his unit the right to secure respectable posts in the regiment of provincial fusiliers.

In this example, free-colored militia service was not being terminated in its entirety. In fact, a number of free-colored companies persisted into the 1820s in Veracruz.[15] What transpired as a result of the military reforms was a rerouting of black troops into integrated forces. But Soto's response shows that some men demonstrated an unyielding commitment to seek service exclusively in *pardo* and *moreno* units of the independent type, regardless of the proposed changes. The case also reveals that colonial whites did not always exert complete control over the decision of whether to create racially segregated companies. It has often been claimed that when whites did not want to serve alongside blacks, they initiated processes to establish separate companies, particularly during the Bourbon reform period.[16] The Veracruz case shows that the inverse could also be true.

It is quite clear in this example that concerns of prestige loomed large in the decision for the grenadiers to seek segregated service. But the currents may have run deeper. The same documents mention that Veracruz's free-coloreds generally expressed such an aversion toward serving in the newly formed integrated units that many hid themselves during times of levy. Others claimed exemption on the false grounds that they were slaves. While we have seen that recruitment into specifically designated, free-colored units likewise held its share of problems, the implication in Soto's writings was that when faced with options, blacks in Veracruz exhibited a greater willingness to join units that, racially speaking, they could call their own.

In the province of Xicayan, the shocks produced by the Bourbon military reforms in the 1780s and 1790s triggered equally insightful responses by free-colored militiamen toward preserving the racial integrity of their forces. A decree passed in 1784 called for the retirement of every free-colored officer in the bishopric of Oaxaca, whether in integrated companies or in those of the independent type. The militiamen were to be thanked for their services and compensated with lifetime use of the *fuero*. Whites were to be eased into the vacated free-colored posts.[17] The law was not immediately implemented in all areas. In some places, free-colored officers were removed from duty only to find their way back into the ranks shortly thereafter. In the town of Guajolotitlan, protracted delays set back the first major steps of reform until 1788. By that time, a host of other damaging legislative measures had been approved. Consequently, when Guajolotitlan's officials finally decided to implement the reform project, they had been authorized to deal a heavy blow to the militia. *Alcalde mayor* Don Amaro González de Mesa proceeded not only to disband the militia's free-colored officers in 1788 but also to dismantle the town's *pardo* companies altogether, removing their war drums and forcing all residents to pay tribute.[18]

Guajolotitlan's free-coloreds were taken aback. They hastily drafted a letter that was promptly dispatched to the capital. Lacking a detailed knowledge of law and legal procedure, the free-coloreds hired an *agente de negocios* (legal representative) to handle their affairs and present a case for viceregal consideration. In the meantime, their woes continued. Virtually every year saw new military inspectors visiting the province, making more modifications and imposing added tribute pressures. In the face of the challenges, many militiamen stubbornly remained in their posts. Additionally, free-coloreds throughout the town began to protest openly that the tribute burden was starting to get out of hand, being charged arbitrarily without warning. They noted that census counts, which normally preceded tribute collections, were not being regularly performed. That further hurt the accuracy of tribute assessment rates, since there was no way to gauge who was truly eligible for collection, or to determine their proper payment obligations. During the visitation of Dn. Bernardino Cuyasendo, many residents angrily testified that they had been charged in excess of five pesos of tribute per year.[19]

Aside from these attempted reforms in Guajolotitlan, between 1792 and 1793 sharper cuts were made into the provincial militia companies throughout the Pacific region, as more than half the units along the *Costa Sur* were abolished.[20] Unlike the case during previous administrations, these reductions and their accompanying personnel changes were taken more seriously than in the early 1780s. That was especially true in Xicayan and Igualapa, where measures to eliminate the free-colored officer corps were finally conducted in systematic fashion.[21] Combined with three years of bad harvests, this backdrop established an atmosphere of widespread free-colored discontent during the late 1780s and early 1790s. Eventually, the simultaneous pushes to implement tribute, alongside the constant tinkering with the free-colored militia design, culminated in disturbances in 1794.

The episodes of change played out badly in the town of Guajolotitlan. When word was announced on January 4, 1794, that all free-colored officers were finally to be replaced with whites, the rank and file responded vehemently. There had been too many abuses and manipulations to bear in recent years; the soldiers adamantly requested that they retain officers of their own race to stave off further problems. The soldiers had a short list of favorites. At the helm was sixty-year-old Lieutenant Policarpio de los Santos, a ruffian of dubious reputation. In the estimation of some townspeople, Policarpio was a lazy petty criminal who lived merely to prey off weaker citizens. In the opinion of others, the lieutenant was one of the few residents unafraid to stand up to the provincial authorities. He had led a successful tribute "rebellion" a few years earlier and was frequently involved upfront in struggles with the *justícia*. Although acting as a militiaman, his past deeds and resistance to tribute collection had managed to reduce the level of tax for all of Guajolotitlan's free-colored population. In that sense, while he undoubtedly abused his militia commission toward selfish ends, he was occasionally willing to jeopardize the benefits derived from his militia standing for the greater good of the free-coloreds in his community. Such sacrifices ultimately reduced his clout with the colonial government. But of course, Policarpio only braved those trials as long as he had something concrete to gain in the process. In any case, his demonstrated willingness to pay a high personal price for the sake of the collective free-colored good spoke volumes of the strength of his racial identity. Policarpio was a consummate risk-taker who, when the timing was right, seemed unafraid to interpret political issues in racial terms.

Apart from Policarpio, the other officers whom the soldiers wanted to retain in their posts were the two Luna brothers, Captain José Luna and Lieutenant Martín Luna. Headed by Policarpio, the angry militiamen marched through the town protesting the latest reform effort, beating their war drums and trying to call out others to join the cause. Meanwhile, news of the attempt to install an all-white militia officer corps reached free-colored workers in the fields, who became equally upset and restless. On the night of January 5, a group of *pardo* and *moreno* townsmen held an all-night vigil at the house of Captain José de Luna. There they prepared two letters for dispatch to other militia captains in the surrounding region. One read as follows:

My esteemed friend and colleague, we would like to inform you that as your associate, we suggest that you request as we have done [here] in not allowing Spaniards to become officers in the [militia] companies under any circumstances. Please forward this message to other captains and provide a swift response.[22]

Anxious authorities, always quick to prejudge, feared that widespread conspiracy and rebellion were brewing. But the truth of the matter was that the free-colored cause was not completely unified. Even within Guajolotitlan, cooler heads begged for calm. Free-colored militia officers Pasqual Mayoral and Vicente Gallardo, who were too ill to stop Policarpio directly, denied him use of their homes and tried their best to limit the disturbances. They alleged that the Luna brothers had simply joined the resistance movement because they were natural-born followers, rather than outright leaders. Mayoral and Gallardo, among others, suspected that Policarpio himself might have been the mastermind behind generating the disquiet. Yet they could not be sure.[23]

Whether ignited by Policarpio or simply fanned by him, the movement was doomed to failure. Although the soldiers whipped up enormous support in Guajolotitlan, there was no guarantee that they could duplicate their success elsewhere. The fatal error committed by Policarpio and his group was assuming that the level of racial agitation they experienced was commonly felt by others. Even if so, there was no reason to believe that other free-coloreds in the province would stand up as boldly to challenge the authorities. Guajolotitlan was a minor town, isolated from the major political and economic centers of the province. According to contemporary observers, the residents' rugged lifestyle and independence promoted obstinacy, which was constantly being manifested when provincial and ecclesiastical authorities tried to impose their will in the town.[24] The letters that Guajolotitlan's militiamen sent out to drum up regional support went to Xamiltepec, Pinotepa del Rey, and Tututepec. In the past, all of those towns had unquestionably defied the provincial authorities to some degree. For instance, some *alcaldes mayores* and *subdelegados* recounted difficulties in collecting tribute there in the early 1790s. However, the level of overt resistance had not reached the same proportions as in Guajolotitlan. Moreover, these centers were more politically connected to the provincial authorities. Xamiltepec was the *cabecera* of the province, housing the *alcalde mayor* himself. The free-colored militia officers surrounding him were more pliant than those in Guajolotitlan, being predisposed to doing the *alcalde mayor*'s bidding.[25] Tututepec was the province's second most important political center, possessing free-colored militia leaders who were also less testy than in Guajolotitlan. Pinotepa del Rey, while not as politically important as either Xamiltepec or Tututepec, still demonstrated its loyalty to the government. The town's free-colored officers immediately denounced the Guajolotitlan movement upon receipt of their letter.

The lesson to be learned regarding racial identity in Xicayan is a mixed one. Undoubtedly, statements issued by men such as Policarpio and his colleagues during the tumult of 1794 compel us to believe that there was a desire to preserve free-colored purity in the corps.[26] This translated into overt racial advocacy and expressions of racial identity. But the situation was primarily local and factionalized even within the town itself. Xicayan demonstrates that free-colored militia experiences could vary widely within the same province. For many years in Guajolotitlan, the militia had played a strong role in trying to soothe some of the demands of the provincial government on the town's free-coloreds. But that was less the case in other areas. Inspiring soldiers to resist provincial authorities on account of race was not enough to surmount these fundamental differences in the terms of service. In other words, an appeal to race alone could not inspire the militiamen in one town to suddenly take a more activist militia role than they had before. This held especially true if the militiamen saw nothing tangible to be derived from the experience, or if they felt that the level of resistance could compromise their own position. Keep in mind that for some soldiers there was more to be gained out of being the *alcalde mayor*'s underling than from trying to serve as advocates for the free-coloreds in their communities, be they militiamen or civilians. Not all free-colored militiamen were Policarpios.

The experiences of the militiamen in rural Xicayan can be compared to the attempts to abolish free-colored militia duty in Mexico City and Puebla. In 1792, under the recommendation of Subinspector General Pedro Gorostiza, Viceroy Revillagigedo proceeded to disband the free-colored militia in the interior provinces, beginning with those two cities. According to Gorostiza, the colony's free-colored units were simply not living up to their original expectations. When they were first placed on the provincial footing in the 1760s, the intention had been to transform the pre-existing free-colored companies into a capable force that could supplement the regular army in times of need and that could equally provide an adequate security force for the interior's cities. In Gorostiza's estimation, the free-colored battalions met neither of those goals. Instead, they represented an incessant drain on the royal treasury. Between Mexico City and Puebla alone, the crown annually spent sixteen thousand pesos on free-colored military expenses. The units were also rumored to be disorderly, provoking problems during mobilizations. They burdened their respective cities with high incidences of crime, reputedly aggravating internal security concerns.

Despite Gorostiza's personal distaste for the free-colored corps, he did not aspire to completely abandon all of the discharged soldiers. He proposed to continue to pay the salaries of militiamen above the rank of second sergeant who had logged a sufficient amount of time in the royal service. Of course, their wage scale would be reduced. Men having served since the 1760s would receive half-salary. Those with at least twenty-five years of duty would be given one-third of their normal pay. As an added bonus, all of the individuals meeting these criteria were to retain their full *fuero* rights and tribute exemption. For the lower, nonsalaried grades, twenty years of service qualified them for tribute relief and *fuero* coverage. Any enlisted man with less time would be fully subjected to tribute and would lose his *fuero* rights. Officers were excluded from that fate. Given their "class," even if they had served for less than one year, they would remain tribute exempt, although without access to the *fuero*.[27]

Just 190 men out of the two battalions qualified for some form of tribute relief or *fuero* coverage, amounting to less than a quarter of both cities' total number of soldiers. Only twenty-nine men retained a salary.[28] There was immediate unrest, as the militiamen felt they had been wronged. Even officers, who received the most complete compensations, felt rebuffed. No one anticipated the haste with which their companies were to be extinguished, nor had anyone seen the move coming. In that sense, the situation differed from Xicayan, where years of embittered reforms served as harbingers of the militia's eventual demise. As if to emphasize the celerity, the viceroy acted with unusual speed on Gorostiza's recommendations. By January 21, 1792, less than three weeks after the subinspector general's initial proposals had been submitted, Revillagigedo had signed a letter of approval regarding the units' extinction.[29] Again, while dealing primarily with expunging the forces in Mexico City and Puebla, the intention was that free-colored service throughout the colony's interior was to be eventually abandoned. Out of necessity, free-colored forces along the coasts were to be retained, since those crucial front-line defensive zones could not be successfully protected without *pardo* services. Nevertheless, their units were not to be left unscathed. Save Veracruz itself, within the year, a broader plan for provincial unit reductions would severely jeopardize the integrity of free-colored service virtually everywhere, radically changing the face of command staffs and officer ranks.

Once the free-colored soldiers in Mexico City and Puebla had recovered from the initial blow, they retaliated. Unlike what took place in Guajolotitlan, their protests never assumed openly aggressive form, nor were there any conspiratorial attempts to rouse the sensitivities of other free-coloreds to resist the change. Possessing considerably more legal experience, finesse, and political acumen, the free-colored militiamen of both cities knew how to resist without appearing to be resisting. Like their rural counterparts, they convened meetings and wrote a series of letters, but these were mailed to the viceroy, to the king, or to whatever royal official they believed would hear their pleas. The militiamen did not step outside of the crown framework in their actions, nor did any of their writings suggest that they were not complying with the viceregal decree to disband their units.

Matters dragged on for nearly two years as the mechanics of the dismantling were being worked out. The arguments the soldiers tried during this period are telling. They resorted to the time-tested method of submitting catalogs of militia services. Mexico City's soldiers related that with more than 183 years of continuous duty, how could the colony do without the capital's free-colored battalion?[30] In Puebla, soldiers boasted of valiant deeds performed in Veracruz, Campeche, and Mexico City.[31] A second approach was to profess effusive love and loyalty for His Majesty. Some self-effacement was thrown in for good measure: "The unit of *pardos* is small, or nothing if judged according to the birth of each of its members, but highly elevated in terms of their honor and mode of thinking."[32] A third tactic involved coaxing the highest crown officials into believing that the viceroy and subinspector general had acted independently to abolish the free-colored militia, without acquiring the king's direct approval. By this method the militiamen argued that the ties of fealty ran directly between the soldiers and the king, without intermediaries. Once the king was made to realize that the units had been eradicated without his permission, the militiamen thought that he would surely reverse the decision. To provide evidence that the high crown had not forsaken them, the soldiers noted that their units were mentioned in the 1793 edition of the *Guía de Forasteros*. Published out of Madrid, the book chronicled features of the New World, providing information on functioning institutions. Since the free-colored units appeared listed there, the soldiers stressed that they must continue to constitute a viable institution in the king's eyes. On these grounds, the militiamen asked for reinstatement to their prior status, fully enjoying all of their old privileges. In fact, Puebla's soldiers dared request even more:

We humbly ask of you the restitution of our companies as they once were, establishing and providing for the *plana mayor* . . . a colonel, lieutenant, sergeant major, and commander, before whom the troops will give complete subordination. We propose to Your Majesty that you do not place a subinspector, or adjutant, or *garzones* in our units, since we all now know how to use weapons. If you agree to the new establishment of our units under these terms which we solicit, the Royal Treasury will save money by not having to pay these useless salaries, and we will be free of the yoke of European officers who have always been our capital enemies, bringing us to ruin, and destroying us as they recently managed to do. In this manner we will better serve Your Majesty, who must consider that although we are *pardo* in color, we are of noble heart to sacrifice our being and lives for the king, as we have done on numerous occasions.[33]

Mexico City also requested that the presence of the cadre be reconsidered. If whites had to be added to their units, the free-colored militiamen preferred selecting their own subinspector, Dn. Simón Enderica, who was a man of their liking.[34] Neither Revillagigedo nor the crown budged on the issue of free-colored reinstatement, much less on questions about the cadre. Under the succeeding administration of Viceroy Branciforte, the soldiers' arguments were re-examined with care.[35] But influenced in part by administrators from the previous viceregal government, Branciforte's investigation concluded that it was best to leave the companies disbanded.

The abolition of the militiamen's companies did not trigger a strident, race-based reaction. When race surfaced in their arguments, it was carefully packaged, largely because of their audience. Aside from simple self-referencing, race was used in a self-deprecating manner, deemed the best way to court the crown. This was quite different from the attempted racial stirring of Guajolotitlan, but quite similar to the heavily subdued racial discussion presented by the *moreno* grenadiers in Veracruz, who were also writing to crown officials. Was race any less important as a rallying factor in Mexico City, Puebla, and Veracruz, than in Guajolotitlan? It is difficult to determine from the available documentation reviewed here. What we can assert confidently is that in all of the cities cited in the above examples, most soldiers would have preferred serving in companies without whites. Perhaps on some level, that had something to do with a spirit of fraternity and *pardo*, or racial bonding. But the main underlying motivation was access to privileges, which was first and foremost on their minds.

Whites brought unwanted competition for rank, prestige, rights, and control. In Guajolotitlan, the motives for promoting racial purity also included the desire to curb future abuses against free-coloreds by the provincial government. With whites as the militia's commanders, the institution could no longer serve as an effective agent in defending free-colored concerns, such as tribute immunity. Along with the militiamen's attempts to coordinate and rally a larger, regional protest in the province of Xicayan, these objectives probably accounted for the added racial emphasis in their arguments. In summary, it would seem fair to posit that in nearly all of the colony's free-colored militia units, a large number of soldiers readily referred to themselves as *pardos, morenos, mulatos,* and so forth. In this manner, they conceived of themselves as free-coloreds under the proper nomenclature assigned to them under the caste system. But the expression of race was ultimately a function of privilege. Whenever race came into play in their writings and requests, it did so in whatever ways would best enhance their positioning to secure privilege. Therefore, rather than blindly accepting the crown-designed caste strictures, free-colored militiamen engaged in adroit maneuvering processes whereby they acknowledged their phenotypic race, through finding ways around the traditional legal and social boundaries associated with being *pardo, moreno,* and *mulato.* Rephrased, they affirmed and even redefined race through eluding the confines of the state-imposed caste framework.[36]

In the years following the administration of Revillagigedo, the remaining militia companies that retained free-colored soldiers continued to bestow tribute exemption and *fuero* rights. Consequently, racial identity, as predicated upon access to privilege, continued to function right up until independence.[37] But there were some changes. After 1797, another set of legal restrictions were issued that limited the number of blacks who could serve as militia officers. At this time, Veracruz became designated as the only city officially able to name *pardo* or *moreno* commandants.[38] As a result, there was further colony-wide diminution in free-colored access to the special benefits of the commissioned posts. Finally, with the creation of the national and civic militias beginning in 1821–22, although many free-coloreds remained in military service, the scope of their privileges became less clear. Changes in military structure, combined with new alterations to the legal status of blacks in the newly formed nation-state, accounted for the ambiguities.[39]

Free-colored militia duty in the late eighteenth and early nineteenth centuries was also marked by an increase in the national and international political awareness of Mexico's blacks. After 1810, participation in the struggle for independence saw many *pardos* and *morenos* side with royalist forces in Veracruz, while in Morelos, free-coloreds fought for national sovereignty alongside the rebels.[40] Whether the independence wars gave rise to a specific free-colored agenda, replete with special demands, is still an open topic for research and debate. Initial indicators suggest that free-colored combatants normally sought improvements in social conditions that were regional in character rather than race-specific.[41]

The Haitian Revolution proved another source of political impact, as free-coloreds in Mexico sustained criticisms brought on by new fears over the potential conflagration of race-based conflicts. Opinions about the value of the militia became decidedly mixed during this period, as traditional mistrusts increased over employing blacks as soldiers. While black militiamen continued to provide important garrison duty in strategic centers such as Veracruz, the soldiers' racial perspective was affected by the debates about Haiti. Some came to increasingly deny their color as a means to avoid the scorn of public suspicions. Others, however, continued to base their expression of race on the effects it had at garnering military privileges.

Some of the new issues that faced the free-colored militia during the latter days of the colonial period were seen vividly in the community of San Fernando Aké, located in the subdelegation of Tizimín (Yucatan). Established in 1795, San Fernando was a community founded completely by a corps of black militia auxiliaries who had served in Santo Domingo, fighting against the French during the Haitian Revolution. The 115 soldiers who first settled the town were an international lot, representing places such as New York, Jamaica, Senegal, the Congo, Guinea, Santo Domingo, and Rio Tinto. After having served in Santo Domingo, the soldiers were shipped to Cuba. For reasons unknown, the Cuban governor suddenly ordered the men to leave, sending them to the Yucatan. The troops received a lukewarm reception in their new home. On the one hand, Mexican colonial officials saw definite utility in having these seasoned soldiers serve as the backbone of a new coastal defense force. On the other, the militiamen were viewed with particular mistrust. Their contact with Haitian rebels had exposed the group to dangerous ideas about freedom and sovereignty. No one could foresee what might result from having the men stationed permanently in the Yucatan. Perhaps that was one of the reasons why Cuba's governor quickly dismissed the soldiers from his colony. He may have realized that the militiamen's unpredictable loyalties were potentially dangerous for rousing other coloreds, especially in a burgeoning plantation society like Cuba. On a similar score, in the Yucatan it was decided that the troops were to be settled in a remote and isolated area of the peninsula, encompassing the site of the old abandoned Indian town of Aké. There they would be close enough to the coast to provide adequate military defense, but far enough from the major cities of Campeche and Mérida to avoid stirring domestic troubles.[42]

The reliability of the military settlement was put to the test in 1806. Correspondence between San Fernando Aké's commissioner and the captain general of the Yucatan reveals that there were serious worries over potential hostilities between the militiamen and the colonial government. According to intelligence reports, the Venezuelan dissident, Francisco Miranda, had recently been spotted in Santo Domingo gathering military reinforcements for his revolutionary cause. Alarmingly, he had been seen recruiting troops near the zone where the soldiers of San Fernando Aké had been stationed a decade earlier. Colonial officials feared that Miranda's next move would be to sail to the Yucatan, where he would add the community of militiamen to his growing armed column. But in the end, the government's apprehension proved groundless. Investigations revealed that while there were numerous internal problems and discontents within the settlement of San Fernando, the militiamen had not been involved in any seditious overseas communications.[43]

What the militiamen did appear to harbor was an acid distaste for whites. Despite the fact that the community had been created to exist in near isolation, it had been growing ever since its foundation. Within a year of settlement, San Fernando had almost doubled in size, taking in some forty-four outsiders. The militiamen themselves controlled the influx of immigrants. They were racially selective, allowing other free-coloreds to settle in the town for a fee. Meanwhile, whites were hastily warded off. A few Indians trickled into the settlement, but the town's racial composition remained primarily colored. Between 1801 and 1806, the community stood at roughly 230 individuals. A low natural birthrate kept numbers relatively stable for the opening decade of the nineteenth century.[44]

The residents' aversion toward whites had political implications. Defining themselves oppositionally in relation to their local white administrators, the militiamen initiated a score of schemes against the town's commissioners, who were among the few *españoles* in residence at the settlement. Surrounded by blacks, commissioners often feared for their lives and overreacted in most situations, sparking additional racial tensions. The predicament was especially true for José Carreño, who served during the years 1806–9. Throughout his tenure he overzealously reported many supposed conspiracies and sought to dilute the community racially by encouraging the greater immigration of whites and Indians. He also proposed the construction of a church, more widespread cultivation of grain, and a ban on firearms and liquor. Carreño's opinions and policies met stiff resistance. The militiamen refused to cooperate in providing community labor. Also, the commissioner's plans for increasing the presence of whites were frustrated, as were his attempts to increase agricultural production. When he tried to place soldiers in jail for alleged crimes, others quickly set them free. To counter Carreño's authority, the militiamen occasionally felt pressed to ally themselves with the region's *subdelegado*, another white government official. But in courting the *subdelegado*, the militiamen effectively sought to increase their own autonomy. Being a more distant authority than the local commissioner, and more sympathetic to the soldiers' cause, the *subdelegado* generally granted the men more maneuvering room for running their own affairs.[45]

Consistent with what we have seen elsewhere in this chapter, the militiamen of San Fernando displayed a fairly high measure of solidarity in their endeavors against the town's commissioners. These were outsiders to the free-colored militia establishment who were seen as aspiring to degrade the soldiers' status and role in the community. The militiamen's unity was derived from both corporate and racial affinities. All of the government's representatives were *españoles*. All of the militiamen were various shades of black. Somatically charged political issues, depicted starkly in black and white, found their way into the case files about the town.[46] However, as has also been discussed in this chapter, when San Fernando's militiamen were not engaged in disputes against their commissioners, their politics were far more fractured. Since the town was composed almost entirely of soldiers, rank played an important role in structuring town relations. The most important individuals were those who had previously held the highest military ranks while serving as auxiliaries in Santo Domingo. Alongside these men was a small group of ambitious upstarts who also called themselves colonels, captains, and sergeants, but who had not been conferred those grades through official channels.

While the military chain of command might have been a potential source of order in the town, in reality, matters were complicated by the militia hierarchy. Each officer became the de facto head of his linguistic group. That is to say that there was an English-speaking camp in San Fernando, pitted against Spanish speakers, Portuguese speakers, and so forth. When not united in their efforts to dislodge the town's commissioners, the militiamen (under the direction of their officers) were pitted against one another for supremacy in the village. According to Carreño's writings, by the end of the first decade of the nineteenth century, the French-speaking faction had begun to predominate in controlling town affairs.

The commissioners could have exploited the natural divisions among the soldiers for better control over San Fernando. In truth, a few of these administrators did make token gestures in that regard. Carreño himself had recruited the services of Casimiro, a black officer who had enjoyed considerable distinction during the militia's stationing in Santo Domingo. For a period of time, Casimiro was able to build a pro-government faction in San Fernando that assisted the commissioners in maintaining the standards of colonial law. Unfortunately, the loyalty of the faction faded. In Carreño's case, his own attitudes, actions, and prejudices were largely to blame. His overt dislike for blacks was seen in his references to them as "cannibals," "ill-mannered," "uneducated," and "ugly."[47] These views clouded his perception of their utility in the enterprise of town government. Although Carreño maintained that Casimiro was important in facilitating town management, and in later years he even pondered the idea of issuing him the official post of *juez*, at the same time Carreño clung tightly to his notions of black inferiority.[48] He was clearly affected by the emerging ideas of the scientific revolution, as well as Enlightenment racial thought, in believing that whites constituted the "head," which gave direction to the colony's blacks and Indians—the constituent "body."[49] As members of Casimiro's pro-government camp splintered in view of these ideas, they joined the town's other militiamen in an increasingly concerted, racialized resistance to the commissioner's will.

San Fernando Aké was definitely an atypical town in early nineteenth-century Mexico. The high number of black foreigners in the community was a novelty. So was the scarce presence of crown administrators, except for in the most remote colonial settings. Additionally, even in coastal communities such as Tamiagua, Guajolotitlan, Igualapa, and Acayucan, one would have been hard-pressed to find a village that was so thoroughly militarized by free-colored soldiers. Moreover, this community had been directly touched, like none other in Mexico, by the circulating ideas of sovereignty that prevailed among the blacks and *mulatos* in Haiti. This combination of factors created a situation whereby there was ample political space and intellectual ground for the development of a special racial consciousness that could transcend the bounds of privilege discussed throughout this manuscript. However, even in San Fernando, the confluence of racial identification with access to privilege seemed to be important toward substantiating racial expressions. Importantly, and as seen elsewhere, the struggle for rights and status in the town best promoted a solidarity based upon corporate and racial ties when the chief foes were not free-colored militiamen.[50]

Conclusion

NEW SPAIN'S free-colored militia came into being in the middle of the sixteenth century under inauspicious beginnings. It was initially unclear what role the soldiers would play, inasmuch as they were primarily auxiliaries, and serving under conditions in which blacks were held in general suspicion. By the beginning of the seventeenth century, the institution began to assume a more definite form, with the emergence of three basic types of units: companies of racially integrated service, companies of the independent type (racially segregated), and companies in former maroon communities. In the period preceding the Bourbon military reforms, all of these units were known collectively as "urban" militia forces. The major zones of free-colored service developed along the Pacific and Gulf coasts, where men mainly served in small rural towns. Units were created in the interior as well, but with lesser prominence. Two of the most important cities of interior service included Mexico City and Puebla.

Precipitated by the Lorencillo pirate raid of 1683 and militia appeals for tribute exemption in the 1670s, the institution increasingly assumed greater social impact as more privileges were granted to the soldiers. Moreover, as additional companies were created at new sites in the late seventeenth century, and as a greater range of military ranks became available, *pardo* and *moreno* participation in the militia establishment steadily increased into the early eighteenth century. In fact, along the rural coasts, it was rumored that there were few communities in which the free-colored male population was not almost completely militarized. Although that is an exaggeration, there were some underlying truths to the observation. Free-colored militia privileges, most notably tribute exemption, had become illegally afforded to civilians in great numbers, creating the false impression that there was a much larger *pardo* troop base than actually existed. The predicament was encouraged by lenient practices of tribute collection. Provincial *alcaldes mayores* feared that if they chose to collect tribute with vigor, mass free-colored migrations, loss of estate labor, and loss of important militia constabulary support would result. Patterns of tribute leniency also evolved in urban settings. But in New Spain's cities, tribute leniency was credited more to the specific problems of collection procedures, including highly effective tax evasions, than to any conscious effort by government officials to reduce the free-colored tribute burden. Mexico City was an exception, since there, collection officers often lightly collected tribute from free-colored plebeians in order to convey the image that the municipal government was a benevolent entity, acting in the best interests of its lower-class citizens. Therefore, ironically, leniency practices in the capital were frequently allowed to endure so as to legitimize the urban administration.

The net effect of the century-long tribute-exemption practices was a gradual reinterpretation of militia privilege into a more generally perceived racial privilege. In the 1770s and 1780s, there were numerous episodes of free-coloreds claiming exemption based on the mere fact that they were *pardos* or *morenos*, not that they were militiamen. Despite serious challenges to claims of tax immunity during the latter half of the eighteenth century, loose tribute-exemption standards were upheld for free-colored militiamen and civilians alike until the 1790s, when, finally, the free-colored militia was dealt fatal blows under the regime of Revillagigedo. Yet even in the early nineteenth century, wherever free-colored units had managed to persist, there was widespread access to tribute relief.

As the free-colored militia continued to develop institutionally, it began to acquire a great deal of internal autonomy, particularly in the century preceding the Bourbon military reforms. With the implementation of the free-colored colonelcy in 1719, free-colored officers became fully responsible for inspecting and training their forces. Meanwhile, thanks to military law codes and years of testy appeals and experimentation, the soldiers' legal petitions became handled, with few intermediaries, by their own commanders. These case files were then sent directly to the military's *auditor de guerra* for final deliberation. In units of the independent type, the absence of white attachés, and the militia's growing involvement in nonmilitary municipal capacities, increased the soldiers' political capital and offered them opportunities to expand their privilege base. As if in a feedback loop, these factors served to strengthen their overall autonomy, especially as the militia's leaders challenged their opponents and pressed for added corporate rights.

Admittedly, there could be less free-colored control in the colony's integrated companies than in the independent ones. The fact that whites and mestizos were able to assume high officer posts worked to reduce *pardo* and *moreno* command authority. Additionally, the influence of the *alcalde mayor*, acting as *capitan aguerra*, was a prominent presence in these units. But despite such potentially militating elements, in certain coastal communities such as Papantla, *pardos* and *morenos* enjoyed inordinately easy access to the uppermost ranks, allowing them to exert wide power over the integrated corps.

The high level of free-colored militia participation found in seventeenth- and early eighteenth-century Mexico runs against what many have previously written about the colonial military establishment. Traditionally perceived as weak, the sweeping reforms of the 1760s have been interpreted as a watershed event for military involvement, with hosts of colonists joining units as never before. Some have even maintained that whatever citizen-based forces were in place beforehand were militias in name only.[1] Pre–Bourbon reform militia units were rumored to have been untrained, undisciplined, and rarely summoned. On the contrary, my assessment of New Spain's free-colored militia prior to the 1760s reveals a corps of troops who, although not heavily involved in military exercises or campaigns, were greatly involved in patrol duties, *vigía* watches, and a panoply of ancillary functions requested by municipal and provincial authorities. Into the early eighteenth century, those tasks cemented the corps into an institution with definite functional meaning. Of course, the scope of the institution's impact was affected by fluctuating degrees of troop participation throughout the colony. Free-colored recruitment patterns show that the militia possessed only a core of individuals resolutely involved in the institution. That included most officers, and, in provincial settings, a number of troops residing nearest to towns bearing a militia headquarters. Apart from these was a mass of troops with varying levels of commitment, many of whom indeed may have been registered solely in name. But regardless of individual shifts in militia resolve, the evidence shows that, especially where free-coloreds were concerned, it would be erroneous to conclude that the militia was an insignificant feature of colonial life in New Spain prior to the 1760s.

In an inversion of the traditional view, the post-1760s era actually witnessed a decline in free-colored troop enrollment in many major areas of service, quite the opposite of the well-documented surges in white and mestizo militia participation in the Americas. The study of the free-colored militia, therefore, corroborates those opinions presented by some of the emerging literature on militarization in the Spanish dominions. There has been an effort to stress that the existing portrait of the military institution does not take into full account the role of peripheral areas. That has led to an overemphasis on the role of the Bourbon military reforms in shaping the military trajectory of the New World. On the other hand, when smaller and less economically vibrant colonial territories are assessed, a different military story emerges. Santo Domingo, for instance, was a sparsely populated imperial possession, but because of strategic circumstances, it was also a highly militarized zone for the duration of the colonial period, not just after the 1760s.[2] In a similar vein, we can posit for New Spain that the existing view of the military institution does not take into account the full impact of the various races that composed its defense. When free-colored participation is factored into the defense of zones such as the Gulf and Pacific coasts, the social reach of the institution increases visibly for Mexico prior to the 1760s. Undoubtedly, the same situation was true for all of Spain's territories in which *pardos* and *morenos* figured prominently into the designs of colonial protection.

Extending the implications of the historical revisionism even further, while it is probably correct to interpret the Bourbon military reform period as an era of definite historical consequence for *pardo* forces, I argue that it is best to view the period as one that mainly challenged an already established, free-colored military order. The autonomy and privilege structures that free-coloreds had been acquiring from the late seventeenth and early eighteenth centuries were abruptly brought into wholesale question and review at this time. From the 1760s until the 1790s, free-colored soldiers were pitted in a sustained struggle against the state to preserve, and in some cases to expand, their perceived rights. The success of their efforts depended upon a unique blend of historical circumstance, timing, geostrategic positioning, and local political posturing. During the politically turbulent 1780s, for instance, a vacuum of leadership at the highest viceregal levels, accompanied by the outbreak of war, offered the free-colored militia units along coast of Veracruz the opportunity to preserve many of the rights they had enjoyed from the outset of the century. It did not hurt their chances that they were located in the most strategically situated zone of the colony, providing them with added leverage in their legal bargaining. Throughout Mexico, the late eighteenth century was a virtual showcase for these types of power feuds.

Turning now to the effects of military duty on the psyche, identity, and social standing of its free-colored participants, let me start by saying that militia service meant many things to its free-colored participants. Some feared the loss of life and limb and sought quick exit at the first opportunity. Others shunned service out of worry over their jobs and families, not wanting to abandon them during campaign seasons. Still more avoided duty, or rushed out of the corps to enhance their chances at "passing" for a lighter hue. While in certain places, such as Puebla, soldiers exhibited a marked tendency to marry white brides at extremely high rates, the free-colored militia was not the best avenue for whitening. Participating in the corps firmly stamped one's *pardoness* on him and his family, adding taints of color to their reputational race.

Militia ties were not particularly coveted for enhancing one's job opportunities, either. An overview of recruitment reveals that while the militiamen were favorably differentiated from most of their black civilian counterparts by being artisans to a greater degree than lowly domestics or servants, the distinction had more to do with the mechanics of the recruitment process itself than with the direct influence of their militia connections. Additionally, the soldiers' occupations were seldom highly distinguished in the view of larger society, even among officers. This meant that there was a ceiling lowered onto their social climbs. In the urban environment, what we find is that the militia overwhelmingly composed the strata of free-coloreds who represented the middle and lower-middle level occupational groups of New Spain's cities. In the countryside there was more occupational parity between soldiers and civilians. As manifested in rural Igualapa, free-colored militiamen were primarily agriculturists, like almost everyone else in the province. Yet, as in the colony's urban centers, these soldiers were again underrepresented in the service sector when compared with civilian blacks.

For those who were eager to achieve significant class mobility that transcended the traditional bounds of free-colored occupational behavior—that is, social whitening—joining the militia was most often a lateral move. A cook who entered the corps as a foot soldier might indeed rise to be a prominent officer: hence, mobility. But his chances of significantly increasing his occupational status and income were slim. Most likely, he would still be employed as a cook despite being promoted to free-colored lieutenant. At best, his ascension to the lieutenant's grade would greatly enhance his standing among other free-coloreds in his city or town, while lightly nudging his place upward in the realm of broader civil society. While there was much to be said about augmenting one's status among free-colored peers, that was certainly not the brusque tearing of class/caste boundaries that has been so often associated with free-colored militia duty.

With that said, there were some remarkable examples of free-colored success within the militia framework. There were the Escobar and Villaseca families in Mexico City, as well as the Santanders and Bertels in Puebla, just to name a few. However, what distinguished those families from the rest was that they entered the corps at a level already several notches above that of the average free-colored recruit. Poised for success in prominent professions such as commerce, they multiplied their accomplishments by exploiting every available opportunity that the militia offered. They found rapid access to the highest militia posts. Tribute-collection commissions, maize collections, extortion rackets—all subsequently provided handsome income supplements. For these men, the militia tie was seen as a status symbol. And they wanted all the trappings. Two successive colonelcies for the Bertel family only solidified their already strong economic base by adding both the link of crown fealty and the power of command over the colony's entire free-colored corps. Exclusive access to royal medals and the right to wear officer uniforms radiated their authority. Equally, the Santanders, with independent fortunes, flaunted their captaincies for social prestige.

Yet these men remained free-coloreds, and publicly so. Even in their highly favored positions, service in the *pardo* militia did not offer a means to escape the confines of race; rather, it better allowed them the ability to negotiate race's meaning. For instance, they were entitled to the *fuero*. Although in practice *fuero* invocations frequently proved a failure, they still presented substantial challenges to the traditional channels of legal authority. Moreover, as a graduated privilege whose value and coverage increased according to rank, the *fuero* worked best for the militia's officers. In this sense, for men such as the Bertels, Escobars, and Santanders, court immunity was seen as a cherished right that proved instrumental toward helping them to define their position in society. Along with their militia *preeminencias*, including relief from debtor's prison and tribute exclusion, their corporate privileges favorably altered their legal position as blacks.

Such statements are of wide consequence. In terms of the broader literature on the African Diaspora and the role of race in the Americas, I believe that the case of the Mexican militia is valuable in illuminating the relationship between racial identity and privilege. Often, the free-colored acquisition of privilege and status has been assessed as either the signaler of a whitening process, or as evidence that "class" supplanted "race" as the principal patterning force of colonial social relations. Hence, social mobility has been repeatedly scrutinized under the terms of the caste versus class debate. The practice of equating class mobility with whitening has persisted as a prominent theme in nineteenth- and twentieth-century Latin American historiography as well.[3] But when status ascension is examined in light of free-colored participation in corporate institutions like the militia, different interpretations result. For families like the Escobars, free-colored social mobility was attained within a free-colored racial framework. That is to say that their class gains did not necessarily trump caste affiliations. Nor did privilege or status gains indicate eager efforts at racial mobility. Instead, social advancement was made on the premise that the family was composed of *pardo* militiamen. Being *pardo* was a necessary part of the success equation. Speaking in more theoretical terms, free-colored participation in racially defined corporate institutions like the militia, and even black confraternities, opened the possibility for a coexistence between caste and class social structures. The two were not mutually exclusive, mainly because the corporate rights of these institutions intervened, offering space for a fluid reconceptualization of caste and class. With corporate institutions as mediators, the boundaries of caste became looser without becoming lost completely. The ensuing situation proved advantageous for many New World blacks. It became truly possible for *mulatos* to become legally free of the burdens traditionally assigned to their caste, while coming to a new, personal understanding of what *mulatoness* meant in the process. In a sense, therefore, the militia example offers some supporting evidence to those who prefer utilizing *calidad* as a proper means of examining colonial society. Essentially, this position, as articulated by Robert McCaa, favors placing a stronger emphasis on understanding how connections between caste and class status defined one's overall social station.[4] But again, what is new through the militia analysis is having the ability to see precisely how *calidad* could be manipulated in ways that would transform, yet not eliminate, the social meaning of blackness.

These points still do not fully answer the question of why race would matter to the most socially mobile members of the free-colored corps. It is not inherently intuitive that color should serve as a natural bonding mechanism, nor even a social distinguisher.[5] Besides, the free-colored categories of *pardo*, *moreno*, and *mulato* were constructs of the colonial regime, created for the crown's own benefit. In response, I ultimately believe that an analysis of the militia provides what Paul Gilroy has termed the "ideological work" behind transforming physical difference into a true racial signifier.[6] Free-colored soldiers consistently subscribed to the racial labeling created for them under the caste system because there were concrete benefits to be derived from institutionally linked racial affiliations. Access to corporate privileges provided the cornerstone for building their racial consciousness. Since being *pardo* or *moreno* in the militia context did not carry the same weight as for those lacking their privileged legal immunities, color status became safer to claim. By referring to themselves in caste-laden nomenclature, the militiamen secured added privileges, or fought to preserve existing benefits. Ultimately, for families like the Escobars, the ensuing position and influence they wielded as "*pardo* militiamen" probably exceeded that which they would have possessed as Escobars in a racially neutered, militia-less form.

On some level, I believe that many of the same principles described above also applied to the militia's rank and file, despite the fact that they were not as socially mobile as the corps' leading families. We have already discussed how the material rewards of militia service, notably in occupational terms, were least for these soldiers. But what baited them and kept them involved in service were tribute immunities and *fuero* rights. The ability of the militia to mediate land claims and influence local politics was an equally strong attraction. As militiamen participated in the institution on those grounds, racially laden language surfaced in their written documents. Scores of appeals for tribute exemption saw soldiers willingly referencing themselves as *pardos*, *morenos*, and *mulatos*. Early eighteenth-century conflagrations in Tamiagua, as well as Domingo Ramos's bold use of the *fuero* to uphold the perceived rights of the *pardo* community in Acayucan, offer other concrete instances in which racial identity was manifested through institutional participation (see Chapters 5 and 6). Even the attempted maneuvers by the soldiers of the Pacific coast to secure farmland in the name of the *república de pardos militares* speaks to an evolving sense of racial consciousness that affected the rank and file (see Chapter 3).

Occasionally, the militiamen's jockeying for benefits led to internal bickering about nuances of color within the free-colored units themselves. *Pardos* sought to deny rights to *morenos*; *mulatos* disdained rights afforded to the *negros*. These fractious disputes serve to reinforce the notion of how expressions of racial identity were strongly predicated upon the heavy desire for privilege. Free-coloreds could become divisible by color when privileges were at stake. However, when threats to the soldiers' rights emanated from outside their institution, the militiamen retaliated, more unified in kind. Unlike internal disputes, confrontations with outsiders jeopardized the basic integrity of privileges for their entire corps—*pardos, morenos,* and *mulatos* alike. In such circumstances, deeper corporate bonds generated a broader racial solidarity. As seen in Guajolotitlan and Tamiagua, sometimes the resistance to outsiders was firm, overt, and highly racialized. The degree of the free-colored population's militarization in a given zone, the scale of the perceived threat to their rights, as well as the scope of collective black involvement in local economic and political endeavors provided key variables that conditioned the strength of the soldiers' racial bonding. When these factors were reduced, confrontations with outsiders were calmer and more racially subdued. When heightened, resistance to outsiders acquired a greater confrontational tone.

It is important to underscore here that sometimes the soldiers' expressions of race involved a degree of personal risk. Again, consider Domingo Ramos's belligerent activities and the hostilities that brewed in Tamiagua. Atop these were the furtive rebellions planned in Guajolotitlan and Acayucan during the 1780s and 1790s, both of which operated on an assumed regional, racial unity. That some militiamen were willing to step outside of their comfort zone, exposing themselves to danger in using their racial/corporate affiliations, implies that racial consciousness had indeed gathered significant strength in certain areas of the colony.

Nevertheless, it must not be forgotten that the defining aspect of a corporate-based racial identity was its conditionality. Even in areas where a militia-inspired racial identity appeared to be entrenched, there was always the chance that members of the corps could backtrack on their declared race. Let's revisit the situation found in Puebla during the mid-1790s, described in Chapters 3 and 6. When Viceroy Revillagigedo threatened to terminate militia duty in the city, the soldiers presented a typical, unified response to preserve their institution, peppered with occasional mentions of racial solidarity. But when the viceroy's machinations finally succeeded and were upheld by his successor, several soldiers tried a different approach. Rather than continuing to describe themselves as *mulatos,* many confessed that they were actually mestizos or *indios caciques,* hoping to find other ways to secure release from the dreaded free-colored tribute burden. Tellingly, overt expressions of free-colored racial affiliation ceased when the benefits of corporate privilege were completely eliminated. We can conjecture that this held true throughout Mexico in the late eighteenth and early nineteenth centuries, wherever free-colored forces were successfully abolished.

Reference Matter

Appendix

TABLE A.1

List of Recruits by Race for the Provincial Regiment of Tampico, Panuco, and the Jurisdiction of Huexutla, 1766

Towns	Whites	Castizos	Mestizos	Pardos	Total	Absentees[a]
Tantoyuca	22	0	0	241	263	80
Tempoal	1	1	0	76	78	23
Ozuluama	6	0	0	168	174	46
Panuco	3	3	6	152	164	55
Tampico	0	0	0	169	169	15
TOTAL	32	4	6	806	848	219

Source: AGN, I.G., vol. 490-A, August 9, 1766, Gorostiza to Villaba.
[a]Denotes men absent at time of recruitment and not included in the regiment.

TABLE A.2

Racial Classification of Officer Corps in the Provinces of Tampico, Panuco, and the Jurisdiction of Huextla, 1766

Towns	White Captains	Pardo Captains	White Lieutenants	Pardo Lieutenants	White 2nd Lieutenants	Pardo 2nd Lieutenants
Tantoyuca	2	0	2	0	3	0
Tempoal	1	0	1	0	1	0
Ozuluama	2	0	3	0	0	2
Panuco	0	1	0	1	1	0
Tampico	1	0	0	1	0	1
Huexutla	2	0	1	0	1	0
TOTAL	8	1	7	2	6	3

Source: AGN, I.G., vol. 490-A, Gorostiza to Marques de Croix, October 17, 1766; AGN, I.G., vol. 490-A, Gorostiza to Villaba, October 1766.

TABLE A.3

Provincial Militia Units in New Spain, 1766

Unit Type and Location	Number of Militiamen
Infantry Regiment of Mexico City	1,000
Infantry Regiment of Tlaxcala	991
Infantry Regiment of Puebla	991
Infantry Regiment of Córdoba	991
Infantry Regiment of Toluca	1,000
Infantry Regiment of Veracruz	530
Infantry Battalion of Oaxaca	465
Pardo Infantry Battalion of Puebla	280
Pardo Infantry Battalion of Mexico City	520
Pardo and Moreno Infantry Companies, Veracruz	438
Dragoon Regiment of Puebla	638
Cavalry Regiment of Querétaro	648
Lancers of Veracruz	714
Regular Cadre for Second Cavalry Regiment	38
TOTAL PROVINCIAL MILITIA	9,224

Source: McAlister, *Fuero Militar*, 94.

TABLE A.4

Provincial Militia Units in New Spain, 1784

Unit Type and Location	Number of Militiamen
Infantry Regiment of Mexico City	1,464
Infantry Regiment of Tlaxcala	1,464
Infantry Regiment of Córdoba and Jalapa	1,464
Infantry Regiment of Toluca	1,464
Infantry Battalion of Oaxaca	758
Dragoon Regiment of Puebla	588
Dragoon Regiment of Valladolid (Michoacán)	588
Infantry Battalion of Valladolid	732
Infantry and Cavalry of the Legión del Principe	758
Infantry and Cavalry of the Legión de San Carlos	928
Pardo Infantry Battalion of Mexico City	758
Pardo Infantry Battalion of Puebla	758
Cavalry Regiment of Querétaro	588
Lancers of Veracruz	400
Cavalry of the Legión del Principe	1,446
Cavalry of the Legión de San Carlos	2,597
TOTAL PROVINCIAL MILITIA	16,755

Source: McAlister, *Fuero Militar*, 95–96.

TABLE A.5

The Militia Forces According to the Crespo Plan

Unit Type and Location	Peacetime Strength	Wartime Strength
Infantry Regiment of Mexico City	833	1,361
Infantry Regiment of Tlaxcala	833	1,361
Infantry Regiment of Córdoba	833	1,361
Infantry Regiment of Toluca	833	1,361
Infantry Battalion of Guanajuato (del Príncipe)	417	681
Infantry Battalion of San Carlos (San Luis Potosí)	417	680
Infantry Battalion of Oaxaca	417	681
Infantry Battalion of Valladolid (Michoacán)	417	681
Pardo Infantry Battalion of Mexico City	417	681
Pardo Infantry Battalion of Puebla	417	680
Regiment of Provincial Grenadiers	1,139	1,139
Regiment of Provincial Light Infantry	1,139	1,139
Cavalry Regiment of Querétaro	361	613
Cavalry Regiment of Guanajuato (del Príncipe)	361	613
Cavalry Regiment of San Carlos (San Luis Potosí)	361	613
Cavalry Regiment of San Luis (San Luis Potosí)	361	613
Dragoon Regiment of Puebla	361	617
Dragoon Regiment of Michoacán	361	617
Dragoon Regiment of Volunteers	617	617
Lancers of Veracruz	180	306
Urban and Coastal Militias (Nonprovincial Forces)	6,693	
Sueltas Companies	22,232	
TOTAL MILITIA STRENGTH	40,000	45,339

Source: Archer, *The Army in Bourbon Mexico*, 25.

TABLE A.6

Militia Units of the Costa Sur, Extending from the Jurisdiction of Acaponeta to Tehuantepec, Proposed Changes in 1793

Location and Division Number	Españoles Companies	Españoles Men	Pardos Companies	Pardos Men	Total Soldiers Companies	Total Soldiers Men
Jurisdiction of Acaponeta, 1st Division	0	0	1	90	1	90
Presidio de Paramita, 1st Division	0	0	1	68	1	68
Jurisdiction of Sentispac, 1st Division	0	0	1	112	1	112
Jurisdiction of Tepic, 1st Division	1	55	4	360	5	415
Compostela, 1st Division	0	0	1	79	1	79
Jurisdictions of Purificacion and Autlan, 2nd Division	0	0	2	224	2	224
Jurisdiction of Amula, 2nd Division	0	0	1	68	1	68
Jurisdiction of Colima, 2nd Division	1	88	5	560	6	648
Partido of Motines, 2nd Division	0	0	1	55	1	55
Partido of Zacatula, 2nd Division	1	55	2	224	3	279
Jurisdiction of Acapulco, 3rd Division	0	0	3	336	3	336
Jurisdiction of Igualapa, 4th Division	1	55	4	448	5	503

TABLE A.6—CONT'D

Location and Division Number	Españoles Compa-nies	Españoles Men	Pardos Compa-nies	Pardos Men	Total Soldiers Compa-nies	Total Soldiers Men
Jurisdiction of Xicayán, 4th Division	1	88	5	560	6	648
Partido of Huamelula, 5th Division	0	0	1	55	1	55
Province of Tehuantepec, 5th Division	1	55	3	336	4	391
TOTAL[a]	6	396	35	3,575	41	3,971

Source: Bandos, vol. 17, exp. 50, Reglamento provisional para el regimen, gobierno y nueva planta de las compañias de milicias de la costa del sur del reyno de Nueva España, dese la jurisdicción de Acaponeta hasta Tehuantepec, October 22, 1793, fs. 216–18.

[a]Prior to the 1793 reforms, there were a total of eighty-three militia companies registered for the Costa Sur. Consequently, the reforms brought a more than 50 percent reduction in the number of companies.

TABLE A.7

Militia Units in Nuevo Santander, Proposed Changes in 1793[a]

Location	No. of Militiamen Compa-nies	No. of Militiamen Men	Location	No. of Militiamen Compa-nies	No. of Militiamen Men
Villa de Valles	1	60	Valle del Maiz	1	60
Aquizmon	1	60	Rio-verde	2	120
Tampamolon y Coscatlan	1	60	TOTAL	6	360

Source: AGN, Bandos, vol. 17, exp. 5, Reglamento provisional para el cuerpo de milicias de caballeria, que con el nombre frontera de la colonia del Nuevo Santander, debe formarse en la jurisdicción de los valles y partido de Rioverde, con el objeto de atender a la defensa de aquel territorio contra los indios gentiles de la expresada colonia, auxiliar a su gobernador, al comandante de la milicia de Sierra Gorda, y a la costa de Tampico en tiempo de guerra, February 19, 1793, fol. 49.

[a]According to the *reglamento*, the principal population base for these companies was to come from the *pardos* and *morenos libres. Españoles* and mestizos could be enrolled as well. Officers were to be whites.

TABLE A.8

Militia Units in Tabasco, Proposed Changes in 1793

Location	Españoles Companies[a]	Españoles Men	Pardos Companies	Pardos Men	Total Soldiers
Tacotalpa	1/9	14	1	112	126
Teapa	1/9	14	1	112	126
Xalapa	1/9	14	1	112	126
Villahermosa	1/9	14	1	112	126
Cunduacan	1/9	14	1	112	126
Xalpa	1/9	14	1	112	126
Nacajuca	1/9	14	1	78	92
Macuspana	1/9	7	1	78	85
Usumacinta, Jonutla	1/9	7	1	78	85
TOTAL[b]	1	112	9	906	1,018

Source: AGN, Bandos, vol. 17, exp. 12, Reglamento provisional para el régimen, gobierno y nueva planta de las milicias de la provincia de Tabasco, May 29, 1793, fol. 103.

[a]There was only one white company in Tabasco, with a small selection of men drawn from each town.

[b]Prior to the 1793 reforms there were 27 militia companies in Tabasco. After the reforms, only 10 remained, representing a more than 50 percent reduction in these units.

TABLE A.9

Militia Units of the Seno Mexicano Extending from Tampico and Panuco to the River of Guazacualco, Proposed Changes in 1793[a]

Location and Division Number	Number of Militiamen Companies	Men
Tampico, 1st Division	1	112
Panuco, 1st Division	1	112
Osuluama and Tantima, 1st Division	1	112
Tantoyucan and Tempoal, 1st Division	1	112
Tamiagua, 2nd Division	2	224
Tuxpan and Tihuatlan, 2nd Division	1	112
Tamapachi, 2nd Division	1	112
Papantla, 2nd Division	1	135
Nautla, 2nd Division	1	84
Misantla and Colipa, 2nd Division	1	84
Alvarado, 3rd Division	2	224
Tacotalpan, 3rd Division	2	270
San Andrés and Tuxtla, 3rd Division	1	135
Cosamaluapan, 3rd Division	2	224
Acayucan, 4th Division	4	448
TOTAL[b]	22	2,500

Source: AGN, Bandos vol. 17, exp. 15, Reglamento provisional para el régimen, gobierno y nueva planta de las compañias de milicias mixtas del seno que comprende la provincia de Tampico y Panuco, hasta el Rio Guazacualco, costas laterales de Veracruz, June 18, 1793, fol. 125.

[a]According to the *reglamento,* the principal population base for these companies was to come from the *pardos* and *morenos libres. Españoles* and mestizos could be enrolled if desired. Officers were to be white.

[b]Prior to the 1793 reforms there were thirty-two companies along the Seno Mexicano. After the reforms there were only twenty-two companies, representing a greater than 25 percent decrease in the number of units.

TABLE A.10

Militia Units in the Yucatan, 1778

Location	Españoles Battalions	Men	Pardos Companies	Men	Racially Mixed Units Companies	Men	Total Soldiers
Mérida	1	676	8	684	0	0	1,360
Campeche	1	676	8	684	0	0	1,360
Bacalar	0	0	0	0	2	126	126
TOTAL	2	1,352	16	1,368	2	126	2,846

Source: AGN, I.G., vol. 394-A, Reglamento para las milicias de infanteria de la provincia de Yucatan y Campeche, 1778, fs. 1–34.

TABLE A.11

The Credit Network of Joseph Escobar the Elder

Debts Owed	Pesos
Tribute arrears	1,100
To Ten. Col. Dn. Francisco Velez de Escalante	2,500
To Dn. Juan Nuñez de Villavicencio	850
To Dn. Nicolas Eguren (mercader)	400
To Dn. Andres de Berno (part of a 6,000-peso loan)	180
TOTAL OWED	5,030

Debts owed to Joseph Escobar

	Pesos
By Dn. Francisco, vecino	800
By Dn. Juan Ozes, vecino	500
By Melchor de la Vega, maestro latonero	100
By Dn. Benito Castañeda	150
By Dn. Joseph Garido y Rivera, asentista de pulque de Xochimilco	44
By Dn. Manuel Maldonado, procurador de la audiencia ordinaria	90
By Dn. Joseph Eubio, maestro tintorero	43
By Juan Velázquez, oficial de hacer cardas, Tacuba	50
By Dn. Juan Manuel de la Cueva, alguacil mayor de Metepec	100
By Dn. Francisco Cuellar, vecino	100
By Alférez Bernardo González, de la compañia de morenos	40
By Dn. Juan Alvarez, alguacil mayor de Istlahuaca	37
By Dn. Juan de Dios, escribano de su majestad, vecino	16
By Dn. Pedro Blanco, portero de Real Sala de Crimen	25
By Ignacio Diaz de la Peña, vecino	140
By Nicolas Villaseñor, vecino	29
By Bachiller Dn. Juan Carro de la Vega, presbytero	72
By Juan de Melgarejo, vecino de San Lazaro	120
By Juan de Aguilar, repartidor de ropa y tirador de oro	100
By Bachiller Dn. Antonio Verdigues, presbytero de arzobispado	26
By Dn. Benito Bermudez de Castro	1,230
By Dn. Salvador de la cruz, caballero, vecino de Tacuba	22
By Dn. Andres Servantes, alcalde mayor de Apa y Tepeapulco	43
By Simon de Huertas, maestro sastre	692
By Dn. Sebastian Avares, dueño de obraje	416
By Dn. Miguel Garcia Arias Rio Jondo, mayordomo del Baton de Sta. Lucia	35
By Miguel Garzes, pardo, sastre	20
By Juan Antonio Arias, pardo, bordador	12
By Dn. Manuel Ordoñes	9
By Dn. Juan Bautista Pavia, dueño de obraje	12
By Doña Josepha Celidonia de Camos	100
By Doña Antonia de Bastida, viuda de Dn. Antonio Orosco, maestro platero	20
By Thomas de la Vega, maestro latonero y dorador	80
By Gregorio Alonso, escribano de su majestad, vecino	200
By Juan Agustin Prieto	500
By Bernardino Calderon, repartidor de ropa del barrio de Sta. Maria Catherina Martin	50
By Joseph de Medina, colector de diezmos del Valle de Amilpas	280
By Juan Arziniesa, soldado de la guardia del Virrey	19
By Antonio Jiminez, soldado de la guardia del Virrey	12
By Antonio de la Peña, soldado de la guardia del Virrey	5
By Juan de Espindola, soldado de la guardia del Virrey	27
By Joachin Alvares, soldado de la guardia del Virrey	13
TOTAL OWED	6,379

Source: AN, vol. 2259, Juan Lopez de Bocanegra (343), fs. 211–12v.

TABLE A.12

Average Age of the Free-Colored Officers by Rank, 1768–72

Location	Rank	Average Age	Location	Rank	Average Age
Veracruz	Captain	42	Ahualulco	Captain	40
	Lieutenant	47		Lieutenant	60
	2nd Lieutenant	36		Alferez	60
	Adjutant	40		Sergeant	28
	Sergeant	35	La Magdalena	Captain	50
Mexico City	Colonel	42		Lieutenant	45
	Sergeant Major	45		Alferez	35
	Captain	36		Sergeant	29
	Lieutenant	37	Izatlan	Captain	44
	2nd Lieutenant	29		Lieutenant	22
	Adjutant	37		Alferez	41
Valladolid	Captain	35		Sergeant	30
	Lieutenant	32	Jamiltepec	Captain	50
	2nd Lieutenant	32		Lieutenant	42
Patzuaro	Captain	44		Alferez	48
	Lieutenant	29	Tutupec	Captain	90
	2nd Lieutenant	26		Lieutenant	45
Guadalajara	Captain	35		Alferez	40
	Lieutenant	44	Cuistla	Captain	n/a
	Adjutant	46		Lieutenant	55
	Alferez	35		Alferez	45
	Sergeant	40	Guajolotitlan,	Captain	80
Compostela	Captain	52	Company 1		
	Lieutenant	52		Lieutenant	55
	Alferez	42		Alferez	45
	Sergeant	32	Guajolotitlan,	Captain	50
Tamazula	Captain	53	Company 2	Lieutenant	48
	Lieutenant	35		Alferez	50
	Alferez	43	Guajolotitlan,	Captain	45
	Sergeant	39	Company 3	Lieutenant	50
Tuscacuesco	Captain	42		Alferez	38
	Lieutenant	46	Pinotepa del Rey	Captain	48
	Alferez	46		Lieutenant	55
	Sergeant	42		Alferez	48
Quautitlan	Captain	50	Cortijos	Captain	70
	Lieutenant	46		Lieutenant	70
	Alferez	37		Alferez	55
	Sergeant	35	Tapestla	Captain	50
Tecolotlan	Captain	51		Lieutenant	45
	Lieutenant	60		Alferez	40
	Alferez	35	San Andres and	Captain	45
	Sergeant	43	Santiago Tuxtla	Lieutenant	70
Hacienda de				2nd Lieutenant	64
Ahuacapan	Captain	30			
	Lieutenant	46			
	Alferez	40			
	Sergeant	33			

Source: AGN, I.G., vol. 252-B, exp. 7, Diego Joaquin Garabito, November 1772; AGN, I.G., vol. 9, fs. 17–47; 62–81; 196–206.

Notes

The following abbreviations are used:

AGEY Archivo Genereal del Estado de Yucatan
AGN Archivo General de la Nación
AHAP Archivo Historico del Ayuntamiento de Puebla
AHV Archivo Historico de Veracruz
AJP Archivo Judicial de Puebla, INAH Puebla
AN Archivo de Notarías del Distrito Federal
BNAH Subdirección de Documentación de la Biblioteca Nacional de Historia
I.G. Indiferentes de Guerra

INTRODUCTION

1. Colin A. Palmer, *Slaves of the White God: Blacks in Mexico 1570–1650* (Cambridge: Cambridge Univ. Press, 1976), 28.

2. The technical term *pardo* refers to the offspring of a black and an Indian, while the *mulato* is the progeny of a white and black union. In less technical circumstances *pardo* often represents a mixed-blood having at least one parent of African descent. *Pardo* and *mulato* became almost interchangeable terms in the eighteenth century. The term *moreno* served to delineate a "pure black" having two black parents. *Moreno* and *negro* were interchangeable. The *morisco*, a less common racial description, referred to the offspring of a Spaniard and a *mulato*. Complete essays on racial categories and the caste system can be found in Leslie B. Rout, Jr., *The African Experience in Spanish America, 1502 to the Present Day* (Cambridge, England: Cambridge Univ. Press, 1976), 126–34; Gonzalo Aguirre Beltrán, *La población negra de Mexico: Estudio etnohistórico*, 3d ed. (Mexico City: Fondo de Cultura Economica, 1989), 153–94; and Magnus Mörner, *Race Mixture in the History of Latin America* (Boston: Little, Brown and Company, 1967), 53–73.

3. Aguirre Beltrán, *La población negra*, 222–30. Some feel that this figure is an exaggeration of the free-colored population. See Herbert S. Klein, *African Slavery in Latin America and the Caribbean* (New York and Oxford: Oxford Univ. Press, 1986), 222. The limitations and advantages of Beltrán's work are discussed in Sherburne F. Cook and Woodrow Borah, *Essays in Population History: Mexico and the Caribbean* (Berkeley:

Univ. of California Press, 1974), 2:180–269. Aguirre Beltrán's 1793 numbers are essentially adaptations of the incomplete yet superb military censuses of 1793. In the Mexican archival holdings, these documents are stored in two repositories, the Padrones section and the Ramo Historia. Aguirre Beltrán, using the summary sheets, has noted that the Padrones portion records 94,597 *pardos* and *morenos* in the colony. After incorporating the information from Ramo Historia, which adds the regions of Alta California, New Mexico, Sonora, Sinaloa, Durango, Mexico City, Tabasco, and Mérida, the figure jumps to 186,977. We can claim with certainty that the Afro-Mexican population numbered at least that amount on the eve of the nineteenth century. See also: "The Foundation of Nuestra Señora de Guadalupe de los Morenos de Amapa, Mexico (1769)," in *Colonial Spanish America: A Documentary History*, ed. Kenneth Mills and William B. Taylor (Wilmington, Del.: Scholarly Resources, 1998), 275. Here, the free-colored population of more than 380,000 was said to represent 6 percent of the colony's inhabitants.

4. Compare with data from Rout, *African Experience*, 134; and Klein, *African Slavery*, 221–25.

5. For some examples, see Philip A. Howard, *Changing History: Afro-Cuban Cabildos and Societies of Color in the Nineteenth Century* (Baton Rouge: Louisiana State Univ. Press, 1998); and Ermila Troconis de Veracoechea, "Tres Cofradías de Negros en la Iglesia de San Mauricio en Caracas." *Montalban UCAB* 5 (1976): 339–76.

6. For more details on Mexican guilds, see Manuel Carrera Stampa, *Los gremios Mexicanos: La organización gremial en Nueva España 1521–1861* (Mexico City: EDIAPSA, 1954).

7. Good discussions of legislative restrictions include *Recopilación de leyes de los reynos de las Indias, 1681*, Libro VII, Titulo V; Palmer, *Slaves of the White God*, 178–86; Rout, *The African Experience*, 126–61; Frederick P. Bowser, *The African Slave in Colonial Peru, 1524–1650* (Stanford: Stanford Univ. Press, 1974), 302–23; Bowser, "Colonial Spanish America," in *Neither Slave Nor Free*, ed. David W. Cohen and Jack P. Greene (Baltimore and London: Johns Hopkins Univ. Press, 1972), 38–42; and Mörner, *Race Mixture*, 35–48, 62–68.

8. Peter Wade, *Race and Ethnicity in Latin America* (London and Chicago: Pluto Press, 1997), 28–30.

9. Proponents of the class position in the caste versus class debate include John K. Chance and William B. Taylor, "Estate and Class in a Colonial City, Oaxaca in 1792," *Comparative Studies in Society and History* 19 (1977): 454–87; Chance and Taylor, "The Ecology of Race and Class in Late Colonial Oaxaca," in *Studies in Spanish American Population History*, ed. David J. Robinson (Boulder, Colo.: Westview Press, 1981), 93–117; and Dennis Nodin Valdes, "The Decline of the Sociedad de Castas in Mexico City" (Ph.D. diss., Univ. of Michigan, 1978). Historians arguing the "estate" or caste position include Mörner, "Economic Factors and Stratification in Colonial Spanish America with Special Regard to Elites," *Hispanic American Historical Review (HAHR)* 63, no. 2 (1983): 335–69; Lyle N. McAlister, "Social Structure and Social Change in New Spain," *HAHR* 43, no. 3 (1963): 349–70; Woodrow Borah and Sherburne Cook, "Sobre las posibilidades de hacer el estudio histórico del mestizaje sobre una base demografica," *Revista de Historia de América* 53/54 (1962): 181–90; and Silvia Arrom, *The Women of Mexico City, 1790–1857* (Stanford: Stanford Univ. Press, 1985). Major challenges and insights into both positions have been posited by Patricia Seed, "The Social Dimensions of Race: Mexico City 1753," *HAHR* 62, no. 4 (1982): 569–606; Rodney D. Anderson, "Race and Social Stratification: A Comparison of Working-Class Spaniards, Indians and Castas in Guadalajara, Mexico in

1821," *HAHR* 68, no. 2 (1988): 209–41; Robert Douglas Cope, *The Limits of Racial Domination: Plebeian Society in Colonial Mexico City, 1660–1720* (Madison: Univ. of Wisconsin Press, 1994); Richard Boyer, *Cast and Identity in Colonial Mexico: A Proposal and an Example* (Storrs, Conn.; Providence, R.I.; and Amherst, Mass.: Latin American Studies Consortium of New England, 1997); Robert H. Jackson, *Race, Caste, and Status: Indians in Colonial Spanish America* (Albuquerque: Univ. of New Mexico Press, 1999); Robert McCaa, Stuart B. Schwartz, and Arturo Grubessich, "Race and Class in Colonial Latin America: A Critique," *Comparative Studies in Society and History* 25 (1979): 421–33; with a reply to this article by Chance and Taylor, "Estate and Class: A Reply," *Comparative Studies in Society and History* 25 (1979): 434–42.

10. Some preliminary observations on black soldiers during the Independence era have been presented by Ted Vincent, "The Blacks who Freed Mexico," *The Journal of Negro History* 79, no. 3 (1994): 257–76.

CHAPTER 1

1. Archivo General de la Nación (AGN), Indiferentes de Guerra (I.G.) vol. 28-B, Correspondencia con los pardos de Veracruz, 1777.

2. AGN, Intestados, vol. 242, fs. 160–65; AGN, I.G. vol. 42, Consulta que hace el Sr. Inspector sobre los malos tratamientos que experimentan los individuos del batallon de pardos de esta capital por las justicias ordinarios, y sus dependientes, June 1778.

3. For an account of the fall of Havana and the implications for Cuba, see Allan J. Kuethe, *Cuba, 1753–1815: Crown, Military, and Society* (Knoxville: Univ. of Tennessee Press, 1986). For other works on reforms in the Spanish Americas, see Kuethe, *Military Reform and Society in New Granada, 1773–1808* (Gainesville: Univ. of Florida Press, 1978); Leon G. Campbell, *The Military and Society in Colonial Peru, 1750–1810* (Philadelphia: The American Philosophical Society, 1978); Campbell, "The Army of Peru and the Túpac Amaru Revolt, 1780–1783," *Hispanic American Historical Review (HAHR)* 56, no. 1 (1976): 31–57; Christon I. Archer, *The Army in Bourbon Mexico, 1760–1810* (Albuquerque: Univ. of New Mexico Press, 1977); Maria del Carmen Velazquez, *El estado de guerra en Nueva España, 1760–1808* (Mexico City: El Colegio de México, 1950); Juan Ortiz Escamilla, "Las guerras Napoleónicas y la defensa de la Nueva España en la provincia de Veracruz, 1793–1810," in *Población y estructura urbana en México, siglos XVIII y XIX*, comp. Carmen Blázquez Domínguez, Carlos Contreras Cruz, and Sonia Pérez Toledo (Xalapa, Veracruz: Universidad Veracruzana, 1996), 213–21; Lyle N. McAlister, *The "Fuero Militar" in New Spain, 1764–1800* (Gainesville: Univ. of Florida Press, 1957), and McAlister, "The Reorganization of the Army of New Spain, 1763–1767," *HAHR* 33, no. 1 (1953): 1–32.

4. Juan Marchena Fernández, *Oficiales y soldados en el ejército de América* (Seville: Escuela de Estudios Hispanoamericanos, 1983), 50–51.

5. Juan Marchena Fernández, *Ejército y milicias en el mundo colonial Americano* (Seville: Editorial Mapfre, 1992), 128.

6. The Callao ships were stationed during the seventeenth century. Campbell, *The Military and Society in Colonial Peru*, 1–6.

7. Among the best works detailing the period before the Bourbon reforms are Marchena Fernández, *Oficiales y soldados;* and Paul E. Hoffman, *The Spanish Crown and the Defense of the Caribbean, 1535–1585: Precedent, Patrimonialism, and Royal Parsimony* (Baton Rouge and London: Louisiana State University Press, 1980).

8. John Lynch, *Spain, 1516–1598: From Nation State to World Empire* (Oxford and

Cambridge, Mass.: Basil Blackwell, 1991); and Lynch, *Bourbon Spain, 1700–1808* (Oxford and Cambridge, Massachusetts: Basil Blackwell, 1989). For a comparative perspective on Spain's defenses in the Indies, see John Robert McNeill, *Atlantic Empires of France and Spain: Louisbourg and Havana, 1700–1763* (Chapel Hill and London: Univ. of North Carolina Press, 1985).

9. Marchena Fernández, "La financiación militar en Indias: Introducción a su estudio," *Anuario de Estudios Americanos* 36 (1979): 81–110; Carlos Marichal and Matilde Souto Mantecón, "Silver and Situados: New Spain and the Financing of the Spanish Empire in the Caribbean in the Eighteenth Century," *HAHR* 74, no. 4 (1994): 587–613; and Engel Sluiter, *The Florida Situado: Quantifying the First Eighty Years, 1571–1651* (Gainesville: Univ. of Florida Press, 1985).

10. Hoffman, *The Spanish Crown*, 235.

11. Marchena Fernández, *Oficiales y soldados*, 16–29.

12. Ibid., 24–29. These were locations where the number of soldiers was high but the financial means to support them was low. For the Mexican case, see Christon I. Archer, "Bourbon Finances and Military Policy in New Spain, 1759–1812," *Americas* 37, no. 3 (1981): 315–50.

13. Marchena Fernández, *Ejército y milicias*, 159.

14. Ibid., 128.

15. Bibiano Torres Ramírez, *La armada de Barlovento* (Seville: Escuela de Estudios Hispano-Americanos de Sevilla, 1981), 212.

16. René Quatrefegas, "The Military System of the Spanish Habsburgs," in *Armed Forces and Society in Spain*, ed. Rafael Bañon Martínez and Thomas M. Barker (New York: Columbia University Press, 1988), 40–42; and Pere Molas Ribalta, "The Early Bourbons and the Military," in *Armed Forces and Society in Spain*, 66–73.

17. Marchena Fernández, *Oficiales y soldados*, 112–13; and Kuethe, *Cuba*, 6–7. Note that the senior officer staff was almost completely manned by penninsulars during the first half of the eighteenth century. See Marchena Fernández, *Ejército y milicias*, 166.

18. *Recopilación de leyes de los Reynos de las Indias, 1681*, Libro III, Titulo X.

19. Archer, "The Officer Corps in New Spain: The Marial Career, 1759–1821," *Jarbuch fur Geschichte von Staat, Wirschaft, und Gesellschaft Lateinamerikas* 19, no. 18 (1982): 138–42.

20. Archer, *The Army in Bourbon Mexico*, 223–53; and Archer, "To Serve the King: Military Recruitment in Late Colonial Mexico," *HAHR* 55, no. 2 (1975): 231–33.

21. Marchena Fernández, *Oficiales y soldados*, 45–50; and Marchena Fernández, *Ejército y milicias*, 13–46. There were some exceptions to the endurance of the *encomendero* armies. In many areas, the *encomienda* system did not end abruptly in 1718 but persisted well into the eighteenth century. In these contexts, *econmendero* forces often remained active. See Virginia Guedea, "La organización militar," in *El gobierno provincial en la Nueva España, 1570–1787*, ed. Woodrow Borah (Mexico City: Universidad Autónoma de México, 1985), 134.

22. Hoffman, *The Spanish Crown*, 41.

23. There is some debate on this issue. See Marchena Fernández, *Ejército y milicias*, 103–9. He argues that there were two types, rural and urban, that were distinguishable by the geographic area in which they served. But in my review of military documents, all units before the 1760s were called "urban" units. Among urban units, there could be distinctions in internal organization, based on geographical location. My views coincide with the opinions of Archer and McAlister. See Christon I. Archer, "The Military," in

Cities and Society in Colonial Latin America, ed. Louisa Schell Hoberman and Susan Migden Socolow (Albuquerque: Univ. of New Mexico Press, 1986), 201–7; and Lyle N. McAlister, *Fuero Militar,* 2.

24. Since the number of participants in the colonial militias was always changing, no comprehensive figures can be provided about their size. Instead, the study of the institution has revolved around the nature of the legislation that structured it. Prior to 1769, crown-directed organizational guidelines were few and not regularly codified. After that period, numerous *reglamentos* appeared throughout the Americas, dictating the precise formulas needed to place these forces on a successful footing. Similarly, the aggressiveness of recruitment efforts was increased, signaling an overall expansion in the influence of the institution in places such as New Granada, Peru, and New Spain.

25. Peter Gerhard, *The North Frontier of New Spain* (Norman and London: Univ. of Oklahoma Press, 1982), 5–19; and Guedea, "La organización militar," 139–41.

26. Presidio soldiers received a unique style of training and discipline; their obligations were formalized in a *reglamento* of 1729. See Gerhard, *The North Frontier,* 141.

27. Bernardo de Gálvez, *Instructions for Governing the Interior Provinces of New Spain, 1786,* trans. and ed. Donald E. Worcester (Berkeley: Quivira Society, 1951), 1–5.

28. Archer, *The Army in Bourbon Mexico,* 2.

29. Velazquez, *El estado de guerra,* 14–16.

30. Juan Juárez Moreno, *Corsarios y piratas en Veracruz y Campeche* (Seville: Escuela de Estudios Hispano-Americanos de Sevilla, 1972); and José Ignacio Rubio Mañé, *El virreinato* (Mexico City: Fondo de Cultura Económica, 1992), vol. 2, *Expansión y defensa,* 92–129.

31. Archer, *The Army in Bourbon Mexico,* 38–60.

32. The Yucatan presented its own special circumstances for defense. It represented a mixture of the northern frontier area and the coasts, since there were hostile Indians to contend with as well. A scheme of ports and presidios was utilized to thwart internal and external threats. See Guedea, "La organización militar," 144–46; Jorge Victoria Ojeda, *Mérida de Yucatan de las Indias: Piratería y estrategia defensiva* (Chalco, Mexico: Ediciones del Ayuntamiento de Mérida, 1995); and Rubio Mañé, *El virreinato,* vol. 3, *Expansión y defensa, segunda parte,* 150–350.

33. Marchena Fernández, *Ejército y milicias,* 129–30.

34. Francisco de Seijas y Lobera, *Gobierno militar y político del reino imperial de la Nueva España (1702),* comp. Pablo Emilio Pérez-Mallaína Bueno (Mexico City: Universidad Nacional Autónoma de México, 1986), 261.

35. Ibid., 400.

36. *Recopilacion de leyes,* Libro VII, Titulo V, fs. 287–91; Palmer, *Slaves of the White God,* 122. The need to constantly repeat the legislation pointed out that it was difficult to enforce.

37. A favorable recommendation from a known Spaniard was helpful in the requests, as was evidence of marriage, which pointed to stability and responsibility in lifestyle. See Palmer, *Slaves of the White God,* 184. For specific cases, see AGN, General de Parte, vol. 3, exp. 332; AGN, General de Parte vol. 5, exp. 1432; AGN, General de Parte vol. 6, exps. 351, 473, 573, 643, 865, 970; AGN, General de Parte vol. 7, exps. 159, 208, 227, 315, 409, 516; AGN, General de Parte vol. 8, exps. 22, 73, 81, 95, 212; AGN, General de Parte vol. 15, exp. 103; AGN, General de Parte vol. 21, exp. 290; AGN, General de Parte vol. 28, exp. 88; AGN, and General de Parte vol. 59, exp. 221; AGN, General de Parte vol. 68, exps. 120, 162.

38. J. I. Israel, *Race, Class and Politics in Colonial Mexico, 1610–1670* (Oxford: Oxford Univ. Press, 1975), 67–68.

39. For general treatment on slave resistance throughout the colony, see Palmer, *Slaves of the White God*, 119–44. For Yanga and the Veracruz, see Adriana Naveda Chavez, *Esclavos negros en las haciendas azucareras de Cordoba Veracruz, 1690–1830* (Xalapa, Veracruz: Universidad Veracruzana, 1987), 123–61; Octoviano R. Corro, *Cimarrones en Veracruz y la fundación de Amapa* (Veracruz: Comercial, 1951); Juan Laurencio, *Campaña contra Yanga en 1608* (Mexico City: Editorial Citlaltepetl, 1974); Gonzalo Aguirre Beltrán, *El negro esclavo en Nueva España* (Mexico City: Fondo de Cultura Económica, 1994), 179–86; and Antonio Carrion, *Historia de la ciudad de Puebla de los Angeles*, 2d ed. (Puebla: Editorial Jose M. Cajica, Jr., S.A., 1970), 2:20–24. For published primary sources on the eighteenth-century maroon society of Mazateopan, see Fernando Winfield Capitaine, *Los cimarrones de Mazateopan* (Xalapa, Veracruz: Gobierno del Estado de Veracruz, 1992).

40. Palmer, *Slaves of the White God*, 125.

41. Carrion, *Historia de la ciudad de Puebla*, 2:2.

42. Palmer, *Slaves of the White God*, 135–36.

43. Israel, *Race, Class and Politics*, 68–75.

44. *Recopilacion de leyes*, Libro VII, Titulo V, fs. 287–89; Israel, *Race, Class and Politics*, 74; and Palmer, *Salves of the White God*, 122.

45. For comparative purposes, the situation may have been less antagonistic in Cuba, as observed by Herbert S. Klein, "The Colored Militia of Cuba: 1568–1868," *Caribbean Studies* 6, no. 2 (1966): 17–18.

46. AGN, I.G., vol. 197-B, Narcisso Sagarra, Ildefonso Silva, and Juan Pastor to Marques de Branciforte, June 25, 1795, Mexico City; Jackie Booker, "Needed but Unwanted: Black Militiamen in Veracruz, Mexico, 1760–1810," *Historian* 55 (winter 1993): 260.

47. Papantla is a representative case. See AGN, I.G., vol. 488-A, Ildefonso Arias de Saavedra to Pedro Mendinueta, January 15, 1788, Papantla.

48. Hoffman, *The Spanish Crown*, 41.

49. The dates of the legislation were December 12, 1608; August 15, 1609; and October 5, 1648. AGN, Civil (libros), vol. 1789, Autos fechos a instancia del sargento mayor y demas capitanes del tercio de pardos y morenos libres de la Puebla, sobre haber preso el alcalde mayor de aquella ciudad al capitan Agustin Rodriguez, 1744, fs. 1–2v.

50. McAlister, *Fuero Militar*, 43.

51. A nice overview provided in Cope, *The Limits of Racial Domination*, 1–26.

52. Archer, *The Army in Bourbon Mexico*, 170–71.

53. AGN, I.G., vol. 296-B, Pedro Montesinos de Lara to Marques de Amarillas, September 25, 1756, Puebla.

54. AGN, I.G., vol. 488-A, Ildefonso Arias de Saavedra to Pedro Mendinueta, January 15, 1788, Papantla.

55. AGN, Tierras, vol. 973, exp. 2, fs. 1–97v, with particular attention to 97–97v.

56. AGN, I.G., vol. 484-A, Tomas Gil de Onzue to Martin Mayorga, June 18, 1781, Tamiagua.

57. AGN, I.G., vol. 497-A, Alonso de la Bargas to Marques de Croix, January 7, 1767, Papantla.

58. AGN, I.G., vol. 488-A, Revista y arreglo de las milicias de Papantla practicada por el Ten. Coronel, Dn. Ildefonso Arias de Saavedra, June 1788, Papantla.

59. AGN, Reales Cédulas Duplicadas, vol. 5, exp. 803, fol. 197, June 13, 1607.

60. Naveda Chavez, *Esclavos negros,* 127–28.

61. Winfield Capitane, *Los cimarrones,* 15–25.

62. For an early eighteenth-century example of free-coloreds serving as militiamen in the frontier presidios of Nayarit, see AGN, General de Parte, vol. 38, exp. 94, fs. 113–16.

63. AGN, I.G., vol. 37-B, Manuel de Neyra, November 20, 1759, Tancitaro; AGN, I.G., vol. 490-A, Sergeant Mayor Phelipe de Neve to Marques de Croix, September 6, 1766, Valladolid.

64. McAlister, *Fuero Militar,* 43.

65. Indians did serve in militia companies but were more commonly used in the northern frontier areas, where they were formed into companies of *indios flecheros.* Tabasco is a notable exception, with Indian *laboríos* serving in their own units by the eighteenth century. For nineteenth-century information on Indian soldiers, see Guy P. C. Thomson, "Los indios y el servicio militar en el México decimonónico: Leva o ciuadanía?" in *Indio, nación y comunidad en el México del siglo XIX,* ed. Antonio Escobar Ohmstede (Mexico City: CIESAS, 1993), 207–51.

66. The problems of seventeenth-century data are discussed in Sherburne F. Cook and Woodrow Borah, *Essays in Population History,* 2:182.

67. Ratios derived from Peter Gerhard, "Un censo de la diócesis de Puebla en 1681," *Historia Mexicana* 30, no. 4 (1981): 534–36. He describes the 1681 population of the diocese as containing 73,875 castes, 37,560 whites, and 318,090 Indians.

68. Ibid. Gerhard's calculations reveal that 3,815 castes lived in these areas, as opposed to 760 whites and 16,350 Indians.

69. Ibid. Combined, the seven parishes stretched for 27,700 square kilometers of coastal territory in the diocese. Gerhard's calculations reveal the caste population to have been 8,195, while there were 3,500 whites and 21,400 Indians.

70. The central coasts are defined in Cook and Borah, *Essays in Population History,* 2:192–97. Their definition excludes areas such as Cozamaloapa and Veracruz, where full eighteenth-century population data does not seem to have been available.

71. The coastal populations of the Intendancy of Oaxaca and the jurisdictions of Tlapa and Ometepec can be calculated from information provided in AGN, Tributos, vol. 34, exp. 7, fol. 160v. The regions defined as Ometepec, Tehuantepec, Xamiltepec, and Guamelula corresponded exactly to the lower coastal area below Acapulco and south to Guatemala. The free-colored population was calculated at 14,277 persons, compared with 5,851 whites. In other words, free-coloreds outnumbered whites by a margin of 2.4 to 1. Again, this placed free-coloreds as the second most numerous population group in the region. Further north along the Pacific coast, in the jurisdiction of Tepic, within the Intendancy of Guadalajara, *mulatos* constituted the largest population group, as revealed by census information from 1789–93. There, whites numbered 1,318 individuals, Indians totaled 1,218, mestizos and the non free-colored *castas* accounted for 383 persons, and *mulatos* numbered 2,096. In other words, *mulatos* equated to roughly 42 percent of Tepic's population. See Pedro Lopez Gonzalez, *La población de Tepic bajo la organización regional, 1530–1821* (Tepic, Nayarit: Universidad Autonoma de Nayarit, 1984), 23.

72. The 1766 military census for the Provincial Regiment of Tampico, Panuco, and Huexutla reveals that out of 848 potential recruits, 806 were free-coloreds. AGN, I.G., vol. 490-A, August 9, 1766, Gorostiza to Villaba.

73. Cook and Borah calculate the presence of free-colored families in the inner plateau area to have been 3.26 percent between 1742 and 1746, as opposed to 18.78 percent of

the families along the central coasts. See Cook and Borah, *Essays in Population History,* 2:202.

74. This is a general rule, but there were instances, such as the militias of San Andres Tuxtla and Santiago Tuxtla, in which companies of the independent type were formed with little regard to demographic realities. Status concerns led whites to form a company of only twelve men, far too small to be of functional value. See AGN, I.G., vol. 213-A, Pedro Echeverri Laguardia, without date, 1759, Santiago Tuxtla.

75. Hoffman, *The Spanish Crown,* 40.

76. AGN, I.G., vol. 33-B, Antonio de Saavedra to Juan Fernando de Palacio, November 12, 1775, Tuxtla; AGN, Civil, legajo, 24, exp. 156, 1762, Acayucan, fs. 1–49; AGN, I.G., vol. 28-B, Correspondencia con varios cuerpos sueltos de milicias urbanas, 1777, Joachin de San Martin to Bucareli, November 12, 1777, Theguantepeque; and AGN, I.G., vol. 28-B, Joachin de San Martin to Bucareli, October 19, 1777, Tecoantepec.

77. For instance, *fuero* rights in Puebla first came about during the administration of the Marqués de Valero, from 1715 to 1722. They had to be reviewed for renewal under subsequent administrations. See AGN, I.G., vol. 197-B, Jose Arellano, Joseph Zambrano, Joaquin Medina, Jose Moreno, July 3, 1794, Puebla.

78. Brígido Redondo, "Negritud en Campeche, de la conquista a nuestros días," in *Presencia Africana en México,* ed. Luz María Montiel (Mexico City: Consejo Nacional para la Cultura y las Artes, 1994), 368.

79. While not always true, it was assumed that when cases were sent through the military legal system, militiamen were to be favored in the final decisions. See AGN, I.G., vol. 197-B, Jose Arellano, Jose Zambrano, Jose Moreno, Jose Ricardo and Ramon Riveros to Branciforte, July 3, 1794, Puebla; AGN, Civil, vol. 130, pt. 2, 1757, Mexico City, fs. 5–14; AGN, I.G., vol. 42-B, Pasqual Cisneros to Antonio Bucareli y Ursua, May 7, 1778, Mexico City; and McAlister, *Fuero Militar,* 6–15.

80. AGN, Reales Cédulas Originales, vol. 154, exp. 34, fs. 49–73v.

81. Juan Juarez Moreno, *Corsarios y piratas en Veracruz y Campeche* (Seville: Escuela de Estudios Hispano-Americanos de Sevilla, 1972), 116–279.

82. Archer, *The Army in Bourbon Mexico,* 39; Juarez Moreno, *Corsarios,* 215; Sergio Florescano Mayet, *El camino Veracruz-Mexico en la epoca colonial* (Xalapa, Veracruz: Universidad Veracruzana, 1987), 104–6.

83. Juarez Moreno, *Corsarios,* 220; Like Mexico City, Puebla may have sent a free-colored contingent. See AGN, I.G., vol. 40-B, Joseph Francisco de Vargas, Joseph Tello, Joseph Zambrano, Joseph Gonzalez, to Croix, October 15, 1768, Puebla.

84. New black units of the independent type were founded in Atrisco, Cholula, Cordoba, and Orizaba, under the classification of *pardo* companies. Integrated units, both new and reformed, came about in the following locations: Zacatlan, Galacingo, Piastla, Acatlan, San Agustin Tlaxco, Tulancingo, Amozoque, Tustepeque, Guatepeque, San Andres Guatusco, Tlapa, Coscatlan, Santa Maria Tlapacoya, Olinala, Songolica, Jaliscoyan, San Andres Asala, Tamiagua, San Andres, Tuxtla, Chetla, San Luis de la Costa, San Angel del Palmar, Allustla, Chilapa, Copalillo, Temalaque, Goaxsingo, Tepeaca, Acacingo, Quichula, Tecamachalco, Chalchicomula, Tehuacan, Jalapa, Maulingo, Perote, Xalcingo, Los Llanos, and Zacapozatla. See AGN, I.G., vol. 46-A, Pedro Montesimos de Lara, October 14, 1758, Puebla.

85. Puebla's companies had been in existence at least from the 1620s.

86. In addition to the struggles to preserve *comandante* status, there were a range of other factors that led to 1683 as being the purported militia founding date. On the one

hand, there was improved record-keeping. Militiamen possessed copies of documents pertaining to their history and services. These were kept in their own repositories, which sometimes served to supplement records kept in official state collections. In subsequent investigations into their histories, as were conducted in appeals for special privileges or in legal disputes, the excellent preservation of records from 1683 and beyond was important in establishing the Lorencillo era as the formative period for the eighteenth-century companies. Another important event was an investigation initiated by the Duke of Albuquerque into the origins of the free-colored militia. Conducted in 1707, and based partially on documents retrieved from militia archives, his study determined 1683 to be the founding date not just for Mexico City's units but also for Puebla and a score of other cities in the diocese of Puebla. This viceregal study was important for cementing the date as the definitive foundation period of the free-colored militia in official circles. AGN, Civil, vol. 130, pt. 2, 1757, Mexico City, fs. 1–18; AGN, I.G., vol. 40-B, Joseph Francisco de Vargas, Joseph Tello, Joseph Zambrano, Joseph Gonzalez, to Croix, October 15, 1768, Puebla; and AGN, I.G., vol. 296-B, Manuel Bertel, September 20, 1756, Puebla.

87. AGN, Civil, vol. 130 pt. 2, 1757, Mexico City, fs. 5–11; AGN, I.G., vol. 40-B, Joseph Francisco de Vargas, Joseph Tello, Joseph Zambrano, Joseph Gonzalez, to Croix, October 15, 1768, Puebla; AGN, I.G., vol. 197-B, Jose Arellano, Jose Zambrano, Jose Moreno, Jose Ricardo, and Ramon Riveros to Branciforte, July 3, 1794, Puebla.

88. Cope, *Limits of Racial Domination*, 125–60; Carlos de Siguenza y Gongora, *Alboroto y motín de Mexico del 8 de junio de 1692*, with a foreword by Irving A. Leonard (Mexico City: Talleres Graficos del Museo Nacional de Arqueologia, Historia, y Etnografia, 1932); Israel, *Race, Class and Politics*, 135–60.

89. For information on the subordinates of the provincial governors, see Woodrow Borah and Sherburne Cook, "Los Auxiliares del Gobernador Provincial," in *El gobierno provincial*, 51–64; María del Refugio González and Teresa Lozano, "La Adminitración de Justicia," in *El gobierno provincial*, 75–105; and Charles R. Cutter, *The Legal Culture of Northern New Spain, 1700–1810* (Albuquerque: Univ. of New Mexico Press, 1995), 92. Note that Indians were supposed to supply thirty-two bailiffs in Papantla in the eighteenth century, but that was not always enough. See AGN, Californias, vol. 58, fs. 44v–49. For information on poor jail facilities and the need to rely on free-colored assistance, see AGN, Criminal, vol. 542, exp. 6, fs. 160–65.

90. For brief samples, see AGN, Criminal, vol. 542, exp. 6, fs. 160–63.

91. Good discussion of the Indian nobility and elite can be found in James Lockhart, *The Nahuas after the Conquest: A Social and Cultural History of the Indians of Central Mexico, Sixteenth through Eighteenth Centuries* (Stanford: Stanford Univ. Press, 1992), 130–40; Nancy Farriss, *Maya Society under Colonial Rule: The Collective Enterprise of Survival* (Princeton: Princeton Univ. Press, 1984), 227–55; and Karen Spalding, *Huarochirí: An Andean Society under Inca and Spanish Rule* (Stanford: Stanford Univ. Press, 1984), 209–13.

92. AGN, Criminal, vol. 542, exp. 6, fol. 162.

93. McAlister, *Fuero Militar*, 50.

94. AGN, Californias, vol. 58, Expediente formado a Msta. de Don Phelipe Izusquiza, jefe de las companias de caballeria de Xicayan sobre que no matriculen en los tributarios los que son soldados, fs. 82–82v.

95. *Alcaldes mayores* were often unsalaried despite legislation to the contrary. Combined with the fact that a great number of officials had paid for their positions outright before assuming office, many of them were primarily interested in finding a means to reap

profit from their tenure. See William B. Taylor, *Magistrates of the Sacred: Priests and Parishioners in Eighteenth-Century Mexico* (Stanford: Stanford Univ. Press, 1996), 402; Woodrow Borah and Sherburne Cook, "El gobernador novohispano (alcalde mayor/corregidor): Consecución del puesto y aspectos económicos," in *El gobierno provincial*, 38–39.

96. Ibid.

97. AGN, Californias, vol. 58, Testimonio al exp. formado a consulta del capitan de regimento . . . Don Joachin Pozos . . . 1784, fs. 44v–49.

98. Ibid., fs. 34–52.

99. In Jalapa, the rounds were carried out after 1:00 A.M. Note that these four cities simply represent the documented cases that I have for night patrols. Other cities would have had similar arrangements as well. The 1683 founding date for the rounds is clearest for Mexico City and Puebla. For more on Jalapa, see AGN, I.G., vol. 232-B, Joseph Ladron de Guvara, Manuel de Rivera, to Croix, August 10, 1770, Jalapa.

100. In 1719, the Tribunal of the Acordada was established to deal with rural banditry and serious property crimes. It was coequal to the Real Sala in appellate authority. But the soldiers continued to fall primarily under the jurisdiction of the Real Sala, which handled lesser crimes. Both courts possessed their own jurisdiction. Gabriel J. Haslip, "Crime and the Administration of Justice in Colonial Mexico City, 1696–1810" (Ph.D. diss., Columbia University, 1980), 91–96.

101. The *traza* model was difficult to maintain and began to fragment in the sixteenth century, as Indian and caste laborers were brought into the city center to provide labor for whites. But the general dimensions of the *traza* could be found as late as 1811. Whites tended to concentrate more heavily in the downtown center, with castes and Indians in the outer areas. See Lourdes Marquez Morfin, "La desigualdad ante la muerte: Epidemias, población y sociedad en la ciudad de Mexico (1800–1850)" (Ph.D. diss., El Colegio de México, 1991), 59.

102. AGN, Civil, vol. 130, pt. 2, 1729, Puebla and Mexico City, fs. 1–15. Sometimes in these situations, the administrators who contracted the soldiers for patrols appointed someone to supervise the militiamen on their rounds. At other times, and depending on the stature of their office, they substituted as the free-colored commander themselves.

103. AGN, I.G., vol. 197-B, Jose Arellano, Jose Zambrano, Jose Moreno, Jose Ricardo, and Ramon Riveros to Branciforte, July 3, 1794, Puebla.

104. AGN, I.G., vol. 231-B, Estados de Fuerza, Regimento de Infanteria Provincial y de Pardos, 1768, Mexico City.

105. AGN, Civil, vol. 130, pt. 2, 1729, Puebla and Mexico City, fol. 1v.

106. Ibid., 6v–7.

107. Ibid., 8–9v.

108. AGN, Civil, legajo 24, exp. 156, 1762, Acayucan, fs. 19v–28v.

109. Molas Ribalta, "The Early Bourbons," in *Armed Forces and Society in Spain*, 70; McAlister, *Fuero Militar*, 1–3; Marchena Fernández, *Ejército y milicias*, 106.

110. Nine integrated, provincial companies were raised in these areas, comprising 679 men: AGN, I.G., vol. 490-A, Gorostiza to Croix, October 17, 1766, Tantoyucan; AGN, I.G., vol. 53-A, Pasqual Cisneros to Thomas Serrada, December 4, 1779; AGN, I.G., vol. 490-A, Gorostiza, Tantoyucan, August 9, 1766.

111. McAlister, *Fuero Militar*, 5.

112. Archer, *The Army in Bourbon Mexico*, 17.

113. Again, except for Veracruz and within isolated pockets along the coasts. Much

of the information on the Bourbon reforms is drawn from Archer, *The Army in Bourbon Mexico*, 8–33. For excellent additional treatment, see McAlister, "The Reorganization of the Army of New Spain," 1–32; Velazquez, *El estado de guerra;* and Josefa Vega Juanino, *La institución militar en Michoacán* (Zamora, Michoacán: El Colegio de Michoacán, 1986).

114. Archer, *The Army in Bourbon Mexico;* Kuethe, *Military Reform and Society in New Granada;* and Campbell, *The Military and Society in Colonial Peru.*

115. From Table 10, the racial status of 880 out of the total 1,347 militiamen could be identified, with 681 (77 percent) of the soldiers recorded as *pardos.* The muster of 1,347 men represents the state of the militia after the reforms of 1780, including troop augmentations in Tampico and Panuco.

116. Apparently, reductions in the number of free-colored militiamen in integrated units were greatest immediately after a military inspector had passed through to reorganize and downsize a region's forces. Thereafter, numbers tended to increase slightly, particularly in areas along the coasts, as the pressure to maintain a strict cap on enrollment subsided. The ebb and flow process would repeat again until the next formal reform process took place.

CHAPTER 2

1. Juarez Moreno, *Corsarios*, 230–33.

2. Quatrefages, "The Military System," 13.

3. Marchena Fernández, *Oficiales y soldados*, 70–87.

4. AGN, I.G., vol. 484-A, Toms Gil de Onzue to Martin Mayorga, June 18, 1781, Tamiagua.

5. These included Veracruz, Mexico City, Puebla, Campeche, and Mérida.

6. AGN, Civil, vol. 87, exp. 5, 1727, Mexico City, fs. 1–47; AGN, Civil (cajas), vol. 224, exp. 152, 1724, Mexico City, fs. 1–31.

7. AGN, Civil, vol. 158, exp. 74, 1761, Mexico City, fs. 1–11.

8. Archivo Historico del Ayuntamiento de Puebla (AHAP), legajo 1255, fs. 72v–77.

9. Documents from 1741 to 1742 and 1756 continue to relate the presence of five companies, albeit at reduced strengths of 500 to 526 men. See AGN, Civil, vol. 130, pt. 2, 1742, Puebla, fs. 1–5; AGN, I.G., vol. 296-B, Dn. Pedro Montesinos Lara to Amarillas, 1756, Puebla.

10. AGN, I.G., vol. 252-B, Nicolas Lopez Padilla, October 13, 1772, Guadalajara.

11. AGN, Civil, vol. 130, pt. 2, 1741, Puebla, fs. 1–5; and AHAP, legajo 1255, fs. 72v–77.

12. Quatrefages, "The Military System," 19–20; and Marchena Fernández, *Oficiales y soldados*, 71–76. Many *reglamentos* speak to the internal militia order as well. For one late eighteenth-century example, see AGN, Reales Cédulas Originales, vol. 229, exp. 24, fs. 44–76v.

13. Guinea was a widely used synonym for Africa in Spain between the sixteenth and nineteenth centuries. See Baltasar Fra Molinero, *La imagen de los negros en el teatro del siglo de oro* (Mexico City and Madrid: Siglo XXI Editores, 1995), 4–6.

14. AGN, I.G., vol. 231-B, Luis Bermudo Sorrano, 1763.

15. AGN, Civil, vol. 158, pt. 7, exp. 16, 1742, Puebla, fol. 8v.

16. Ibid.

17. Considering that one ducat approximated 1.4 pesos, the amount totaled just over 1,000 pesos per year. For more on currency, see Barnes Thomas, Thomas Naylor, and

Charles W. Polzer, *Northern New Spain: A Research Guide* (Tucson: Univ. of Arizona Press, 1981), 66–67.

18. AGN, Civil, vol. 158, pt. 7, exp. 16, 1742, Puebla, fs. 1–9.

19. AGN, I.G., vol. 197-B, Jose Arellano, Joaquin Medina, Josef Zambrano, Jose Moreno, July 3, 1794, Puebla; Civil, vol. 158, pt. 7, exp. 16, 1742, Puebla, fs. 10–10v; AGN, I.G., vol. 296-B, Relación de los meritos y servicios de Nicolas Bertel, June 8, 1743, Madrid.

20. Archivo Judicial de Puebla, INAH-Puebla (AJP), exp. 2968, fol. 3, 1724, Puebla. Bertel tallied the worth of the Guevara family furniture in 1724, estimated at 3,824 pesos. The family itself was worth over 40,000 pesos.

21. AGN, Civil, vol. 158, pt. 7, exp. 16, 1742, Puebla, fs. 8–9.

22. AGN, Civil (libros), vol. 1789, Nicolas Bertel, May 21, 1744, Puebla.

23. AGN, Civil, vol. 130, pt. 2, exp. 3, 1742, Puebla, fs. 1–25; AGN, I.G., vol. 296-B, Relacion de los meritos y servicios de Nicolas Bertel, June 8, 1743, Madrid.

24. AGN, I.G., vol. 296-B, King Ferdinand VI to Manuel Joseph Bertel, January 20, 1748, without location.

25. AGN, I.G., vol. 296-B, Documentos pertenecientes al tercio del batallon de pardos de Puebla. Representaciones de su coronel, Manuel Bertel, y evidencias tomadas en el asunto sobre el arreglo de dicho cuerpo, fol. 29, 1756.

26. There was evidence of the existence of a lieutenant colonel, but it is unclear as to when the post developed, or if the colonel *agregado* was implemented to replace the lieutenant colonel. The *sargento mayor* may have doubled as the lieutenant colonel.

27. AGN, I.G., vol. 231-B, Luis Bermudo Sorrano, 1763.

28. AGN, I.G., vol. 213-A, Dn. Pedro Echeverri Laguardia, 1759, Santiago Tuxtla.

29. AGN, I.G., vol. 422-A, Francisco Cañaveral y Ponce, June 5, 1781, Mexico City.

30. AGN, I.G., vol. 233-B, loose leaves, 1774–75, Mexico City, Puebla. Twenty officerships were available in Puebla, nine were vacant. Twenty-seven officerships were available in Mexico City, eight were vacant.

31. AGN, I.G., vol. 231-B, Estados de fuerza, regimento de infanteria provincial y de pardos, Mexico City, 1768; and AGN, Civil, vol. 130 pt. 2, 1741, Puebla, fs. 1–5.

32. AGN, I.G., vol. 9, Hojas de servicio de jefes y oficiales de los regimentos de caballeria provincial de Queretaro, batallon de pardos de Mexico, compañía de Valladolid, regimentos de comercio de Mexico, Puebla, y otros cuerpos, 1766–96.

33. For examples, see NCOs in AGN, I.G., vol. 231-B, Estados de fuerza . . . pardos, Mexico City, 1768; AGN, I.G., 233-B, loose leaves, Jalapa, Mexico City, Puebla, 1774–75.

34. AGN, Civil, vol. 224, exp. 152, 1724, Mexico City, fs. 1–31; AGN, Civil, vol. 158, pt. 7, exp. 16, 1742, Puebla, fs. 1–16.

35. For examples for Veracruz in 1763–64, see General de Parte, vol. 47, exp. 182–83, fs. 97v–98v; AGN, General de Parte, vol. 47, exps. 206, 209, 210, fs. 115v–118. There is some consultation in these appointments with the governor of Veracruz. AGN, General de Parte, vol. 29, exp. 33, deals with an *alférez* nomination in Puebla in 1732. The *sargento mayor*'s influence is predominant, but the *justicia mayor* performs the final naming of the post. AGN, I.G., vol. 296-B, Pedro Montesinos Lara to Amarillas, 1756, Puebla, discusses the greater autonomy afforded to free-colored officers in promotions.

36. For Michoacán, see AGN, I.G. 296-B, Martin de Reynoso Mendoza y Luyando to the Marques de Amarillas, October 7, 1758, Valladolid.

37. Some examples for the post-1760s pattern include Veracruz, Acapulco, Guadalajara, Acayucan, Oaxaca, and Tulancingo. See AGN, General de Parte, vol. 47, exp. 124,

fs. 63–63v; AGN, General de Parte, vol. 47, exp. 146–48, fs. 78v–80v; AGN, General de Parte, vol. 47, exp. 156–58, fs. 84–86; AGN, General de Parte, vol. 47, exps. 224–28, fs. 129–30v; AGN, General de Parte, vol. 47, exp. 238, 134v–35v; AGN, I.G., vol. 293-A, exp. 5, Joseph Gil Taboada, March 4, 1763, Acayucan; AGN, I.G., vol. 490-A, Pedro Sarrio to Croix, October 20, 1766, Oaxaca; Archer, *The Army in Bourbon Mexico*, 136–37.

38. This seemed to be the case with Guadalajara in 1772. See AGN, I.G., vol. 252-B, exp. 7, Diego Joaquin Garabito, November 1772, Guadalajara. Tuxtla also provides another example: AGN, I.G., vol. 33-B, Arreglo de las compañías de milicias de Tuxtla por el sargento mayor de la plaza de Veracruz, Dn. Antonio Saavedra, 1776.

39. AGN, I.G., vol. 33-B, Arreglo de las companias de milicias de Tuxtla por el sargento mayor de la plaza de Veracruz, Dn. Antonio Saavedra, 1776.

40. Unfortunately, given that most military-related documents in the Mexican archives possess precious little information on the period preceding the Bourbon reforms, a full assessment of officer careers for earlier years is not possible. But some trends for the decades prior to the 1760s can be inferred from the data provided here.

41. Veracruz and Tuxtla correspond to the Gulf coast. Mexico City, Michoacán, and Oaxaca account for the interior. Xicayan, Tehuantepec, and New Galicia correspond to the Pacific coast.

42. AGN, Archivo Historico de la Hacienda, vol. 85, exp. 15, fs. 14–17.

43. AGN, I.G. 497-A, Pie de lista de los oficiales, sargentos, tambores, cabos, y soldados de expresada compania [Mexico City] con distincion de sus nombres, estatura, edad, estado, y oficio, 1767.

44. To qualify as a member of Puebla's elite, a financial worth of twenty thousand pesos was deemed the minimum prerequisite. See Guy P. C. Thomson, *Puebla de los Angeles: Industry and Society in a Mexican City, 1700–1850* (Boulder, San Francisco, and London: Westview Press, 1989), 74–82. Information on the Santanders comes from AJP, exp. 3108, fs. 1–277; 1730, Puebla. For the material cited here, see fs. 14v–21 and 31–32v.

45. AGN, Criminal, vol. 447, exp. 7, fs. 149–61.

46. AGN, vol. 296-B, Lista de individuos vecinos de esta ciudad de Valladolid, y de su . . . orden, entresacados del padron general que se ha echo a efecto de cumplir el superior mandato de el excelentissimo Marques de las Amarillas, virrey, gobernador, y capitan general de esta Nueva España, 1759. See also Vega Juanino, *La Institución Militar*, 119–51.

47. Thomson, *Puebla*, 93.

48. These cities were sampled between 1766 and 1770.

49. Marchena Fernández, *Ejército y milicias*, 130; and McAlister, *Fuero Militar*, 93.

50. Archer, *The Army in Bourbon Mexico*, 38–60. Most military planners felt that the city could not withstand a siege for more than a few days. If San Juan Ulúa were taken, the remaining soldiers in the port would have to retreat.

51. Antequera initially came into being in the sixteenth century as a stronghold for the conquest of the Zapotec and Mixtec Indians but soon became a commercial and administrative center. According to Chance and Taylor, it was "the only town of any importance between Puebla and the territory of Guatemala." See John K. Chance and William B. Taylor, *Race and Class in Colonial Oaxaca* (Stanford: Stanford Univ. Press, 1978), 7.

52. McAlister, *Fuero Militar*, 94; and Marchena Fernández, *Ejército y milicias*, 130.

53. AGN, I.G., vol. 490-A, Sarrio to Croix, September 29, 1766, Oaxaca.

54. There were six companies created in all, four for whites, one for mestizos, and another for free-coloreds. The free-colored company contained one hundred men.

55. AGN, I.G., vol. 9, fol. 79; AGN, I.G., vol. 296-B, Martin de Reynoso Mendoza y Luyando to the Marques de Amarillas, October 7, 1758, Valladolid; AGN, I.G., vol. 252-B, Francisco Galmido to Antonio Maria Bucareli, December 4, 1772, Guadalajara; AGN, I.G., vol. 37-B, Manuel de Neyra, November 20, 1759, Tancitaro; and Vega Juanino, *La institución militar*, 39.

56. AGN, I.G., vol. 252-B, exp. 7, Nicolas Lopez Padilla, October 13, 1772, Guadalajara; AGN, I.G., vol. 197-B, Diego Joaquin Garabito, November 1772, location unavailable.

57. AGN, I.G. 296-B, Martin de Reynoso Mendoza y Luyando to the Marques de Amarillas, October 7, 1758, Valladolid.

58. McAlister, *Fuero Militar*, 94–95; Marchena Fernández, *Ejército y milicias*, 130.

59. William B. Taylor, *Drinking, Homicide, and Rebellion in Colonial Mexican Villages* (Stanford: Stanford Univ. Press, 1979), 114–16; and AGN, I.G., vol. 490-A, Pedro Sarrio to Croix, September 29, 1766, Oaxaca.

60. AGN, I.G., vol. 53-A, Matias de Armona to Mayorga, June 2, 1781, Mexico City.

61. AGN, Californias, vol. 58, Captain Blas Antonio Perez, fs. 53–56, June 18, 1782, Sn. Andres Tuxtla.

62. Ibid.; Tuxtla's militias had been around since 1703: AGN, I.G., vol. 33-B, Antonio de Saavedra to Juan Fernando de Palacio, November 12, 1775, Tuxtla.

63. For the Rosario and Figueroa cases, as well as more on Tuxtla, see AGN, I.G., vol. 33-B, Arreglo de las companias de Tuxtla por el sargento mayor de plaza de Veracruz, Dn. Antonio Saavedra, 1776.

64. AGN, I.G., vol. 42-B, Representacion de Francisco Suarez, Coronel del Battallon de Pardos de Mexico, pidiendo a S.M. se le aumente el sueldo 10 pesos annuales que goza y quejandose del maltrato que se les da a los pardos, December 26, 1777, Mexico City.

65. Much inappropriate behavior was uncovered during Gorostiza's 1768 militia inspection. See AGN, I.G., vol. 40-B, Informaciones hechas por el sargento mayor del ejército, Dn. Pedro Gorostiza, y ajuste general de cuentas del batallon de milicias de pardos de esta capital de Mexico, de orden del inspector general de infanteria, Marques de la Torre, 1768, Mexico City.

66. AGN, Archivo Hisotirco de la Hacienda, vol. 85, exp. 15, fs. 1–4v.

67. AGN, Civil, vol. 130 pt. 2, 1757, Mexico City, fs. 8v–9v.

68. These individuals were Captain Joseph Escobar (1st company), Lieutenant Lorenzo Escobar (3rd company), Captain Lazaro Escobar (4th company), Lieutenant Mariano Escobar (4th company), Lieutenant Antonio Escobar (5th company). See AGN, Archivo Historico de Hacienda, vol. 94, unnumbered pages.

69. Archivo de Notarías del Distrito Federal, Mexico City (AN), vol. 1655, Juan Clemente Guerrero (254), fs. 13–17v.

70. AN, vol. 2259, Juan Lopez de Bocanegra (343), fs. 211–12v.

71. AN, vol. 2259, Juan Lopez de Bocanegra (343), fs. 163–63v; 249v–250v.

72. Thomson describes the middle class in nearby Puebla as possessing resources between 2,000 and 40,000 pesos. Elites commanded wealth that often extended well over 100,000 pesos. Thomson, *Puebla*, 74–91. For more on the elite, see Doris M. Ladd, *The Mexican Nobility at Independence, 1780–1826* (Austin: Univ. of Texas Press, 1976).

73. AN, vol. 2259, Juan Lopez de Bocanegra (343), fs. 163, 201–14; AN, vol. 1660, Juan Clemente Guerrero (254), fs. 358–63v.

74. AGN, Matrimonios, vol. 203, exp. 1, fol. 7, 1735.

75. AGN, I.G., vol. 497-A, Juan Fernando de Palacio, February 1, 1767, Mexico City.

76. Valdes, "The Decline of the Sociedad de Castas," 118–25; and Ben Vinson III, "Race, Class, and the Use of Physical Space in Mexico City's Cuartel 23, 1811" (Master's thesis, Columbia Univ., 1993).

77. AGN, I.G., vol. 501-A, Pedro Garibay, March 10, 1772, Mexico City; AGN, I.G., vol. 501-A, Pedro Garibay, April 1, 1772, Mexico City; and AGN, Criminal, vol. 680, exp. 2, fs., 5–10v.

78. For more on Lazaro Escobar, see AGN, Inquisición, vol. 1043, exp. 2, fs. 2–8. Here, he demonstrates having a friendship with two Europeans, with whom he collaborates in trying to find buried treasure.

79. AGN, Matrimonios, vol. 159, exp. 75, fs. 1–9; AGN, Matrimonios, vol. 117, exp. 16, fs. 56–58; AGN, Matrimonios, vol. 33, exp. 61, fs. 257–60; and AGN, Archivo Historico de Hacienda, vol. 94, unnumbered pages.

80. Marchena Fernández, *Oficiales y soldados*, 141–50.

81. Note that one company captain did not report his age.

82. The companies of Guajolotitlan in Xicayan provide an excellent example. Several families in this town, including the Mayoral, de los Santos, and Roman clans, vied for ranking militia posts. See AGN, I.G., vol. 483-A, carpeta 2, Francisco Marti to Francisco Antonio Crespo, May 29, 1784, Oaxaca, fs. 39–57.

83. Mogol appears to have been a location in New Granada.

84. AGN, Civil, legajo 101, exp. 3, fs. 1–5.

85. AGN, I.G., vol. 42-B, Suarez to Bucareli, December 26, 1777, Mexico City.

86. AGN, I.G., vol. 40-B, Torre and Gorostiza to Croix, 1768, Mexico City, fs. 5v–25v.

87. Archer, *The Army in Bourbon Mexico*, 254–77.

88. AGN, Civil, vol. 224, exp. 152, Mexico City, 1763, fs. 1–27.

89. Guadalupe was involved in a fight with Ignacio Eusevio Alsate in 1758 about "contributions" paid by some members of the militia to avoid patrol duty. AGN, Civil, vol. 23, pt. 3, exp. 136, no. 9, Mexico City, 1758, fs. 1–27.

90. AGN, Archivo Historico de la Hacienda, vol. 85, exp. 15, fs. 1–26.

91. AGN, Civil, vol. 224, exp. 152, Mexico City, 1763, fs. 1–27.

92. AGN, Criminal, vol. 447, exp. 7, fs. 149–61. For example, in February of 1770, Suarez ordered Captain Sedeño and his wife to leave the militia barracks where they had been residing. He needed their room for military purposes. Sedeño prepared to see the viceroy about the matter, uttering to his wife, "Dame la ropa que voy a ver al excellentissimo señor virrey, porque ese perro lobo me quiere quitar la casa." Suarez overhead the comment, and the men began fighting in the barracks.

93. AGN, Archivo Historico de la Hacienda, vol. 85, exp. 15, fs. 1–13v.

94. AGN, I.G., vol. 40-B, Informaciones hechas por el sargento mayor del ejército ... 1768, Mexico City.

95. AGN, Archivo Historico de la Hacienda, vol. 85, exp. 15, fs. 2–3v and 21–22v.

96. AGN, I.G., vol. 42-B, Pasqual Cisneros, September 17, 1778, Mexico City.

97. AGN, I.G., vol. 96-A, Francisco Manuel Suarez, February 28–29, 1768, Mexico City.

98. AGN, I.G., vol. 40-B, Torre and Gorostiza to Croix, fs. 1–61, 1768, Mexico City.

99. AGN, I.G., vol. 42-B, Pasqual Cisneros, September 17, 1778, Mexico City.

100. AGN, I.G., vol. 197-B, Pedro Gorostiza to Revillagigedo, 1792, Mexico City; and AGN, Correspondencia de Virreyes, vol. 167, fs. 130–31.

101. AGN, Reales Cédulas Originales, vol. 229, exp. 24, fol. 46; AGN, I.G., vol., 28-B,

Cisneros to Bucareli, May 12, 1777, Mexico City; AGN, I.G., vol. 28-B, Tineo to Bucareli, November 3, 1777, Mexico City; AGN, I.G., vol. 28-B, Cinseros to Bucareli, October 4, 1777, Mexico City.

102. AGN, I.G., vol. 307-B, Correspondencia de Puebla 1785–90, Camunez to Valcarcel, October 29, 1788, Puebla.

103. AGN, I.G., vol. 306-A, exp. 4, Expediente promovido por Don Pedro Camuñez, subinspector del batallon de pardos de Puebla sobre las dificultades que pulsa a cerca del fuero y privilegios que debe gozar dicho batallon, 1782, Puebla and Mexico City.

104. AGN, I.G., vol. 42-B, Instancia del subinspector de pardos de Puebla solicitando se le costee un asesor y un escribano para que no padezcan dilacion las causas criminales, 1779, Mexico City and Puebla; and AGN, I.G., vol. 79-B, Mayorga to Camuñez, November 28, 1781, Mexico City.

105. AGN, I.G., vol. 79-B, Mayorga to Camuñez, August 29, 1781, Mexico City; and AGN, I.G., vol. 306-A, Camuñez to Valcarcel, May 16, 1781, Puebla.

106. AGN, I.G., vol. 42-B, Sobre milicianos pardos de Puebla que soliciten vender sombreros en el baratillo, January 1778, Puebla and Mexico City.

107. AGN, I.G., vol. 197-B, Josef Zambrano and Joaquin Medina, November 26, 1793, Puebla; and AGN, I.G., vol. 197-B, Narcisso Segarra, January 31, 1793, Mexico City.

108. AGN, I.G., vol. 502-A, exp. 8, De comandante de las milicias de Acayucan, representa que a aquella tropa le obligan a contribuir para pagar el vigía de la barra de Goazacoalcos, lo cual costeaban antes los parrdos libres, y tambien a estar sugeta en lo civil y criminal al alcalde mayor, September 1786, Acayucan. While the document alludes to many matters, the key observation is that Commander Roncali is head of all militia forces in the province, regardless of color or status.

109. AGN., I.G., vol. 28-B, Correspondencia con Varios Cuerpos Sueltos de Milicias Urbanas, 1777, Joachin de San Martin to Bucareli, November 12, 1777, Theguantepeque; AGN, I.G., vol. 28-B, Joachin de San Martin to Bucareli, October 19, 1777, Tecoantepec.

110. AGN, I.G., vol. 28-B, Correspondencia con el Battalon de Pardos de Puebla, 1777, Pasqual Cisneros, October 4, 1777, Mexico City. For more comparative information, see Booker, "Needed but Unwanted," 265; and AGN, Archivo Historico de la Hacienda, vol. 94, Militia Salary and Expense Sheets, 1777–82, unnumbered pages, no expediente reference.

111. Frederick J. Shaw, "The Artisan in Mexico City (1824–1853)," in *El trabajo y los trabajadores en la historia de México,* comp. Elsa Cecilia Frost, Michael C. Meyer, and Josefina Zoraida Vázquez (Mexico City and Tucson: El Colegio de Mexico and Univ. of Arizona Press, 1979), 415; and Haslip, "Crime and the Administration of Justice," 63.

112. The salary problems were greatest with the regular army, as seen in Marchena Fernández, *Oficiales y soldados,* 322–27; Marchena Fernández, *Ejército y milicias,* 86–89. The militia salary documents I have reviewed all point to consistent, uninterrupted payments; see AGN, Archivo Historico de la Hacienda, vol. 94, Militia Salary and Expense Sheets, 1777–82, unnumbered pages, no expediente reference. I propose that after the 1760s, salaries were paid with more frequency than in earlier periods. This meant that free-colored soldiers might have had greater access to a regular paycheck than lower-class, free-colored civilians, whose employment patterns were uneven.

113. AGN, I.G., vol. 307-A, Instancia de los oficiales del batallon de pardos de esta capital sobre que so se les descuente de sus sueldos para los fondos de invalidos y monte pio militar, September 1784, Mexico City; and Archer, "Bourbon Finances," 340.

114. Thomson, *Puebla,* 83.

115. Haslip, "Crime and the Administration of Justice," 59.

116. Thomson, *Puebla*, 83.

117. Haslip, "Crime and the Administration of Justice," 59; and AGN, Californias, vol. 58, Expediente formado a consulta del cap. de regimento de . . . Don Joachin de Pozos . . . 1784, fs. 44v–49.

118. AGN, I.G., vol. 42-B, Dn. Francisco Manuel Suarez, December 26, 1777, Mexico City.

119. Linda Arnold, *Bureaucracy and Bureaucrats in Mexico City, 1742–1835* (Tucson: Univ. of Arizona Press, 1988), 131–52.

120. Archer, "Bourbon Finances," 349.

121. AGN, Archivo Historico de la Hacienda, vol. 94, Militia Salary and Expense Sheets, 1777–82, unnumbered pages, no expediente reference; and AGN, I.G., vol. 28-B, Pasqual Cisneros, October 31, 1773, Mexico City.

122. AGN, I.G. 28-B, Pasqual Cisneros, October 4, 1777, Mexico City.

123. AGN, Correspondencia de Diversas Autoridades, vol. 37, exp. 42, fs. 75–76v, 162–63v, 208–208v, 388–89; AGN, Correspondencia de Diversas Autoridades, vol. 36, exp. 61, fs. 305, 316–17, 333–333v.

124. AGN, I.G., vol. 40-B, Ramon Luis Barrales to Marques de la Torre, October 12, 1768, Mexico City.

125. The barracks and bivouacs were located in the barrio del Zapo, as well as in locations near the Puente de Peredo and the Puente de Larendo. The only private individual who rented space to the militiamen was Dn. Vicente Roldan, who rented a home at an unspecified site.

126. In actuality 1,481 pesos were spent on repairs for free-colored units only, while another 3,975 pesos were for both white and free-colored units. AGN, I.G., vol. 147-B, exp. 13, fs. 1–33.

127. 1 *carga* = 12 *arrobas*.

128. AGN, I.G., vol. 147-B, Croix, February 3, 1767, Mexico City; and AGN, I.G., vol. 147-B, Posada to Florez, June 22, 1789, Mexico City.

129. *Mezcal* was a liquor distilled from agave; pulque was fermented from the maguey plant.

130. Excellent treatment of finances as well as a more complete overview of the Nuevos Impuestos can be found in Archer, "Bourbon Finances," 315–50.

CHAPTER 3

1. Klein, "The Colored Militia," 17–27; Booker, "Needed but Unwanted," 275–76; Christon I. Archer, "Pardos, Indians, and the Army of New Spain: Inter-Relationships and Conflicts, 1780–1810," *Journal of Latin American Studies* 6, no. 2 (1974): 231–55; George Reid Andrews, *The Afro-Argentines of Buenos Aires, 1800–1900* (Madison: Univ. of Wisconsin Press, 1980), 113–37; Peter M. Voelz, *Slave and Soldier: The Military Impact of Blacks in the Colonial Americas* (New York and London: Garland Publishing, 1993); Allan J. Kuethe, "The Status of the Free-Pardo in the Disciplined Militia of New Granada," *Journal of Negro History* 56, no. 2 (1971): 105–17; Rout, *The African Experience*, 150–51; McAlister, *Fuero Militar*, 43–54; and Jorge I. Domínguez, "International War and Government Modernization: The Military—A Case Study," in *Rank and Privilege: The Military and Society in Latin America*, ed. Linda Alexander Rodríguez (Wilmington, Del.: Scholarly Resources, 1994), 5–9.

2. Andrews, *Afro-Argentines*, 132–33.

3. Henry William Hutchinson, *Village and Plantation Life in Northeastern Brazil* (Seattle: Univ. of Washington Press, 1957), 99.

4. Klein, "The Colored Militia," 26.

5. In medieval times, the *hidalguía* was also a way of separating "those who fought from those who worked." Discussed in Anderson, "Race and Social Stratification," 216–17.

6. For problems with the use of the *hidalguía* for free-coloreds in Mexico, see AGN, I.G., vol. 42-B, Representacion de Francisco Suarez, coronel del batallon de pardos de Mexico, pidiendo a S.M. se le aumente el sueldo de 10 pesos annuales que goza, quejandose del matrato que se les da a los pardos, exp. 6, September 1778, Mexico City. For examples of use of the *hidalguía* in public documents, see also AGN, Civil, vol. 158, pt. 7, exp. 14, 1761, Mexico City, fs. 1–11; AGN, Civil, vol. 224, exp. 152, 1763, Mexico, fs. 1–27.

7. Superb recent treatment of the evolution of the black image as manifested in Spanish theatrical productions in the sixteenth and seventeenth centuries can be found in Fra Molinero, *Imagen de los negros*. The literature on the topic is vast, but see also Aguirre Beltrán, *La población negra*, 153–72; Israel, *Race, Class and Politics*, 73–74.

8. Cope points to a greater acceptance of the mestizo until the end of the sixteenth century, when more rigid laws were created to control them. Despite restrictive legislation, mestizos emerged as the most favored of the *castas*, constituting the majority of their economically successful individuals. Cope, *Limits of Racial Domination*, 17–19.

9. Archer, *The Army in Bourbon Mexico*, 224. For comparative information on Brazil, see Henrik Kraay, "Soldiers, Officers, and Society: The Army in Bahia, Brazil, 1808–1889" (Ph.D. diss., University of Texas at Austin, 1995), 223–29.

10. In Mexico, the career of the renowned *mulato* painter Juan Correa stands out as a significant example. Elisa Vargas Lugo and Gustavo Curiel, *Juan Corrrea: Su vida y su obra* (Mexico City: Universidad Nacional Autónoma de México, 1991).

11. Archer, "To Serve the King," 235.

12. Archivo Historico del Ayuntamiento de Puebla (AHAP), legajo 1255, fs. 72v–76v.

13. AGN, Civil, vol. 158, pt. 7, exp. 74, 1761, Mexico City, fs. 1–11; and Haslip, "Crime and the Administration of Justice," 40.

14. In Mexico City, each of the six free-colored rifle companies was supposed to have 75 men apiece. The company of grenadiers ideally contained 65 men. Adding the command staff of 5 officers, the free-colored total should have been 520. This complete muster received the title of battalion. Crown officials strictly expressed that they wanted only one free-colored battalion in the city. By contrast, the white provincial units of Mexico City between 1766 and 1777 totaled two battalions at 515 men apiece, distributed into five companies per battalion. Both battalions comprised a regiment of whites, containing 1,030 soldiers and officers, plus a veteran cadre of 12 men. In Puebla, the composition and structure of the free-colored forces more closely resembled the city's whites than in Mexico City. After 1766, Puebla's whites and free-coloreds had their own separate battalion, consisting of six companies at 610 men apiece. AGN, I.G., vol. 231-B, Regimento de infanteria provincial y batallon provincial de pardos, estados de fuerza, 1768, Mexico City; AGN, I.G., vol. 231-B, El sargento mayor del regimento infanteria provincial y de pardos, 1768, Puebla.

15. McAlister, *Fuero Militar*, 94.

16. Booker, "Needed but Unwanted," 263.

17. McAlister, *Fuero Militar*, 94.

18. Miguel Ángel Cuenya Mateos, "Epidemias y salubridad en la Puebla de los Ángeles, 1650–1833," in *Limpiar y obedecer: La basura, el agua, y la muerte en la Puebla de los Ángeles, 1650–1925*, comp. Rosalva Loreto and Francisco J. Cervantes B. (Puebla: Claves Latinoamericanas, Universidad Autónoma de Puebla, and Colegio de Puebla, 1994), 102–5. For detailed analysis of similar problems in nearby Cholula during the same period, see Elsa Malvido, "Factores de despoblación y de reposición de la población de Cholula (1641–1810)," in *Historia y población en México*, ed. Thomas Calvo (Mexico City: El Colegio de México, 1994), 90–101.

19. Enrique Florescano and Susan Swan, *Breve historia de la sequía en Méxcio* (Xalapa, Veracruz: Universidad Veracruzana, 1995), 177.

20. For the 1770 figure, see Booker, "Needed but Unwanted," 263.

21. Haslip, "Crime and the Administration of Justice," 64.

22. AGN, I.G., vol. 485-A, Ana Josefa Montiel, para que se licencie del servicio a su marido Joseph Ignacio Sayas, soldado del batallon de pardos de Puebla, March 1784, Puebla; and AGN, I.G., vol. 485-A, Escrito de Maria Jacinta Salazar para que se licencie el servicio a su hijo, Manuel Muñoz, sargento del batallon de pardos de Puebla, March 1784, Puebla.

23. AGN, Correspondencia de Diversas Autoridades, vol. 36, exp. 61, fs. 316–17, 333–333v; and Archer, *The Army in Bourbon Mexico*, 41–60, 236–53.

24. For more details, see Archer, "To Serve the King," 234–35.

25. After the 1760s, the influence of the veteran cadre was important in this form of recruitment, but can still be considered "internal" to the militia's design.

26. AGN, I.G. 28-B, Cisneros to Bucareli, March 24, 1777, Mexico City; and AGN, I.G., vol. 252-B, Nicolas Lopez Padilla, October 13, 1772, Guadalajara.

27. AGN, I.G., vol. 490-A, Phelipe de Neve to Marques de Croix, September 6, 1766, Valladolid.

28. Although as evidenced in Mexico City in 1762, the active approach could occasionally be used for mass recruitment. Colonel Suarez requested the authority to consult the city's tribute lists to refill the 150 men lost from his units in recent years, AGN, Civil, vol. 158, pt. 7, exp. 74, 1761, Mexico City, fs. 1–11.

29. AGN, Bandos, vol. 17, exp. 15, fs. 111–42; and AGN, I.G., vol. 252-B, Nicolas Lopez Padilla, October 13, 1772, Guadalajara.

30. AGN, I.G., vol. 296-B, Pedro Montesinos Lara to Revillagigedo the elder, July 31, 1755, Puebla.

31. Archer, *The Army in Bourbon Mexico*, 238–39; and AGN, I.G., vol. 394-A, Reglamento para las milicias de infanteria de la provincia de Yucatan y Campeche, 1778, Madrid, fs. 3–4. Legally designated areas of tobacco production included Yucatán, Orizaba, Córdoba, Teusitlán, and Jalapa. These were the zones endorsed by the royal monopoly, specified in the royal decrees of 1764. See Susan Deans-Smith, *Bureaucrats, Planters, and Workers: The Making of the Tobacco Monopoly in Bourbon Mexico* (Austin: University of Texas Press, 1992), 16.

32. AGN, I.G., vol. 533-A, Pasqual Cisneros to Thomas Serrada, December 4, 1779, Mexico City; AGN, I.G., vol. 296-B, Don Pedro Montesinos Lara to Revillagigedo the elder, July 31, 1755, Puebla; and AGN, I.G., vol. 28-B, Cisneros to Bucareli, March 24, 1777, Mexico City.

33. AGN, Alcaldes Mayores, vol. 2, exp. 384, unnumbered pages.

34. AGN, Matrimonios, vol. 91, exp. 1, fs. 1–18.

35. AGN, Ramo Civil, vol. 72, exp. 94, 1763, Puebla, fol. 2v.

36. Ibid., fol. 9.

37. Ibid., fs. 1–12.

38. AGN, I.G., vol. 296-B, Documentos pertenecientes al tercio del batallon de pardos de Puebla, Representaciones de su coronel Manuel Bertel, y evidencias tomadas en el asunto sobre el arreglo de dicho cuerpo, Manuel Bertel, September 20, 1756, Puebla.

39. AGN, I.G. 40-B, Privilegios, obligaciones y orden que deberan observar las milicias de Veracruz, Croix, 1767, Mexico City.

40. Douglas Cope, in *Limits of Racial Domination*, 82–84, notes that passing may not have been as widespread as once thought. In his view, the benefits of a color transformation were slight when compared with the efforts involved in changing one's social networks to be in accord with a new racial status. However, passing was still an aspect of colonial society, and free-coloreds often found easy entry into the ranks of white military units.

41. Valdes, "The Decline of the Sociedad de Castas," 201–2.

42. Thomson, *Puebla*, 93–94.

43. AGN, I.G., vol. 307-B, Sobre maltratamientos por el alcalde ordinario de Cordoba, Don Diego Lemayo a los soldados pardos del batallon de Puebla, Rafael y Juan de Tapia, 1790, Puebla.

44. See sample service records in AGN, I.G. vol. 9, Hojas de servicio de jefes y oficiales de los regimentos de cabelleria provincial de Queretaro, batallon de pardos de Mexico, compañía de Valladolid, regimentos de comercio de Mexico, Puebla, y otros cuerpos, 1766–96.

45. Subdirección de Documentación de la Biblioteca Nacional de Historia (BNAH), Archivo Judicial de Puebla, rollos 43–45, Tributos, 1795, Puebla, unpaginated. My numbers come from comparing names from the list of soldiers registered in Veracruz's *fijo* regiment in 1794–95 with those of the Battalion of Puebla, 1792.

46. BNAH, Archivo Judicial de Puebla, rollo 2, Batallón fijo de pardos y morenos de Veracruz sobre averiguar la lista de pardos tributarios. Incluye lista de los que han servido en Puebla a dicho batallón, 1794, Puebla, fol. 45.

47. Jalapa possessed a population of just under 4,000 in 1777, compared with the midcentury populations of Mexico City (112,926 persons) and Puebla (52,717 persons). See Deans-Smith, *Bureaucrats, Planters, and Workers*, 110. Free-colored men of all ages numbered 157 individuals. Most likely, the militia employed almost the full adult muster. For a detailed population analysis of Jalapa during this period, see Matilde Souto Mantecón and Patricia Torres Meza, "La población de la antigua parroquia del pueblo de Xalapa (1777)," in *Población y estructura urbana*, 88–109.

48. As seen in Chapter 1, Tuxtla serves as an excellent example of the effects of the policy changes. In the prereform units of Santiago and San Andrés Tuxtla, there existed two free-colored companies with no cap on enrollment. Their rosters logged 177 troops in 1759. By 1774, there were 241 men in the units. In essence, the entire free-colored, adult male population was enrolled. After Bourbon military reforms were brought to the region in 1775, the forces were reduced to a single company of 100 men, amid much protest from the free-coloreds who were cut from duty. See AGN, I.G., vol. 33-B, Saavedra to Dn. Juan Fernando de Palacio, November 12, 1775, Tuxtla; and AGN, Californias, vol. 58, fs. 53–56.

49. These figures are based on rates for Acayucan prior to the 1790s. AGN, I.G., vol. 502-A, Dn. Diego Avete y Maestre, July 27, 1784, Acayucan.

50. In addition to relief from the *vigía* fee, the men who actually performed the *vigía*

were compensated with a small daily salary of two reales. Officers were relieved from *vigía* payment altogether because the crown deigned that their time commitment and responsibility to their units merited exclusion. AGN, I.G., vol. 53-A, Dn. Matias de Armona to Martin Mayorga, September 16, 1780, Sn. Andres Tuxtla.

51. Remember that these are broad generalities. There were regional variations to the collection of the *vigía*. For example, in Tabasco, free-colored militia officers were responsible for collecting *vigía* both from civilians and soldiers. However, in almost every circumstance reviewed for this book, Tabasco included, militia *vigía* collections were taken by militia officers themselves.

52. AGN, Civil, legajo 24, exp. 156, fs. 32v–34, 49v.

53. AGN, I.G., vol. 33-B, Saavedra to Dn. Juan Fernando de Palacio, November 12, 1775, Tuxtla.

54. AGN, Tierras, vol. 973, exp. 2, fs. 1–24v.

55. Ibid.

56. For an excellent model, see Sonia Pérez Toledo and Herbert S. Klein, *Los hijos del trabajo: Los artesanos de la ciudad de México, 1780–1853* (Mexico City: El Colegio de México and Universidad Autónoma Metropolitana Iztapalapa, 1996), 54–57. See also Jorge González Angulo Aguirre, *Artesanado y ciudad a finales del siglo XVIII* (Mexico City: Fondo de Cultura Económica, 1983), 30–35.

57. Given the difficulties in determining the precise status of many occupations, scholars have been reluctant to hierarchically arrange occupations according to skill, although some noteworthy attempts have been made. One excellent effort is Sonia Pérez Toledo and Herbert S. Klein, "La población de la ciudad de Zacatecas en 1857," *Historia Mexicana*, vol. 41, no. 1 (1992): 77–102. For information on delineation by class, see Seed, "The Social Dimensions of Race," 569–606; Chance and Taylor, *Race and Class*; Timothy E. Anna, *The Fall of Royal Government in Mexico City* (Lincoln and London: Univ. of Nebraska Press, 1978), 8–25. Anna uses Villoro's conception of the classes. For a critique of the "class" method in favor of "stratification," see Anderson, "Race and Social Stratification," 212.

58. Seed, "Social Dimensions of Race"; Chance and Taylor, *Race and Class*; and Thomson, *Puebla*.

59. Seed, "Social Dimensions of Race"; and Felipe Castro Gutiérrez, *La extinción de la artesanía gremial* (Mexico City: Universidad Autónoma de México, 1986). The 1753 census was taken after the 1749 agricultural crisis and is incomplete, offering a view of only three-quarters of the central area of the city. This was predominantly a Spanish residential area. Nonetheless, the census is among the best existing documents we have for occupational patterns in Mexico City for the eighteenth century, allowing for full views of race and occupation.

60. Ninety-one militiamen were *sastres*, while sixty-two were *zapateros*.

61. Seed, "Social Dimensions or Race," 580.

62. Castro Gutiérrez, *Extinción de la artesanía*, 97, 172–80. His work identifies only forty-six free-colored artisans. Of these, seventeen (37 percent) were *sastres*, five were *zapateros* (10.9 percent), and two were *herreros* (4.3 percent).

63. John E. Kicza, *Colonial Entrepreneurs: Families and Business in Bourbon Mexico City* (Albuquerque: Univ. of New Mexico Press, 1983), 209–11; and Pérez Toledo, *Los hijos del trabajo*, 74.

64. Pérez Toledo, *Los hijos del trabajo*, 136–38.

65. Ibid., 74–80.

66. González Angulo Aguirre, *Artesanado y ciudad*, 30, 153–55.

67. Ibid., 57; Haslip, "Crime and the Administration of Justice," 70–71; Luis González Obregon, *La vida de Mexico en 1810* (Mexico City: Colección Metropolitana, 1975), 15–16; and Fanny Calderón de la Barca, *Life in Mexico, The Letters of Fanny Calderón de la Barca,* ed. Howard T. Fisher and Marion Hall Fisher (New York: Doubleday and Company, Inc., 1966), 91–92.

68. González Angulo Aguirre, *Artesanado y ciudad*, 156.

69. Pérez Toledo, *Los hijos del trabajo*, 78–79.

70. Thomson, *Puebla*, 96; Carmen Aguirre Anaya and Alberto Carabarin Gracia, "Formas artesanales y fabriles de los textiles de algodón en la ciudad de Puebla, siglos XVIII y XIX," in *Puebla de la colonia a la revolución: Estudios de historia regional,* ed. Colomba Salazar Ibarguen (Puebla: Centro de Investigaciones Historicas y Sociales, Instituto de Ciencias de la Universidad Autonoma de Puebla, 1987), 134–36. For detailed descriptions of textile manufacturing, see Manuel Miño Grijalva, *La manufactura colonial: La constitución técnica del obraje* (Mexico City: El Colegio de México, 1985), 89–145, Isabel González Sánchez, "Sistemas de trabajo, salarios y situación de los trabajadores agrícolas, 1750–1810," in *La clase obrera en la historia de México,* 6th ed., ed. Carmen Valcarce (Mexico City: Siglo XXI Editores, 1990), 1:150–72.

71. AGN, Alcaldes Mayores, vol. 2, exp. 254, Joseph Enereno to Bucareli, December 21, 1771, Puebla.

72. Five of Puebla's six parish censuses have been analyzed here, given the difficulty in determining race in the sixth parish.

73. Thomson, *Puebla*, 69. For more, see Miguel Marín Bosch, *Puebla Neocolonial 1777–1831, Casta, ocupación y matrimonio en la segunda ciudad de Nueva España* (Zapopan, Jalisco: El Colegio de Jaliso, 1999).

74. Ibid. Thomson's study of four parishes in Puebla yields the same results.

75. David A. Brading, "Grupos étnicos: Clases y estructura ocupacional en Guanajuato," in *Historia y población*, 256. Free-coloreds were involved in the mining professions at rates of 60 percent of their population, higher than any other racial category. In terms of tailoring and shoemaking, they composed 36 percent of all the city's *zapateros* and 12 percent of the city's *sastres*. Surprisingly, they played a smaller role as servants than they did as *zapateros*. Only 28 percent of the city's servants were free-coloreds.

76. Chance and Taylor, *Race and Class*, 148–49.

77. Precise numbers for free-coloreds are not available in Chance and Taylor's work, but to give a sense of the dimensions of the occupations of *sastres, tejedores*, and *zapateros*, these three professions accounted for 37.5 percent of all the city's artisans. Chance and Taylor, *Race and Class*, 141, 160.

78. For excellent treatment of the occupational situation in Orizaba, see Guillermina del Valle Pavón, "Distribución de la población en el espacio urbano de Orizaba en 1791," in *Población y estructura urbana*, 129–51. See also Deans-Smith, *Bureaucrats, Planters, and Workers*, 108.

79. There is debate as to what occupations were the most important, in numerical terms, in Orizaba. Deans-Smith ranks tobacco workers as the most prominent, employing 182 persons, followed by commerce (140 *vecinos*), and tailoring (76 *vecinos*). Deans-Smith, *Bureaucrats, Planters, and Workers*, 108. Del Valle Pavón, using the same census source, tallies commerce and transportation as the leading occupational sector, accounting for 334 individuals. This was followed by agriculture (232 *vecinos*) and tobacco (138 *vecinos*). Del Valle Pavón, *Distribución de la población*, 133–38. Furthermore,

she categorizes the leading artisan category as that of dress and clothing, including *zapateros*.

80. For good discussion of Michoacán, see Claude Morin, *Michoacán en la Nueva España del siglo XVIII: Crecimiento y desigualdad en una economía colonial* (Mexico City: Fondo de Cultura Económica, 1979), 92–126. For *obrajes* and looms, see pages 121–26.

81. Morin, *Michoacán*, 117. For more on Michoacán's tithe returns, see Juan Carlos Garavaglia and Juan Carlos Grosso, "La región de Puebla/Tlaxcala y la economía novo-hispana (1670–1821)," *Historia Mexicana* 35, no. 4 (1986): 554–58.

82. Morin, *Michoacán*, 122–24.

83. María Ofelia Mendoza Briones, "Pertenencia étnica e interlocución al sistema colonial en Michoacán: 1766–1767," *Tzintzun* 23 (1996): 14–15; for comparative purposes and a look at the slave condition, see Maria Guadalupe Chávez Carbajal, *Propietarios y esclavos negros en Michoacán (1600–1650)* (Morelia, Michoacán: Universidad Michoacana de San Nicolás de Hidalgo, 1994). Her interpretation differs from the standard view by alleging that free-blacks found ready entry into the artisan class. However, neither Chavéz Carbajal nor Mendoza Briones provides any statistical evidence to support their claims.

84. To be precise, 58 percent of white militiamen were in these upper-level posts.

85. Vega Juanino, *La institución militar*, 119–57.

86. Discussions of resistance and enrollment difficulties in Michoacán can be found in AGN, I.G., vol. 37-B, Informe del alcalde mayor de Tancitaro en la provincia de Michaocán sobre la imposibilidad de formar milicias en aquella jurisdicion, November 20, 1759; AGN, I.G. vol. 490-A, Phelipe Neve to Marques de Croix, September 6, 1766, Valladolid; and AGN, I.G., vol. 37-B, Informe del alcalde mayor de Cuiceo de la Laguna sobre no poderse formar mas milicias que la compañía establecida, October 10, 1758.

87. Reinhard Liehr, *Ayuntamiento y oligarquía en Puebla, 1787–1810*, trans. Olga Hentschel (Mexico City: Secretaría de Educación Pública, 1976), 2:86.

88. There were a total of 1,044 men in the companies. Thomson, *Puebla*, 93–94.

89. The 1791 census counts the following: Whites = 201, Mestizos = 313, *Castizos* = 107, *Chinos* = 8, Free-Coloreds = 5407. AGN, Padrones, vol. 18, fs. 209–305v. There were 2,075 Indian tributaries in 1801. See Peter Gerhard, *Geografía histórica de la Nueva España, 1519–1821* (Mexico City: Universidad Nacional Autónoma de México, 1986), 155. Keep in mind that the number of tributaries is only a partial glimpse at the actual number of the indigenous population. Women were half-tributaries and children were not counted. Indians must have totaled at least five thousand individuals by 1801.

90. While in other regions in Mexico the *estancia* was synonymous for ranch, in Igualapa, *estancias* tended to resemble townships in terms of their size, organization, and function. The depiction of the *estancia* as a ranch is perhaps best seen in Morelos: Cheryl English Martin, *Rural Society in Colonial Morelos* (Albuquerque: Univ. of New Mexico Press, 1985), 13. None of the four *estancias* in Igualapa seemed to fit this model. See AGN, Padrones, vol. 18, fs. 209–305v.

91. Unfortunately, the census does not provide information on female occupations. This research is based only on male employment.

92. Whites made beneficial use of their small presence in the province. In 1791, we see that they firmly amassed among themselves the lion's share of professional careers. The range and diversity of the Spanish labor pool in Igualapa was impressive. In contrast to the situation observed for free-coloreds, there were twenty-six different professions recorded for a working white male population of only 66 individuals. For comparative

purposes, note that there were 117 working mestizos placed in just ten professions. *Castizos* numbered 33 men in only seven different job types. All ecclesiastical, medical, and administrative positions went to whites, except for two posts as *mayordomos de estancia* (ranch overseers), one of which went to a free-colored and the other to a mestizo. All commerce passed through white hands. That was true even at the level of shopkeeper, except for the occasional mestizo cashier. There seemed to be slightly more opportunities for the castes in educational careers. There were four *maestros de escuela* (schoolteachers) in the province, only one of whom was labeled a Spaniard. The others included a member from each of the non-Indian racial mixtures, including one *mulato*, a mestizo and one *castizo*. Without further evidence, one might be inclined to speculate that education was segregated, with the races ministering to their own kind. On the whole, the occupational structure of the province reveals a clearly distinguishable elite that was thoroughly white in racial presence. Many of these individuals hailed directly from Spain and were often routed into prestigious offices. Of course, not all whites were elite. A significant number were simple farmers, and there was even a servant. But by and large, they controlled economic and political affairs in Igualapa. Under them were the mestizos, *castizos,* and free-coloreds, all of whom provided the hands that labored the province. Except for very slight differences in one or two middle-status jobs, these groups were occupationally almost indistinguishable, apart from the fact that free-coloreds were the most likely to be simple farmers. For *castizos* and mestizos, the occupation of *labrador* employed between 72 and 78 percent of their number, as opposed to more than 90 percent for free-coloreds.

93. The numbers are more difficult to acquire, but in 1777 Puebla had at least 2,930, blacks and *mulatos*, and many more *pardos* among its 12,670 "*castas.*" During the militia levy of that year, free-colored commanders were able to fill their battalion, meaning that there were a maximum of 610 *pardos, morenos*, and *mulatos libres* in the services. See Thomson, *Puebla*, 63; and AGN, I.G., vol. 28-B, Correspondencia con el batallon de pardos de Puebla, 1777.

94. In other contexts the same provinces are referred to as Pánuco (Tampico) and Guazacualco (Acaycuan).

95. *Filastica* was used for cordage. AGN, I.G., vol. 53-A, Armona to Mayorga, June 2, 1781, Mexico City.

96. AGN, I.G., vol. 53-A, Thomas Serrada, December 1, 1780, Tampico.

97. By military law, militiamen were under special obligation to secure licenses before contracting marriage. The policy was imposed more stiffly on white officers than for white NCOs and free-colored militiamen. The objective of the policy was to allow crown representatives and high military officers the chance to review the credentials of brides beforehand, checking to see that they were of proper station and race for marriage. Investigations were made into their family histories so as to ensure that their parents were honorable, and preferably of noble or *hidálgo* origin. For commissioned officers and others receiving a regular military salary, the proposed bride had to be able to provide a substantial dowry, ranging between one thousand and twenty-five hundred pesos minimum. In some cases, the investigation process took years to complete. The brides' requirements were less stringent for lower-ranking NCOs. Soldiers, and especially officers, who refused to abide by the rules could be demoted, refused their salary, or ejected from military duty altogether. For free-coloreds, the principal design of the law was to control the proliferation of interracial marriages, although there was occasional concern over maintaining proper "class" criteria, as written in the laws for Yucatan. The passing of the

Real Pragmatica (1778) gave free-colored officers rights to interfere with the marriage choice of their children, also a move to ensure that they preserved their proper place in society. Until 1803, free-colored officers were the only black group covered under the Pragmatica. But military license laws, as they applied to free-colored militiamen, had as their ulterior motive the desire to restrict free-colored exogamy to suitable white women in areas where they were few. Examples include the coasts of Veracruz, Tabasco, Nuevo Santander, and the Pacific littoral zones. However, based on the evidence reviewed here, the effects of these laws were negligible, and free-colored militiamen married whomever they pleased without securing licenses. For that reason, the data appearing in the marriage tables was unaffected by license laws. For more, see AGN, I.G., vol. 214-A, Tineo to Mayorga, May 28, 1780, Mexico City; AGN, I.G., 394-A, Reglamento para las milicias de infanteria de la provincia de Yucatan y Campeche, 1778, Madrid, fs. 16–19; AGN, Bandos, vol. 17, exp. 15, Reglamento provisional para el régimen, gobeirno y nueva planta de las compañías de milicias mixtas del seno que comprehende la provincia de Tampico, Pánuco, hasta el Rio Guazacualco, costas laterales de Veracruz, fs. 122–122v; AGN, Bandos, vol. 17, exp. 12, Reglamento Provisional para el régimen gobierno y nueva planta de las milicias de la provincia de Tabasco, fs. 100–100v; AGN, Bandos, vol. 17, exp. 5, Reglamento provisional para el cuerpo de milicias de caballeria que con el nombre de la frontera de la colonia del Nuevo Santander debe formarse . . . fs. 45v–46; and AGN, Bandos, vol. 17, exp. 50, Reglamento provisional para el régimen, gobierno y nueva planta de las compañías de milicias de la costa del sur del reyno de Nueva España desde la jurisdiccion de Acaponeta hasta la de Tehuantepec, fs. 213v–14.

98. See Brading, "Grupos étnicos," 258–59; Marcelo Carmagnani, "Demografía y sociedad: La estructura social de los centros mineros del norte de México, 1600–1720," in *Historia y población*, 130–34; Patrick J. Carroll, "Los mexicanos negros: El mestizaje y los fundamentos olvidados de la 'raza cósmica,' una perspectiva regional," *Historia Mexicana* 44, no. 3 (1995): 411–19; and Cecilia Rabell, "Matrimonio y raza en una parroquia rural: San Luis de la Paz, Guanajuato, 1715–1810," in *Historia y población*, 168–83; 199–201.

99. Thomson, *Puebla*, 63.

100. Ibid., 66; Liehr, *Ayuntamiento y oligarquía*, 1:81–82.

101. Thomson, *Puebla*, 66.

102. McCaa, "Calidad, Clase, and Marriage in Colonial Mexico: The Case of Parral, 1788–90," *HAHR* 64, no. 3 (1984): 477–501.

103. The best regional studies of intermarriage, which provide detailed data on endogamy/exogamy trends for all of New Spain's racial groups, include Carroll, "Mexicanos negros," vi–x, 411–19; Souto Mantecón and Torres, "La población de la antigua parroquia," 95–96, Chance and Taylor, *Race and Class*, 136–37; Brading, "Grupos étnicos," 258–59; Marcelo Carmagnani, "Demografía y sociedad," 130–34; Cope, *Limits of Racial Domination*, 78–85; Juan Javier Pescador, *De bautizoados a fieles difuntos: Familia y mentalidades en una Parroquia urbana, Santa Catarina de México, 1568–1820* (Mexico City: El Colegio de México, 1992), 145–81; Thomas Calvo, "Familias y sociedad: Zamora (Siglos XVII–XIX)," in *Historia de la familia*, comp. Pilar Gonzalbo (Mexico City: Instituto Mora, 1993), 129–40; McCaa, "Calidad, Clase, and Marriage," 493–97, 499–501; David J. Robinson, "Patrones de Población: Parral a fines del Siglo XVIII," in *Demografía histórica de México, siglos XVI–XIX*, comp. Elsa Malvido and Miguel Ángel Cuenya (Mexico City: Instituto Mora, 1993), 199–210; and Rabell, "Matrimonio y raza," 168–83; 199–201.

104. For a good schematic design of spatial race distribution in rural settings, see Patrick J. Carroll, *Blacks in Colonial Veracruz: Race, Ethnicity, and Regional Development* (Austin: Univ. of Texas Press, 1991), 115–16.

105. Brígida von Mentz, *Pueblos de indios, mulatos y mestizos, 1770–1870* (Mexico City: CIESAS, 1988), 82–85.

106. This is a low figure based on the numbers of Mentz's typology of rural townships. The percentage would have applied more to townships than to *haciendas*, plantations, and *estancias*. Fewer Indians resided on these estates because labor structures were weighted to attract coloreds and blacks; however, Indians were still found there nevertheless. Von Mentz, *Pueblos de indios*, 83; and Carroll, *Blacks in Colonial Veracruz*, 115.

107. The classic statement of free-colored assimilation in Mexico is Aguirre Beltrán, "The Integration of the Negro," 11–27. On the role of blacks in the process of *mestizaje*, see Carroll, "Mexicanos Negros," 403–38. For theoretical information and case studies on assimilation, consult Leo Spitzer, *Lives in Between, Assimilation and Marginality in Austria, Brazil, and West Africa, 1780–1945* (Cambridge, England: Cambridge Univ. Press, 1989). Whitening is discussed in other contexts: Carl N. Degler, *Neither Black nor White: Slavery and Race Relations in Brazil and the United States* (New York: Macmillan, 1971; repr., Madison: Univ. of Wisconsin Press, 1986); Thomas E. Skidmore, *Black into White: Race and Nationality in Brazilian Thought* (New York: Oxford Univ. Press, 1974); and Winthorp Wright, *Café con Leche: Race, Class, and National Image in Venezuela* (Austin: Univ. of Texas Press, 1990). For legal boundaries on interracial marriages, see Rout, *The African Experience*, 140–45; Mörner, *Race Mixture*, 36–39; Socolow, "Acceptable Marriage Partners: Marriage Choice in Colonial Argentina, 1778–1810," in *Sexuality and Marriage in Colonial Latin America*, ed. Asunción Lavrin (Lincoln and London: Univ. of Nebraska Press, 1992), 210–13; and Seed, *To Love, Honor, and Obey in Colonial Mexico: Conflict over Marriage Choice, 1574–1821* (Stanford: Stanford Univ. Press, 1988). For discussion of marriage as a social improvement strategy for black slaves in Peru, see Christine Hunefeldt, *Paying the Price of Freedom: Family and Labor among Lima's Slaves, 1800–1854*, trans. Alexandra Stern (Berkeley, Los Angeles, and London: Univ. of California Press, 1994), 129–66. Note that exogamy rates have also been used to discuss the weaknesses of the caste system. Successful intermarriages, particularly in the eighteenth century, have been used to show that racial boundaries were not as tight as the laws stipulated and were increasingly difficult to maintain.

108. In most areas, the number of exogamous unions rarely exceeded 50 percent for any racial group, even in the late eighteenth century. Broadly speaking, Indian endogamy was greatest, followed sequentially by whites, mestizos, and coloreds. Obviously, there were variations to the model. Mestizo and *castizo* exogamy sometimes outpaced that of coloreds, as seen in Antequera during the seventeenth century and in Guanajuato during the late eighteenth century. In places like Zamora and Charcas, Indian endogamy could be lower than that of whites. In Mexico City, Indian endogamy rates were even less than those of mestizos. For more, see Carroll, "Mexicanos negros," vi–x, 411–19; Souto Mantecón and Torres, "La población de Xalapa," 95–96, Chance and Taylor, *Race and Class*, 136–37; Brading, "Grupos étnicos," 258–59; Carmagnani, "Demografía y sociedad," 130–34; Cope, *Limits of Racial Domination*, 78–85; Pescador, *De bautizoados a fieles difuntos*, 145–81; Calvo, "Familias y sociedad," 129–40; McCaa, "Calidad, Clase, and Marriage," 493–97, 499–501; Robinson, "Patrones de población," 199–210; and Rabell, "Matrimonio y raza," 168–83; 199–201.

109. Even though sexual imbalances ran high, contributing to a larger number of

men than women, in places such as Mexico City, blacks were still involved in endogamous marriage relationships at rates of 86 percent. *Mulatos* were less endogamous but nevertheless married other people of color at rates of 52 percent. Most black endogamy was ethnically based. For example, Angolans petitioned to marry other Angolans at rates of 73 percent. Similar trends could be detected for the Bakongo, Bran Biafra, and Gelofe ethnic groups, among others. See Herman L. Bennett, "Lovers, Family, and Friends: The Formation of Afro-Mexico, 1580–1810" (Ph.D. diss., Duke University, 1993), 65–69, 90–91. There are a number of criticisms about the high proportion of black endogamy observed for the period. Some point out that illegitimacy and consensual unions for Afro-Mexicans was high during these times, implying that an understanding of intimate relationships is incomplete and skewed when based upon marriage data alone. In other words, marital endogamy probably appeared so prevalent because instances of Afro-Mexican marriage were so low prior to the eighteenth century. See Seed, *To Love, Honor, and Obey*, 25–26. Another interpretation places a premium on the need for more inclusive analysis of areas outside of Mexico City to reach a better understanding of Afro-Mexican endogamy patterns. Blacks in places like Jalapa, particularly slaves, frequently sought exogamous relationships (marital and consensual) so that their children would be born free. In the Spanish Americas, children assumed the status of the mother (slave or free). In an environment like that of Jalapa, where slave men outnumbered women at ratios of three to one, the decision to choose a partner for such reasons led to a number of racial intermarriages. Furthermore, given the structural imbalances induced by the slave trade, Carroll observes that slaves were faced with two basic options: "to marry outside of the slave population, or simply not marry at all." Carroll, "Mexicanos negros," 411. See also Chávez Carbajal, *Propietarios y esclavos*, 104–5, 115–17.

110. Secondary and tertiary pushes of slave shipments continued to be brought into certain areas of Veracruz, but after 1710 much of the fresh arrival of African-born slaves had ceased. Naveda Chavez, *Esclavos negros*; Carroll, *Blacks in Colonial Veracruz*, 37–39.

111. Cope, *Limits of Racial Domination*, 83.

112. For Cope, ethnic categories are broader in scope than the racial designations of the *sociedad de castas*. *Mulatos*, blacks, *pardos*, and *moriscos*, for instance, because of their African-based heritage, would fall into the same ethnic category. *Pardos* with Indian parents would also fall under the ethnic category that grouped mestizos and *indios*. For more on ethnicity, see Wade, *Race and Ethnicity*, 19–24.

113. Cope, *Limits of Racial Domination*, 82.

114. Carroll, "Mexicanos negros," 411; and Brading, "Grupos étnicos," 258.

115. Cope, *Limits of Racial Domination*, 78, 56–67.

116. For examples, see Ricardo Pozas, *Juan the Chamula: An Ethnological Re-creation of the Life of a Mexican Indian* (Berkeley, Los Angeles, and London: Univ. of California Press, 1962); and Ramón Gutiérrez, *When Jesus Came, the Corn Mothers Went Away* (Stanford: Stanford Univ. Press, 1991), 203–6.

117. Men desiring to whiten through marriage were perhaps the least affected by exogamous unions. Particularly, free-colored men aspiring to have their racial category recast in public documents because they married white or *mestiza* women were to be found sadly mistaken. Most official records reported the husband and wife's racial status individually, unaffected by one another. A smaller selection of census and parish registers record that when a free-colored man married lighter, his wife often assumed *his* racial status, rather than having her color "upgrade" his own. The contexts where this "racial drift," or adscripted race occurred were not always consistent, but in situations in which

the change did happen, it served as a means for municipal and clerical officials to force the caste system into working by correcting color imbalances after marriage. If ideal racial matches did not take place with respect to the class standing of the couple, these officials could still pretend that they did. Cope has observed similar trends in his work. He adds a corollary. Plebeian, light-skinned husbands who were not white could be demoted to their wives' racial category if the women were *mulattas* or mestizas. While his sample is small, he believes that racial alterations took place because enumerators were interested in preserving the integrity of the major racial groups over the smaller ones. This is to say that mestizos and *mulatos*, two of the most used classifications under the caste system in the late seventeenth century, took precedence over *castizos, moriscos,* and *albinos,* which were lesser used categories. See AHAP, legajo 1385, fs. 68–103; Chance and Taylor, *Race and Class,* 171–72; McCaa, "Calidad, Clase, and Marriage," 497–99; and Cope, *Limits of Racial Domination,* 70–78.

118. Voelz, *Slave and Soldier,* 420; Edward Brathwaite, *The Development of Creole Society in Jamaica, 1770–1820* (Oxford: Clarendon Press, 1985), 106; and Orlando Patterson, *The Sociology of Slavery* (London: Fairleigh Dickenson Univ. Press, 1967), 162.

CHAPTER 4

1. A notable exception includes Bowser, *The African Slave,* 301–10.

2. Ross Hassig, *Trade, Tribute, and Transportation, The Sixteenth-Century Political Economy of the Valley of Mexico* (Norman: University of Oklahoma Press, 1985); Spalding, *Huarochirí*; Alonso de Zorita and José Miranda, *El tributo indígena en la Nueva España durante el siglo XVI* (Mexico, 1952).

3. Arij Ouweneel, "Growth Stagnation, and Migration: An Explorative Analysis of the *Tributario* Series of Anáhuac (1720–1800)," *HAHR* 71, no. 3 (1991): 540.

4. *Recopilacion de Leyes,* Libro VII, Titulo V, fol. 285v.

5. Charles Gibson, *The Aztecs under Spanish Rule: A History of the Indians of the Valley of Mexico, 1519–1810* (Stanford: Stanford Univ. Press, 1964), 194–203.

6. Bowser, *The African Slave,* 303.

7. *Recopilacion de Leyes,* Libro VII, Titulo V, fs. 285–285v.

8. Bowser, *The African Slave,* 23, AGN, Bandos, vol. 17, exps. 55 and 56.

9. Bowser, *The African Slave,* 23, 303–7.

10. Rout, *The African Experience,* 150.

11. AGN, Californias, vol. 58, exp. 1, fs. 6–8, 70; AGN, Civil, vol. 130 pt. 2, 1757, Mexico City, fs. 5–11.

12. Gibson, *The Aztecs,* 205. New Spain's Indian tribute practices appear to have differed from those of the Andes, where tribute rates varied according to the wealth of the Indians. In New Spain, if an Indian community was enduring economic hardship, its tribute rate would be lowered until the community could recover its financial base.

13. Ibid., 205, 209. Indian communities seem to have paid *alcabala,* although there is mention that one of the many rights of living in a *pueblo de indios* was exemption from sales taxes. Although they were charged many fees, they were still relieved from a multitude of other payments. See William B. Taylor, "Indian Pueblos of Central Jalisco on the Eve of Independence," in *Iberian Colonies, New World Societies: Essays in Memory of Charles Gibson,* ed. Richard L. Garner and William B. Taylor (University Park, Pennsylvania: State College, 1985), 166.

14. AGN, Tributos, vol. 40, exp. 9, fs. 88–95.
15. AGN, Tributos, vol. 34, exp. 7, fol. 162v.
16. AGN, Californias, vol. 58, fs. 44v–49.
17. Gibson, *Aztecs*, 251.
18. AGN, Tributos, vol. 40, exp. 9, fs. 89–95.
19. AGN, Bandos, vol. 17, exps. 55–56.
20. *Alcaldes mayores* also were called *gobernadores* and *corregidores*. After the institution of the intendancy system in the 1780s, *subdelegados* replaced the *alcaldes mayores*. The key distinctions to be made between the *alcaldes mayores* and their subordinates was their relationship with local towns. The *alcalde mayor* was a more distant authority, often a foreigner to the province, if not to the colony. His term was for an average length of three to five years in the eighteenth century. After serving in one post, he might be rotated elsewhere. Many *alcaldes mayores* were absentees, preferring to live in Mexico City rather than in their provinces. Others lived in the *cabeceras*. The *alcalde mayor* represented the supreme judicial and administrative authority at the provincial level. By contrast, the *tenientes* were drawn from the population of local notables. Although appointed to serve under the administration of a particular *alcalde mayor*, they could serve in succession in the same area, making them more attuned to local affairs. For excellent detail on these posts, see Borah, "El gobernador novohispano," 37–50; and Taylor, *Magistrates of the Sacred*, 345–69.
21. Ouweneel, "Growth, Stagnation, and Migration," 543. There were exceptions, and in some cases, *matrículas* were annual affairs.
22. In general, attempts were made to keep mestizos separated from tribute registers. Exceptions include mestizos tributed in Sn. Andres Tuxtla, AGN I.G., vol. 33-B, Arreglo de las companias de milicias de Tuxtla por el sargento mayor de la plaza de Veracruz, Dn. Antonio Saavedra, 1776; in Tacotalpa (Tabasco) AGN, Tributos, vol. 40, exp. 9, fs. 97–100, and Nochistlan (Oaxaca), AGN, I.G., vol. 483-A, Francisco Marti to Crespo, May 29, 1784, Oaxaca.
23. AGN, Bandos, vol. 17, exps. 55 and 56.
24. Taylor, "Indian Pueblos of Central Jalisco," 166.
25. Ibid.
26. Gibson, *The Aztecs*, 200, AGN, Tributos, vol. 40, exp. 9, fs. 89–95.
27. The case of Xicayan is a good example, AGN, Tributos, vol. 34, exp. 7, fs. 118–78.
28. Gibson, *The Aztecs*, 205; AGN, Tributos, vol. 34, exp. 7, fs. 133–78.
29. AGN, Californias, vol. 58, fs. 253v–56v.
30. Taylor, *Magistrates of the Sacred*, 402, Borah, "El gobernador novohispano," 37–50.
31. An example in Guachinango: AGN, Tributos, vol. 40, exp. 15, fs. 260–64v.
32. Carmen Yuste, "Las autoridades locales como agentes del fisco en la Nueva España," in *El gobierno provincial*, 113.
33. Michael T. Ducey, "Viven sin ley ni rey: Rebeliones coloniales en Papantla, 1760–1790" in *Procesos rurales e historia regional*, ed. Victoria Chenaut (Mexico City: CIESAS, 1996), 19–20.
34. Ibid.
35. AGN, Californias, vol. 58, fs. 15v–23.
36. Ibid., 82–117v.
37. AGN, Bandos, vol. 17, exps. 55–56.

38. AGN, Californias, vol. 58, fs. 82–117v; and AGN, I.G., vol. 53-A, Armona to Mayorga, September 9, 1781, Sn. Andres Tuxtla. Note that Tuxtla's *mulatos blancos* were not included in white units because the government resisted their incorporation.

39. Palmer, *Slaves of the White God*, 183.

40. John J. TePaske and Herbert S. Klein, *Ingresos y egresos de la real hacienda de Nueva España*, 2 vols. (Mexico City: Instituto Nacional de Antropologia e Historia, 1986); TePakse, *Real hacienda de Nueva España: La real caja de México* (Mexico City: Instituto Nacional de Antropologia e Historia, 1976).

41. Carlos Ruiz Abreu, *Comercio y milicias de Tabasco en la colonia* (Villahermosa, Tabasco: Instituto Cultural de Tabasco, 1989); Peter Gerhard, *The Southeast Frontier of New Spain* (Princeton: Princeton Univ. Press, 1979), 42; AGN, Bandos, vol. 17, exp. 55, fol. 246v.

42. AGN, Tributos, vol. 48, exp. 8.

43. Zimapan was an exception: TePaske and Klein, *Ingresos y egresos*, 1:1–23 (Zimapan); Colima was another exception: Juan Carlos Reyes, "Tributarios negros y afromestizos: Primeras notas sobre un padrón Colimense de 1809," in *III Encuentro nacional de afromexicanistas*, ed. Luz Ma. Martínez Montiel and Juan Carlos Reyes (Colima: Gobierno del Estado de Colima, 1993), 126–32.

44. For additional raw data, consult TePaske and Klein, *Ingresos y egresos*.

45. Florescano and Swan, *Breve historia de la seqía*, 54; Richard Boyer, "Mexico in the Seventeenth Century: Transition of a Colonial Society," *HAHR* 57, no. 3 (1977): 477.

46. Richard Boyer, *La gran inundación: Vida y sociedad en la ciudad de Mexico (1629–1638)*, trans. Antonieta Sánchez Mejorada (Mexico City: Secretaría de Educación Publica, 1975); Florescano and Swan, *Breve historia de la seqía*, 174.

47. Herbert S. Klein and John J. TePaske, "The Seventeenth-Century Crisis in New Spain: Myth or Reality?" *Past and Present* 90 (February 1981): 120–21.

48. AGN, Tributos, vol. 48; Gibson, *Aztecs*, 199.

49. J. I. Israel, "Mexico and the 'General Crisis' of the Seventeenth Century," *Past and Present* 63 (May 1974): 40; and Boyer, "Mexico in the Seventeenth Century," 472.

50. Israel, *Race, Class and Politics*, 193–94; Torres Ramírez, *La armada de Barlovento*.

51. Apart from these years and the stretch from 1621 to 1640, there remain only three years unaccounted for in the collection of back taxes: 1619–20, 1606–7, and 1610–11.

52. Israel, *Race, Class and Politics*, 252–54.

53. Israel notes that from 1661–63, Mexican agriculture experienced a severe blow because of drought. Moreover, silver was in crisis in the 1660s due to the sluggish distribution of mercury, creating a further crisis in specie. Israel, *Race, Class and Politics*, 261–62. This context emphasizes the importance of the previous decade in sustaining and increasing free-colored tribute revenues.

54. Aguirre Beltrán, *La población negra*.

55. Ibid., 206–7. Beltrán says that slaves numbered 18,569 at this time.

56. Aguirre Beltrán's 1793 figures are more reliable, based on the excellent yet incomplete census of Revillagigedo. Cook and Borah, *Essays in Population History*, 2:180–269, have better general figures for Mexico's eighteenth-century black population. They also reveal the limitations of Aguirre Beltrán's work.

57. AGN, General de Parte, vol. 33, exp. 77–78, fs. 68–87.

58. Rout, *The African Experience*, 150.

59. The level of corsair aggression increased significantly after 1628, with the capture of the Spanish treasure fleet that had set sail from Veracruz for Europe. Having experi-

enced tremendous success, pirate enterprises became bolder. Raiders were no longer content with reaping the small rewards of assaulting weak towns and isolated vessels. Campeche and Veracruz now became favorite targets. The mid-seventeenth century witnessed the successful capture of Jamaica by the British, who converted the island into a base of operations against Spanish possessions. The island of Tris (known as Isla del Carmen), in the Laguna de Términos, also served as an important base for corsair activity until the early eighteenth century. It wasn't until 1717, after a major Spanish offensive and the establishment of the Presidio del Carmen, that the pirate threat was reduced along the southeastern coast of New Spain. See Redondo, *Negritud en Campeche*, 86; Juarez Moreno, *Corsarios*, 11–42; Rubio Mañe, *El virreinato*, 2:92–118; AGN, I.G., vol. 53-A, Armona to Mayorga, September 16, 1780, Sn. Andres Tuxtla.

60. AGN, Californias, vol. 58, exp. 1, fs. 1–5; AGN, General de Parte, vol. 33, exps. 77–78, fs. 68–87; AGN, Tributos, vol. 40, exp. 11, fs. 182–92v; Recopilacion de Leyes, Libro VII, Titulo V, fol. 287v; and AGN, Reales Cédulas Originales, vol. 11, exp. 113, fs. 316–17. This last document intimates that the tribute exemption process in Veracruz may have been initiated as early as 1669, sparked by the appeals of militia captains Diego Pérez and Francisco de Torres. However, the preponderance of evidence from other sources confirms that the 1676 petition was the definitive effort that secured the privilege.

61. AGN, I.G., vol. 492-A, exp. 3, Testimonio de las diligencias practicadas en el superior gobierno por representacion que hicieron a su ex. a los pardos y demas milicianos de la provincia de Goazacoalcos sobre la reelevacion de pasar al puerto de Veracruz cada que haiga novedad de hostilidades, por los fundamentos que expresan, 1767; and AGN, I.G., Tributos, vol. 40, exp. 11, fs. 167–233.

62. AGN, Tributos, vol. 34, exp. 7, fs. 163–73.

63. The term "contract" is used in the petition of the militiamen of Tamiagua: AGN, Californias, vol. 58, exp. 1, fs. 23–62.

64. AGN, Tributos, vol. 40, exp. 1, 1677. This document mainly discusses Indian exemption in Tabasco.

65. AGN, General de Parte, vol. 47, exp. 50, fs. 30–32v; AGN, General de Parte, vol. 35, exp. 180, fs. 141–42.

66. AGN, I.G., vol. 502-A, Diego Avete y Maestre, July 27, 1784, Acayucan.

67. AGN, Tributos, vol. 34, exp. 7, 163–73.

68. Some examples of women using the poverty argument in military contexts: AGN, I.G., vol. 485-A, Maria Jacinta Salazar to Valcarcel, Puebla, 1782; AGN, I.G., vol. 485-A, Anna Joséfa Montiel to Valcarcel, 1782, Puebla; AGN, I.G., vol. 307-B, Leberina Azebedo to Rivas, October 13, 1785, Mexico City.

69. While the geography argument is made in the initial petition, these details become clearer in a second appeal for privileges made by the militiamen in 1707: AGN, I.G., vol. 492-A, exp. 3, Testimonio de las diligencias practicadas . . . 1767.

70. AGN, Tributos, vol. 40, exp. 11, fs. 182–92v.

71. AGN, Californias, vol. 58, exp. 1, fs. 6, fol. 23.

72. See also Archer, *The Army in Bourbon Mexico*, 39.

73. AGN, I.G., vol. 492-A, exp. 3, Juan Francisco Ramirez de Castron to Pedro Madraso Escalera, April 20, 1697, Acyaucan. Note that the *vigía* was considered the critical element of the defense scheme in this letter.

74. AGN, Tributos, vol. 34, exp. 3, fs. 71–72.

75. AGN, I.G., vol. 33-B, Arreglo de las compañías de milicias de Tuxtla, por el Sargento Mayor de la plaza de Veracruz, Dn. Antonio Saavedra, 1776, fs. 33–35. Note that in

Tuxtla unpaid errand boys tended to be *indios*, whereas the salaried ones tended to be mestizos or *pardos*.

76. AGN, Bandos, vol. 17, exp. 15; AGN, Tributos, vol. 40, exp. 9, fs. 115–19; AGN, Tributos, vol. 34, exps. 5–6, fs. 106–17v; and AGN, Tributos, vol. 34, exp. 3, fs. 60–93.

77. Gerhard, *The Southeast Frontier*, 35–53; AGN, Tributos, 40, exp. 9, fs. 115–19; Carlos Ruiz Abreu, *Comercio y milicias de Tabasco*, 24–30.

78. AGN, Tributos, 40, exp. 9, fs. 115–19. As in Tabasco, opposition to the militiamen's tribute exemption requests also took place in Sn. Andres Tuxtla, where the *alcalde mayor* and priest teamed up against the militiamen's pleas in the 1770s: AGN, I.G., vol. 53-A, Armona to Mayorga, September 16, 1780, Sn. Andres Tuxtla.

79. AGN, Civil, vol. 130, pt. 2, 1757, Mexico City, fs. 11–14; Californias vol. 58, fs. 37–43.

80. AGN, Civil, vol. 130, pt. 2, exp. 3, 1742, Puebla, fs. 1–25.

81. AGN, I.G., vol. 296-B, Relación de los meritos y servicios de Nicolas Bertel, June 8, 1743, Madrid.

82. AGN, Civil, vol. 130, pt. 2, 1757, Mexico City, fs. 11–14.

83. Ibid., fs. 5–18.

84. AGN, I.G. 502-A, Thomas Roncali to Mayorga, February 13, 1783, Acayucan.

85. Marchena Fernández, *Ejército y milicias*, 103; and Hoffman, *The Spanish Crown*, 39–40.

86. For Tabasco, Tuxtla, and the Veracruz coastal areas of Pánuco, Tampico, and Tantoyuca, see AGN, Tributos vol. 40, exp. 9, fs. 105–13; AGN, Californias, vol. 58, fs. 53–56; AGN, Tributos, vol. 40, exp. 15, fs. 259–74. For Xicayan, see AGN, Tributos, vol. 34, exp. 7, fs. 118–78v.

87. Marchena Fernández, *Ejército y milicias*, 105.

88. AGN, Padrones, vol. 18, fs. 209–305v.

89. Archer, *The Army in Bourbon Mexico*, 223–53; Archer, "To Serve the King," 227–31; and McAlister, "The Reorganization of the Army of New Spain," 23.

90. AGN, I.G., vol. 33-B, Antonio de Saavedra to Dn. Juan Fernando de Palacio, November 12, 1775, Tuxtla.

91. Archer, *The Army in Bourbon Mexico*, 233–35. For instances of success in meeting the desired recruitment criteria, see AGN, I.G., 232-B, Dionisio Hurtado, August 14, 1769, Orizaba; and AGN, I.G., 232-B, Thomas Serrada, July 8, 1781.

92. AGN, Padrones, vol. 18, fs. 209–305v.

93. There were forty-seven men at the rank of second sergeant and above. AGN, I.G., 483-A, Francisco Marti to Francisco Antonio Crespo, May 29, 1784, Oaxaca.

94. AGN, I.G., vol. 33-B, Antonio de Saavedra to Juan Fernando de Palacio, November 12, 1775, Tuxtla.

95. AGN, I.G., vol. 307-B, Juan de Riva to Martin Mayorga, December 10, 1780, Mexico City.

96. AGN, I.G., vol. 307-B, Posada to Mayorga, April 21, 1781, Mexico City.

97. AGN, I.G., vol. 422-A, Francisco Cañaveral y Ponce to Martin Mayorga, April 4, 1781, Acapulco.

98. AGN, Tributos, vol. 40, exp. 8, fs. 76–81.

99. AGN, General de Parte, vol. 38, exp. 229, fs. 113–16.

100. AGN, I.G., vol. 492-A, Martín de Solis, June 2, 1679, Mexico City.

101. AGN, I.G., vol. 492-A, Jacobo Ramires Montejano to Martin de Solis, September 26, 1763, fs. 31v–34v. Here, tribute law is reinterpreted by the *alcalde mayor* in Acayu-

can. He allows tribute payments to be made casually, whenever free-coloreds felt it was possible to pay.

102. Gerhard, *The North Frontier*, 140. The naval department was founded in 1768.

103. AGN, Californias, vol. 58, fs. 143–274.

104. For comparative purposes, see how *pardo* causes were supported by military officers in New Granada: Kuethe, "The Status of the Free-Pardo," 111.

105. Taylor, *Magistrates of the Sacred*, 40. Keep in mind that although the purpose of placing soldiers in administrative posts was to foster harmony between the military and the colonial government, as well as to ease the implementation of the Bourbon military reforms, rarely were these objectives achieved. Archer shows the contentiousness that existed between the military and administrative spheres: Archer, *The Army in Bourbon Mexico*, 106–67; 61–79.

106. Tabasco and Mérida were united for fiscal purposes in 1787. At that time, Yucatan's Intendant decreed that all of Tabasco's militiamen were to be subjected to tribute. However, from 1788 to 1791, Tabasco's governor, Francisco de Amusquibar, successfully protested the levy by showing the poverty of the province's residents and stressing how the new tax might cause considerable discord. He also eloquently demonstrated how Tabasco's militiamen had proven their worth in past operations, performing exemplary duties in subduing the Indian populace. In return for their work, they had enjoyed tribute exemption for years. AGN, Tributos, vol. 40, exp. 9, fs. 81–159v. While this document marks an instance in which a provincial governor came to the aid of free-colored militiamen and their privileges, there may have been many other reasons behind Amusquibar's support, including personal feuds that he had with other administrators. For more examples of officers and officials upholding free-colored military privileges, see AGN, Tributos vol. 40., exp. 15, fs. 259–74; AGN, Tributos vol. 40, exp. 11, fs. 167–233 (here, the *teniente general* of Tamiagua supports his militiamen); AGN, Tributos vol. 34, exp. 3, fs. 60–71 (here, Tehuantepec's militia colonel pleads against charging free-colored soldiers tribute in 1784–86, and actually obstructs the collection process); and AGN, Californias, vol. 58, fs. 83–117v (here, Xicayan's *sargento mayor* and other white officers attempt to preserve tribute exemption for free-colored soldiers enrolled in white units).

107. Archer, *The Army in Bourbon Mexico*, 223–25.

108. AGN, I.G., vol. 502-A, Thomas Roncali to Mayorga, February 13, 1783, Acayucan.

109. AGN, Tributos, vol. 34, exp. 7, fs. 169–73; AGN, I.G., vol. 252-B, Nicolas Lopez Padilla, October 13, 1772, Guadalajara; AGN, I.G., vol. 296-B, Pedro Montesinos, to Marquez de Amarillas, September 25, 1756.

110. AGN, I.G., vol. 492-A, Maritn de Solis, June 2, 1679, Mexico City; AGN, I.G., vol. 502-A, Pedro Moscoso, February 7, 1782, Acayucan.

111. English Martin, *Rural Society*, 149–53.

112. AGN, Padrones, vol. 18, fs. 209–305v.

113. AGN, Californias, vol. 58, expediente formado a msta. de Don Phelipe Izusquiza, gefe de las companias de caballeria de Xicayan sobre que no matriculen en los tributarios los que son soldados, 1780; AGN, Tributos, vol. 34, exps. 4–6, fs. 106–17v; AGN, Tributos, vol. 40, exp. 9, fs. 81–159v.

114. In Veracruz, Patrick Carroll has traced a shift in labor patterns from slaves to free workers. He notes a strong transition from slave to free workers between 1630 and 1720, intensifying after 1720. However, a glance at Adriana Naveda Chavez's work on the 18 sugar haciendas registered in the area of Cordoba in 1788 reveals that although free-

coloreds represented approximately 28 percent of the free-labor force, they constituted only 9 percent of total workers. Here, the majority of laborers continued to be slaves. In the smaller ranchos near Cordoba, of which 145 were registered in 1788, the percentage of free-coloreds was smaller, representing just over 7 percent of the labor force. None of the *rancho* workers were slaves. The patterns found in Naveda Chávez's study are repeated farther north in the Huasteca. Antonio Escobar notes that in 1743, almost half the hacienda residents were either *pardo* or *mulato*, the majority being slaves. In all, there were 878 hacienda residents, of whom 132 were pardos and 392 mulatos. Of the mulatos, 277 were slaves. Interestingly, although slaves may have constituted the core work force on haciendas in the Huasteca and near Cordoba, evidence suggests that the *alcaldes mayores* did not radically alter their disposition toward extending privileges to free-coloreds in these areas for fear of losing those free-coloreds that did play important labor roles on the estates. Carroll, *Blacks in Colonial Veracruz*, 61–78; Naveda Chavez, *Esclavos negros*, 54–55; Antonio Escobar Ohmestede, "La población en el siglo XVIII y principios del siglo XIX: Conformacion de una sociedad multiétnica en las Huastecas?" in *Polación y estructura urbana*, 277–91. For information on the transition from slave to free-labor in Michoacán, see Morin, *Michoacán*.

115. AGN, Californias, vol. 58, fs. 83–85v.

116. AGN, I.G., vol. 497-A, Bargas al Marques de Croix, January 7, 1767.

117. AGN, Tributos, vol. 40, exp. 9, fs. 89–95.

118. AGN, Tributos, vol. 34, exp. 7, fs. 118–78v.

119. For Guachinango, see AGN, Tributos vol. 40, exp. 11, fs. 167–233. Here, the *teniente general* suspended tribute payment in the late 1780s. The document also makes references to customary tribute exemptions in the jurisdictions of Papantla and Chicontepec. For Pánuco and Tampico, see AGN, Tributos, vol. 40, exp. 15, fs. 270–74. For Xicayan, see AGN, Tributos, vol. 34, exp. 7, fs. 118–78v. For Tehuantepec, see AGN, Tributos, vol. 34, exp. 3, fs. 60–93. For Tabasco, see AGN, Tributos vol. 40, exp. 9, fs. 121–27.

120. AGN, Tributos vol. 40, exp. 9, fs. 149–52.

121. AGN, Tributos vol. 34, exp. 7, fs. 163–73.

122. This was true in Xicayan: AGN, Californias, vol. 58, fs. 90v–94v.

123. Arrom, *The Women of Mexico City*, 106; Archer, *The Army in Bourbon Mexico*, 225.

124. For excellent treatment of "passing" in Mexico City, see Valdes, "The Decline of the Sociedad de Castas." Passing was commonplace in the region of Puebla as well: AGN, I.G. vol. 296-B, Manuel Bertel, September 20, 1756, Puebla.

125. Cope, *The Limits of Racial Domination*, 33–35.

126. Ibid., 39; Haslip, "Crime and the Administration of Justice."

127. Cope, *Limits of Racial Domination*, 38–39.

128. AGN, Tributos, vol. 34, exp. 4, fs. 94–105.

129. E. P. Thompson, *Customs in Common: Studies in Traditional Popular Culture* (New York: New Press, 1993).

130. AGN, I.G., vol. 252-B, Nicolas Lopez Padilla, October 13, 1772, Guadalajara. The 360 tributaries include the area of Acaponeta.

131. AGN, I.G., vol. 307-B, Juan de Riva to Martin Mayorga, December 10, 1780, Mexico City.

132. Throughout their history, the *pueblos de indios* demonstrated an ability to adapt to external forces of change. As Bernardo García Martínez observes for Puebla's Sierra Norte, resiliency persisted in these towns as long as essential community functions re-

mained basically the same in the face of change. *Pueblos* lost cohesion when there was a crisis of government, particularly involving difficulties in getting Indian notables to accept high posts. Nancy Farriss agrees with this viewpoint, stressing that migrations from *pueblos de indios* occurred when there were problems at the "center," defined as the core group of esteemed village elders and officials. Also damaging to the *pueblos* were the numerous struggles for *cabecera* status by the *sujeto* towns. Bernardo García Martínez, *Los pueblos de la sierra: El poder y el espacio entre los indios del norte de Puebla hasta 1700* (Mexico City: El Colegio de Mexico, 1987), 268–79; Farriss, *Maya Society*, 199.

133. AGN, I.G., vol. 502-A, Diego Avete y Maestre, July 27, 1784, Acayucan; and AGN, Tributos, vol. 34, exp. 7, 129–31. In the Tributos document it is observed that even the proximity of a principally black town to a *pueblo de indios* did not foster better, more responsible behavior among free-coloreds.

134. Farriss, *Maya Society*, 256–85; Asunción Lavrin, "Rural Confraternities in the Local Economies of New Spain: The Bishopric of Oaxaca in the Context of Colonial Mexico," in *The Indian Community of Mexico: Fifteen Essays on Land Tenure, Corporate Organizations, Ideology and Village Politics*, ed. Arij Ouweneel and Simon Miller (Amsterdam: Centro de Estudios y Documentación Latinoamericanos, 1990), 239; and Taylor, *Drinking, Homicide, and Rebellion*, 20–24, 27.

135. For information on the evolution of the system of Indian government, see Lockhart, *Nahuas*, 14–58; Gibson, *The Aztecs*, 66–193; Farriss, *Maya Society*, 227–55.

136. Spanish administrators tolerated abuses by Indian officials as long as they did not translate into fundamental changes in the structure of government, and as long as the accretion of Indian power did not threaten the influence of the *teneintes de justica*, priests, and *alcaldes mayores*. Taylor, *Magistrates of the Sacred*, 385.

137. Ducey, "Viven sin ley," 17–30; and Taylor, *Drinking, Homicide, and Rebellion*, 113–51.

138. García Martínez, "Pueblos de Indios, Pueblos de Castas: New Settlements and Traditional Corporate Organization in Eighteenth-Century New Spain," in *The Indian Community*, 105.

139. Of course, flight from these settlements certainly took place, and unfair tribute pressure was oftentimes the motive behind the moves. This was especially true when famine and epidemic struck, since tribute burdens increased on the survivors, who then became accountable for paying the tribute of the deceased. Nevertheless, current research reveals that apart from the Yucatan and selected communities near Mexico City, the number of Indian migrants remained small. Decisions to move out of the *pueblos* were made individually, rather than being collective responses to changes in tribute methods. See García Martínez, *Los Pueblos*, 215, 262, 267; Farriss, *Maya Society*, 205; and Taylor, *Drinking, Homicide, and Rebellion*, 25–26.

140. Farriss, *Maya Society*, 205–6, 208; García Martínez, *Los pueblos*, 264–65.

141. Taylor, "Indian Pueblos," 163–65.

142. English Martin, *Rural Society*, 168–69.

143. John Tutino, *From Insurrection to Revolution in Mexico: Social Bases of Agrarian Violence, 1750–1940* (Princeton: Princeton Univ. Press, 1986), 66.

144. Research is revealing that these settlements were highly complex communities with tremendous regional variance. Scholars are just now beginning to unravel the details and synthesize the regional cases. William B. Taylor perhaps put it best when he noted that rural studies have recently started to move away from the investigation of landlords and *encomenderos* as the central figures of allegedly "inward-oriented" pueblo

histories. Taylor, "Conflict and Balance in District Politics: Tecali and the Sierra Norte de Puebla in the Eighteenth Century," in *The Indian Community*, 270–71. Important toward rethinking *pueblo* life is reconsidering the effects of the demographic devastation sustained by the indigenous population during the sixteenth and early seventeenth centuries. Many Indian towns were left partially populated at best, while others were completely extinguished. In their wake, the vacated sites continued to retain the names of the former *pueblos*. When these settlements were later refounded, they were given the titles and institutional apparatus of the *pueblos de indios*, although in many instances these towns were populated almost wholly by *castas*. Consequently, on the surface these *pueblos* appeared to be direct descendants of their pre-Hispanic ancestors, but in practice they were completely different entities. In lowland coastal regions, where Indian decline was acute and where free-coloreds thrived, it was unsurprising to find *pardos* and *mulatos* forming the majority population in such settlements. See García Martínez, "Pueblos de Indios," 103–16. For additional references, see Mentz, *Pueblos de indios*; and Rudolf Widmer Sennhauser, "Autoconsumo y mercado: La producción textil como estrategia de los campesinos de Acayucan y Jicayan (1770–1830)," in *Anuario X Instituto de Investigaciones Histórico-Sociales, Universidad Veracruzana* (Xalapa, Veracruz: Universidad Veracruzana, 1995), 19–29.

145. AGN, Tributos vol. 40, exp. 9, fs. 105–13.

146. AGN, Tributos vol. 40, exp. 9, 98–98v.

147. Farriss, *Maya Society*, 215–16; García Martínez, "Pueblos de Indios," 103–4.

148. Marichal and Souto Mantecón, "Silver and Situados," 586–613.

149. AGN, I.G., 492-A, Jacobo Ramirez Motejano, September 26, 1763, Acayucan.

150. Ibid., and AGN, Tributos, vol. 40, exp. 9, fs. 105–13; AGN, General de Parte, vol. 47, exp. 50, fs. 30v–32.

151. Fabian de Fonseca and Carlos de Urrutia, *Historia general de real hacienda* (Mexico City: Vicente G. Torres, 1845), 4:436, 475–76.

152. Ibid., 440–41, 450. According to Fonseca and Urrutia's summaries, the total tribute revenues received from 1750 to 1790 were: 1750–60 = 6,512,970 pesos; 1760–70 = 5,962,200 pesos; 1770–80 = 7,882,610 pesos; and 1780–90 = 8,409,180 pesos.

153. Arnold, *Bureaucracy and Bureaucrats*, 81–83. There were some proposals to reform the *matricula* process: Vicente Rodriguez Garcia, *El fiscal de real hacienda en Nueva España (Don Ramón de Posada y Soto, 1781–1783)* (Oviedo: Secretariado de Publicaciones de la Universidad de Oviedo, 1985), 120–22.

154. McAlister, "The Reorganization of the Army of New Spain," 12–13.

155. Archer, *The Army in Bourbon Mexico*, 8–37.

156. McAlister, "The Reorganization of the Army of New Spain," 28–30.

157. Ibid., 25–26.

158. AGN, Tributos, vol. 40, exp. 5, fs. 63–66v. Here, the 1767 law is dated December 4, 1767. See also: McAlister, *Fuero Militar*, 44; AGN, Californias, vol. 58, fs. 37–43.

159. AGN, I.G., vol. 307-B, Galvez to Croix, November 21, 1770.

160. AGN, I.G., vol. 307-B, Croix, 1770, Mexico City; McAlister dates this same law as 1771, McAlister, *Fuero Militar*, 46.

161. McAlister, *Fuero Militar*, 46.

162. Taylor, *Drinking, Homicide, and Rebellion*, 135.

163. Ducey, "Viven sin ley," 24.

164. AGN, General de Parte, vol. 47, exp. 50, fs. 30–32v; AGN, Californias, vol. 58, fs. 1–70; AGN, Tributos, vol. 34, exp. 3, fs. 77–82; AGN, Tributos, vol. 34, exps. 5–6, fs. 106–

17v; AGN, I.G., vol. 307-B, Riva to Mayorga, December 10, 1780, Mexico City. Information from these sources demonstrates the free-colored militiamen's methods of obtaining tribute exemption during the Bourbon reform period.

165. AGN, Criminal, vol. 542, exp. 6, fs. 211–26v.

166. AGN, I.G., vol. 502-A, Pedro Moscoso, February 7, 1782, Acayucan.

167. AGN, Californias, vol. 58, fs. 111–111v.

168. AGN, Californias, vol. 58. fs. 82–117v; AGN, I.G., vol. 483-A, Francisco Marti to Crespo, May 29, 1784, Mexico City.

169. AGN, I.G., vol. 307-B, Mayorga to Juan de la Riva Aguero, May 30, 1781, Mexico City; AGN, I.G., vol. 307-B, Mayorga to Riva, March 15, 1782, Mexico City.

170. Ideally, Mayorga did not want free-coloreds mixed in with white provincials. AGN, I.G., vol. 307-B, Posada to Mayorga, April 21, 1781, Mexico City.

171. AGN, Reales Cédulas Originales, vol. 122, exp. 153, fol. 279.

172. AGN, Reales Cédulas Originales, vol. 122, exp. 55, fs. 102v–3.

173. AGN, I.G., vol. 307-B, Cordoba to Villaurrutia and Beleña, March 21, 1787, Mexico City; AGN, I.G., vol. 307-B, Valdes, September 1, 1787, San Ildefonso; AGN, Reales Cédulas, Originales, vol. 138, exp. 2, fs. 2–2v; McAlister, *Fuero Militar*, 51.

174. McAlister, "The Reorganization of the Army of New Spain," 16.

175. Archer, *The Army in Bourbon Mexico*, 19–26.

176. AGN, I.G., vol. 422-A, Rafael Vasco to Mayorga, September 18, 1782, Acapulco.

177. AGN, Tributos, vol. 40, exp. 14, fs. 254–56v; AGN, General de Parte, vol. 47, exp. 50, fs. 30v–32; McAlister, *Fuero Militar*, 50.

178. An excellent example of soldiers pressing to serve only in their locality is AGN, I.G., 492-A, exp. 3, Testimonio de las diligencias practicadas . . . 1767.

179. AGN, I.G., vol. 307-B, Posada to Mayorga, April 21, 1781, Mexico City.

180. McAlister, *Fuero Militar*, 51. In Michoacán there were changes to free-colored tribute policies. Although provincial soldiers were exempt, after May 8, 1782, other free-coloreds certainly were not, even those serving as veterans in regular army regiments. See AGN, Tributos, vol. 40, exp. 12, fs. 233–39.

181. AGN, I.G., vol. 483-A, Francisco Marti to Crespo, May 29, 1784, Oaxaca. This document shows that the urban and *sueltas* units formed here in the 1760s and 1770s did not always enjoy exclusion. Marti also called for additional clarifications on the tribute exemption policies for Oaxaca's urban companies.

182. Reversals in Puerto Escondido are discussed in: AGN, Tributos, vol. 34, exps. 5–6, fs. 114–17v. Problems with the implementation of tribute on account of debates by bureaucrats over exemption status in Puerto Escondido and Xicayan are discussed in AGN, Tributos, vol. 34, exp. 7, fs. 174–78v.

CHAPTER 5

1. McAlister, *Fuero Militar*.

2. Ibid., 6; and Ladd, *The Mexican Nobility*, 6.

3. David A. Brading, *Miners and Merchants in Bourbon Mexico, 1763–1810* (Cambridge, England: Cambridge Univ. Press, 1971), 20–21; Ladd, *The Mexican Nobility*, 6.

4. McAlister, *Fuero Militar*, 7–11; AGN, I.G., vol. 394-A, Reglamento para las milicias de infanteria de la provincia de Yucatan y Campeche, 1778, Madrid, fs. 12–14; AGN, I.G., vol. 51-A, Reglamento provicional de Cordoba y Jalapa, January 1775, unnumbered folios.

5. McAlister, *Fuero Militar*, 68.

6. AGN, Californias, 58, fs. 35v–36.

7. McAlister, *Fuero Militar*, 44; AGN, Californias vol. 58, fs. 37–43.

8. AGN, Californias, vol. 58, fs. 37–43.

9. Booker, "Needed but Unwanted," 268–69.

10. AGN, Californias, vol. 58, fs. 37–43.

11. AGN, I.G. 42-B, Consulta que hace el sr. Inspector sobre los malos tratamientos que experimentan los individuo del batallon de pardos de esta capital por las justicias ordinarios, y sus dependientes, June 1778, Puebla; AGN, Criminal, vol. 450, exp. 12, fs. 171–191.

12. AGN, Criminal, vol. 450, exp. 17, fs. 238–68v.

13. Booker, "Needed but Unwanted," 269.

14. AGN, Bandos, vol. 17, exp. 12, Reglamamento provisional para el régimen, gobierno y nueva planta de milicias de la provincia de Tabasco, fol. 101.

15. There are differences between my conclusions and those of Archer and Booker. Both ascertain that Revillagigedo eliminated the *fuero* for blacks. Indeed, Archer mentions that Revillagigedo's ambition was to eliminate the *fuero* for all creole militia forces. See Archer, "Pardos, Indians, and the Army of New Spain," 240. However, after reexamining the ordinances/*reglamentos* produced during this period, I cannot fully share their conclusions. I agree that Revillagigedo aggressively downsized militia forces in the colony in general and sought to purge free-coloreds from service. But I find that when free-coloreds remained in the military in spite of Revillagigedo's policy initiatives, their *fuero* rights were upheld. Some examples include Tabasco, where nine out of ten companies were slated as free-colored units after 1793, as well as Nuevo Santander, Veracruz, and the Costa Sur. McAlister, examining the same documents, draws similar conclusions. McAlister, *Fuero Militar*, 66–68.

16. Voelz, *Slave and Soldier*, 415–27; Domínguez, "International War," 1–8; Booker, "Needed But Unwanted," 267; Rout, *The African Experience*, 150–51; and Kuethe, "The Status of the Free-Pardo," 109–10.

17. Kuethe, "The Status of the Free-Pardo," 110.

18. AGN, Californias, vol. 58, fs. 34–35.

19. AGN, Criminal, vol. 450, exp. 12, fs. 190–190v. A full explanation of the *sumaria* is in Cutter, *Legal Culture*, 105–24.

20. McAlister, *Fuero Militar*, 7.

21. AGN, I.G., vol. 42-B, Valcarcel to Bucareli, June 1778, Mexico City.

22. AGN, I.G., vol. 42-B, Consulta que hace el inspector sobre los malos tratamientos . . . June 1778, Mexico City.

23. Charles Gibson, *Spain in America* (New York: Harper and Row, 1966), 109–10; and Cutter, *Legal Culture*, 110. Sample judicial procedures are found in Cutter, *Legal Culture*, 105–46; Haslip, "Crime and the Administration of Justice," 165–69; and Teresa Lozano Armendares, *La criminalidad en la ciudad de Mexico, 1800–1821* (Mexico City: Universidad Nacional Autónoma de México, 1987), 165–69.

24. In colonial Mexico the jail was seen more as a holding space until a different sentence was decided, rather than an end for punishment itself. Lozano Armendares, *Criminalidad*, 177.

25. AGN, I.G., vol. 100-A, exp. 50, Causa de Francisco Patiño Soldado pardo procesado y castigado por la Acordada, February 20, 1780 to June 26, 1780, Mexico City; Pati-

ño's time in jail was actually short in comparison with other cases. In more serious crimes, such as homicides, there are instances of custody being dragged out for more than ten years before any clear resolution of jurisdiction was made. For example, see AGN, Criminal, vol. 450, exp. 9, fs. 121–67. Here, a tavern brawl over a racial slur resulted in homicide. Militiaman Joseph Florez killed Joseph Alvarez for calling him a *negro*. In addition to the time spent in jail, the pattern of custody is interesting when compared with that of Patiño. Shortly after the murder, Florez sought initial sanctuary in the church, before being transferred to his barracks. After a year he was brought back into church custody, where he remained for four years. Finally he was sent to the *Real Carcel*, where he spent another four years. Flight to a religious building was a common first point of refuge for lucky criminals who were able to reach one. Some might escape military and civil justice altogether after hiding out in the church. In Florez's case, it facilitated his eventual custody to the militia barracks and helped him secure his full *fuero* rights. Therefore, he was in a more advantageous legal position than Patiño. In the end, however, the value of being tried under military court was debatable. It is true that Florez was eventually exonerated and freed by decree of the *auditor de guerra*. He also avoided corporal punishment. But before this decision was reached, his own colonel had recommended a two-year labor sentence in the *presidio* of Veracruz. Moreover, reaching the *auditor*'s final decision took nearly a decade.

26. Certain officials were singled out for particularly malicious behavior, such as Don Raphael Lucero. In one incident, a soldier in the 7th company of fusiliers related how he was apprehended for innocently standing in front of the door of his home. Lucero and his patrol asked the soldier what he was doing out so late. The militiaman responded that he was enjoying the night air. At that point a minister from Lucero's entourage approached him with a weapon and smashed his face. In the frenzy, the militiaman invoked military privilege and tried to show his credentials but was rudely carted off to jail. The soldier's captain rushed to his aid the next morning. Once Lucero had gotten word of the officer's arrival, he ordered him to sit down. Then he signaled for the jail-keepers to take the prisoner downstairs, where he was issued fifty lashes. Smeared in blood, the militiaman was handed over to his captain. Lucero was responsible for many more such incidents, and in several instances he requested that soldiers pay a fine upon release. AGN, I.G., vol. 42-B, Consulta que hace el inspector sobre los malos tratamientos . . . June 1778, Mexico City. Similar woes were told by free-colored militiamen in Puebla, Querétaro, Cordoba, and Atlixco, as successive administrations of *alcaldes ordinarios* were credited with abuses and extortion throughout the 1770s and 1780s. AGN, I.G., vol. 486-A, Pedro Camuñez, September 11, 1779, Puebla; AGN, I.G., vol. 307-B, Sobre maltratamientos por el alcalde ordinario de Cordoba, Don Diego Lemayo a los soldados pardos del batallon de Puebla, Rafael y Juan de Tapia, 1790; AGN, Criminal, vol. 450, exp. 17, fs. 238–68v; AGN, I.G., vol. 306-A, Representación de Don Pedro Camuñez, subinspector del battalon de pardos de Puebla que trata sobre que los Ayuntamientos de Cordoba y Atlixco no les guardan a los individuos de dicho cuerpo el fuero que gozan, January 1782; AGN, Criminal, vol. 450, exp. 12, fs. 171–91.

27. AGN, I.G., vol. 42-B, Benito Tineo to Pasqual Cisneros, May 1, 1778, Mexico City.

28. Haslip, "Crime and the Administration of Justice," 159–63; Haslip, "Criminal Justice and the Poor in Late Colonial Mexico City," in *Five Centuries of Law and Politics in Central Mexico*, ed. Ronald Spores and Ross Hassig (Nashville: Vanderbilt Univ. Publications in Anthropology, 1984), 111, 126.

29. AGN, I.G., vol. 100-A, Incidencia de la causa formada en Puebla contra Joseph Ignacio Corbello y Joseph Francisco Castillo, soldados de aquel batallon de pardos, por robos y homicidios.

30. AGN, I.G., vol. 307-B, Causa remitida por la real sala del crimen contra Joseph Anzures soldado del battalon de pardos de Mexico, February 1790, Mexico City.

31. AGN, Criminal, vol. 450, exp. 13, fs. 192–95v.

32. Haslip, "Crime and the Administration of Justice," 234–39.

33. AGN, I.G., vol. 307-B, Causa formada contra el teniente de pardos de Puebla, Ignacio Domínguez, por homicidio, February 1790, Puebla. For more on Camuñez, see AGN, I.G. 486-A, Dna. Joaquina Carpintero y Oropesa, sobre se le devuelvan tres mil pesos que se embargaron a su difunto marido, Dn. Pedro Camuñes, subinspector del batallon de pardos de Puebla; and AGN, I.G., 100-A, Sobre pension annual de cien pesos a cada de las tre hijas de Dona Joaquina Guzman Carpintero, viuda del ten. coronel, subinspector de pardos de Puebla, Dn. Pedro Camuñez.

34. AGN, I.G., vol. 100-A, Instancia de Ignacio Rosario, soldado pardo de Tuxtla sobre la prision que sufre, 1791, Tuxtla.

35. AGN, I.G., vol. 306-A, Expediente promovido por Juana Maria Esquivel para que se le declare el real indulto a su hijo José Ignacio Pantoja, soldado del batallon de pardos de esta capital, February 1782, Mexico City.

36. AGN, I.G., vol. 96-A, Francisco Manuel Suarez to Croix, February 28–29, 1768, Mexico City.

37. AGN, Civil, vol. 130 pt. 2, exp. 480, 1726 Puebla, fs. 1–25v.

38. AGN, I.G., vol. 42-B, Consulta que hace el sr. Inspector sobre los malos tratamientos . . . June 1778, Mexico City.

39. Haslip, "Crime and the Administration of Justice," 200–209.

40. AGN, Civil, vol. 130 pt. 2, exp. 480, 1726, Puebla, fs. 26–27.

41. AGN, I.G., vol. 53-A, Lista o prontuario de los informes, mapas, y documentos que ha presentado el coronel Don Matias de Armona en virtud de la insepccion que ha pasado a las provincias del seno mexicano, 1781–82.

42. Ibid.; AGN, Civil, legajo 24, exp. 156, 1762, Acayucan, fol. 49v.

43. AGN, Civil, legajo 24, exp. 156, 1762, Acayucan, fol. 4.

44. Ibid., fol. 32.

45. Ibid., fs. 1–60.

46. Domingo Ramos's testimony is found ibid., fs. 30v–32v.

47. Ibid., fs. 3–3v.

48. Prior to its incorporation in the Intendancy of Veracruz, Tamiagua belonged to the province of Guachinango.

49. AGN, I.G., vol. 231-B, Luis Bermudo Sorrano, 1763, Tamiagua.

50. AGN, I.G., vol. 484-A, Tomas Gil de Onzue to Martin Mayorga, June 18, 1781, Tamiagua.

51. AGN, Tributos, vol. 40, exp. 11, fs. 194–194v; and AGN, Bandos vol. 17, exp. 15, Reglamento provisional para el régimen, gobierno y nueva planta de las compañias de milicias mixtas del seno que comprende la provincia de Tampico y Panuco, hasta el Rio Guazacualco, costas laterales de Veracruz, June 18, 1793, fol. 125.

52. AGN, Padrones, vol. 18, fs. 116–85v.

53. AGN, Californias, vol. 58, fol. 70. 1 *arroba* = 25 pounds.

54. Jorge Sada, *Los pescadores de la laguna de Tamiahua* (Mexico City: Secretario de Educación Pública, 1984), 26–29.

55. Initiated in the late sixteenth century, the *composición de tierras* was a scheme designed to raise revenue for the Spanish crown, declaring that any lands that had been settled without a crown title had to be formalized with the purchase of a royal deed. Many of the funds raised by the *composición* paid for New World defenses, such as the Armada de Barlovento.

56. AGN, Tierras, vol. 1458, exp. 7, fs. 23–33.

57. Ibid., fs. 37–37v.

58. Ibid., fol. 80.

59. Ibid., fs. 78v–81.

60. Ibid.

61. Ibid., fs. 37–37v.

62. Ibid., fs. 12–16. One excellent example of how the free-coloreds viewed the town's history is the account of eighty-year-old Gaspar de los Reyes: AGN, Tierras, vol. 1458, exp. 7, fs. 13–13v.

63. Ibid., fs. 44–47.

64. Ibid., fs. 86–88v.

65. Ibid., fs. 86–90v.

66. Ibid., fs. 16v–17.

67. Ibid., fs. 89–93v.

68. Ibid., fs. 1–97v. There are many references to this terminology in these folios. Note that there is occasional variation in the reference. Sometimes free-coloreds are described as the *vecindad de pardos milicianos,* and sometimes simply as *mulatos* or *pardos,* but the frequency of the reference to the *vecindad de pardos libres militares* is unique in the documents reviewed for this manuscript.

69. Ibid., fs. 47–60.

70. Ibid., fs. 16v–17.

71. Another account says that the captain of the whites, Juan Francisco Thello, was the person wounded: Ibid., 55v–58.

72. Ibid., fol. 58.

73. Kuethe, "The Development of the Cuban Military as a Sociopolitical Elite, 1763–83," *HAHR* 61, no. 4 (1981): 695; and Archer, *The Army in Bourbon Mexico.*

CHAPTER 6

1. Aguirre Beltrán, *La poblacíon negra,* 172–73; 153–79. His analysis traces change from the sixteenth and seventeenth centuries, in which racial nomenclature tended to be more derogatory, into the eighteenth century, where more euphemistic terms became standard.

2. Recopilacion de Leyes, Libro VII, Titulo V, fs. 285–91.

3. AGN, Civil, vol. 224, exp. 152, 1724, Mexico City, fol. 5v.

4. AGN, Civil, vol. 130 pt. 2, 1729, Puebla and Mexico City, fol. 12.

5. AGN, Californias, vol. 58, fs. 82–117v; and AGN, I.G., vol. 53-A, Armona to Mayorga, September 9, 1781, Sn. Andrés Tuxtla.

6. For a brief example of how gradations of color among free-coloreds caused jealousies in rural Guajolotitlan, see AGN, Criminal, vol. 542, exp. 6, fs. 262–65.

7. Both Ambrosio de Pino and Gregorio Albis were described as *negro/moreno* in color, hailing from the "Reynos de Castilla." They were not *mulatos* from Mexico.

8. San Joseph was also reportedly from the "Reynos de Castilla."

9. In 1724 there was no lieutenant colonel. The sergeant major would have been second in command. The importance of Mexico City's free-colored militia in the 1720s and 1730s was marked. As we have seen, Mexico City's colonel held supervisory powers over all the free-colored troops in the viceroyalty. That is why the *comandante* post of Mexico City offered added prestige, even over *comandantes* in Veracruz or Puebla.

10. AHAP, legajo 1255, fs. 72v–76v.

11. AGN, Civil, vol. 224, exp. 152, 1724, Mexico City, fs. 1–31; AGN, Civil, vol. 130 pt. 3b, exp. 29, no. 7, 1726, Mexico City, fs. 1–5.

12. It is unclear, but *pardos* may have been separated from *morenos* and *mulatos* into their own separate company, sometime before 1741. See AGN, General de Parte, vol. 33, exps. 77–78, fs. 68–87.

13. AGN, Reales Cédulas Originales, vol. 62, exp. 58, fs. 180–180v; AGN, Reales Cédulas Originales, vol. 62, exp. 65, fol. 199; and AGN, General de Parte, vol. 33, exps. 77–78, fs. 68–87.

14. AGN, I.G., vol. 40-B, exp. 1, Jose Antonio de Soto, Francisco Xavier Buenvecino, y Jose Morantes, Sobre levantar una compania de 50 pardos milicianos, 1769, Veracurz, fs. 1–12.

15. Archivo Historico de Veracruz (AHV), caja 139, vol. 184, 1822, fs. 41–45; AHV, caja 139, vol. 184, 1822, fs. 188–94.

16. McAlister, *Fuero Militar*, 43.

17. AGN, I.G., vol. 483-A, Crespo to Marti, December 23, 1784.

18. Information on the 1788 reforms and the subsequent division of militia companies into the 4th and 5th divisions of the Costa Sur can be found in AGN, I.G., vol. 422-A, Instrucción para las milicias de la 4ta y 5ta Division de la costa del sur de N.E., 1788.

19. AGN, Criminal, vol. 542, exp. 6, fs. 262–65.

20. The *Costa Sur* was a synonym for the Pacific coast region. AGN, Bandos, vol. 17, exp. 50, Reglamento provisional para el regimen, gobierno y nueva planta de las compañías de milicias de la costa del sur del reyno de Nueva España, dese la jurisdiccion de Acaponeta hasta Tehuantepec, October 22, 1793.

21. AGN, I.G. 422-A, Ordenes y demas relativo al establecimiento de la 4ta division en la jurisdicion de Igualapan y Xicayan, correspondiente a la intendencia de Oaxaca y Puebla, 1793–94.

22. AGN, Criminal, vol. 542, exp. 6, fol. 217.

23. Ibid., fs. 222–25v.

24. AGN, Criminal, vol. 542, exp. 6, fs. 160–63v; AGN, Tributos, vol. 34, exp. 7, fs. 119–31.

25. AGN, Tributos, vol. 34, exp. 7, fs. 119–119v; AGN, Criminal, vol. 542, exp. 6, fs. 160–63v.

26. On June 14, 1794, Policarpio and the Luna brothers wrote another letter, this time while in jail in Oaxaca City (Antequera), which also clearly expressed their racial views and disagreement with having whites governing free-colored militia companies. See AGN, Criminal, vol. 542, exp. 6, fol. 261.

27. AGN, I.G., vol. 197-B, Gorostiza to Revillagigedo, January 2, 1792, Mexico City.

28. AGN, I.G., vol. 197-B, Gorostiza to Revillagigedo, March 16, 1792, Mexico City.

29. AGN, I.G., vol. 197-B, Revillagigedo, January 21, 1792, Mexico City.

30. AGN, I.G., vol. 197-B, Narcisso Segarra, Ildefonso Silva, Juan Pastor, undated, Mexico City.

31. AGN, I.G., vol. 197-B, Jose Arellano, Joseph Zambrano, Joaquin Medina, Jose Moreno, July 3, 1794, Puebla.

32. Ibid.

33. AGN, I.G., vol. 197-B, Josef Zambrano and Joaquin Medina, November 26, 1793, Puebla.

34. AGN, I.G., vol. 197-B, Narcisso Segarra, January 31, 1793, Mexico City.

35. AGN, Correspondencia de Virreyes, vol. 178, fs. 95–96v.

36. This discussion assumes that there was some difference in the meaning of race and caste, which is not an easy point to prove for colonial Latin America. *Raza, casta,* and even *calidad* were used quite interchangeably in the colonial documentation of New Spain. Throughout this manuscript, I have also used these terms rather synonymously, given the colonial examples. However, as is discussed by Wade, caste may have more appropriately referred to the state's attempt to legislate and control groups that had been assigned labels based upon status and descent. Color, or race, loomed large in preparing these labels. See Wade, *Race and Ethnicity in Latin America,* 29. If this view is accepted, then the caste system dealt more with the effort to control populations, while race served as a tool in the process. Therefore, the two terms can be viewed independently, with race referring primarily to phenotype, and caste to the legal and social boundaries attached to race. By the same token, *calidad* could be examined independently also. Following the research of McCaa, *calidad* would include other determinants to one's caste designation, such as dress, speech patterns, and so forth. See McCaa, "Calidad, Clase, and Marriage."

37. For instance, Dn. Ramon Sandoval, a captain in the *pardo* company of the Yucatan, received full use of uniform and criminal *fuero* upon retirement in 1818. See Archivo General del Estado de Yucatán (AGEY), Apartado Colonial, Reales Cédulas, vol. 4, exp. 33. While his color is questionable, his free-colored subordinates would have most likely had the similar privileges, of course with extended benefits prior to retirement.

38. AGN, Correspondencia de Virreyes, vol. 187, fol. 113. There is evidence that other areas retained some black officers, such as the Yucatan and perhaps Jalapa.

39. AHV, caja 139, vol. 184, 1822, fs. 41–45; AHV, caja 139, vol. 184, 1822, fs. 188–94.

40. Ted Vincent, "The Blacks Who Freed Mexico," *Journal of Negro History* 79, no. 3 (1994): 257–76.

41. Mentz, *Pueblos de indios.*

42. AGEY, Apartado Colonial, Fondo Militar, vol. 1, exp. 22, fs. 1–3v; AGEY, Apartado Colonial, Fondo Militar, vol. 1, exp. 13. The soldiers who populated San Fernando Aké were just a few of a larger cohort of similar black auxiliaries who, following the Treaty of Basel (1795), left Santo Domingo after it fell under French control. These men were initially sent to Cuba but were rerouted to other crown holdings, such as Guatemala. See Rout, *The African Experience,* 154–56.

43. AGEY, Apartado Colonial, Fondo Militar, vol. 1, exp. 22.

44. Ibid., exp. 7.

45. Ibid., exp. 6.

46. Ibid., exp. 7.

47. Perhaps one of the more telling of Carreño's statements was when he proffered an explanation as to why the birth rate was so low among blacks in San Fernando. Apart from the factor of climate, Carreño believed that the law of nature "is not content [to have] what is ugly exist in abundance." Ibid., exp. 7, fol. 1v.

48. The *juez* was to be a newly created post that was a cross between a judge and a town superintendent. Ibid., exp. 6, fs. 5–7v.

49. Ibid., exp. 7, 1v–2v; ibid., exp. 6, fs. 5–7v.

50. For more on blacks in the Yucatan and a brief account of San Fernando Aké, see Francisco Fernández Repetto and Genny Negroe Sierra, *Una población perdida en la memoria: Los negros de Yucatán* (Mérida: Universidad Autonoma de Yucatán, 1995). Documentation on the town is sparse. The community allegedly persisted until the advent of the Caste Wars, when it was reputedly destroyed in conflicts with Indians. Additional documentation includes AGEY, Apartado Poder Ejecutivo, Ramo Milicias, vol. 34, exp. 2; and ibid., vol. 2., exp. 15.

CONCLUSION

1. Archer, *The Army in Bourbon Mexico*; Kuethe, *Military Reform and Society in New Granada;* and Campbell, *The Military and Society in Colonial Peru.*

2. During the 1720s, 127 out of every thousand residents were soldiers or militiamen, a massive amount even when compared with "post-militarization" Cuba and Chile, which respectively possessed an average of 36 and 32 soldiers per thousand inhabitants in 1800. See Margarita Gascón, "The Military of Santo Domingo, 1720–1764," *HAHR* 73, no. 3 (1993): 431–52; and Domínguez, *Insurrection or Loyalty: The Breakdown of the Spanish American Empire* (Cambridge, Massachusetts: Harvard Univ. Press, 1980), 74–81.

3. For some examples, see Degler, *Neither Black nor White*; Skidmore, *Black into White*; Peter Wade, *Blackness and Race Mixture: The Dynamics of Racial Identity in Colombia* (Baltimore and London: Johns Hopkins University Press, 1993), 3–47; and Aline Helg, "Race in Argentina and Cuba, 1880–1930: Theory, Policies, and Popular Reaction," in *The Idea of Race in Latin America*, 37–69.

4. McCaa, "Calidad, Class, and Marriage," 477–501.

5. Wade, *Blackness and Race Mixture*, 344.

6. Paul Gilroy, *'There Ain't no Black in the Union Jack': The Cultural Politics of Race and Nation* (London: Hutchinson, 1987), 39.

Selected Bibliography

ARCHIVAL SOURCES

Archivo General del Estado de Yucatán—Mérida: Apartado Colonial, Reales Cedulas, vol. 4. Apartado Colonial, Fondo Militar, vol. 1. Apartado Poder Ejecutivo, Ramo Milicias, vols. 2, and 34.

Archivo General de la Nación—Mexico City: Alcaldes Mayores, vol. 2. Archivo Historico de la Hacienda, vols. 85 and 94. Bandos, vol. 17. Californias, vol. 58. Civil (libros), vol. 1789. Civil (en cajas), legajos 23, 24, 72, 87, 101, 130, 158, and 224. Correspondencia de Diversas Autoridades, vols. 36 and 37. Correspondencia de Virreyes, vols. 167, 178, and 187. Criminal, vols. 447, 450, 542, and 680. General de Parte, vols. 3, 5, 6, 7, 8, 15, 28, 29, 33, 38, 47, 59 and 68. Indiferentes de Guerra, vols. 9, 28-B, 33-B, 37-B, 40-B, 42-B, 46-A, 51-A, 53-A, 79-B, 96-A, 100-A, 147-B, 197-B, 213-A, 214-A, 231-B, 224, 231-B, 232-B, 233-B, 252-B, 293-A, 296-B, 306-A, 307-B, 394-A, 416-A, 422-A, 483-A, 484-A, 485-A, 486-A, 488-A, 490-A, 492-A, 497-A, 501-A, 502-A, and 533-A. Inquisición, vol. 1043. Matrimonios, vols. 33, 91, 117, 159, and 203, Padrones, vol. 18. Reales Cedulas Duplicadas, vol. 5. Reales Cedulas Originales, vols. 62, 122, 138, 154, and 229. Tierras, vols. 973 and 1458. Tributos, vols. 34, 40, and 48.

Archivo Historico del Ayuntamiento de Puebla—Puebla: legajos 1255, 1384, 1385, 1387, 1388, 1389, and 1390.

Archivo Historico de Veracruz—Veracruz: caja 139, vol. 184.

Archivo Judicial de Puebla—INAH-Puebla: expedientes 2968 and 3108.

Archivo de Notarías del Distrito Federal—Mexico City: vols. 1655, 1660, and 2259.

Mapoteca Orozco y Berra—Mexico City: Colleción Orozco y Berra, 1152.

Subdirección de Documentación de la Biblioteca Nacional de Historia—Mexico City: Archivo Judicial de Puebla, rollos 2, 43, 44 and 45.

PUBLISHED PRIMARY SOURCES

Calderón de la Barca, Fanny. *Life in Mexico, The Letters of Fanny Calderón de la Barca*. Ed. Howard T. Fisher and Marion Hall Fisher. New York: Doubleday and Company, 1966.

Fonseca, Fabian de, and Carlos de Urrutia. *Historia general de real hacienda*. 4 vols. Mexico City: Vicente G. Torres, 1845.

Gálvez, Bernardo de. *Instructions for Governing the Interior Provinces of New Spain, 1786*. Trans. and ed. Donald E. Worcester. Berkeley: Quivira Society, 1951.

González Obregon, Luis. *La vida de Mexico en 1810*. Mexico City: Colección Metropolitana, 1975.

Recopilación de leyes de los reynos de las Indias. 4 vols. Madrid: Julián de Paredes, 1681; facsimile reprint, Madrid: Ediciones Cultura Hispánica, 1973.

Seijas y Lobera, Francisco. *Gobierno militar y político del reino imperial de la Nueva España*. Comp. Pablo Emilio Pérez-Mallaína Bueno. Mexico City: Universidad Nacional Autónoma de México, 1986.

Siguenza y Gongora, Carlos. *Alboroto y motín de Mexico del 8 de junio de 1692*. With a foreword by Irving A. Leonard. Mexico City: Talleres Graficos del Museo Nacional de Arqueologia, Historia, y Etnografia, 1932.

Winfield Capitaine, Fernando. *Los cimarrones de Mazateopan*. Xalapa, Veracruz: Gobierno del Estado de Veracruz, 1992.

Zorita, Alonso de, and José Miranda, *El tributo indígena en la Nueva España durante el siglo XVI*. Mexico, 1952.

SECONDARY SOURCES

Aguirre Anaya, Carmen, and Alberto Carabarin Gracia. "Formas artesanales y fabriles de los textiles de algodón en la ciudad de Puebla, siglos XVIII y XIX." In *Puebla de la colonia a la revolucíon: Estudios de historia regional*, ed. Colomba Salazar Ibarguen, 125–54. Puebla: Centro de Investigaciones Historicas y Sociales, Instituto de Ciencias de la Universidad Autonoma de Puebla, 1987.

Aguirre Beltrán, Gonzalo. "The Integration of the Negro into the National Society of Mexico." In *Race and Class in Latin America*, ed. Magnus Mörner, 11–27. New York: Columbia Univ. Press, 1970.

———. *La población negra de Mexico: Estudio etnohistórico*. 3d ed. Mexico City: Fondo de Cultura Economica, 1989.

———. *El negro esclavo en Nueva España*. Mexico City: Fondo de Cultura Económica, 1994.

Anderson, Rodney D. "Race and Social Stratification: A Comparison of Working-Class Spaniards, Indians and Castas in Guadalajara, Mexico in 1821." *Hispanic American Historical Review* 68, no. 2 (1988): 209–43.

Andrews, George Reid. *The Afro-Argentines of Buenos Aires, 1800–1900*. Madison: Univ. of Wisconsin Press, 1980.

Angulo Aguirre, Jorge González. *Artesanado y ciudad a finales del siglo XVIII*. Mexico City: Fondo de Cultura Económica, 1983.

Anna, Timothy E. *The Fall of Royal Government in Mexico City*. Lincoln and London: Univ. of Nebraska Press, 1978.

Archer, Christon I. "Pardos, Indians, and the Army of New Spain: Inter-Relationships and Conflicts, 1780–1810." *Journal of Latin American Studies* 6, no. 2 (1974): 231–55.

———. "To Serve the King: Military Recruitment in Late Colonial Mexico." *Hispanic American Historical Review* 55, no. 2 (1975): 226–50.

———. *The Army in Bourbon Mexico, 1760–1810*. Albuquerque: Univ. of New Mexico Press, 1977.

————. "Bourbon Finances and Military Policy in New Spain, 1759–1812." *Americas* 37, no. 3 (1981): 315–50.

————. "The Officer Corps in New Spain: The Marial Career, 1759–1821." *Jarbuch fur Geschichte von Staat, Wirschaft, und Gesellschaft Lateinamerikas* 19, no. 18 (1982): 137–57.

————. "The Military." In *Cities and Society in Colonial Latin America*, ed. Louisa Schell Hoberman and Susan Migden Socolow, 197–226. Albuquerque: Univ. of New Mexico Press, 1986.

Arnold, Linda. *Bureaucracy and Bureaucrats in Mexico City, 1742–1835*. Tucson: Univ. of Arizona Press, 1988.

Arrom, Silvia. *The Women of Mexico City, 1790–1857*. Stanford: Stanford Univ. Press, 1985.

Barnes, Thomas, Thomas Naylor, and Charles W. Polzer. *Northern New Spain: A Research Guide*. Tucson: Univ. of Arizona Press, 1981.

Bennett, Herman L. "Lovers, Family, and Friends: The Formation of Afro-Mexico, 1580–1810." Ph.D. diss., Duke University, 1993.

Booker, Jackie. "Needed but Unwanted: Black Militiamen in Veracruz, Mexico, 1760–1810." *Historian* 55 (winter 1993): 259–76.

Borah, Woodrow, and Sherburne Cook. "Sobre las posibilidades de hacer el estudio histórico del mestizaje sobre una base demografica." *Revista de Historia de América* 53/54 (1962): 181–90.

————. "Los auxiliares del gobernador provincial." In *El gobierno provincial en la Nueva España, 1570–1787*, ed. Woodrow Borah, 51–64. Mexico City: Universidad Autónoma de México, 1985.

————. "El gobernador novohispano (alcalde mayor/corregidor): Consecución del puesto y aspectos económicos." In *El gobierno provincial en la Nueva España, 1570–1787*, ed. Woodrow Borah, 37–50. Mexico City: Universidad Autónoma de México, 1985.

Bowser, Frederick P. "Colonial Spanish America." In *Neither Slave Nor Free*, ed. David W. Cohen and Jack P. Greene, 19–58. Baltimore and London: Johns Hopkins Univ. Press, 1972.

————. *The African Slave in Colonial Peru, 1524–1650*. Stanford: Stanford Univ. Press, 1974.

Boyer, Richard. *La gran inundación: Vida y sociedad en la ciudad de Mexico (1629–1638)*. Trans. Antonieta Sánchez Mejorada. Mexico City: Secretaría de Educación Publica, 1975.

————. "Mexico in the Seventeenth Century: Transition of a Colonial Society." *Hispanic American Historical Review* 57, no. 3 (1977): 455–78.

————. *Cast and Identity in Colonial Mexico: A Proposal and an Example*. Storrs, Conn.; Providence, R.I.; and Amherst, Mass.: Latin American Studies Consortium of New England, 1997.

Brading, David A. *Miners and Merchants in Bourbon Mexico, 1763–1810*. Cambridge, England: Cambridge Univ. Press, 1971.

————. "Grupos étnicos: Clases y estructura ocupacional en Guanajuato." In *Historia y población en México*, ed. Thomas Calvo, 240–60. Mexico City: El Colegio de México, 1994.

Brathwaite, Edward. *The Development of Creole Society in Jamaica, 1770–1820*. Oxford: Clarendon Press, 1985.

Calvo, Thomas. "Familias y sociedad: Zamora (siglos XVII–XIX)." In *Historia de la familia*, comp. Pilar Gonzalbo, 126–49. Mexico City: Instituto Mora, 1993.

Campbell, Leon G. "The Army of Peru and the Túpac Amaru Revolt, 1780–1783." *Hispanic American Historical Review* 56, no. 1 (1976): 31–57.

———. *The Military and Society in Colonial Peru, 1750–1810.* Philadelphia: American Philosophical Society, 1978.

Carmagnani, Marcelo. "Demografía y sociedad: La estructura social de los centros mineros del norte de México, 1600–1720." In *Historia y población en México*, ed. Thomas Calvo, 122–62. Mexico City: El Colegio de México, 1994.

Carrera Stampa, Manuel. *Los gremios Mexicanos: La organización gremial en Nueva España 1521–1861.* Mexico City: EDIAPSA, 1954.

Carrion, Antonio. *Historia de la ciudad de Puebla de los Angeles.* 2d ed. Puebla: Editorial Jose M. Cajica Jr., S.A., 1970.

Carroll, Patrick J. *Blacks in Colonial Veracruz: Race, Ethnicity, and Regional Development.* Austin: Univ. of Texas Press, 1991.

———. "Los mexicanos negros: El mestizaje y los fundamentos olvidados de la "raza cósmica," una perspectiva regional." *Historia Mexicana* 44, no. 3 (1995): 403–38.

Castro Gutiérrez, Felipe. *La extinción de la artesanía gremial.* Mexico City: Universidad Autónoma de México, 1986.

Chance, John K., and William B. Taylor. "Estate and Class in a Colonial City, Oaxaca in 1792." *Comparative Studies in Society and History* 19 (1977): 454–87.

———. *Race and Class in Colonial Oaxaca.* Stanford: Stanford Univ. Press, 1978.

———. "Estate and Class: A Reply." *Comparative Studies in Society and History* 25 (1979): 434–42.

———. "The Ecology of Race and Class in Late Colonial Oaxaca." In *Studies in Spanish American Population History*, ed. David J. Robinson, 93–117. Boulder, Colo.: Westview Press, 1981.

Chávez Carbajal, Maria Guadalupe. *Propietarios y esclavos negros en Michoacán (1600–1650).* Morelia, Michoacán: Universidad Michoacana de San Nicolás de Hidalgo, 1994.

Cook, Sherburne F., and Woodrow Borah. *Essays in Population History: Mexico and the Caribbean.* Berkeley: Univ. of California Press, 1974.

Cope, Robert Douglas. *The Limits of Racial Domination: Plebeian Society in Colonial Mexico City, 1660–1720.* Madison, Wis.: Univ. of Wisconsin Press, 1994.

Corro, Octoviano R. *Cimarrones en Veracruz y la fundación de Amapa.* Veracruz: Comercial, 1951.

Cuenya Mateos, Miguel Ángel. "Epidemias y salubridad en la Puebla de los Ángeles, 1650–1833." In *Limpiar y obedecer: La basura, el agua, y la muerte en la Puebla de los Ángeles, 1650–1925,* comp. Rosalva Loreto and Francisco J. Cervantes B., 69–126. Puebla: Claves Latinoamericanas, Universidad Autónoma de Puebla, and Colegio de Puebla, 1994.

Cutter, Charles R. *The Legal Culture of Northern New Spain, 1700–1810.* Albuquerque: Univ. of New Mexico Press, 1995.

Davis, Darién J. "Introduction: The African Experience in Latin America—Resistance and Accommodation." In *Slavery and Beyond: The African Impact on Latin America and the Caribbean*, ed. Darién J. Davis, xxi–xxvi. Wilmington, Del.: Scholarly Resources, 1995.

Deans-Smith, Susan. *Bureaucrats, Planters, and Workers: The Making of the Tobacco Monopoly in Bourbon Mexico*. Austin: University of Texas Press, 1992.

Degler, Carl N. *Neither Black nor White: Slavery and Race Relations in Brazil and the United States*. New York: Macmillan, 1971; repr., Madison: Univ. of Wisconsin Press, 1986.

Domínguez, Jorge I. *Insurrection or Loyalty: The Breakdown of the Spanish American Empire*. Cambridge, Mass.: Harvard Univ. Press, 1980.

————. "International War and Government Modernization: The Military—A Case Study." In *Rank and Privilege: The Military and Society in Latin America*, ed. Linda Alexander Rodríguez, 1–9. Wilmington, Del.: Scholarly Resources, 1994.

Ducey, Michael T. "Viven sin ley ni rey: Rebeliones coloniales en Papantla, 1760–1790." In *Procesos rurales e historia regional*, ed. Victoria Chenaut, 15–49. Mexico City: CIESAS, 1996.

English Martin, Cheryl. *Rural Society in Colonial Morelos*. Albuquerque: Univ. of New Mexico Press, 1985.

Escobar Ohmestede, Antonio. "La población en el siglo XVIII y principios del siglo XIX: Conformacion de una sociedad multiétnica en las Huastecas?" In *Población y estructura urbana en México, siglos XVIII y XIX*, comp. Carmen Blázquez Domínguez, Carlos Contreras Cruz and Sonia Pérez Toledo, 277–99. Xalapa, Veracruz: Universidad Veracruzana, 1996.

Farriss, Nancy. *Maya Society under Colonial Rule: The Collective Enterprise of Survival*. Princeton: Princeton Univ. Press, 1984.

Fernández Repetto, Francisco, and Genny Negroe Sierra. *Una población perdida en la memoria: Los negros de Yucatán*. Mérida: Universidad Autonoma de Yucatán, 1995.

Florescano, Enrique, and Susan Swan. *Breve historia de la sequía en Méxcio*. Xalapa, Veracruz: Universidad Veracruzana, 1995.

Florescano Mayet, Sergio. *El camino Veracruz-Mexico en la epoca colonial*. Xalapa, Veracruz: Universidad Veracruzana, 1987.

"The Foundation of Nuestra Señora de Guadalupe de los Morenos de Amapa, Mexico (1769)." In *Colonial Spanish America: A Documentary History*, ed. Kenneth Mills and William B. Taylor, 274–81. Wilmington, Del.: Scholarly Resources, 1998.

Fra Molinero, Baltasar. *La imagen de los negros en el teatro del siglo de oro*. Mexico City and Madrid: Siglo XXI Editores, 1995.

Garavaglia, Juan Carlos, and Juan Carlos Grosso. "La región de Puebla / Tlaxcala y la economía novohispana (1670–1821)." *Historia Mexicana* 35, no. 4 (1986): 549–600.

García Martínez, Bernardo. *Los pueblos de la sierra: El poder y el espacio entre los indios del norte de Puebla hasta 1700*. Mexico City: El Colegio de Mexico, 1987.

————. "Pueblos de Indios, Pueblos de Castas: New Settlements and Traditional Corporate Organization in Eighteenth-Century New Spain." In *The Indian Community of Mexico: Fifteen Essays on Land Tenure, Corporate Organizations, Ideology and Village Politics*, ed. Arij Ouweneel and Simon Miller, 103–16. Amsterdam: Centro de Estudios y Documentación Latinoamericanos, 1990.

Gascón, Margarita. "The Military of Santo Domingo, 1720–1764." *Hispanic American Historical Review* 73, no. 3 (1993): 431–52.

Gerhard, Peter. *The Southeast Frontier of New Spain*. Princeton: Princeton Univ. Press, 1979.

————. "Un censo de la diócesis de Puebla en 1681." *Historia Mexicana* 30, no. 4 (1981): 530–60.

———. *The North Frontier of New Spain.* Norman and London: Univ. of Oklahoma Press, 1982.

———. *Geografía histórica de la Nueva España, 1519–1821.* Mexico City: Universidad Nacional Autónoma de México, 1986.

Gibson, Charles. *The Aztecs under Spanish Rule: A History of the Indians of the Valley of Mexico, 1519–1810.* Stanford: Stanford Univ. Press, 1964.

———. *Spain in America.* New York: Harper and Row, 1966.

Gilroy, Paul. *'There Ain't no Black in the Union Jack': The Cultural Politics of Race and Nation.* London: Hutchinson, 1987.

González, María del Refugio, and Teresa Lozano. "La adminitración de justicia." In *El gobierno provincial en la Nueva España, 1570–1787,* ed. Woodrow Borah, 75–105. Mexico City: Universidad Autónoma de México, 1985.

González Sánchez, Isabel. "Sistemas de trabajo, salarios y situación de los trabajadores agrícolas, 1750–1810." In *La clase obrera en la historia de México,* 6th ed., ed. Carmen Velcarce, 125–72. Mexico City: Siglo XXI Editores, 1990.

Guedea, Virginia. "La organización militar." In *El gobierno provincial en la Nueva España, 1570–1787,* ed. Woodrow Borah, 125–48. Mexico City: Universidad Autónoma de México, 1985.

Gutiérrez, Ramón. *When Jesus Came, the Corn Mothers Went Away.* Stanford: Stanford Univ. Press, 1991.

Haslip, Gabriel J. "Crime and the Administration of Justice in Colonial Mexico City, 1696–1810." Ph.D. diss., Columbia University, 1980.

———. "Criminal Justice and the Poor in Late Colonial Mexico City." In *Five Centuries of Law and Politics in Central Mexico,* ed. Ronald Spores and Ross Hassig, 107–26. Nashville, Tenn.: Vanderbilt Univ. Publications in Anthropology, 1984.

Hassig, Ross. *Trade, Tribute, and Transportation: The Sixteenth-Century Political Economy of the Valley of Mexico.* Norman: University of Oklahoma Press, 1985.

Helg, Aline. "Race in Argentina and Cuba, 1880–1930: Theory, Policies, and Popular Reaction." In *The Idea of Race in Latin America, 1870–1940,* ed. Richard Graham, 37–69. Austin: Univ. of Texas Press, 1990.

Hoffman, Paul E. *The Spanish Crown and the Defense of the Caribbean, 1535–1585: Precedent, Patrimonialism, and Royal Parsimony.* Baton Rouge and London: Louisiana State University Press, 1980.

Howard, Philip A. *Changing History: Afro-Cuban Cabildos and Societies of Color in the Nineteenth Century.* Baton Rouge: Louisiana State Univ. Press, 1998.

Hunefeldt, Christine. *Paying the Price of Freedom: Family and Labor among Lima's Slaves, 1800–1854.* Trans. Alexandra Stern. Berkeley, Los Angeles, and London: Univ. of California Press, 1994.

Hutchinson, Henry William. *Village and Plantation Life in Northeastern Brazil.* Seattle: Univ. of Washington Press, 1957.

Israel, J. I. "Mexico and the 'General Crisis' of the Seventeenth Century." *Past and Present* 63 (May 1974): 33–57.

———. *Race, Class and Politics in Colonial Mexico, 1610–1670.* Oxford: Oxford Univ. Press, 1975.

Jackson, Robert H. *Race, Caste, and Status: Indians in Colonial Spanish America.* Albuquerque: Univ. of New Mexico Press, 1999.

Juarez Moreno, Juan. *Corsarios y piratas en Veracruz y Campeche.* Seville: Escuela de Estudios Hispano-Americanos de Sevilla, 1972.

Keen, Benjamin. *The Aztec Image in Western Thought.* New Brunswick, N.J.: Rutgers Univ. Press, 1971.

Kicza, John E. *Colonial Entrepreneurs: Families and Business in Bourbon Mexico City.* Albuquerque: Univ. of New Mexico Press, 1983.

Klein, Herbert S. "The Colored Militia of Cuba: 1568–1868." *Caribbean Studies* 6, no. 2 (1966): 17–27.

———. *African Slavery in Latin America and the Caribbean.* New York and Oxford: Oxford Univ. Press, 1986.

Klein, Herbert S., and John J. TePaske. "The Seventeenth-Century Crisis in New Spain: Myth or Reality?" *Past and Present* 90 (February 1981): 116–35.

Kraay, Henrik. "Soldiers, Officers, and Society: The Army in Bahia, Brazil, 1808–1889." Ph.D. diss., University of Texas at Austin, 1995.

Kuethe, Allan J. "The Status of the Free-Pardo in the Disciplined Militia of New Granada." *Journal of Negro History* 56, no. 2 (1971): 105–17.

———. *Military Reform and Society in New Granada, 1773–1808.* Gainesville: Univ. of Florida Press, 1978.

———. "The Development of the Cuban Military as a Sociopolitical Elite, 1763–83." *Hispanic American Historical Review* 61, no. 4 (1981): 695–704.

———. *Cuba, 1753–1815: Crown, Military, and Society.* Knoxville: Univ. of Tennessee Press, 1986.

Knight, Alan. "Racism, Revolution, and Indigenismo: Mexico, 1910–1940." In *The Idea of Race in Latin America, 1870–1940*, ed. Richard Graham, 70–113. Austin: Univ. of Texas Press, 1990.

Ladd, Doris M. *The Mexican Nobility at Independence, 1780–1826.* Austin: Univ. of Texas Press, 1976.

Laurencio, Juan. *Campaña contra Yanga en 1608.* Mexico City: Editorial Citlaltepetl, 1974.

Lavrin, Asunción. "Rural Confraternities in the Local Economies of New Spain: The Bishopric of Oaxaca in the Context of Colonial Mexico." In *The Indian Community of Mexico: Fifteen Essays on Land Tenure, Corporate Organizations, Ideology and Village Politics*, ed. Arij Ouweneel and Simon Miller, 224–49. Amsterdam: Centro de Estudios y Documentación Latinoamericanos, 1990.

Liehr, Reinhard. *Ayuntamiento y oligarquía en Puebla, 1787–1810.* Trans. Olga Hentschel. Mexico City: Secretaría de Educación Pública, 1976.

Lockhart, James. *The Nahuas after the Conquest: A Social and Cultural History of the Indians of Central Mexico, Sixteenth through Eighteenth Centuries.* Stanford: Stanford Univ. Press, 1992.

Lopez Gonzalez, Pedro. *La población de Tepic bajo la organización regional, 1530–1821.* Tepic, Nayarit: Universidad Autonoma de Nayarit, 1984.

Lozano Armendares, Teresa. *La criminalidad en la ciudad de Mexico, 1800–1821.* Mexico City: Universidad Nacional Autónoma de México, 1987.

Lynch, John. *Bourbon Spain, 1700–1808.* Oxford, and Cambridge, Mass.: Basil Blackwell, 1989.

———. *Spain, 1516–1598: From Nation State to World Empire.* Oxford, and Cambridge, Mass.: Basil Blackwell, 1991.

Malvido, Elsa. "Factores de despoblación y de reposición de la población de Cholula (1641–1810)." In *Historia y población en México*, ed. Thomas Calvo, 63–121. Mexico City: El Colegio de México, 1994.

Marchena Fernández, Juan. "La financiación militar en Indias: Introducción a su estudio." *Anuario de Estudios Americanos* 36 (1979): 81–110.

——. *Oficiales y soldados en el ejército de America.* Seville: Escuela de Estudios Hispanoamericanos, 1983.

——. *Ejército y milicias en el mundo colonial Americano.* Seville: Editorial Mapfre, 1992.

Marichal, Carlos, and Matilde Souto Mantecón. "Silver and Situados: New Spain and the Financing of the Spanish Empire in the Caribbean in the Eighteenth Century." *Hispanic American Historical Review* 74, no. 4 (1994): 587–613.

Marín Bosch, Miguel. *Puebla Neocolonial 1777–1831: Casta, ocupación y matrimonio en la segunda ciudad de Nueva España.* Zapopan, Jalisco: El Colegio de Jaliso, 1999.

Marquez Morfin, Lourdes. "La desigualdad ante la muerte: Epidemias, población y sociedad en la ciudad de Mexico (1800–1850)." Ph.D. diss., El Colegio de México, 1991.

McAlister, Lyle N. "The Reorganization of the Army of New Spain, 1763–1767." *Hispanic American Historical Review* 33, no. 1 (1953): 1–32.

——. *The "Fuero Militar" in New Spain, 1764–1800.* Gainesville: Univ. of Florida Press, 1957.

——. "Social Structure and Social Change in New Spain." *Hispanic American Historical Review* 43 (1963): 349–70.

McCaa, Robert, Stuart B. Schwartz, and Arturo Grubessich. "Race and Class in Colonial Latin America: A Critique." *Comparative Studies in Society and History* 25 (1979): 421–33.

——. "Calidad, Clase, and Marriage in Colonial Mexico: The Case of Parral, 1788–90." *Hispanic American Historical Review* 64, no. 3 (1984): 477–501.

McNeill, John Robert. *Atlantic Empires of France and Spain: Louisbourg and Havana, 1700–1763.* Chapel Hill and London: Univ. of North Carolina Press, 1985.

Mendoza Briones, María Ofelia. "Pertenencia étnica e interlocución al sistema colonial en Michoacán: 1766–1767." *Tzintzun* 23 (1996): 9–29.

Miño Grijalva, Manuel. *La manufactura colonial: La Constitución técnica del obraje.* Mexico City: El Colegio de México, 1985.

Molas Ribalta, Pere. "The Early Bourbons and the Military." In *Armed Forces and Society in Spain,* ed. Rafael Bañon Martínez and Thomas M. Barker, 51–80. New York: Columbia University Press, 1988.

Moreno, Juan Juárez. *Corsarios y piratas en Veracruz y Campeche.* Seville: Escuela de Estudios Hispano-Americanos de Sevilla, 1972.

Morin, Claude. *Michoacán en la Nueva España del siglo XVIII: Crecimiento y desigualdad en una economía colonial.* Mexico City: Fondo de Cultura Económica, 1979.

Mörner, Magnus. *Race Mixture in the History of Latin America.* Boston: Little, Brown and Company, 1967.

——. "Economic Factors and Stratification in Colonial Spanish America with Special Regard to Elites." *Hispanic American Historical Review* 63, no. 2 (1983): 335–69.

Naveda Chávez, Adriana. *Esclavos negros en las haciendas azucareras de Cordoba Veracruz, 1690–1830.* Xalapa, Veracruz: Universidad Veracruzana, 1987.

Ortiz Escamilla, Juan. "Las guerras Napoleónicas y la defensa de la Nueva España en la provincia de Veracruz, 1793–1810." In *Población y estructura urbana en México, siglos XVIII y XIX,* comp. Carmen Blázquez Domínguez, Carlos Contreras Cruz, and Sonia Pérez Toledo, 213–21. Xalapa, Veracruz: Universidad Veracruzana, 1996.

Ouweneel, Arij. "Growth, Stagnation, and Migration: An Explorative Analysis of the

Tributario Series of Anáhuac (1720–1800)." *Hispanic American Historical Review* 71, no. 3 (1991): 531–77.

Palmer, Colin A. *Slaves of the White God: Blacks in Mexico 1570–1650.* Cambridge, Mass.: Harvard Univ. Press, 1976

Patterson, Orlando. *The Sociology of Slavery.* London: Fairleigh Dickenson Univ. Press, 1967.

Pérez-Rocha, Emma, and Gabriel Moedano Navarro. *Aportaciones a la investigación de archivos del México colonial a la bibliohermerografía afromexicanista.* Mexico City: Instituto Nacional de Antropología y Historía, 1992.

Pérez Toledo, Sonia, and Herbert S. Klein. "La población de la ciudad de Zacatecas en 1857." *Historia Mexicana* 41, no. 1 (1992): 77–102.

———. *Los hijos del trabajo: Los artesanos de la ciudad de México, 1780–1853.* Mexico City: El Colegio de Mexico and Universidad Autónoma Metropolitana Iztapalapa, 1996.

Pescador, Juan Javier. *De bautizoados a fieles difuntos: Familia y mentalidades en una parroquia urbana, Santa Catarina de México, 1568–1820.* Mexico City: El Colegio de México, 1992.

Pozas, Ricardo. *Juan the Chamula: An Ethnological Re-creation of the Life of a Mexican Indian.* Berkeley, Los Angeles, and London: Univ. of California Press, 1962.

Quatrefegas, René. "The Military System of the Spanish Habsburgs." In *Armed Forces and Society in Spain*, ed. Rafael Bañon Martínez and Thomas M. Barker, 1–50. New York: Columbia University Press, 1988.

Rabell, Cecilia. "Matrimonio y raza en una parroquia rural: San Luis de la Paz, Guanajuato, 1715–1810." In *Historia y población en México*, ed. Thomas Calvo, 163–204. Mexico City: El Colegio de México, 1994.

Redondo, Brigido. *Negritud in Campeche.* Campeche: Ediciones de la LIV Legislatura, 1994.

———. "Negritud en Campeche, de la conquista a nuestros días." In *Presencia Africana en México*, ed. Luz María Montiel, 337–421. Mexico, City: Consejo Nacional para la Cultura y las Artes, 1994.

Reyes, Juan Carlos. "Tributarios negros y afromestizos: Primeras notas sobre un padrón Colimense de 1809." In *III Encuentro nacional de afromexicanistas*, ed. Luz Ma. Martínez Montiel and Juan Carlos Reyes, 126–32. Colima: Gobierno del Estado de Colima, 1993.

Robinson, David J. "Patrones de población: Parral a fines del siglo XVIII." In *Demografía histórica de México, siglos XVI–XIX*, comp. Elsa Malvido and Miguel Ángel Cuenya, 179–216. Mexico City: Instituto Mora, 1993.

Rodriguez Garcia, Vicente. *El fiscal de real hacienda en Nueva España (Don Ramón de Posada y Soto, 1781–1783).* Oviedo: Secretariado de Publicaciones de la Universidad de Oviedo, 1985.

Rout, Jr., Leslie B. *The African Experience in Spanish America, 1502 to the Present Day.* Cambridge, England: Cambridge Univ. Press, 1976.

Rubio Mañé, José Ignacio. *El virreinato.* Vol. 2, *Expansión y defensa.* Mexico City: Fondo de Cultura Económica, 1992.

———. *El virreinato.* Vol. 3, *Expansión y defensa, segunda parte.* Mexico City: Fondo de Cultura Económica, 1992.

Ruiz Abreu, Carlos. *Comercio y milicias de Tabasco en la colonia.* Villahermosa, Tabasco: Instituto Cultural de Tabasco, 1989.

Sada, Jorge. *Los pescadores de la laguna de Tamiahua.* Mexico City: Secretario de Educación Pública, 1984.

Seed, Patricia. "The Social Dimensions of Race: Mexico City 1753." *Hispanic American Historical Review* 62, no. 4 (1982): 569–606.

———. *To Love, Honor, and Obey in Colonial Mexico: Conflict over Marriage Choice, 1574–1821.* Stanford: Stanford Univ. Press, 1988.

Shaw, Frederick J. "The Artisan in Mexico City (1824–1853)." In *El trabajo y los trabajadores en la historia de México*, comp. Elsa Cecilia Frost, Michael C. Meyer, and Josefina Zoraida Vázquez, 399–418. Mexico City and Tucson: El Colegio de Mexico and the Univ. of Arizona Press, 1979.

Skidmore, Thomas E. *Black into White: Race and Nationality in Brazilian Thought.* New York: Oxford Univ. Press, 1974.

Sluiter, Engel. *The Florida Situado: Quantifying the First Eighty Years, 1571–1651.* Gainesville: Univ. of Florida Press, 1985.

Socolow, Susan Migden. "Acceptable Marriage Partners: Marriage Choice in Colonial Argentina, 1778–1810." In *Sexuality and Marriage in Colonial Latin America*, ed. Asunción Lavrin, 209–51. Lincoln and London: Univ. of Nebraska Press, 1992.

Souto Mantecón, Matilde, and Patricia Torres Meza. "La población de la antigua parroquia del pueblo de Xalapa (1777)." In *Población y estructura urbana en México, siglos XVIII y XIX*, comp. Carmen Blázquez Domínguez, Carlos Contreras Cruz, and Sonia Pérez Toledo, 87–110. Xalapa, Veracruz: Universidad Veracruzana, 1996.

Spalding, Karen. *Huarochirí: An Andean Society under Inca and Spanish Rule.* Stanford: Stanford Univ. Press, 1984.

Spitzer, Leo. *Lives in Between: Assimilation and Marginality in Austria, Brazil, and West Africa, 1780–1945.* Cambridge, England: Cambridge Univ. Press, 1989.

Taylor, William B. *Drinking, Homicide, and Rebellion in Colonial Mexican Villages.* Stanford: Stanford Univ. Press, 1979.

———. "Indian Pueblos of Central Jalisco on the Eve of Independence." In *Iberian Colonies, New World Societies: Essays in Memory of Charles Gibson*, ed. Richard L. Garner and William B. Taylor, 161–83. University Park, Pa.: State College, 1985.

———. "Conflict and Balance in District Politics: Tecali and the Sierra Norte de Puebla in the Eighteenth Century." In *The Indian Community of Mexico: Fifteen Essays on Land Tenure, Corporate Organizations, Ideology and Village Politics*, ed. Arij Ouweneel and Simon Miller, 270–94. Amsterdam: Centro de Estudios y Documentación Latinoamericanos, 1990.

———. *Magistrates of the Sacred: Priests and Parishioners in Eighteenth-Century Mexico.* Stanford: Stanford Univ. Press, 1996.

TePakse, John J. *Real hacienda de Nueva España: La real caja de México.* Mexico City: Instituto Nacional de Antropologia e Historia, 1976.

TePakse, John J., and Herbert S. Klein. *Ingresos y egresos de la real hacienda de Nueva España.* Mexico City: Instituto Nacional de Antropologia e Historia, 1986.

Thompson, E. P. *Customs in Common: Studies in Traditional Popular Culture.* New York: New Press, 1993.

Thomson, Guy P. C. *Puebla de los Angeles: Industry and Society in a Mexican City, 1700–1850.* Boulder, Colo., San Francisco, and London: Westview Press, 1989.

———. "Los indios y el servicio militar en el México decimonónico: Leva o ciuadanía?" In *Indio, nación y comunidad en el México del siglo XIX*, ed. Antonio Escobar Ohmstede, 207–51. Mexico City: CIESAS, 1993.

Torres Ramírez, Bibiano. *La armada de Barlovento*. Seville: Escuela de Estudios Hispano-Americanos de Sevilla, 1981.

Troconis de Veracoechea, Ermila. "Tres Cofradías de Negros en la Iglesia de San Mauricio en Caracas." *Montalban UCAB* 5 (1976): 339–76.

Tutino, John. *From Insurrection to Revolution in Mexico: Social Bases of Agrarian Violence, 1750–1940*. Princeton: Princeton Univ. Press, 1986.

Valdes, Dennis Nodin. "The Decline of the Sociedad de Castas in Mexico City." Ph.D. diss., Univ. of Michigan, 1978.

Valle Pavón, Guillermina del. "Distribución de la población en el espacio urbano de Orizaba en 1791." In *Población y estructura urbana en México, siglos XVIII y XIX*, comp. Carmen Blázquez Domínguez, Carlos Contreras Cruz, and Sonia Pérez Toledo, 129–69. Xalapa, Veracruz: Universidad Veracruzana, 1996.

Vargas Lugo, Elisa, and Gustavo Curiel. *Juan Corrrea: Su vida y su obra*. Mexico City: Universidad Nacional Autónoma de México, 1991.

Vega Juanino, Josefa. *La institución militar en Michoacán*. Zamora, Michoacán: El Colegio de Michoacán, 1986.

Velazquez, Maria del Carmen. *El estado de guerra en Nueva España, 1760–1808*. Mexico City: El Colegio de México, 1950.

Victoria Ojeda, Jorge. *Merida de Yucatan de las Indias: Piratería y estrategia defensiva*. Chalco, Mexico: Ediciones del Ayuntamiento de Merida, 1995.

Vincent, Ted. "The Blacks Who Freed Mexico." *Journal of Negro History* 79, no. 3 (1994): 257–76.

Vinson III, Ben. "Race, Class, and the Use of Physical Space in Mexico City's Cuartel 23, 1811." Master's thesis, Columbia Univ., 1993.

Voelz, Peter M. *Slave and Soldier: The Military Impact of Blacks in the Colonial Americas*. New York and London: Garland Publishing, 1993.

Von Mentz, Brígida. *Pueblos de indios, mulatos y mestizos, 1770–1870*. Mexico City: CIESAS, 1988.

Wade, Peter. *Blackness and Race Mixture: The Dynamics of Racial Identity in Colombia*. Baltimore, Md., and London: Johns Hopkins University Press, 1993.

———. *Race and Ethnicity in Latin America*. London and Chicago: Pluto Press, 1997.

Widmer Sennhauser, Rudolf. "Autoconsumo y mercado: La producción textil como estrategia de los campesinos de Acayucan y Jicayan (1770–1830)." In *Anuario X Instituto de Investigaciones Histórico-Sociales, Universidad Veracruzana*, 19–28. Xalapa, Veracruz: Universidad Veracruzana, 1995.

Wright, Winthorp R. *Café con Leche: Race, Class, and National Image in Venezuela*. Austin: Univ. of Texas Press, 1990.

Yuste, Carmen. "Las autoridades locales como agentes del fisco en la Nueva España." In *El gobierno provincial en la Nueva España, 1570–1787*, ed. Woodrow Borah, 107–23. Mexico City: Universidad Autónoma de México, 1985.

Index

In this index an "f" after a number indicates a separate reference on the next page, and an "ff" indicates separate references on the next two pages. A continuous discussion over two or more pages is indicated by a span of page numbers, e.g., "57–59."